RISE AND FALL OF THE IMPERIAL GUPTAS

RISE AND FALL OF THE IMPERIAL GUPTAS

ASHVINI AGRAWAL

MOTILAL BANARSIDASS
PUBLISHERS (P) LTD.
DELHI

First Edition: Delhi, 1989

MOTILAL BANARSIDASS
Bungalow Road, Jawahar Nagar, Delhi 110 007
Branches
Chowk, Varanasi 221 001
Ashok Rajpath, Patna 800 004
24 Race Course Road, Bangalore 560 001
120 Royapettah High Road, Mylapore, Madras 600 004

ISBN: 81-208-0592-5

PRINTED IN INDIA
BY JAINENDRA PRAKASH JAIN AT SHRI JAINENDRA PRESS, A-45 NARAINA INDUSTRIAL AREA, PHASE I, NEW DELHI 110 028 AND PUBLISHED BY NARENDRA PRAKASH JAIN FOR MOTILAL BANARSIDASS PUBLISHERS PRIVATE LIMITED, DELHI 110007.

To the Sacred Memory of

My Mother

SHRIMATI VIDYAVATI AGRAWAL

माता किल मनुष्याणां दैवतानां च दैवतम्

PREFACE

THE PRESENT WORK primarily formed the author's thesis on which the degree of Doctor of Philosophy was awarded by the Panjab University, Chandigarh in 1980. Both of my examiners Prof. U.V. Singh of the Kurukshetra University and Prof. Upendra Thakur of the Magadh University, Bodh Gaya, besides my teacher and superviser Prof. V. C. Pandey had recommended its publication by the University. But before it could be sent to the press the new edition of the *Corpus Inscriptionum Indicarum*, Vol. III revised by Late Dr. D. R. Bhandarkar and edited by Dr. B. Ch. Chhabra and Dr. G. S. Gai was released in 1981 and in December of the same year Vol. III of the *Comprehensive History of India*, edited by Late Dr. R. C. Majumdar, also came out. These works coupled with some epoch making discoveries of fresh source material, made it not only a desideratum but a necessity to completely revise the whole thesis and make it upto-date in the light of fresh evidence, which in a way amounted to the rewriting of almost entire work. This process took an unduly long period of eight years during which we were benefited by two more works on the subject—*Imperial Gupta Epigraphs* by Dr. P. K. Agrawala and the *Catalogue of the Gupta Gold Coins of the Bayana Hoard in the National Museum* by Dr. B. Ch. Chhabra. Though its publication was delayed, but it gives us the satisfaction of presenting to the world of scholars an uptodate work studied from a fresh point of view and revised in the light of the latest discoveries, like the Risthal inscription of Prakāśadharmā.

The necessity of a new work on the subject may be questioned, because many standard works have been written on the history of the imperial Guptas. However, the continuous discovery of the new source material, particularly epigraphic and numismatic, makes a fresh study of the subject, of perennial interest and it hardly needs any justification. There are many problems which are still unsolved and there are some regarding which there is a sharp difference of opinion. Moreover, new material is being constantly discovered and made available through archaeological excavations. The new facts thus brought to light have to be incorporated by assigning them a proper place in the history of this period.

After the present work was undertaken many new inscriptions came to light, which have given an entirely new course to the history of this period by revealing hitherto completely unknown facets of the past. The most important of these is the Risthal stone slab inscription of the Aulikara ruler Prakāśadharmā, the predecessor of Yaśodharman Vishṇuvardhana, which has revealed for the first time that the Hūṇa emperor Toramāṇa was not only utterly defeated in the battle field by the Aulikara hero, but was also deprived of his title of 'overlord of kings'. Two inscriptions of the reign of emperor Budhagupta have brought interesting facts to light. The Shankarpur copper-plate indicates that the founder of the main dynasty of the Maukharis was a feudatory of the emperor Budhagupta. Similarly the Mathura stone image inscription of Budhagupta's reign proves that his empire extended so far in the north and it pointedly goes against the theory of the division of the Gupta empire between Purugupta and Skandagupta or between any of their successors.

A lot of misunderstanding still prevails even in scholarly circles with regard to the problems like the predecessors of the Guptas in Magadha, and the political map of India at the time of the rise of the Guptas. I have striven to present the facts correctly in the light of the latest researches and tried to rectify the errors regarding the part played by the Nāgas and the Vākāṭakas in Gupta history. Similarly the place of the Muruṇḍas has been much misunderstood and misrepresented. Though there is not a single coin or inscription of any Muruṇḍa ruler, writer after writer has placed them as rulers of the Gangetic valley, on the evidence which does not stand even a minute's scrutiny. It is astonishing that some writers still go on harping on the thoroughly discredited evidence of the Sanskrit works like the *Kṛishṇacharitam* and the *Kaumudīmahotsava*.

The controversy regarding the original home of the Imperial Guptas has been re-examined and the facts have been straightened. An absolutely fresh and original approach has been made regarding the caste of the Guptas. It has been shown on the strength of the epigraphic evidence that Dhāraṇa was not the *gotra* of the Guptas, but it was that of a family of Nāgas. It has also been shown that Dhāraṇa was a *gotra* amongst the Brahmans and the attempt to connect it with some low castes is misleading and baseless.

In dealing with Samudragupta, a fresh attempt has been made to discuss the nature and extent of his southern conquests, as also regarding his relations with the foreign powers in the West. The researches of Prof. K.D. Bajpai have thrown some fresh light on the identification of some rulers like Maṇṭrarāja. New evidence on the Śaka ruler Śridharavarman has been carefully examined and his relations with Samudragupta have been discussed. The untenability of the identification of Kācha with Bhasma mentioned in the Buddhist work *Āryamañjuśrīmūlakalpa* has been brought to fore, by showing that the account of this Buddhist work is full of contradictions and can not be relied upon for drawing important historical conclusions. Likewise the historicity of Rāmagupta has been reexamined in the light of his Durjanpur (Vidiśā) Jain images inscriptions and his historicity established. Some writers are still not reconciled to the view that Govindagupta succeeded his father Chandragupta II. This point has been thoroughly discussed.

The problem of a war of succession after the death of Kumāragupta I, between his sons—Skandagupta, Purugupta and Ghaṭotkachagupta of the Tumain inscription has been reviewed thoroughly in the Appendix to chapter X. New light has been thrown on the disputed status of Skandagupta's mother and the proper interpretation of a passage in the Bhitari inscription has been pointed out.

The amazing fresh light thrown on the history of the Hūṇas in India by the Risthal stone-slab inscription of Prakāśadharmā and Sanjeli copper-plates of Mahārāja Bhūta has been fully discussed to straighten many problems and misconceptions regarding the downfall of the Gupta dynasty. It has been shown in the epilogue that it were not the Hūṇas but the rise of feudatories like the Maukharis which was really responsible for pulling down the mighty edifice of the Gupta empire.

It now remains, to perform my most pleasant and bounden duty to express my deep and sincere gratitude to all those but for whose valuable help and guidance this work would not have seen the light of the day. There are no adequate words to express my gratitude to my teacher and guide Professor V.C. Pandey, formerly Professor and Head of the Department of Ancient Indian History, Culture and Archaeology, Panjab University, Chandigarh, who suggested this topic for research. He has most gladly extended his expert guidance and kind advice at all stages of my work, and never spared any pains in solving my difficulties. I shall be indulging in no mere formality, when I say that he has been to me literally a true philosopher, friend and guide. My father Prof. Jagannath Agrawal has helped me very often by explaining many a difficult passage in Sanskrit inscriptions as well as in literary works. He has been going through the entire manuscript of the work and making valuable suggestions and corrections. To express my thanks to him shall be undermining my respect for him. My head is bowed with affection and respect for him.

I am highly grateful to Prof. U.V. Singh of the Kurukshetra University and Prof. Upendra Thakur of the Magadha University, Bodh Gaya, who examined my thesis and besides recommending its publication gave some valuable suggestions. I am equally indebted to Prof. K.D. Bajpai, formerly Tagore Professor at the Sagar University, Prof. Lallanji Gopal of Banaras Hindu University, Prof. Ajay Mitra Shastri of Nagpur University and Prof. O.P. Bharadwaj of Kurukshetra University for affectionately providing me with expert guidance and help in this work from time to time, and I must place on record my heart-felt gratitude to these savants.

I must express my deep sense of gratitude to Dr. S.L. Dogra, Librarian, V.V.B.I.S. & I.S., Hoshiarpur, for providing me all necessary library facilities and help during the course of my research.

It would be no mere formality to express my indebtedness to my wife Achala Agrawal, M.A. for her help by keeping me free from the domestic worries and constantly reminding me to devote to my research work.

To Messrs Motilal Banarsidass, the internationally famous firm of Indological Publishers, I am deeply beholden for undertaking this publication, and doing such a fine job in bringing it out.

In spite of best efforts some errors have crept in and I crave the indulgence of readers for them.

Chandigarh
July 1, 1988

ASHVINI AGRAWAL

CONTENTS

ABBREVIATIONS

ABORI	*Annals of the Bhandarkar Oriental Research Institute*, Poona.
AHD	*Ancient History of the Deccan* by G.J. Dubreuil.
AIG	*Age of the Imperial Guptas* by R.D. Banerji.
AIHC	*Aspects of Indian History and Civilization* by Buddha Prakash.
AIU	*Age of Imperial Unity* Ed. by R.C. Majumdar.
AMMK	*Āryamañjuśrīmūlakalpa.*
AO	*Acta Orientalia*, Leiden.
AOR	*Annals of Oriental Research*, Madras.
API	Allahabad Stone Pillar Inscription of Samudragupta.
As. Res.	*Asiatic Researches.*
ASI.AR	*Archaeological Survey of India, Annual Reports.*
ASWI	*Archaeological Survey of Western India.*
BAIHA	*Bulletin of Ancient Indian History and Archaeology*, Sagar University, Sagar.
Bayana Hoard	*Catalogue of the Gupta Gold Coins in Bayana Hoard* by A.S. Altekar.
BDCRI	*Bulletin of the Deccan College Post-Graduate and Research Institute*, Poona.
BIA	*Bibliography of Indian Archaeology.*
BMC. GD	*See CCGD.*
Bom. Gaz.	*Bombay Gazeteer.*
BPI	Bhitari Pillar Inscription of Skandagupta.
BRAAH	*Buddhist Remains in Andhra and Andhra History* by K.R. Subramaniam.
BRBPP	*Bihar Rāshṭrabhāshā Parishad Patrikā.*
Brihat.	*Bṛihatsaṁhitā* of Varāhamihira.
BSOAS	*Bulletin of the School of Oriental and African Studies*, London.
BV	*Bhāratīya Vidyā*, Bombay.
CA	*Classical Age* Ed. by R.C. Majumdar.

CCA	*Catalogue of the Coins of Ancient India* by J. Allan.
CCAD, WK	*Catalogue of the Coins of the Andhra Dynasty, the Western Kshatrapas etc.* by E.J. Rapson.
CCCM	*Catalogue of the Coins in the Central Museum Lahore* by C.J. Rodgers.
CCGD	*Catalogue of the Coins of the Gupta Dynasties and of Śaśāṅka, King of Gauḍa* by J. Allan.
CCIM	*Catalogue of the Coins in Indian Museum, Calcutta* by V.A. Smith.
CHB	*Comprehensive History of Bihar* Ed. by B.P. Sinha.
CHI	*Comprehensive History of India*, Vol. II Ed. by K.A.N. Sastri; and Vol. III Ed. by R.C. Majumdar.
CII	*Corpus Inscriptionum Indicarum.*
Coinage	*Coinage of the Gupta Empire* by A.S. Altekar.
DHM	*Dynastic History of Magadha* by B.P. Sinha.
DKA	*Dynasties of the Kali Age* by F.E. Pargiter.
DKM	*Decline of the Kingdom of Magadha* by B.P. Sinha.
E & W	*East and West*, Rome.
EECA	*Early Empires of Central Asia* by W.M. McGovern.
EHAC	*Early History of the Andhral Country* by K. Gopalachari.
EHI	*Early History of India* by V.A. Smith.
EHNI	*Early History of North India* by S. Chattopadhyaya.
EI	*Epigraphia Indica.*
GE	*Gupta Empire* by R.K. Mookerji
G.S.	*Gupta Saṃvat.*
Gup. Sam.	*Gupta Sāmrājya* by P.L. Gupta.
HB	*History of Bengal* Ed. by R.C. Majumdar.
HDS	*History of Dharmaśāstra* by P.V. Kane.
HEDA	*History of Early Dynasties of Andhradesa* by B.V. Krishnarao.
HG	*A History of the Guptas* by R.N. Dandekar.

HI	*History of India, 150 A.D. to 350 A.D.* by K.P. Jayaswal.
HIG	*A History of the Imperial Guptas,* by S.R. Goyal.
HIIA	*History of Indian and Indonesian Art* by A.K. Coomaraswami.
HNEI	*History of North-Eastern India* by R.G. Basak.
HP	*Hindu Polity* by K.P. Jayaswal.
HSAJIS	*Haryana Sahitya Akademi Journal of Indological Studies,* Chandigarh.
IA	*Indian Antiquary,* Bombay.
IC	*Indian Culture,* Calcutta.
IGTT	*Imperial Guptas and Their Times* by S.K. Maity.
IHI	*Imperial History of India* by K.P. Jayaswal.
IHQ	*Indian Historical Quarterly,* Calcutta.
IMC	*See CCIM.*
JA	*Journal Asiatique,* Paris.
JAHRS	*Journal of the Andhra Historical Research Society,* Rajahmundry.
JAIH	*Journal of Ancient Indian History,* Calcutta.
JAOS	*Journal of American Oriental Society.*
JARS	*Journal of the Assam Research Society,* Gauhati.
JASB	*Journal of the Asiatic Society of Bengal,* Calcutta.
JBBRAS	*Journal of the Bombay Branch of the Royal Asiatic Society,* Bombay.
JBORS	*Journal of the Bihar and Orissa Research Society,* Patna.
JBHU	*Journal of Benaras Hindu University,* Varanasi.
JBRS	*Journal of the Bihar Research Society,* Patna.
JESI	*Journal of the Epigraphical Society of India.*
JGJRG	*Journal of the Ganganath Jha Research Institute,* Allahabad.
JIH	*Journal of Indian History,* Trivandrum.
JNSI	*Journal of the Numismatic Society of India,* Varanasi.
JOI	*Journal of the Oriental Institute,* Baroda.

JOIVU	*Journal of the Oriental Institute, Venkateshvara University*, Tirupati.
JOR	*Journal of Oriental Research*, Madras.
JPASB	*Journal and Proceedings of the Asiatic Society of Bengal*, Calcutta.
JRI	Junagadh Rock Inscription of Skandagupta.
JRAS	*Journal of the Royal Asiatic Society*, London.
JRASB	*Journal of the Royal Asiatic Society of Bengal*, Calcutta.
JRASB.L	*Journal of the Royal Asiatic Society of Bengal, Letters*, Calcutta.
JUB	*Journal of the University of Bombay*, Bombay.
JUPHS	*Journal of the U.P. Historical Society.*
KURJ	*Kurukshetra University Research Journal*, Kurukshetra.
MASI	*Memoirs of the Archaeological Survey of India.*
MPI	Mehrauli Pillar Inscription of Chandra.
MR	*Modern Review*, Calcutta.
MS	*Mālava Saṃvat.*
NC	*Numismatic Chronicle.*
NIA	*New Indian Antiquary*, Bombay.
NPP	*Nāgarī Prachāriṇī Patrikā*, Varanasi.
NS	*Numismatic Supplement.*
NUJ	*Nagpur University Journal*, Nagpur.
OHRJ	*Orissa Historical Research Journal*, Bhuvaneshvar.
PAIOC	*Proceedings, All India Oriental Conference*, Poona.
PHAI	*Political History of Ancient India by H.C. Raychaudhuri.*
PIHC	*Proceedings, Indian History Congress.*
PPHC	*Proceedings, Punjab History Conference*, Patiala.
Pra. Bha. Iti.	*Prāchīna Bhārata kā Itihāsa* by V.C. Pandey.
RHC	*Readings in History and Culture* by B.P. Sinha.
RPHI	*Readings in Political History of India* by R.C. Majumdar (Ed. S.P. Gupta).
SAIS	*Studies in Ancient Indian Seals* by K.K. Thaplayal.

Śat. Br.	*Śatapatha Brāhmaṇa.*
Sel. Ins.	*Select Inscriptions,* Vols. I & II, by D.C. Sircar.
SGH	*Studies in Gupta History* by S.K. Aiyangar.
SIHC	*Studies in Indian History and Civilization* by Buddha Prakash.
S.S.	*Śaka Saṃvat.*
THAI	*A Tribal History of Ancient India* by K.K. Dasgupta.
VGA	*The Vākāṭaka-Gupta Age* by A.S. Altekar & R.C. Majumdar.
VIJ	*Vishveshvaranand Indological Journal,* Hoshiarpur.
VOJ	*Vienna Oriental Journal,* Vienna.
V.S.	*Vikrama Saṃvat.*
ZDMG	*Zeitschrift der Deutschen Morgenlandischen Gesellschaft.*

TABLE OF TRANSLITERATION

a	ā	i	ī	u	ū	e	ai	o	au
अ	आ	इ	ई	उ	ऊ	ए	ऐ	ओ	औ
ṛi	ṛī	lṛi	lṛī	ṁ	ḥ				
ऋ	ॠ	ऌ	ॡ	*anusvara*	*visarga*				
ka	kha	ga	gha	ṅ					
क	ख	ग	घ	ङ					
cha	chha	ja	jha	ñ					
च	छ	ज	झ	ञ					
ṭa	ṭha	ḍa	ḍha	ṇa					
ट	ठ	ड	ढ	ण					
ta	tha	da	dha	na					
त	थ	द	ध	न					
pa	pha	ba	bha	ma					
प	फ	ब	भ	म					
ya	ra	la	va						
य	र	ल	व						
śa	sha	sa	ha						
श	ष	स	ह						

CHAPTER I:

SOURCES

THE VEIL OF OBLIVION that shrouded the glorious past of India was lifted slowly after the last quarter of the 18th century with the arduous work of many scholars working to reconstruct the history of India. The ancient literature was forgotten by our own countrymen for centuries and indigenous pandits were completely ignorant of our ancient alphabet. No wonder the attempts of Ferozeshah Tughlaq failed to get deciphered the Topra and Meerut edicts of Aśoka which he brought to Delhi. Later Akbar also met with no success in the same attempt. The credit for pioneer work in this direction goes to Western scholars like William Jones, Wilkins and James Prinsep, whose work was later carried forward by a host of other scholars, Western as well as Indian, such as Alexander Cunnigham, George Bühler, J.F. Fleet, V.A. Smith, R. Hoernle, H. Lüders, J. Ph. Vogel, E.J. Rapson, Sten Konow, F.W Thomas, E. Hultzsch, R.G. Bhandarkar, Bhagwan Lal Indraji, Bhau Daji, D.R. Bhandarkar, R.D. Bannerji, R.C. Majumdar, A.S. Altekar, V.V. Mirashi, B. Ch. Chhabra. It is due to their hard labour that we have ample material for the reconstruction of our ancient history. Though much has been written since then but a critical study and proper interpretation of the material made available till today is still a desideratum. For the convenience of treatment, we may divide the survey of our source material into the following categories:

1. Inscriptions.
2. Seals and Sealings.
3. Coins.
4. Literature.

INSCRIPTIONS

Inscriptions form the most important source material for the reconstruction of the political history of ancient India and more particularly of the Gupta period. Before the discovery and decipherment of the Gupta inscriptions we did not know the name of a single Gupta king. There is no reference to any Gupta king in Sanskrit literature not even in the *Purāṇas*. The latter do mention the name of the Gupta dynasty and the territory under their early sway, but they do not supply any genealogical or chronological information. The order of succession has been determined entirely on the basis of genealogies contained either in their inscriptions or in their seals.

The publication in 1888, of a volume of inscriptions of the Gupta period edited by J. F. Fleet[1] is a landmark in the history of study about the Gupta dynasty. In Fleet's work for the first time we come across all the historical material available at that time collected at one place and presented in a very critical and methodical manner. Considerable progress in the study and discovery of Gupta inscriptions has been made since the publication of Fleet's work and we are fairly better equipped to reconstruct the history of the imperial Guptas on a much firmer ground than were the scholars of the 19th century. The Gupta inscriptions which consist both of royal and private records and are found on stone slabs, stone pillars, pedestals of statues, copper plate grants and even on an iron pillar, may be classified as follows:

a. Praśastis: These are eulogistic accounts of kings composed by the court poets, highlighting their achievements. They are particularly valuable being the official records prepared with great precision by the court officials who had first hand knowledge of all the events. They are often accompanied by genealogical lists. The Allahabad stone pillar inscription of Samudragupta[2], the Mehrauli iron pillar inscription of Chandra[3], the Bhitari pillar inscription[4], and the Junagadh rock inscriptions[5], of Skandagupta, the Risthal stone slab inscription of Prakāśadharmā[6] and the Mandasor stone pillar inscription of Yaśodharman[7], are good examples of royal eulogies. Here we get details not only of the conquests of the territories of the kings dethroned or subdued, but also information about the personal accomplishments and character of the monarch, who is the hero of the document. In the Allahabad inscription, for instance, after describing the conquests in the Deccan and in north India by Samudragupta, its author Harisheṇa goes on to mention in detail the personal accomplishments of the king such as his sharp and mature intellect and proficiency in the fine arts of music and poetry, in which he set the pace for others. The Mehrauli pillar inscription narrates the exploits of Chandra who won fame in battle against the confederacy of foes in south Bengal and conquered distant Bactria after crossing the seven months of the river Indus; and also performed deeds of equal valour in the South. About his person we are told that he carried the beauty of countenance like the beauty of full moon. The Bhitari inscription enlightens us about Skandagupta's achievements on the battlefield against such formidable foes as the Hūṇas and the Pushyamitras and supplies a vivid picture of his personality. While it speaks of his outstanding bravery, it also emphasises his great humility. There was not a trace of pride or conceit in him, in spite of his brilliant victories in war. He has been called the "sole hero" of the Gupta dynasty who firmly established the tottering fortunes of his family. These statements are further corroborated by the Junagadh rock inscription of Skandagupta, in which he has been described to have curbed the pride of his enemies, who raised their heads like serpents, only to be crushed and have their venom taken out. He was the voluntary choice of the goddess of fortune, from among other aspirants for the throne. It also speaks about his reorganisation of the entire administrative set up by appointing really capable officers to hold the key positions. The recent discovery of the Risthal stone slab inscription of Prakāśadharmā is an important addition to the inscriptions of this category. It almost revolutionises our ideas about the rise and decline of the Hūṇa power in India and supplies for the first time the urgently needed evidence for the ancestry of Yaśodharman. In the Mandasor pillar inscription, the poet Vāsula has eulogised the virtuous conduct of the emperor Yaśodharman and narrated his glorious achievements as a sovereign who ruled over territories which were not enjoyed even by the kings of the Gupta family and who compelled Mihirakula to pay obeisance at his feet. This inscription gives a clear idea of the extent of his empire.

However, we have to exercise a fair amount of caution in extracting historical information from these eulogies. Being compositions of grateful proteges, they are likely to be partial.

While they may exaggerate their good qualities and achievements, they may just ignore their shortcomings. At the same time we must not try to underrate these accounts, as has been done by some modern writers who see Samudragupta's defeat and discomfiture in his Southern campaign, even when the writer of the *Praśasti* is actually speaking of his policy of a traditional righteous conqueror in restoring the defeated kings to their thrones. There is no room likewise for being sceptic about the limits of the empire of Yaśodharman, when the author has so specifically mentioned its boundaries from east to west and north to south.

b. Inscriptions in Religious Monuments: To this category belong the inscriptions which record the construction of religious monuments such as temples, stūpas and setting up of flagstaffs as well as the construction of works of public utility for religious merit. Apart from giving us a peep into the religious life of those times, they supply other valuable historical information. For example, the Mandasor inscription of M.S. 524[8], which records the construction of a stūpa, throws new light on the achievements of Chandragupta II and his son Govindagupta. Before the discovery of this inscription, the name of Govindagupta was known only from the Vaiśālī seal of his mother Mahādevī Dhruvasvāminī and he was regarded only as governor of the province of Vaiśālī. But this inscription shows that most probably he was an imperial sovereign who ruled between G.S. 93 and 96. The Mandasor inscription dated M.S. 529[9], records the construction of a temple of the god Sun. Besides giving an account of the city of Daśapura, it supplies us a date 493 in the reign of Kumāragupta I in a reckoning other than the Gupta era and thus it helped Fleet in solving the knotty problem of the epoch of the Gupta era. Further it supplies the history of the local dynasty of Varman rulers of Daśapura who were feudatories of the Guptas, atleast during the reign of Kumāragupta I. The stone Boar inscription at Eran[10] records the construction of a temple of the Boar incarnation of Vishṇu, in the first year of Toramāṇa's rule. It indirectly speaks of the transference of the sovereignty over this region from the Guptas to the Hūṇas within one generation. The fragmentary stone inscription of Samudragupta from Eran, not only enlightens us about his munificient gifts of gold, but also affords a peep into his selection and anointment to the throne by his father himself. Other inscriptions recording the construction of religious monuments in the Gupta period are the following:

(i) The Mathura pillar inscription of the year 61[11], which supplies us the earliest known date for Chandragupta II and throws welcome light on the history of the worship of Lakulīśa.

(ii) Udayagiri cave inscription of Sanakānīka Mahārāja dated 82[12], records the excavation of a cave-temple by a Sanakānīka feudatory of Chandragupta II.

(iii) Udayagiri undated cave inscription of Vīrasena Śāba, the minister of foreign affairs of Chandragupta II Vikramāditya.[13] It records the excavation of a cave-temple dedicated to Śiva.

(iv) Bilsad stone pillar inscription dated 96[14], records the building of a lofty gateway and an alms-house at the temple of the god Kārttikeya, by a learned and pious Brahman Dhruvaśarman.

(v) Tumain stone inscription dated 116[15], mentions the construction of a lofty temple.

(vi) Kahaum stone pillar inscription dated 141[16], records the installation of this stone pillar together with the images of the five chief *tīrthaṁkaras* namely Ādinātha, Neminātha, Śāntinātha, Supārśva and Mahāvīra.

(vii) Rajghat (Varanasi) stone pillar inscription dated 159.[17] This is the second record proving the inclusion of Varanasi region in Budhagupta's empire.

(viii) Eran stone pillar inscription of Budhagupta dated 165[18], is the oldest epigraph in the Indian history in which the name of a week day along with the date G. S. 165 has been recorded.

(ix) Khewra (Kura) inscription of Toramāṇa[19], records the construction of a monastery.

(x) Gwalior stone inscription of Mihirakula[20], tells us about the building of a temple of the god Sun.

(xi) Mandasor stone slab inscription dated 589[21], of the reign of Yaśodharman, records the construction of a well, by the younger brother of Dharmadosha, a minister of Yaśodharman.

c. Inscriptions on Pedestals of Images: A good number of epigraphs recording the installation of images of deities are found on the pedestals of these statues and supply us very interesting and important historical information. For instance, the

Sarnath Buddha images dated 154[22] and 157[23] discovered during the excavations of 1914-15 at Sarnath, throw new light on the Gupta history and chronology. After the discovery of these inscriptions, it became clear for the first time that there was another Kumāragupta besides Kumāragupta I, the son of Chandragupta II Vikramāditya and that Budhagupta was not a mere ruler of Malwa as supposed by Fleet, but an emperor ruling over the heart of the Gangetic plain. Recent discovery of the Vidiśā Jain image inscriptions of Mahārājādhirāja Rāmagupta[24] has settled the long standing controversy about the historicity of this monarch, giving him a place amongst the imperial Gupta rulers. The inscription on the pedestal of Buddha image from Mankuwar[25] supplies a very late date for the rule of Kumāragupta I. The use of the title Mahārāja instead of Mahārājādhirāja for Kumāragupta I has given rise to the mistaken notion that Kumāragupta had suffered some reverses shortly before or about the date of this inscription. Following are the other image inscriptions found so far:

(i) Udayagiri cave inscription of the G. S. 106[26], records the engraving of an image of the Jain *Tīrthaṁkara* Pārśva.

(ii) Mathura Jain image inscription dated 107[27]. It records the dedication of a statue of Jina.

(iii) Mathura pedestal inscription of the reign of Kumāragupta I, dated 125[28]. It records the installation of the image of standing Buddha.

(iv) Mathura inscription of the reign of Budhagupta, dated the year 161[29]. It records the installation of four images of the Buddha.

d. Land Grants: Quite a good number of inscriptions consist of land grants. They are engraved on copper plates (*tāmra-patras*) with the exception of the Bihar stone pillar inscription[30]. The records of land grants consist of two distinct types: (a) those which record the gifts of land by the rulers to Brahmanas and religious institutions like temples, monasteries etc., for their maintenance; and (b) those which record the transfer of land by sale by the government for religious purposes. The first type gives us information about the pedigree of the donor king, the names of important administrative officers, the revenue system of the state concerned, the religious sect patronised etc. Sometimes we get very important historical information from the land grants. The Gunaighar copper plate of Vainyagupta[31] records the grant of land to a Buddhist monastery. It shows that the Gupta kings were liberal in their religious outlook and patronised other faiths like Buddhism. Similarly the Poona copper plates of the regnal year 13[32] and the Riddhapur copper plates of the regnal year 19[33] give information that the Vākāṭaka queen Prabhāvatīguptā, the wife of Rudrasena II, was the daughter of Chandragupta II by his Nāga queen Kuberanāgā. This information enabled us for the first time to identify Devagupta of the Chammak[34] and other Vākāṭaka copper plates, with Chandragupta II Vikramāditya, instead of Devagupta of the Later Gupta dynasty. This also placed the chronology of the Vākāṭakas on a sound footing.

As examples of the transfer of land by sale by the government, mention may be made of five copper plate grants from Damodarpur[35], and Kulaikuri copper plate inscription dated 120.[36] These inscriptions may be regarded as having been drawn up roughly in six parts. The first part contains the prayer of the applicant for the purchase of land, and the names of the ruling emperor and the high officers of the local administration. It also contains the date. The second part consists of the statement of the object for which the land is needed. Along with it is the mention of the prevalent price at which the land is sold by the government. Next we are informed that the application is referred to the keepers of land-records whose approval appears to be necessary for the transfer at the mentioned price. The fourth part embodies the sanction of the state authorities to the sale of land and instructions issued to the local revenue officers to measure out the land and give its possession to the applicant. The local officers then measured the land and handed over its possession to the applicant. At the end we find the usual imprecatory and laudatory verses. Following are the other copper-plate grants known to us so far:

(i) Nalanda (spurious) copper plate of Samudragupta.[37] This is a forged charter, as is indicated by the use of the bipartite *ya* instead of the tripartite one and the abrupt change from genetive to nominative in the genealogical portion. It purports to record a grant of two villages to a brahman named Jayabhaṭṭasvāmin.

(ii) Gaya (spurious) copper plate of Samudragupta.[38] This is also a forged document as clearly revealed by the use of bipartite *ya* and the abrupt change from genetive to nominative. It also purports to record a grant of a village named Revatikā to a brahman named Gopasvāmin.

(iii) Dhanaidah copper plate inscription dated 113[39], records the sale of one *kulyāvāpa* of land to a brahman named Varāhasvāmin at the market price, by orders of the *Āyuktaka*.

(iv) Baigram copper plate grant of the year 128[40]. This records the request for the transfer by sale of some land for the maintenance of a temple of Govindasvāmin.

(v) Khoh copper plate of Mahārāja Hastin dated 156.[41] This is a charter of grant of land written in accordance with the injunctions in the *Yājñavalkya Smṛiti*. It records the grant of a village to certain brahmans by the Parivrājaka king Hastin, who was a feudatory of the imperial Gupta dynasty.

(vi) Paharpur copper plate grant of the year 159.[42] This is the record of sale of some land to a brahman Nāthasvāmin and his wife Rāmī for making a gift of it to a Jain monastery at Vaṭagohāli, in the Rajshahi district of Bangladesh.

(vii) Khoh copper plate of Mahārāja Hastin dated 163.[43] This charter records the grant of an *agrahāra* named Korpirika by the Parivrājaka king Hastin, for the increase of his religious merit.

(viii) Shankarpur copper plate of Budhagupta and Harivarman dated 168.[44] The object of the inscription is to record the grant of a village Chitrapalya to a brahman Gosvāmin by Mahārāja Harivarman.

(ix) Nandpur copper plate inscription of the year 169.[45] This is also a sale deed in favour of *Vishayapati* Chhatramaha for making a gift of four *kulyāvāpas* of land to a brahman whose name in the inscription is damaged.

(x) Bhamodarmohtta copper plate inscription of Droṇasiṁha dated 183.[46] This is a record of grant of the village—Trisaṃgamaka, by the Maitraka king Droṇasiṁha of Valabhī to the temple of the goddess Pāṇḍurājā for providing materials of worship and for the upkeep of the temple.

(xi) Majhagwan-copper plate inscription of Mahārāja Hastin dated 191.[47] This records the grant of a village to three brahmans by Mahārāja Hastin in the year A.D. 510.

(xii) Three Copper Plate inscriptions from Sanjeli: Of the three plates, discovered very recently, and each recording a grant, the first was issued in the year 3 by Mahārāja Bhūta who was governing the *vishaya* of Śivabhogapura when *Paramabhaṭṭāraka Mahārājādhirāja* illustrious Toramāṇa was ruling over the earth. The second plate was also issued by Mahārāja Bhūta meditating on the feet of a *Paramabhaṭṭāraka*, whose name is not mentioned, in the year 6. The first records the levying of certain taxes to meet the expenses of worship of the god Jayasvāmin and repair of his temple and the second records the grant of two villages alongwith taxes and a farm-house in favour of the same temple.

The third plate issued in the year 19 by Mahārāja Mātṛidāsa, son of Mahārāja Bhūta, records the grant of a village to the god Syāmi-Nārāyaṇa.[48]

(xiii) Jagdishpur (Rajshahi) copper plate inscription.[49]

e. Inscriptions Recording Donations: The fifth category comprises of the inscriptions recording the donations given to the religious institutions, such as temples and *vihāras* or to the brahmans and Buddhist mendicants by individuals. They provide us information about the prevalent religious trends of those times, incidently giving important historical data also. For example the Indore copper plate[50] which records a private donation to a temple of the god Sun, supplies a late date—A.D. 465-66—for the reign of Skandagupta. There are the following inscriptions of this type :

(i) Gadhwa stone inscription dated 88.[51] It tells us about the establishment of an alms-house.

(ii) Sanchi railing inscription dated 93[52], informs us that on behalf of the Gupta emperor Chandragupta II and on his own behalf one of his military officers donated 25 golden coins and some property named Iśvaravāsaka which had been purchased with the money provided by the royal family. From half of this five monks were to be fed and a lamp lighted at the *stūpa* for the religious merit of Chandragupta II and by means of the other half similar acts were to be performed for the merit of that army officer.

(iii) Gadhwa stone inscription dated 98.[53] It records the donation of 12 *Dīnāras* to an alms-house.

(iv) Gadhwa undated stone inscription of Kumāragupta I[54], records two donations—one of ten and the other of three *Dināras* to the alms-house at Gadhwa which seems to have been a very important charitable establishment.

(v) Karmadanda lingam inscription dated 117[55], records a gift of unspecified nature for the worship of god Śiva named as Pṛithivīśvara.

f. Memorial Stone Pillar Inscriptions: Putting up of memorial records on stone in memory of departed relatives is a fairly old custom in India. In the year 52 of the reign of Western Kshatrapa ruler Rudradāman I, i.e. in A.D. 130, as many as four memorial stones were set up in the small village of Andhau near Bhuj in Kutch.[56] In the Gupta period we have so far come across the following memorial records:

(1) Supia stone pillar inscription dated 141[57], records that this *gotra-śailikā* 'i.e. 'a small stone memorial' was set up by a person named Varga-grāmika. It has also been called a *vala-yashṭi.* An interesting point regarding this inscription is the mention of Ghaṭotkacha as the founder of the Gupta dynasty, and the kings Chandragupta II and Kumāragupta have been referred to only by their *birudas*—Vikramāditya and Mahendrāditya.

(ii) Eran stone pillar inscription dated 191.[58] The stone pillar bearing this inscription has been worshipped as a *Śivaliṅga* from time out of memory. Fleet published this inscription which records that Mahārāja Goparāja, a feudatory of the Gupta sovereign Bhānugupta, was killed here in a battle with an unspecified enemy; and his wife immolated herself on the funeral pyre. This is the sole reference to the custom of *satī* in the Gupta inscriptions. The pillar was recently dug up to the foundation and it was discovered that it was put up much earlier, during the rule of Śaka Śrīdharavarman, in order to commemorate the heroic death of some warriors in a battle, the details of which have not been given.

g. Inscription of Unspecified Nature: A fragmentary inscription on red sand stone was discovered from Mathura.[59] The extent portion of the inscription contains a part of the genealogy of the imperial Guptas and mentions the name of Samudragupta. Fleet assigned it to Chandragupta II. The object of the inscription is lost in the broken portion.

Seals and Sealings

Just like the inscriptions, seals and sealings[60] too form an important source of historical information for the Gupta history. Sometimes they constitute the solitary source of information. Relevant to the present discussion are the seals which were attached to the copper plates recording grants of lands.

The most notable instance of such a seal is the well known Bhitari seal of Kumāragupta III, made of an alloy of copper, silver and a small quantity of gold.[61] Presumably, this seal was attached to some copper plate recording a grant of land which has now been lost, perhaps irretrievably. The discovery of this seal in 1889, is a landmark in the reconstruction of the Gupta history. Upto that time, the last known emperor of the imperial Gupta line was Mahārājādhirāja Skandagupta, the son and successor of Kumāragupta I. But this seal carried the genealogy further, adding two more generations and three new names of rulers viz. Purugupta son of Kumāragupta I, his son Mahārājādhirāja Narasiṁhagupta whose son and successor was Mahārājādhirāja Kumāragupta who has now to be designated as Kumāragupta III. As the name of Skandagupta who is known to have ruled from G.S. 136 to 148 is omitted in the Bhitari seal, it gave rise to a big problem for the historians of the Gupta dynasty. There has been a sharp difference of opinion among them regarding the reason for this omission. Some have suggested that Skandagupta was not entitled to succeed his father as he was not the son of the chief queen. This led to a war of succession and the division of the empire between Skandagupta and Purugupta. Others propose to identify the two as one and the same person. These theories will be discussed in their proper place.

Of the clay sealings of this period we have a fairly good number discovered during the course of archaeological excavations at Basarh (Vaiśālī), Bhita, Nalanda and Rajghat (Varanasi). Some sealings written in the Gupta Brāhmī have been discovered from sites like Sunet and Sanghol in Punjab, but in the absence of any positive evidence it is difficult to connect them with the imperial Guptas. Clay was used in ancient India for sealing official communications or parcels of documents sent through messengers. Sometimes these served the purpose of tokens of permit or of identity.[62] Nalanda has yielded a number of sealings of the Gupta emperors Budhagupta, Narasiṁhagupta, Kumāragupta III as well as fragments of those of Vainyagupta and Vishṇugupta besides the sealings of various administrative officers, mentioned by name or by designation or by both. Sealings of the latter type belonging to the Gupta age, have been found at Bhita also. Another class of clay sealings from some of these sites appears to be intended for dissemination of moral teachings.

The clay sealings of the emperors Budhagupta[63], Narasiṁhagupta[64], Kumāragupta III[65], Vishṇugupta[66], and Vainyagupta[67], presumably belong to the official communications that were addressed to the authorities of the Nalanda University. They have provided valuable historical information. The discovery of the clay sealing of Budhagupta furnished evidence for the first time regarding the exact place of Budhagupta in the genealogy of the imperial Gupta dynasty, and helped to correct some erroneous notions. In the absence of such information, Fleet had designated him as a local ruler of Malwa. But this sealing from Nalanda proved that he was a son of Mahārājādhirāja Purugupta and belonged to the imperial Gupta family.

The clay sealings of Mahārājādhirāja Narasiṁhagupta and Mahārājādhirāja Kumāragupta III from Nalanda not only confirm the existence of these two Gupta emperors who had first become known from the Bhitari seal, but also enable us to correct the names of the queens of Purugupta and of Narasiṁhagupta. The name of the former had been doubtfully read as Vatsadevī by Hoernle[68] and Fleet[69] on the Bhitari silver seal but the Nalanda sealing clearly gives Chandradevī[70]. Similarly the name of Narasiṁhagupta's queen on the Bhitari seal had been read as Śrimatīdevī by Hoernle[71] and Mahālakshmīdevī by Fleet[72], but according to the Nalanda sealing the correct name is Śrīmitradevī[73].

The clay sealings of Vainyagupta and Vishṇugupta from Nalanda have added two more names to the list of imperial Gupta rulers and have enabled us to correct two mistakes in Gupta numismatics. The gold coins bearing the name Vishṇu[74] attributed to Vishṇuvardhana Yaśodharman by Hoernle[75], can now be safely attributed to this imperial Gupta ruler. Similarly the gold coins attributed to Chandragupta III by Allan, have now been correctly assigned to Vainyagupta.

The clay sealing of Mahādevī Dhruvasvâmini from Basarh is equally informative. It has supplied the name of another son of Chandragupta II and Dhruvadevī viz. Govindagupta, whom we now know from the Mandasor inscription dated M.S. 524[76], as a powerful ruler and the envy of even Indra, the lord of the gods. Some scholars regard him as an imperial ruler who succeeded his father Chandragupta II and preceded Kumāragupta I[77]. Others, however, contest this view[78].

Another seal from Basarh, supplies the name of Śrī Ghaṭotkachagupta who is evidently different from Mahārāja Ghaṭotkacha, the son and successor of Mahārāja Gupta, the founder of the Gupta dynasty[79]. Śrī Ghaṭotkacha of the Basarh seal may be identified with the prince mentioned in the Tumain inscription dated G.S. 116[80].

The fragmentary Nalanda sealing of Mahārājādhirāja Vainyagupta does not contain the names of any of his predecessors or successors; and that makes it very difficult to assign a definite place to this ruler in the imperial Gupta genealogy and chronology. In all probability he is not different from Vainyagupta of the Gunaighar copper plate grant of the year 188[81], although the title Mahārāja given to Vainyagupta in this inscription creates some doubt regarding the identity of the two.

The discovery of the sealings of so many Gupta rulers from Nalanda may be taken as an indication of the active association of these rulers with this famous seat of learning and also as a proof of the patronage bestowed by them on this great institution.

Besides the seals and sealings of individual rulers and the members of their families, a large number of these discovered from Basarh, Nalanda and Bhita throw welcome light on the administrative set up of the Gupta period. The more important among these are given below:

a. *Seals from Basarh*[82]

(i) *Kumārāmātyādhikaraṇasya.*
'Of the office of the *Kumārāmātya*.'

(ii) *Yuvarājapādīya-kumārāmātyādhikaraṇasya.*
'Of the office of the *kumārāmātya* attached to the heir-apparent.'

(iii) *Śrī-para* [*mabhaṭṭāraka*] *pādīya kumārāmātyādhikaraṇasya.*
'Of the office of the *kumārāmātya* attached to the illustrious the Supreme lord.'

(iv) *Yuvarāja-bhaṭṭāraka-pādīya-balādhikaraṇasya.*
'Of the war office (headed by) the lord heir apparent.'

(v) *Śrī raṇa-bhāṇḍāgārādhikaraṇasya.*
'Of the office of the military stores.'

(vi) *Daṇḍapāśādhikaraṇasya.*
'Of the office of Police'.

(vii) *Mahāpratihāra-taravara Vinayaśūrasya.*
'Of Vinayaśūra, the chief chamberlain and prefect of police.'

(viii) *Tīra-bhukty-uparik-ādhikaraṇasya.*
'Of the office of *Uparika* of Tīra-Bhukti.'

(ix) *Tīrabhuktau vinaya-sthiti-sthāpakādhikaraṇasya.*
'Of the office of moral education and discipline in Tīra-bhukti.'

(x) *Śreshṭhi-sārthavāha-kulika-nigamasya.*
'Of the corporation of the bankers, traders and artisans.'

b. Seals from Nalanda[83]

(i) *Rājagṛihe vishayādhikaraṇasya.*
'Of the district office in Rājagṛiha.'

(ii) *Gayā vishayādhikaraṇasya.*
'Of the district office in Gayā.'

(iii) *Śoṇāntarāla vishayā-dhikaraṇasya.*
'Of the district office in Śoṇa-*doab*.'

(iv) *Magadha-bhuktau kumārāmātyādhikaraṇasya.*
'Of the office of the *Kumārāmātya* in the Division of Magadha.'

(v) *Śrāvastī bhuktau nayādhikaraṇasya.*
'Of the court of law in the Śrāvastī Division.'

(vi) *Dharmādhikaraṇasya.*
'Of the Court of Justice.'

(vii) *Mahābhāṇḍārika Śri Bhadrabhānoh.*
'Of the honourable Bhadrabhānu, the Chief Keeper of Stores.'

c. Sealings from Bhita[84]

(i) *Mahāśvapati Mahādaṇḍanāyaka Vishṇurakshita-pādānugṛihītakumārāmātyādhikaraṇasya.*
'Of the office of the *Kumārāmātya* favoured by the feet of Vishṇurakshita the great commander of the Horse and the great commander of the army.

(ii) *Mahārāja Śaṅkarasiṁha-pādīya Āyuktādhikaraṇasya.*
'Of the office of the *Āyukta* attached to Mahārāja Śaṅkarasiṁha.'

(iii) *Amāty=eśvarachandrasya.*
'of the minister Īśvarachandra.'

COINS

Numismatic evidence is an important and indispensable source of the Gupta history, next only to the inscriptions. The first hoard of the Gupta gold coins was found in 1783[85], from Kalighat near Calcutta. At that time these coins were taken as a mere treasure of gold, and were presented to the Directors of the East India Company by Warren Hastings, the then Governor General of India. A small number of them ultimately found their way to the British Museum, London, the Ashmolean Museum, Oxford, and the Public Library, Cambridge. The rest of them were melted away. These coins were examined by Payne Knight who failed to decipher the legends on them and called them close imitations of Greek coins. It was Marsden who successfully read the legends Chandra and *Śrī-Vikrama* on them[86]. In 1832, Wilson contributed a paper on the subject whose plates were drawn by James Prinsep.[87] Neither Wilson nor Prinsep could make much of it at that time except for reading letters *pa*, *ra* and *ka* on the reverse of the standard type of Samudragupta, without completing the word *prākramaḥ*. However, by 1835 considerable progress had been made in deciphering Gupta Brāhmī letters, and Prinsep was successful in reading some of the marginal inscriptions on these coins. In course of time more hoards of the Gupta gold-coins came to light in the later half of the 19th century and first half of the 20th century. Important amongst these were Bharsar (1851), Jessore (1852), Allahabad (1864), Hugali (1883), Tanda (1885), Kotwa (1886), Basti (1887), Hajipur (1893), and Tekri Debra (1912).[88] In 1884 the *Catalogue of the Coins of Gupta*

Dynasty was published by V.A. Smith for the first time[89]. It was improved with great labour by the same author and it appeared with additions in 1889 in the *Journal of the Royal Asiatic Society*[90]. It was followed by the *Catalogue of the Coins of the Gupta Dynasties, in the British Museum,* by John Allan, published in 1914. Like the Corpus of Fleet on the Gupta inscriptions this was the first comprehensive work of very high merit on the Gupta numismatics brought out with meticulous care and scholarly labour. The discoveries continued even after the publication of Allan's Catalogue like Kasarva (1912), Sakori (1914), Mithathal (1915), Bamnala (1940), Bayana (1946), Kusumbhi (1947), Khairatal (1948), and Kumarkham (1952).[91] The Bayana hoard is the most important. It contained about 2100 gold coins of which only 1821 were recovered. A.S. Altekar published a splendid catalogue of this hoard.[92] In 1957 an exhaustive and up to date work *The Coinage of the Gupta Empire* was presented to the world of numismatists by the same eminent scholar[93]. In the new publication Altekar included all varieties of the Gupta coinage—gold, silver and copper coins.

In some cases the coins constitute the primary evidence. The importance of coins for the study of economic conditions is too obvious. The vast number and varieties of the Gupta gold coins by themselves indicate the high state of economic prosperity under the imperial Guptas proving their regime literally as the golden age of India.

The coins throw a flood of light on the political, cultural and the religious history of the time. The legends on the coins are a sort of written source material, though often too small to give details. But nonetheless they solve many riddles of history. The metrical legends on the Gupta coins show high literary taste of the rulers who issued them, and eloquently speak of their many deeds of religious merit and of valour on the battlefield.

The internal evidence contained in the different coin-types of each ruler has its own importance. They supply many unknown facts of history. For example Chandragupta-Kumāradevī type of gold coins throw light on the rise of the Guptas to imperial position. Similarly the *Aśvamedha* type of Samudragupta and Kumāragupta I, reveal the performance by these rulers of the horse-sacrifices which are not mentioned in their inscriptions. Besides providing new facts they corroborate the information obtained from epigraphic and literary sources. For example, Harisheṇa states in the Allahabad inscription of Samudragupta that the latter put to shame the divine musicians Nārada and Tumburu by his musical skill. The statement is corroborated by the lyrist type coins of Samudragupta. The copper coins of Rāmagupta from Malwa help in proving the historicity of this ruler, first known from *Devīchandraguptam*. The large variety in the types of coins of one ruler is an index of the comparative prosperity of the reign. Samudragupta issued seven different types, Chandragupta II issued eight, Kumāragupta I—fifteen and Skandagupta—five while the later rulers of the dynasty were content with one or two types each only.

The figures and other symbols on the coins reveal the religious leanings of the rulers. They also throw light on various aspects of culture such as costume, furniture, weapons of war, etc. A.K. Narain has rightly said, "These portraits sometimes tell the historian of the time range of a king's reign, and moreover they may betray more convincingly than even a biography, the character and personality of the king."[94]

The style and fabric, metallurgy and metrology of the coins also indirectly furnish useful historical evidence. The fine fabric and high artistic merit of the coins indicate the political stability and the progress in art. However, it is not quite safe always to draw definite conclusions on this basis only. Metrology however may prove safer. Its fluctuations may reflect political and economic situations and their effect. The early Gupta kings followed the Kushāṇa and Roman standard of 121 grains for their gold coins, most probably because it was well established in the Roman and Kushāṇa empires and had acquired an international recognition[95]. Gradually the weight standard of the gold coins was increased from the time of Chandragupta II till it came to 144 grains, the Indian standard of *suvaraṇa*, in the time of Skandagupta. His successors continued to issue the coins in *suvarṇa* standard only. Metallurgy is an equally noteworthy point in the Gupta gold coins. The coins of Chandragupta I contained 90% pure gold, that of Samudragupta and Chandragupta II 85% to 90% pure gold, that of Kumāragupta I, Skandagupta, Budhagupta, Prakāśāditya etc. contain 75% to 80% pure gold. Only the coins of Narasiṁhagupta, Kumāragupta II and Vishṇugupta are heavily adulterated. They contain 54% and 43% pure gold respectively[96]. Many writers have argued that the deteriorating political and economic condition of the Gupta empire was responsible for the adulteration. However, this was not the case in our opinion. The higher percentage of alloy in the coins of the latter Guptas was probably due to the desire to have a coin of traditional weight of *suvarṇa* as described in our ancient law-books[97], but containing only 112-113 grains of pure gold as before, so that the metal value of the coin remained the same. The theory of critical, political and economic condition may be true for the latest rulers like Vishṇugupta.

The geographical distribution and provenance of different types of coins also provide valuable evidence for reconstructing the history of the issuer. Though the existence of coins in a particular area may not positively indicate the political authority of the issuer in that area but it definitely throws light on many other facts. The existence of a large number of Roman gold coins in India, for instance, proves the flourishing trade between India and the West. Whereas the existence of gold coins may not prove the political authority of the king who issued them, over that area, it is not so with the coins of inferior metals like copper or even silver, as they seldom travelled far from their home province. For example, the silver coins of Chandragupta II, Kumāragupta I and Skandagupta issued in Surāshṭra from the beginning of the fifth century were close imitations of the popular currency of that province, Hemi-Drachmas of the Śaka currency and were undoubtedly issued by the Gupta rulers after the conquest of Surāshṭra. Similarly the copper coins issued by Rāmagupta, Chandragupta II and Kumāragupta I formed the popular currency of Malwa and were issued according to the local needs and tradition of the province. This indicates the conservatism in regard to the types and fabric of coin in a particular area, even after the change of political authority. Though a numismatist faces some limitations when interpreting the evidence provided by coins, there is no doubt that the proper interpretation gives very useful results for the reconstruction of history.

Silver Coins:

The startling discoveries in this field of numismatics of the Gupta period have made it necessary to discuss the silver coinage under a separate heading. It was a well established belief up to very recent times that Chandragupta II was the first Gupta ruler to issue silver currency and even that after the conquest of Surāshṭra following the pattern of Śaka silver coinage. However, the discovery of two silver coins belonging, one each to Chandragupta I and Samudragupta has given a new turn to the theories and ideas about the silver coinage of the Guptas. The first of these coins is of *King and Queen* type and exactly resembles its counterpart in gold. Its discovery was reported by A.L. Srivastava in 1975.[98] The other one is the *Lyrist* type of Samudragupta published by Upendra Thakur.[99] The most significant fact brought forth by these discoveries is that the Gupta emperors issued coins in all the three metals from the very beginning and that the gold coins being precious have survived in larger number. However, during the 1987 session of the Numismatic Society of India at Patna we had a chance to examine about two dozen silver coins of the types mentioned above, with the coin-dealers attending the conference. We dare say, all of them appeared to us to be recent forgeries. The presence of three silver coins amongst these, with the name of Kanishka and Kushāṇa obverse and the reverse of Kumāragupta's *Apratigha* type with the legend *apratigha* confirmed our suspicion about their being forged issues. A. S. Altekar had expressed the same opinion as early as 1959 about the Lyrist type of Samudragupta's silver coin.[100]

Coin Types:

The following coin types of the Gupta rulers in gold, silver and copper are known so far:

Cold Conins

Chandragupta I:

i. King and Queen type: [101] On the obverse of these coins Chandragupta and Kumāradevī are shown standing facing each other. Under the left arm of the king *Chandra* is written vertically and outside the standard, also written vertically, is *gupta*.

On the left hand side margin *Śrī Kumāradevī* is written. The reverse shows goddess sitting on lion. The legend on this side is *Lichchhavayaḥ* i.e. 'the Lichchhavis'. Chandragupta I seems to have issued coins of this type only.

Samudragupta:

i. Archer type: In this type which became the most popular type with all the imperial Gupta rulers down to Vishṇugupta, the king is shown standing with bow in the left hand and an arrow in the right. The *Garuḍa* emblem is found on the left hand side. Under the king's left arm is written *Saṃudra*. The circular legend is *Apratiratho vijitya kṣhitiṃ sucharitair=divaṃ jayati*, i.e. 'Having conquered the earth, the invincible one wins heaven by meritorious deeds'. On reverse is shown a goddess sitting on throne holding cornucopiae. The legend is *Apratirathaḥ* i.e. 'Matchless warrior'.

ii. Standard type: On the obverse of this type of coins the king is shown standing to the left, holding a standard in the left hand and offering oblation in fire with the right hand. *Samudra* is written under the left arm. These coins were perhaps issued on the pattern of Kushāṇa gold coins of this type, but their individuality is brought to fore by the metrical circular legend in chaste Sanskrit, typical of the gold issues of the imperial Guptas. It reads, *Samara-śata-vitata-vijayo-jita-ripur=ajito-divam-jayatī* i.e. 'The invincible (king) who has won victories in a hundred battles and conquered the enemies, now wins the heaven.' The reverse shows the goddess as in the Archer type and the legend *Parākramaḥ*. This type seems to have been discontinued very soon as we have only one specimen of this type belonging to Chandragupta II and none after that.

iii. Battle-axe type: On the obverse of this type, the king is shown standing with his right hand resting on the waist and having *parśu* (battle-axe) in the left hand. There is a dwarf attendant in his front looking at the king. A crescent-topped standard is between the two. *Samudra* is written under the arm of the king. The circular legend is *Kṛitānta-paraśur=jayatyajita-rājajetājitaḥ* i.e. 'wielding the battle-axe of Kṛitānta, the unconquered conqueror of unconquered kings, is victorious! The reverse shows goddess sitting on throne and the legend is *Kṛitāntaparśuḥ*.

iv. Tiger slayer type: These coins depict the king standing to the left trampling upon and shooting at a tiger by his bow. The crescent topped standard is shown between the king and the tiger. The legend on obverse is *Vyāghraparākramaḥ*, 'Valiant like a tiger'. On the reverse goddess Gaṅgā is shown standing on a crocodile. The legend on this side is *Rājā Samudraguptaḥ*.

v. Lyrist type: This type, which testifies to Samudragupta's skill in music, depicts Samudragupta wearing waist-cloth (*dhotī*), seated on a couch and playing upon the lute (*Vīṇā*). The legend is *Mahārājādhirāja-Śrī-Samudraguptaḥ*. On the reverse of this type goddess Lakshmī is shown sitting on a wicker stool. The legend to the left is *Samudraguptaḥ*.

vi. Aśvamedha type: Evidently these coins were issued to commemorate the performance of the horse-sacrifice by Samudragupta, a fact mentioned in the inscriptions of his successors. The obverse of these coins shows an uncaparisoned horse, standing before the sacrificial post (*yūpa*). The circular legend reads, *Rājādhirājaḥ pṛithivīmavitvā* (or *vijitya*) *divaṁ jayaty=āhṛita-vājimedhaḥ*[102] i.e. 'The king of kings, who had performed the *vājimedha* (*aśvamedha*) sacrifice, wins heaven after protecting (or after conquering the earth)'. On the reverse of this type the crowned queen is shown holding a *chaurī* over her right shoulder in her right hand and a towel in her left hand. The legend is *Aśvamedha parākramaḥ* i.e. 'One who has the prowess to perform *aśvamedha* sacrifice.'

vii. Kâcha type[103]: These are a very close copy of the standard type coins of Samudragupta, with the only difference that the king is shown on obverse holding a wheel-(*chakra*)-surmounted standard and the name under the king's arm is *Kācha* instead of Samudra. The circular legend is *Kācho gāmavajitya divaṃ karmabhir-uttamair=jayati* i.e. 'Having conquered the earth Kācha wins the heaven by excellent deeds.' On the reverse the legend is *Sarvarāj=ochchhettā* i.e. 'Exterminator of all kings'.

Chandragupta II:

i. Archer type: Same as that of Samudragupta. On the obverse *Chandra* is written vertically under the left arm of the king and the circular legend is *Deva-Śrī-mahārājādhirāja-śrī-Chandragupataḥ*. The legend on the reverse is *Śrī Vikramaḥ*.

ii. Lion slayer type: This type closely resembles the Tiger slayer type of Samudragupta, but here instead of a tiger, Chandragupta is shown slaying a lion with his bow and arrow. These coins have been divided into three classes viz. Lion combatant type, Lion trampler type and Lion retreating type.[104] The legend on the obverse of the first two classes is *Narendrachandraḥ prathitaraṇo raṇe jayatyajeyo bhuvi siṁhavikramaḥ* i.e. 'The moon among the kings who is famous for his warfare, who is invincible in battle and who has the prowess of a lion, is victorious on this earth.' In some cases the legend on the third class of this type is given as: *Mahārājādhirāja śrī Chandraguptaḥ* or *Deva-śrī-mahārāja Chandraguptaḥ*, instead of the meterical one. The legend on the reverse invariably reads *Siṁhavikramaḥ* i.e. 'Having the valour of lion.'

It has been suggested that this type was issued by Chandragupta after his conquest of Gujrat, which is the home of lions in India.

iii. The Horseman type: This is one of the new types introduced by Chandragupta II who was probably a skilled horseman. On the obverse of these coins, the king is shown riding a caparisoned horse, sometimes carrying weapons like bow and arrow or sword. On the reverse the goddess is shown sitting on a wicker-stool. The obverse legend is *Paramabhāgavata-Mahārājādhirāja-Śrī-Chandraguptaḥ* i.e. 'The great devotee of Vishṇu the Emperor Chandragupta'. On the reverse is inscribed *Ajitavikramaḥ* i.e. 'Of invincible valour'.

iv. Chhatra type: On the coins of this type the king is shown standing to left offering oblations upon an altar with his right hand, while his left hand rests upon the hilt of his sword. A dwarf attendant, holding a parasol (*Chhatra*) over the king's head is shown at the back of the king. The reverse has the goddess Lakshmī, standing on a lotus. The coins of this type have been divided into two classes. In one class the legend on the obverse is in prose, while in the second class it is metrical. On the coins of first class we find written, *Mahārājādhirāja-Śrī-Chandraguptaḥ*, 'King of kings, His Majesty Chandragupta.' The second class has the legend *Kshitimavajitya sucharitair=divaṁ jayati Vikramādityaḥ* i.e. 'Having conquered the earth, Vikramāditya wins the heaven by his meritorious deeds.' The reverse legend on both the classes is *Vikramādityaḥ*.

v. Couch type: On the coins of this type, the king is shown seated upon a couch with a flower in his hand. The obverse legend reads either *Devaśrī-mahārājādhirāja-śrī-Chandraguptasya* or *Paramabhāgavata-mahārājādhiraja-Śri-Chandraguptaḥ*. On some of these coins occurs the legend *Rūpākṛitī*, which has given rise to a controversy amongst the scholars as to its exact meaning. The legend on the reverse is *Śrī-Vikramaḥ*.

vi. King and Queen on couch type: Only one coin of this type is known so far.[105] On its reverse the king and the queen are shown sitting on a couch. The king is offering an object to the queen.[106] The legend on the margin is *Śrī-Vikramaḥ*. On the other side the king is shown standing, holding a standard in the right hand. *Garuḍa* standard is seen behind his right hand. Under his left arm is written *Chandra*. The circular legend is *Para(?) mabhāga...Śrī-Chandragupta*.

vii. Chakravikrama type: Only two coins of this type are known so far. On their obverse is the deity *Chakrapurusha* (personification of *Chakra* of god Vishṇu) standing to the right within a wheel and offering three round objects to the king, who is shown standing in front of the deity, extending his right hand to receive the divine gift. There is no legend on this side. The reverse depicts goddess Lakshmī standing on lotus. Legend on the right is *Chakravikrama(ḥ)*. Though the name of the issuer is not given on this type, but the epithet *Vikrama* makes it almost certainly an issue of Chandragupta II who used it on all varieties of his coins in combination with *Ajit*, *Siṁha* etc.

viii. Standard type: There is only one coin of this type which is similar to the standard type of Samudragupta. *Chandragu(pta)* is written on its obverse. vertically under the left arm of the king and the circular legend is, *Vasudhā vijitya jayata tradava pṛithavaśvaraḥ* which has been restored by A. S. Altekar as *Vasudhāṁ vijitya jayati tridivaṁ pṛithivīśvaraḥ (puṇyaiḥ)*[107] i.e. 'Having conquered the globe, the lord of the earth (now) wins heaven by meritorious deeds. The legend on the reverse is *Paramabhāgavāta*.

Kumāragupta I:

Kumāragupta issued the largest varieties, and some of them are superb artistic productions.

i. Archer type: They are similar to the archer type coins of Chandragupta II and are found in a large number. Under the king's left arm is written vertically *Kumāra* or sometimes only *Ku.* On some specimens even that is missing. On the reverse the legend is *Śrī-Mahendraḥ*. They have been divided into many classes on the basis of their obverse circular legends which variously read as follows:

a. *Mahārājādhirāja-Śrī-Kumāraguptaḥ.*
'King of kings, the illustrious Kumāragupta.'
b. *Guṇeśo mahītalam......jayati Kumāraḥ.*
'Prominent in merit......Kumāra conquers the world.'
c. *Vijitāvanir=avanipatiḥ Kumāragupto divaṁ jayati.*
'King Kumāragupta who has conquered the earth, wins heaven.'
d. *Jayati mahītalaṁ Śrī-Kumāraguptaḥ.*
'The illustrious Kumāragupta conquers the earth.'
e. *Jāyati mahītālaṁ Śrī-Kumāraguptaḥ sudhanvī.*
'The excellent archer, the illustrious Kumāragupta conquers the earth.'
f. *Paramarājādhirāja-Śrī-Kumāraguptaḥ.*
'The illustrious Kumāragupta, the highest king of kings.'

ii. Horseman type: The obverse of these coins is the same as that of the horseman type of Chandragupta II. On the reverse of some of these coins we however find a goddess feeding a peacock, which is an innovation of Kumāragupta. The obverse legends on this type are:

a. *Pṛithivītal-āmbaraśaśī Kumāragupto jayaty-ajitaḥ.*
'The moon in the firmament of the earth, the invincible Kumāragupta is victorious.'
b. *Jayati nṛipo=ribhir-ajitaḥ.*
'Victorious is the king who is never defeated by the enemies.'
c. *Kshitipatir-ajito vijayī Kumāragupto*[108] *divaṁ jayati.*
'The unconquered and victorious king Kumāragupta wins the heaven.'
d. *Guptakula-vyoma-śaśī jayaty=ajeyo' jita Mahendraḥ.*
'The unconquered and invincible Mahendra, who is a moon in the sky of the Gupta family, is victorious.'

e. *Guptakul-āmalachandro Mahendrakarm-ājito jayati.*
'The spotless moon (in the firmament) of the Gupta family, the invincible hero who is valorous as Indra, is victorious.'

f. *Kshitipatir-ajito vijayī Kumāragupto jayaty-ajitaḥ.*
'The invincible and victorious king Kumāragupta carries the day, being undefeated.'

g. *Pṛithivītaleśvarendraḥ Kumāragupto jayaty-ajitaḥ.*
'The lord of the rulers of this earth, the invincible Kumāragupta is victorious.'

The legend on the reverse of this type is *Ajitamahendraḥ*.

iii. Swordsman type: This is a new type introduced by Kumāragupta I. It shows on obverse the king standing to the right offering oblations on the altar before him with his right hand, and the left hand resting on the hilt of his sword, hanging by his side. *Garuḍa* standard is in front of the king. The letter *Ku* is written by the side of sword. The circular legend is, *Gāmavajitya sucharitaiḥ Kumāragupto divaṁ jayati.* 'Having conquered the earth, Kumāragupta wins the heaven by his meritorious deeds.' The reverse shows goddess Lakshmī sitting on a lotus. The legend on this side is *Śrī-Kumāraguptaḥ.*

iv. Lion-slayer type: The coins of this type are similar to that of lion-slayer type of Chandragupta II, but of only two classes viz. lion-combatant type and lion-trampler type. Lion-retreating type has not been found. The legends on the obverse are as follows:

a. *Kshitipatir-ajita-Mahendraḥ Kumāragupto divaṁ jayati.*[109]
'Kumāragupta, unconquered Mahendra, the lord of earth, wins heaven.'

b. *Kumāragupto vijayī siṁha-Mahendro divaṁ jayati.*[110]
'The victorious Kumāragupta, lion-like Mahendra, wins the heaven.'

c. *Kumāragupto yudhi siṁhavikramaḥ.*
'Kumāragupta, who is as valorous in the battle as a lion.

d. *Sākshādiva Narasiṁho siṁha-Mahendro jayatyaniśam.*
'Narasiṁha, as it were incarnate, the lion-like Mahendra is ever victorious.'

The legend on the reverse is *Śrī-mahendrasiṁhaḥ* or *Siṁha-mahendraḥ*.

v. Tiger-slayer type: Kumāragupta revived this type first issued by his grandfather, Samudragupta but Kumāragupta's issues have a new reverse, with a goddess standing on crocodile and feeding a peacock. The legend on the obverse is almost the same and reads *Śrīmān vyāghra-bala-parākramaḥ* i.e. 'The glorious (king) whose prowess is like that of a tiger. The reverse legend is, *Kumāragupto'dhirājā*.

vi. Elephant-rider type: This is an innovation of Kumāragupta, which shows on obverse, the king riding a caparisoned elephant and holding a goad in his right hand. Behind the king is seated an attendant holding an umbrella over his head. The circular legend seems to be *Kshataripu-Kumāragupto rājatrātā jayati ripūn* i.e. 'Kumāragupta, who has destroyed his enemies and protects (subordinate) kings, is victorious over his foes.' The reverse depicts goddess Lakshmī standing on a lotus and holding a lotus stalk in her right hand. The legend is *Śrī-Mahendragajaḥ* i.e. 'The elephant of the illustrious Mahendra.'

vii. Elephant-rider lion-slayer type: This is almost the same type as (vi) mentioned above with an addition that the king is shown holding a dagger to attack the lion which is shown in front of the elephant. The legend is uncertain but restored by A. S. Altekar, on conjecture, reads as, *Kshataripu Kumāragupto rājatrātā jayati ripūn*, the same as that of elephant-rider type On the reverse of this type, goddess Lakshmī is shown standing on a lotus with some indistinct object in her hand and a peacock looking towards it. The legend on this side is *Siṁhanihnatā Mahendragajaḥ* i.e. 'The elephant of king Mahendra, destroyer of lion.'

viii. Khaḍgatrātā type:[111] This type is also a new addition to the Gupta gold coins, and was issued only in the time of Kumāragupta I. The obverse shows the king riding a horse and attacking a rhinoceros with sword. The circular legend is (Bharatā?) *khaḍgatrātā Kumāragupto jayaty-aniśaṁ* i.e. 'Ever victorious is the lord Kumāragupta, who is saviour of rhinoceroses.' This type has a unique reverse which depicts the goddess Gaṅgā standing on an elephant-headed crocodile with a lotus stalk in its trunk. Behind the goddess is a female attendant holding a *chhatra* (parasol) in her right hand. The legend is *Śrī-*

Mahendrakhaḍga i. e. 'The illustrious Mahendra (saviour of) rhinoceros.'

ix. Aśvamedha type: This type is similar to the Aśvamedha type of Samudragupta, but somehow crudely executed. Allan had doubtfully read the legend on its obverse as *Jayati divaṁ Kumāra* and *Aśvamedha* between the horse's feet.[112] Altekar has restored it as *Devo = jitaśatruḥ Kumāragupto = dhirājā*[113] i.e. 'King Kumāragupta, the supreme lord, who has conquered his enemies.' What was read as *aśvamedha* by Allan, has been read as *Kumāra* by Altekar. The latter seems to be right. The reverse legend on these coins is *Śrī-aśvamedha-Mahendraḥ.*

x. Kārtikeya type:[114] This is an innovation of Kumāragupta himself. This type, which is one of the finest types issued by the Gupta emperors, was perhaps issued in honour of god Kārtikeya, also a synonym of Kumāra. On the obverse of this type, the king is shown feeding a peacock, the mount of the god Kàrtikeya, whose figure appears on the reverse. The obverse legend has been read by A.S. Altekar[115] as *Jayati svaguṇair-guṇa...Mahendrakumāraḥ* and translated as 'Victorious is Mahendrakumāra by his own merits.' Allan who could not read it properly in his *BMC. GD.* later restored it with the help of a better specimen as *Jayati svaguṇair-guṇarāśi Mahendra-kumāraḥ*. The legend on the reverse is *Śrī-Mahendra Kumāraḥ.*

xi. Chhatra type: This type is a close copy of the *chhatra* type of Chandragupta II. The obverse legend on the available specimens is incomplete. It begins with *Jayati mahītalaṁ*..... The legend on the reverse is *Śrī-Mahendrāditya.*

xii. Apratigha type[116]: This is a highly enigmatic and controversial type which depicts on its obverse three figures, a male (king?) standing in the centre, another male figure[117] on the left and a female in *vitarka mudrā* on the right. The legend written vertically on the right and left of the central figure is *Kumāra* and *guptaḥ*. The circular legend has not been read satisfactorily so far.[118] On the reverse the goddess Lakshmī is shown sitting on a lotus. The legend is read as *Śrī-pratāpa* by Allan and S.V. Sohoni, While Altekar and others have read it as *Apratighaḥ.*

xiii. Lyrist type: The obverse of this type resembles the obverse of the lyrist type coins issued by Samudragupta. It shows the king sitting on a couch and playing upon a lute. The legend on this side is *Mahārājādhirāja-Śrī-Kumāraguptaḥ*. On the reverse a lady is shown sitting at ease on a couch and holding a flower in her right hand. The legend is *Śrī-Kumāragupta*. A. S. Altekar thinks that this lady is the queen of Kumāragupta, and not a goddess as is usual on the Gupta gold-coins.

xiv. King and Queen type: This is a close copy of the king and queen type of Chandragupta I. On the obverse the king is depicted as presenting a bunch of flowers to the queen. The legend is indistinct. The reverse shows the goddess sitting on lion as in its prototype and the legend is *Śrī-Kumāraguptaḥ*.

xv. Repousse coins of Garuḍa type: Some coins of repousse type were discovered from Khairatal hoard which have Garuḍa with outstretched wings and the legend *Mahendrāditya* on one side and the other side is blank. These coins have caused a lot of controversy amongst the scholars. In all probability they are not the imperial Gupta issues and have nothing to do with Kumāragupta.[119]

Skandagupta:

i. Archer type: This type, which was perhaps the most common type of Skandagupta and the only known type of his successors, is similar to the Archer type of Chandragupta II. On the obverse the king is standing to the left with bow and arrow. The *Garuḍa* standard is in the centre. *Skanda* is written vertically under the left arm of the king. The circular legends on obverse are of two types viz.

a. *Jayati mahītalaṁ* (*Skandaguptaḥ*) *sudhanvī*.
'The excellent archer, Skandagupta conquers the earth.'

b. *Parahitakārī rājā jayati divaṁ Śrī-Kramādityaḥ*.
'The illustrious king Kramāditya, the benefactor of others, wins the heaven.'

The reverse of this type shows the goddess Laksmī sitting on a lotus. The legend is either *Śrī-Skandaguptaḥ* or *Kramādityāḥ*.

ii. King and queen type:[120] These coins are quite similar to the coins of Chandragupta I and Kumāradevī type. On the obverse the king is shown standing on left, holding a bow and an arrow, facing the queen who is shown standing to right with a lotus in her left hand. The *Garuḍa* standard is shown in the centre. The legend is uncertain. Altekar has doubtfully restored it as *Jayati mahītalaṁ......sudhanvī*. The reverse shows the goddess Lakshmī seated on a lotus. The legend is *Śrī-Skanda-guptaḥ*.

iii. Chhatra type: The discovery of a solitary specimen of this type from the Bayana hoard gave rise to a controversy about its attribution, since the name of Skandagupta is not found on the coin.[121] It is exactly a copy of the Chhatra type of Chandragupta II. The legend on the obverse is indistinct. On the reverse is written *Kramādityaḥ*.

iv. Horseman type: There is just one coin of this type similar to that of the horseman type of Chandragupta II and Kumāragupta I. Since it has the legend *Kramāditya* on reverse, it has been attributed to Skandagupta. The legend on the obverse is indistinct.

Ghaṭotkachagupta:

i. Archer type: Only two coins of this ruler are known so far. Both are of archer type. The name *Ghaṭo* is inscribed under the king's arm on the obverse and his *birud Kramāditya* on the reverse.

Purugupta:

The coins on which Allan had read *Pura* have now been assigned to Budhagupta by S. K. Saraswati, who has read the name *Budha* instead of *Pura*.[122]

Prakāśāditya:

Some gold coins bearing the legend *Śrī-Prakāśāditya* on reverse and ......*vijitya vasudhāṁ divaṁ jayati* 'having conquered the earth, he wins heaven' written on the obverse have been discovered. They depict on the obverse king on horse-back attacking a lion in front of him, with a sword. *Garuḍa* standard is shown on the right. The reverse has the goddess Lakshmī sitting on a lotus. Since the name of the king is not given on these coins, they have given rise to a lot of controversy. Smith, Allan, Altekar and some other scholars have doubtfully assigned them to Purugupta. Since the coins cannot be removed far from the time of Skandagupta, we have placed them close to his coinage.[123]

Kumāragupta II:

i. Archer type: Coins of archer type with legend *Mahārājādhirāja Śrī-Kumāraguptaḥ* on obverse and *Kramāditya* on the reverse are attributed to him.

Budhagupta:

i. Archer type: Same as other coins of this type. *Budha*[124] written under the left arm of the king. The reverse legend is *Śrī-Vikrama*.

Vainyagupta:

i. Archer type: Same. *Vainya*[125] written under the left arm of the king and the legend *Dvādaśādityaḥ* on the reverse.

Narasiṁhagupta:

i. Archer type: *Nara* written under the king's arm on the obverse and *Bālādityaḥ* on the reverse.

Kumāragupta III:

i. Archer type: *Ku* under the king's arm on the obverse and *Śrī-Kramādityaḥ* on the reverse.[126]

Vishṇugupta:

i. Archer type: *Vishṇu* is written under the left arm of the king on the obverse and *Śrī-Chandrāditya* on the reverse.[127]

SILVER COINS :

Chandragupta I:

Only one coin of Chandragupta I, in silver, has been found so far. It is an exact copy of the king and queen type gold coins issued by Chandragupta I. It may be a forgery.

Samudragupta:

The only known silver coin of Samudragupta is a copy of the lyrist type of gold coin of this ruler. A.S. Altekar, who examined this coin as early as 1959, took it to be an ancient forgery.

Recently Upendra Thakur has opined that it is a genuine coin issued by the Gupta sovereign.

Chandragupta II:

Silver coins of Chandragupta II were probably issued after his conquest of Western India, as they are a close copy of the Śaka silver coinage. They depict on the obversehte bust of the king with long hair and the date in the Gupta era given behind the king's head. The reverse shows Garuḍa with outstretched wings.[128] There is a cluster of dots above on the right. Two types of legends are found on the reverse.

a. *Paramabhāgavata - mahārājādhirāja - Śrī - Chandragupta-Vikramāditya* i.e. 'The illustrious Chandragupta Vikramāditya, king of kings, (and) a devotee of Vishṇu.' and b. *Śrī-Gupta-kulasya Mahārājādhirāja-Śrī-Chandragupta Vikramāṅkasya* i.e. '(The coin) of the illustrious Chandragupta Vikramāṅka, the king of kings, of the illustrious Gupta family.'

Kumāragupta I:

i. Western Indian coins: They are similar to the type described above and were issued on the pattern of the Śaka coinage. On the reverse of some specimens a trident is found in place of Garuḍa. The legend is *Paramabhāgavata-Mahārājādhirāja-Śrī-Kumāragupta-Mahendrāditya.* Some specimens bear *Rājādhirāja* in place of *Mahārājādhirāja.*

ii. Madhyadeśa type coins: They were perhaps issued for circulation in the central provinces of the Gupta empire and present some marked differences from the Western type coins. On the obverse of these coins the bust of king does dot look like Śaka portraits as the moustaches are missing and the nose is flat. The date is found in front of the king's head. The reverse has a fantailed peacock in place of Garuḍa. The prose legend is also replaced by a metrical one, which reads, *Vijit=āvanir-avani-patiḥ Kumāragupto divaṁ jayati.* 'King Kumāragupta, who has conquered the earth, wins heaven.' It is same as on the gold coins of archer type of this ruler.

Skandagupta:

i. Garuḍa type: The obverse of this type has the bust of king with date behind his head. The reverse shows Garuḍa standing facing, on a wavy line. The circular legend is *Paramabhāgavata Mahārājādhirāja Śrī-Skandagupta Kramādityaḥ.*

ii. Bull type: The obverse is same as in (i). On the reverse is shown a recumbent bull to right. The legend is same as in the *Garuḍa* type.

iii. Altar type: Obverse as above. The reverse has an altar in the centre with three flames rising above it. The circular legend is either *Paramabhāgavata Śrī-Vikramāditya-Skandaguptaḥ* or *Paramabhāgavata Śrī-Skandaguptaḥ Kramādityaḥ.*

iv. Madhyadeśa type: They are the exact copy of this type of coins issued by Kumāragupta I. The legend is also same, only the name of Kumāragupta is replaced by that of Skandagupta.

Budhagupta:

His silver coins of only Madhyadeśa type are known so far. They are exactly similar to that type of Kumāragupta I and Skandagupta. The legend is also same but contains the name of Budhagupta in place of Kumāragupta or Skandagupta.

Copper Coins

Samudragupta:

Two copper coins of this ruler were referred to by R. D. Banerji, which according to him bore on obverse the figure of Garuḍa above and *Samudra* written below. The reverse was completely illegible.

Rāmagupta:

Only copper coins of this ruler are known so far, which were discovered from Vidiśā-Eran area of Madhya Pradesh. The obverse of these coins has five different types which variously depict, a lion sitting to left, a lion standing, Garuḍa with outstretched wings, a vase, and a vase with flowers hanging down its edge. The reverse of all the coins shows a crescent above and *Rāmagupta* or a part of it written below.

Chandragupta II:

As many as six[129] types of his copper coins are known. All of them have the same reverse i.e. Garuḍa with outstretched wings above and *Mahārāja Śrī-Chandragupta* or a part of it written below. The obverse shows the following types:

i. Chhatra type: The king with a dwarf attendant behind, holding an umbrella. This is the exact copy of his Chhatra type gold coins.

ii. King standing type: King standing to left with right hand raised.

iii. Archer type: It is same as the Archer type gold coins of Chandragupta II.

iv. Bust type: Bust of the king to left, holding a flower in the uplifted right hand.

v. Chakra type: A wheel or *chakra* in the upper half and *Chandra* or *gupta* written in the lower half.

vi. Vase type: A vase or *Kalaśa* with flowers hanging down from its edge.

Kumāragupta I:

i. Chhatra type: This type is a close copy of the *Chhatra* type coins of Chandragupta II, the only difference being that the name of the king is written in two lines instead of one.

ii. Standing king type: The obverse shows the king standing wearing a waist cloth. Altekar thinks that he is offering oblations on an altar on one coin while on an other he is holding a bow and an arrow.[130] He also called the latter type as Archer type. Since the coins are not very clear we combined the two into one type. On the reverse Garuḍa is shown standing facing in the upper half and *Kumāragupta* is written in the lower half.

iii. Altar type: The obverse of this type has an altar above and *Śrī Ku* written below. On the reverse is goddess sitting on some indistinct object, which is a lion according to Allan and a stool according to Smith. Altekar has rightly pointed out that it is not possible to define this object definitely from these specimens.

LITERATURE

a. *Sanskrit Literature*:

The Purāṇas: When the history of the Guptas first began to be studied, the only literary source known to the writers were the Purāṇas, which contained in their *vaṁśānucharita* (the account of the dynasties) section a bare mention of the Gupta dynasty and the regions of northern India over which its rule was known to have extended. Even the definitely established text of the verse containing this reference became available only in 1913 when F. E. Pargiter published a critically edited text of the *vaṁśānucharitas* in the various Purāṇas under the title *The Purāṇa Text of the Dynasties of the Kali Age*. The relevant verse runs as follows:

Anugaṅgā Prayāgaṁ cha Sāketaṁ Magadhāṁstathā,
etān janapadān sarvān bhokshyante Guptavaṁśajāḥ.[131]

According to this verse the kings born of the Gupta family are said to enjoy Prayāga on the Ganges, Sāketa and Magadha. This verse can be very helpful in determining the original homeland of the Guptas.

The Purāṇas do not mention any of the Gupta kings. However, Dashrath Sharma[132] is of the opinion that the names of Chandragupta II, Kumāragupta I, and Skandagupta have been mentioned in the following lines of the *Vishṇu Purāṇa*:

i. *Anugaṅgā Prayāgam cha Māgadhā Guptāścha Magadhān bhokshyanti.*
ii. *Kosal-Oḍrā-Tāmraliptān samudrataṭapurīṁ cha Devarakshito rakshyshyati.*
iii. *Kalingaḥ Māhishkaṁ Mahendraḥ.*

To these we may add one line from the *Vāyu Purāṇa*, which runs thus: *Etān janapadān sarvān pālayishyati vai Guhaḥ.*[133]

The *Vishṇu* and the *Vāyu Purāṇas* therefore yield the following valuable information bearing on the history of the Guptas: 'The Guptas of Magadha shall rule over Magadha from Prayāga along the Ganges. Devarakshita i.e. Devagupta = Chandragupta II will protect Kosala, Oḍra, Tāmraliptas and the city on the sea-coast i.e. Purī; Kaliṅga and Māhishaka will be enjoyed by Mahendra i. e. Kumāragupta; and Guha i.e. Skandagupta will rule over all of these.'

Kālidāsa: The most brilliant luminary in the firmament of the classical Sanskrit poetry and drama, is the author of two epic poems—the *Kumārasambhava* and the *Raghuvaṁśa*; two lyrics—the *Ritusaṁhāra* and the *Meghadūta*; and three dramas—*Mālavikāgnimitra*, *Vikramorvaśī* and *Abhijñānaśākuntalam*. Although Kālidāsa's date has been a subject of long-drawn controversy, in all likelihood he lived during the classical age of the Guptas. While his works are a rich mine of information for the cultural history of this period, they also throw considerable and very welcome light on the political history of the imperial Gupta family. His *Raghuvaṁśa* contains a good number of verses which particularly illumine the reigns of Samudragupta and Chandragupta II Vikramāditya. In the fourth canto of the *Raghuvaṁśa* he covertly refers to the handing over of the empire to Samudragupta by his father (iv. 1), the rejoicings of the people on his accession to the throne (iv. 3), the jealousy of the tributary kings (iv. 2) and their subjugation by Samudragupta who easily established his control over the enemies and made his position very firm on the throne (iv. 4), and undertook a military campaign of conquest in the traditional manner of the *digvijaya*. The earlier portion of this canto i.e. from verse iv. 28 to iv. 50 seems to refer to the conquests of Samudragupta, and we can notice a clear resemblance between this part of the *Raghuvaṁśa* and the Allahabad pillar inscription of Samudragupta. From verse iv. 51 onwards we have the echoes of the victories of Chandragupta II, right up to verse iv. 79. We can clearly discern here an account of the military exploits of Chandragupta II, as briefly hinted at in the Mehrauli pillar inscription, which speaks of Chandra's crossing the seven mouths of the Indus, and conquering the Bactrians. Kālidāsa mentions Raghu conquering the Pārasīkas and the Hūṇas. In all probability, we have here a reference to the clash of the victorious armies of Chandragupta II with the Sassanians and with the Hūṇas who were trying to secure a foothold in these regions.

In the *Raghuvaṁśa* we also find some clear references to the Gupta coinage. In vi. 4 Kālidāsa says, "His splendour was in a great measure comparable with the god Kārtikeya (riding) on the back of the peacock." We find an exact representation of this idea on a variety of Kumāragupta's gold coins. Further there is an unmistabable link between the rhinoceros type of gold coins of Kumāragupta and verse ix. 62 of the *Rughuvaṁśa*.

Similarly there is an obvious allusion to the lyrist type gold coins of Samudragupta in *Raghuvaṁśa*, xix. 13.

The repeated mention of Mahendra in the *Vikramorvaśī* clearly looks like a reference to Kumāragupta I whose *birud* was Mahendrāditya. There are quite a number of similarities of verbal expressions occurring in the works of Kālidāsa and Gupta inscriptions and coins. If properly collected and explained these are a substantial addition to our knowledge of the Gupta history.

Chaturabhāṇi: The next important source in Sanskrit, are the four *Bhāṇas* (monologues)—the *Padmaprābhṛitaka* of Śūdraka, the *Dhūrta-viṭasaṁvāda* of Iśvaradatta, the *Ubhayābhisārikā* of *Vararuchi* and the *Pādatāḍitaka* of Śyāmilaka. These were published in 1922 by M. R. Kavi and S. K. Ramnath Sastri who had discovered the manuscript containing the text of these plays. However, the importance of the discovery for the history of ancient India was not realised till F.W. Thomas wrote an illuminating note in the *JRAS*, 1925-26, and described their language as the 'very ambrosia of Sanskrit prose.' Their historical content was later on brought out by Jagannath Agrawal, who pointed to the mention of Kumāragupta I in the *Ubhayābhisārikā*, of Skandagupta in the *Pādatāḍitaka*; as also to that of the high ranking officer called *Kumārāmātya*.[134]

Harshacharita: In the *Harshacharita* of Bāṇa, there is a reference to the incident which has been dramatised by Viśākhadatta in his play *Devīchandraguptam*. Bāṇa states that Chandragupta disguised as a fair lady, killed the lord of the Śakas, who was coveting the wife of another person.[135] Obviously Bāṇa is referring to the Śaka king demanding the surrender of the queen Dhruvasvāminī, the wife of Rāmagupta. Bāṇa's reference is important in as much as it supports the story of the *Devīchandraguptam* and points to its historicity.

Devīchandraguptam: Fragments of this Sanskrit drama—*Devīchandraguptam* of Viśākhadatta, as preserved in the *Nāṭyadarpaṇa* of Rāmachandra and Guṇachandra and the *Śṛiṅgāraprakāśa* of the Paramāra emperor Bhoja, were first noticed by Sylvain Levi.[136] However, the historical information revealed by these fragments was highlighted by A. S. Altekar and D. R. Bhandarkar.[137] These fragments revealed the existence of the king Rāmagupta, who preceded Chandragupta II.

Harivaṁśa: In the Sanskrit literature of the Jains, the *Harivaṁśa Purāṇa* by Jinasena, who finished his work in the Śaka year 705 or A.D. 783, there is mention of the Gupta kings who are assigned a total period of 231 years for their rule.[138] Jinasena has not mentioned the names of any of the Gupta kings nor any events of their times. The contribution of this writer to the Gupta history is thus very much limited.

Kuvalayamālā: The Kuvalayamālā of Udyotana Sūri who wrote in c. A.D. 779 also makes mention of kings Devagupta, Devarāja and Harigupta, who can possibly be connected with the Gupta dynasty.

Kāvyalaṅkārasūtravṛitti: This work of Vāmana quotes the following verse:

> *So = yaṁ samprati Chandragupta-tanayaḥ Chandraprakāśo yuvā,*
> *Jāto bhūpatirāśrayaḥ kṛitadhiyām dishṭyā kṛitārtha-śramaḥ.*

Although neither its authorship nor its source has been indicated by Vāmana, the work from which it has been quoted must be earlier than the eighth century A.D. It has been a moot problem as to who is the young ruler Chandraprakāśa. We shall discuss it later on.

Tiloyapaṇṇatti: *Tiloyapaṇṇatti*,[139] a Jain work on cosmography in Prākṛit written by Jadivāsula (Yativṛishabha), contains some information on the chronology of ancient India. We are told that Pālaka, son of the king of Avanti was anointed in the year of Mahāvīra's *nirvāṇa* (demise). He ruled for sixty years. After him the king of Vijaya family ruled for 155 years. Then the Muruṇḍas ruled for 40 years followed by Pushyamitras for 30 years. After them Vasumitra and Agnimitra ruled for 60 years, the Gāndharvas for a hundred years, Naravāhana for forty years, Āndhrabhṛitayas for 242 years, after whom came the Guptas who ruled for 231 years. According to this work the Gupta rule commenced (60+155+40+30+60+100+40+242) i.e. 727 years after the death of Mahāvīra, which is placed in 467 B.C. by Charpantier. Therefore, according to *Tiloyapaṇṇati* the Gupta rule began in A.D. 260 and lasted upto 491. The Jain tradition dates the event of Mahāvīra's death in 527 B.C. According to this view the commencement of the Gupta rule shall have to be placed in 727 – 527 = A.D. 200, which is too early.

Chandragarbhaparipichchhā: A Buddhist work in Sanskrit, the *Chandragarbhaparipichchhā*, mentions a king named Mahendrasena of Kausāmbī whose territories were invaded by Yavanas, Palhīkas and Śakunas. The young son of Mahendrasena who was only twelve years of age, lead the armies of his father and inflicted a crushing defeat on the foreign invaders. King Mahendrasena of this account has been taken by K.P. Jayaswal as Kumāragupta I, whose son Skandagupta is known to have defeated the Hūṇas. However, there are important discrepancies between this account and the known facts of the Gupta history. Kauśāmbī was never the capital of the Guptas nor were any Pahlavas or Yavanas on the borders of the Gupta empire, who could threaten an invasion of India.

Auchityavichāracharchā: In this work a play, *Kuntaleśvaradautyam*, now lost, is quoted by Kshemendra who attributes it to Kālidāsa and quotes two verses from it which throw light on the relationship of the Guptas with some ruling houses of the south.[140]

Kāvyamīmāṁsā: Rājaśekhara has quoted a verse as an instance of an account of an actual event. It tells us that a king named Śarmagupta with his courage shattered, retired from the Himalayas after having surrendered his queen Dhruvasvāminī.[141] This seems to refer to the story dramatised in Devīchandraguptam.

Kathāsaritasāgara: In the *Kathāsaritasāgara* of Somadeva, there is an echo perhaps of the Gupta kings, Kumāragupta I and Skandagupta in the XVIII *lambaka*. We are told that the king Mahendra, having anointed his son Vikramāditya as ruler, himself retired to Varanasi along with his queen. Vikramāditya easily destroyed all the barbarian tribes such as the Kāmbojas, the Yavanas, the Hūṇas, the Tokharians and the Persians. This account tallies in some respect with the account of Skandagupta's wars and conquests as described in the Junagadh rock inscription and may possibly have a kernel of historical facts, but one cannot reconcile the reference to the Yavanas, Tokharians and Persians with established facts of the Gupta history.

Rājataraṅgiṇī: Kalhaṇa mentions that king Vikramāditya of Ujjain appointed Mātṛigupta as the king of Kashmir. After the death of his patron Mātṛigupta abdicated in favour—of Pravarasena II. However, all these identifications of Vikramāditya with

Chandragupta II and Mātṛigupta with Kālidāsa are highly doubtful.[142]

Āryamañju-śrīmūlakalpa: Another Sanskrit work which is often pressed into service to yield historical material for the Gupta period, is the *Āryamañju-śrīmūlakalpa*, a Mahāyānist Buddhist work which appears to have been written before the tenth century A.D. Although profusely praised by Jayaswal, who published a critical edition of its historical portion and hailed it as a mine of information, appears to us of little value for the history of the Guptas. The only piece of intelligible information is given in verse 646, where the kings Samudra, Vikrama, Mahendra and Sa (Skanda) are mentioned, without any mention of the name of the dynasty, the extent of their dominions or any events of their time. Strangely enougn we are told in the next verse 647, that his name will be Devarāja, he will have several names, he will be the best, wise and religious king. His younger successor will be Bala. Now, these details are not at all applicable to Skandagupta. We cannot regard this work as a reliable source. It can be said to supply, at the most, stray references only.

Gāthāsaptaśatī: The Prākṛit anthology—the *Gāthāsaptaśatī* of the Sātavāhana king Hāla, contains a verse making mention of king Vikramāditya who gave away lacs in charity. Some scholars are inclined to find in this verse an echo of the phrase—*Anekago-śatasahasra-hiraṇya-koṭipradasya* which is applied in the Gupta inscriptions to Samudragupta[143] and in the Poona and Riddhapur copper plate inscriptions of the Vākāṭaka queen regent Prabhāvatīguptā to her father Chandragupta II.[144] We cannot be sure whether this verse formed an integral part of Hāla's work or has been inserted later on, as Hāla flourished long before the Gupta times.[145]

There are three other Sanskrit texts which are some times mentioned as sources of the Gupta history. These are—*Kaumudīmahotsava*, *Kṛishṇacharitam* and *Kaliyugarājavṛittānta*. We have shown at the relevant places that all of these are either spurious or they have no bearing on the history of the Guptas.

b. *Foreign Accounts*:

Fa-hien: Besides Indian writings, we have the accounts of some foreign visitors. First of all we have to note the record of

Fa-hien, a Chinese pilgrim who travelled in India during A.D. 399-414. Fa-hien's work known as *Fo-kuo-ki* (Record of Buddhist kingdoms) is written in Chinese. It was translated into French by Rcinusat Klaproth and Landresse in 1836. S. Beal published his first version in English in 1869 under the title *Buddhist Pilgrims*. A much improved translation was published by him in 1885. This was called *Buddhist Records of the Western World*. In 1897 was published another translation by Giles. The latest and the most useful is the translation by Legge published in 1886. However, it may be noted that Fa-hien does not supply any information about the political history of the time of his visit. He was so much unconcerned with the world that he does not even mention the name of the ruling Gupta monarch.

Hiuen Tsang: The other Chinese pilgrim, Hiuen Tsang who came to India in A.D. 629 wrote a more detailed account of contemporary India in his work *Si-yu-ki*. But so far as the Gupta dynasty is concerned, we have only a single reference to a late Gupta king Bālāditya who is said to have defeated the Hūṇa ruler Mihirakula.

I-tsing: The account of this Chinese pilgrim, who visited India in A.D. 671-72, throws some welcome light on the problem of the original home of the Guptas. In his account of the travels of the former Chinese pilgrims, I-tsing refers to a statement in the itinerary of the Korean pilgrim Hwui-lun, where it is stated that a king Che-li-ki-to (Śrī Gupta) got a temple constructed at Mi-li-kia-si-kia-po-no for the Chinese pilgrims and donated 24 villages for its maintenance.[146] This work has been translated into English by S. Beal and into French by Chavannes, whose rendering is slightly different from that of Beal.

Alberuni: A Muslim scholar Alberuni came to India with the invader, Mahmud of Ghazni. He seems to have toiled hard to acquaint himself with India. He studied Sanskrit language and has written in detail about ancient India in his book *Kitab-ul-Hind*. Speaking of various eras used in India, he mentions the Gupta era, the epoch of which he places 241 years after that of the Śaka era. This reference has helped the modern scholars in arriving at the epoch of the Gupta era, though it has created some confusion also.

Mujmal-ut-Tawārīkh: It was translated into Persian from an Arabic work, by Abul Hasan Alī. The original Arabic work is generally considered to be a translation of some original Sanskrit text. Its story seems to have been based on the Rāmagupta episode and the two characters Rawaal and Barakmaris are identified with Rāmagupta and Vikramāditya i.e. Chandragupta II, respectively.

References

1. *Corpus Inscriptionum Indicarum*, III, published in 1888. It was revised by D.R. Bhandarkar and brought upto date by the editors B. Ch. Chhabra and G.S. Gai. The revised edition was published in 1981.
2. Chhabra & Gai (ed.), *CII*, III, (1981), 203ff.
3. *Ibid.* 257ff.
4. *Ibid.* 312ff.
5. *Ibid.* 296ff.
6. *JESI*, X, 96-103.
7. Fleet, *CII*, III, (1888), 146ff.
8. *EI*. XXVII, 12ff.
9. Chhabra & Gai (ed.), *CII*, II1, (1981), 322ff.
10. Fleet, *CII* III (1888), 158ff.
11. Chhabra & Gai (ed.) *CII* III (1981), 234ff.
12. *Ibid.* 242ff.
13. *Ibid.* 255ff.
14. *Ibid.* 267ff.
15. *EI*, XXVI, 115ff. & Chhabra & Gai (ed.), *CII*, III, (1981), 276ff.
16. Chhabra & Gai (ed.), *CII*, III, (1981), 305ff.
17. *Ibid.* 334ff.
18. *Ibid.* 339ff.
19. *EI*, I, 239ff.
20. Fleet, *CII*, III, (1888), 161ff.
21. *Ibid.* 152. Though strictly speaking the MPI, BPI, JRI and the Risthal Stone Slab inscription also fall in this category but these have been placed under the *Praśastis*, because of their special importance as such.
22. *ASI. AR*, 1914-15, 124; Chhabra & Gai (ed.), *CII*, III, (1981), 321ff.
23. Chhabra & Gai (ed.), *CII*, III, (1981), 332ff.
24. *Ibid.*, 231ff.
25. *Ibid.* 291ff.
26. Fleet, *CII*, III, (1888), 258ff.
27. Chhabra & Gai (ed.), *CII*, III, (1981), 272ff.
28. *Ibid.* 287ff.
29. *JESI*, 1X, 6ff.
30. *Op. cit.* 345ff.
31. *IHQ*, VI, 45ff.
32. *EI*, XV, 41ff.

33. *JPASB. NS.* XX, 58ff.
34. Fleet, *CII*, III, (1888), 235ff.
35. Chhabra & Gai (ed.), *CII*, III, (1981), 282, 288; 335, 342 & 360.
36. *IHQ*, XIX, 12ff.
37. *Op. cit.*, 224ff.
38. *Ibid.* 228ff.
39. *Ibid.* 273ff.
40. *EI*, XXI, 78ff.
41. Fleet, *CII*, III, (1888), 93ff.
42. *Op. cit.*, XX, 61ff.
43. *Op. cit.* 100ff.
44. *JESI*, IV, 62ff. The date of the inscription was read as 166 by B.C. Jain, but has been corrected by the editor K.V. Ramesh. *cf.* ibid.
45. *EI*, XXIII, 52ff.
46. *Ibid.*, XVI, 18ff.
47. Fleet, *CII*, III, (1888), 106ff.
48. *Maharaja Sayajirao University Archaeology Series No.* 14.
49. Gupta, P.L., *Gupta Sāmrājya*, 22.
50. Chhabra & Gai (ed.), *CII*, III, (1981), 308ff.
51. *Ibid.*, 244ff.
52. *Ibid.*, 247ff.
53. *Ibid.*, 270ff.
54. *Ibid.*, 293ff.
55. *EI*, X, 71ff. & Chhabra & Gai (ed.), *CII*, III, (1981), 280ff.
56. The inscriptions on these stones have been published by R.D. Banerji in *EI*, XVI.
57. Chhabra & Gai (ed.), *CII*, III, (1981), 317ff.
58. *Ibid.* 352ff.
59. *Ibid.* 252ff.
60. On the use of seals in ancient India, see Fleet, J.F., *Epigraphy, Imperial Gazetteer of India, The Indian Empire*, II, 1907, 29-34 & 37-39; Bloch, T., *ASI. AR*, 1903-04, 101; and Marshall, John, Sir, *ASI. AR*, 1911-12, 44-46.
61. Smith, V.A., *JASB*, LVIII, (Old Series), 1889, 84-105.
62. The necessity of such tokens is indicated by a verse of the *Mahābhārata*, where it is mentioned that during the seige of Dvāravatī by the Śālvas, exit from and entry into the city was permissible only on the possession of a seal. cf. *Mahābhārata*, III.15.19.
63. Chhabra & Gai (ed.), *CII*, III, (1981), 350.
64. *Ibid.* 354.
65. *Ibid.* 355.
66. *Ibid.* 364ff.
67. *Ibid.* 319ff.
68. *JASB*, LVIII, (1889), 84-105.
69. *IA*, XIX, (1890), 227,
70. *Cf ASI.. AR*, 1934-35, 63
71. *JASB*, LVIII, (1889), 84-105.

72. *IA*, XIX, 227.
73. *Cf. ASI.AR*, 1934-35, 63.
74. Allan, J., *CCGD*, 145-46 & LXI.
75. *Ibid.* LXI & fn. 2.
76. *EI*, XXVII, 12ff.
77. Agrawal, Jagannath, *PAIOC*, 1968, 339-43.
78. Sircar, D.C., *IHQ*, XXIV, 71ff.
79. *Cf.* Allan, J., *CCGD*, XVI-XVII.
80. Garde, M.B., *EI*, XXVI, 115ff.
81. Bhattacharya, D.C., *IHQ*, VI, 45-60.
82. Bloch, T., *ASI. AR*, 1903-04, 81-122; and Spooner, D.B., *ASI. AR*, 1913-14, 98f.
83. Shastri, Hiranand, *MASI*, LXVI, 49-53.
84. Marshall, John, Sir, *ASI. AR*, 1911-12, 44-60.
85. Allan, J., *CCGD*, CXXIV.
86. *Numismata Orientalia*, 1823, 726ff.
87. *Asiatic Researches*, XVII.
88. Allan, J. *CCGD*, CXXIVff.; Kotwa is mentioned in *JRAS*, 1893, 47.
89. *JASB*, 1884, 119ff. with four plates.
90. *JRAS*, 1889, 1-159, with five plates.
91. *Bayana Hoard*, VIII-IX and 361.
92. *Catalogue of the Gupta Gold Coins in the Bayana Hoard*, 1954.
93. *The Coinage of the Gupta Empire*, 1957.
94. *JNSI*, XVIII, 159.
95. *Bayana Hoard*, CXXI.
96. Cunningham, A., *Coins of Medieval India*, 1894, 16; Sinha, B.P., *DKM*, Appendix, 1 a, b, c; Maity, S.K., *JNSI*, XVIII, 187ff.
97. *Manu*, VIII. 134.
98. *JNSI*, XXXVII, 83-84.
99. *E & W*, XXIV, 121ff.
100. *AIG*, 214.
101. Although there is a sharp difference of opinion regarding the attribution of these coins, but the weight of evidence certainly leads to the conclusion that they are the issues of Chandragupta I.
102. Allan read this legend as *Rājādhirājaḥ pṛithivīmavitvā divam jayatyaprativāryavīryaḥ*, *CCGD*, 21. It was corrected by Venis with the help of better specimens in *JASB*, 1914, 205.
103. Because of their controversial attribution, they have been mentioned separately by A.S. Altekar in his *Coinage* and John Allan in *CCGD*. Since we attribute them to Samudragupta, we have placed them here.
104. Cf. *Coinage*, 105ff.
105. *Ibid.* 138.
106. Hoernle thought it was a wine-cup and the scene depicted a drinking-scene, *JASB*, 1888, 129-30; A.S. Altekar has pointed out that such a thing would be against 'Hindu taste' and identifies the object as a *Sindūradānī*, *Coinage*, 140; P.L. Gupta, however, takes it to be a part of crescent topped

standard and thinks that the king is empty handed and talking to the queen, *Gupta Sāmrājya*, 162.

107. *Op. cit.*, 141.

108. John Allan in *CCGD*, 70, has given the reading *Mahendrasiṁho* instead of *Kumāragupto*.

109. Complete legend is not available on any coin of this type, though there can hardly be any doubt in this restoration. *Cf. CCGD* CXVIII and *Coinage*, 186.

110. As restored by John Allan, *CCGD*, CXVIII.

111. Both Allan and Altekar have called it as Rhinoceros-slayer type and they have been followed by most of the scholars. However, we prefer to agree with S.V. Sohoni (*JNSI*, XVIII, 178ff.) and call it *Khaḍgatrātā* type, which is the correct rendering of the legend.

112. *CCGD*, CXVI.

113. *Coinage*, 200.

114. John Allan has named it as Peacock type, *CCGD*, XCII. However, Kārtikeya is more appropriate, as pointed out by A.S. Altekar *Cf. Coinage*, 203, fn. 1.

115. *Op. cit.*, 204.

116. Allan has called it Pratāpa type (*CCGD*, XCII) since he read the legend on its reverse as *Śrī-pratāpa*. Altekar has given his reading as *Apratigha*. Sohoni has recently (*JNSI*, XXIII, 347) agreed with Allan's reading on the reverse as *Śrī-pratāpa*.

117. Some scholars were of the view that the figures on both the sides were that of females. Cf. Hoernle, *JASB*, 1883, 144 and Smith, V.A., *JRAS*, 1889, 109 etc. However it has been pointed out by competent authorities like Allan and Altekar, that the figure on the left is that of a male and not female.

118. V.V. Mirashi read it as *Pratāpaparamādhāraḥ śrī prathamakramākramavapuḥ*. *JNSI*, XII, 68-71. S.V. Sohoni has read it as .... *Pratāpa parameśvaraḥ śrī prathitakularupadṛiptaḥ nirupamaguṇamahārṇṇavaḥ aprativāryavīryaḥ*. *JNSI*, XXIII, 345. Both Allan and Altekar think that it is not possible to restore it properly from the available specimens.

119. For various views on this topic see papers mentioned in the bibliography.

120. Allan and Altekar have called this type as the king and Lakshmī type. But we prefer to agree with V.A. Smith and Jagannath Agrawal, who have called it king and queen type. For discussion see *JNSI*, VIII, 48ff. and Jai Prakash Singh, *JNSI*, XXXI, 155ff.

121. For different views see Altekar, A.S, *Coinage*, 248; Gupta, P.L., *JNSI*, XIV, 99-102.

122. *IC*, I, 691-92.

123. As for fuller discussion, see infra.

124. Read by S.K. Saraswati, *op. cit.*

125. Rapson hesitatingly read it *Chandra*, *NC*, 1891, 57. He was followed by Allan, *CCGD*, 144. D.C. Ganguli was the first to read it correctly, *IHQ*, 1934, 195.

126. We are inclined to assign the coins of class II of this type to Kumāragupta III and of class I to Kumāragupta II.

127. The attribution of these coins was a riddle for a long time. Hoernle had assigned them to Yaśodharman Vishṇuvardhana. Altekar first assigned them to Vishṇugupta of the Later Gupta dynasty, but after the publication of the fragmentry Nalanda clay sealing of Vishṇugupta of the imperial family he changed his view and assigned the coins to him. *JNSI*, III, 57 and *ibid.* 103.

128. Smith and Thomas called it peacock. *cf. JRAS*, 1889, 120.

129. P.L. Gupta has mentioned eight types. cf. *Gupta Sāmrājya*, 94-95.

130. *Coinage*, 237.

131. *DKA*, 53. There are incorrect and corrupt variants of this verse in the *Bhāgavata* and the *Vishṇu Purāṇas*. But these are to be rejected outright and speculations based on them will be mere conjectures. There is need for correcting one word in Pargiter's text, namely *anugaṅgā*, the grammatical correct form of which is *anugaṅgam*. On this point see Kaiyyaṭa on *Mahābhāshya*, II.i.2.

132. *IHQ*, XXX, 377.

133. *DKA*, 54.

134. *JOI*, XV, 375-78. A critical and greatly improved edition of the Chaturbhāṇī was brought out by V.S. Agrawala and Moti Chandra, Bombay, 1959.

135. cf. *Aripure cha parakalatrakāmukaṁ kāminīveśaguptaś-Chandraguptaḥ Śakapatimaśātayat*. *Harshacharita*, VI, 199-200, Nirnaya Sagar Press, Bombay, 1946.

136. *JA*, CCIII, 201; Sarasvati, R., *IA*, LII, 181ff.; Raghvan, V., *JBHU*, II, 23ff.

137. JBORS, XIV, 223ff.; *ibid.* XV, 134ff. and *Mālavīya Commemoration Volume*, 189ff.

138. Attention was first drawn to this reference by K.B. Pathak, who wrote an article on Gupta chronology in *IA*, XLVI, 287ff.

139. Ed. A.N. Upadhyaya and H.L. Jain, Sholapur, 1956.

140. See Kshemendra's *Auchityavichāracharchā* and also V. Raghvan's article in *B.C. Law Volume*, II.

141. *Kāvyamīmāṁsā*, IX.

Dattvā ruddhagatiḥ khasādhipataye devīṁ Dhruvasvāminīm,
yasmāt khaṇḍitasāhaso nivavṛite śrī śarmagupto nṛipaḥ |
tasminneva Himālaye giriguhākoṇakvaṇatkinnare,
gīyante tava Kārttikeya-nagara-strīṇāṁ gaṇaiḥ kīrtayaḥ ||

142. *Cf. Rājataraṅgiṇī* of Kalhaṇa, III. 129, 204, 231, 287.

143. Bilsad inscription of Kumāragupta I, *CII*, III, (1981), 267ff.; and Bhitari pillar inscription of Skandagupta, *ibid.* 312ff.

144. Sircar, D.C., *Sel. Ins.*, 412 & 416.

145. See Mirashi, V.V., *Studies in Indology*, I, 99ff.

146. For discussion see infra.

CHAPTER II:

THE POLITICAL CONDITION OF INDIA BEFORE THE RISE OF THE GUPTAS

THE POLITICAL PICTURE of India towards the close of the second and the beginning of the third century A.D., reflects the decline of two great powers—the Kushāṇas in the north and the Sātavāhanas in the south. The Kushāṇa empire was breaking up as a result of the awakening amongst the Indian people to rid themselves of the foreign yoke. The Bhāraśiva Nāgas in the eastern half and the Yaudheyas in the north-western part succeeded in carving out independent principalities for themselves. Their example was followed by the people in the contiguous regions who strove to overthrow the foreign rule. The Kushāṇas were not in a position to prevent this erosion of their hold on India as they were threatened from the west by the newly rising power of the Sassanians in Iran. Thus placed between the onslaughts on both sides the Kushāṇa empire crumbled to pieces. In the south too, owing to the weakness of the later Sātavāhana rulers, their feudatories and governors weaned themselves away from the central authority and laid the foundations of small independent states. A detailed survey of this scene is essential for a proper understanding of the rise and consolidation of the Gupta empire. We shall conduct our survey according to the following regional divisions:

i. Northern India;
ii. Western India;
iii. Eastern India;
iv. The Deccan; and
v. Southern India.

NORTHERN INDIA

The Kushāṇas

The history of the Panjab, Sind and Afghanistan subsequent to the death of Vāsudeva I is highly obscure and controversial due to scarcity of literary and epigraphical evidence. Some references in the Chinese literature and a large number of coins belonging to this period found in the Panjab and Afghanistan are our only sources which enable us to draw an outline of the history of this period. Another difficulty that confronts us is the sharp controvery regarding the chronology of the imperial Kushāṇas. The date of Kanishka is still a matter of great dispute and the more authoritative pronouncements place it as far apart as A.D. 78 and A.D. 144.[1] Accepting the date of Kanishka somewhere between these two, we can say that the rule of Vāsudeva I came to an end the sometimes between A.D. 180 and 240. After his death the Kushāṇa power declined rapidly and they lost their hold over the interior of India. In the south-eastern Panjab and the Gangetic plains, some old ruling powers and some new ones took advantage of the weakening of the Kushāṇa power and reasserted their supremacy once again, while the pressure of the rising power of the Sassanians in the west completed the process of disintegration. Having established himself as the emperor of Iran in A.D. 224, Ardashir conquered the eastern regions of Seistan, Khorasan, Merv and Balkh and appointed his governors over these provinces with authority to issue their own coinage.[2] The coins of Sassanian governors with the titles *Kushāṇashāh* and *Kushāṇashāhānushāh* clearly prove Sassanian supremacy over the Kushāṇas in the region of Balkh.[3] However, it seems that the Kushāṇas continued to rule in Bactria as the feudatories of the Sassanians as is indicated by the titles 'King of Kushàṇas' and 'King of Kushāna kings'.

The Sassanid king Varahrān II (A.D. 276-293) made extensive conquests in the east. His brother Hormizd held the viceroyalty of this region. Hormizd rebelled against his brother in A.D. 283 and the Śakas and the Kushāṇas helped the rebel in a hope to regain their independence. But Varahrān II successfully crushed the revolt and extended his authority beyond Makran upto the lower Indus region. Even the Kshatrapas of Western India (Avanti) were his subordinates according to Herzfeld,[4] but R.C. Majumdar has questioned the verasity of this view.[5]

However, the independent rule of the Kushāṇas seems to have continued in western Panjab and Kabul valley, because the independent king *Kushāṇashāh* mentioned in the Paikuli inscription can be no other than one of the later Great Kushāṇas. We have other evidence too, for the continuation of independent Kushāṇa rule in this region. A large number of gold coins similar to those of the Great Kushāṇas with legends Kanishka, Vasu or Vāsudeva have been found in the Panjab and Afghanistan. They have been assigned to the Kushāṇa rulers Kanishka III, Vāsudeva II and Vāsudeva III (?).[6] We also know that the Sassanid king Hormizd (A.D. 302-309) married a daughter of the Kushāṇa king of Kabul valley.[7] This matrimonial alliance further indicates that the Kushāṇas were maintaining their political hold over this region at least upto the beginning of the fourth century A.D.

Along with the coins of the later Great Kushāṇas are found gold coins closely resembling those of Kanishka III and Vāsudeva II bearing dynastic names Śāka and Shīlada and legends such as *Sya* (Sasya), *Sayatha, Sita* and *Sena* which represent the personal names or parts thereof. Three names Bhadra, Bacharṇa and Pāsana have been found on Shīlada coins. They were probably Kushāṇa rulers of Śāka and Shīlanda clans who ruled over western and central Panjab respectively.[8] The Śāka coins cannot be ascribed to Śaka rulers as the name of the Śaka people has never been spelled with long *ā*.[9] The name of another tribe Gaḍahara or Gaḍakhara is also known from the coins of two of its rulers named Peraya and Kirada. They have been classed with the Kidāra Kushāṇas by some scholars,[10] but A.S. Altekar and R.C. Majumdar have put them with Śākas and Shīladas, and assigned to them the period from the second half of the third century to the first half of the fourth century A.D. Gaḍaharas seem to have ruled along with Shīladas in central Panjab. The occurrence of the name of Samudra on a Gaḍahara coin has been taknn to indicate that they had acecpted Samudragupta's overlordship.[11]

In the middle of the fourth century new developments took place in the whole of this region when the Kushāṇas had to abandon Bactria under the mounting pressure of the Juan-Juan (White Hūṇas) and move into the Gandhāra region. We are told by the Chinese writer of *Wes-shu* (Annals of Wei dynasty) and Ma Twan Lin[12] that Ta Yueh Chi (Great Kushāṇas) with their capital at Lou-Kieu-chi (Balkh) were threatened by a tribe Juan-Juan and were exposed to their raids. They migrated to the west. Their king Ki-to-lo (Kidāra) raised an army, crossed the

Hindukush and conquered Gandhāra and five kingdoms north of it. Thus it seems that Kidāra established his rule over the Kabul valley in the middle of the fourth century A.D. and not in the fifth century A.D. as held by Cunningham. Ammianus, an officer in the Roman army records that Shapur II was occupied in wars with Chionites and Euseni (Cuseni) on his eastern frontier from 350 to 358 A.D. In 358 he made peace with them and started war against Rome.[13] It seems that the movements of these tribes on his eastern frontier forced Shapur II to wage war against the Kushāṇas and their leader Kidāra was forced to acknowledge Shapur II's suzrainty and even to send contingents to help his overlord against the Romans. Chionites of Ammianus have been identified with Juan-Juan of the Chinese sources.[14] An inscription of the 47th year of Shapur (A.D. 356), found at Persepolis[15] also corroborates the statement of Ammianus. But soon after this Kidāra again asserted his independence as we find him fighting against the Sassanians once again in A.D. 367-68. Shapur II was defeated twice and even had to fly for his safety from the battlefield. Though Kidāra had established his independent rule in Kabul and Panjab in the third quarter of the fourth century his successors again acknowledged the Sassanian supremacy which continued almost till the end of the century. The last vestige of the Kushāṇa rule vanished as a result of the Hūṇa invasion.

The Madrakas

To the east of the Gaḍaharas in the central Panjab, between the rivers Chenab and Ravi, there was the kingdom of the Madrakas. They are known to us from pretty early times, from the references in Sanskrit literature.[16] In the Milindapañho, Sākala (Sialkot) is mentioned as their capital. Przyluski[17] and Tarn[18] think that they were barbarians who entered India shortly before the Achaemenian period. But their mention in the older *Upanishads* contradicts such a view, and shows that they were Aryans of blue-blood. No inscriptions or coins of this tribe have been found so far. But their mention in the Allahabad pillar inscription among tribes which acknowledged Samudragupta's suzerainty, shows that they had asserted their independence after the decline of the Kushāṇa power, and had probably played a conspicuous role in its overthrow. No further details of their history can, however, be given in the present state of our knowledge.

The Yaudheyas

The Yaudheyas are an ancient warlike people of the Panjab. They are mentioned by the famous Sanskrit grammarian Pāṇini, who lived in the 6th century B.C.,[19] amongst those communities who earned their living by the profession of arms (*āyudhajīvī-saṁgha*). They figure in the *Mahābhārata*, in the account of Nakula's conquests described in the *Sabhāparva*, where they are associated with Rohtak and the adjacent region. Their kingdom was rich in agricultural produce. They gave a stiff fight to Nakula but were overpowered.[20] They also find mention in the *Purāṇas*,[21] the *Harivaṁśa* and the *Bṛihatsaṁhitā* of Varāhamihira, but these works furnish little information of historical value. K.P. Jayaswal, A.S. Altekar and K.K. Dasgupta are inclined to connect them with an unnamed tribe mentioned by Arrian.[22] However, much more useful and reliable evidence is furnished by their coins, coion moulds and seals discovered almost all over the region which extends from the Sutlej to the Yamunā. These have been found from Sunet in the Ludhians district of Punjab, in Rohtak and Hissar districts of Haryana, in Dehradun and Saharanpur districts of U.P., Rajasthan and as far north as the erstwhile State of Bahawalpur now in Pakistan. Their coins discovered in Rohtak bearing the legend *Yaudheyānāṁ Bahudhānyake* in characters of the second century B.C. supply us the name of their country as Bahudhānyaka which as stated above is mentioned in the *Mahābhārata*. The script of thsee coins shows that the Yaudheyas were ruling in this part of Haryana in the second-first centuries B.C.[23] The Yaudheyas soon extended their state northwards upto the river Sutlej as indicated by the find of their coins and seals from Sunet, only 4 Kms. from Ludhiana and towards the south-east where a stone inscription of a Yaudheya chief has been found at Bijayagadh in the Bharatpur district of Rajasthan.

By the second century A.D. the Yaudheyas had built up such a formidable military strength, that even the Mahākshatrapa Rudradāman speaks of them in a language expressive of awe. In his Girnar rock inscription the Yaudheyas are spoken of as an invincible people who had proclaimed their title of 'the brave' amongst all ruling powers.[24] However, during the period of Kushāṇa ascendancy, the Yaudheyas seem to have lain low. The coins with the legend *Bhagavato svāmino Brahmaṇyasya Kumārasya,* most probably belong to this period, when the Yaudheyas dedicated their realm to their tutelary deity.[25] But as soon as the Kushāṇa empire began to show signs of decay, the Yaudheyas once again raised their head and inflicted a crushing defeat on the Kushāṇas. In memory of this victory they struck coins with the legend *Yaudheya-gaṇasya-jaya* "Victory of the Yaudheya republic". The seals with the legend *Yaudheyānāṁ jayamantra-dharāṇāṁ* also echo their great victory.[26] By the time of the rise of Samudragupta, Yaudheyas were once again a power of count, and are enumerated amongst those tribal states which agreed to pay tribute to the Gupta emperor.[27]

The Kuṇindas

To the north-east of the Yaudheyas, the Kuṇindas occupied the area between the upper courses of the rivers Beas and Yamunā, in the foothills of the Shivaliks. They are mentioned as Kulinda, Kauṇinda, or Kaulinda in the *Mahābhārata*[28] at several places. The *Rāmāyaṇa,*[29] *Bṛihatsaṁhitā*[30] and *Vishṇu Purāṇa* also refer to them. Kulindrene of Ptolemy has been identified with the Kuṇinda country.

Besides these references, Kuṇindas are known to us from their copper and silver coins, discovered in the Kangra district at Jawalamukhi, and Tapa Mewa; in Punjab at Ropar and Sunet, in Haryana at Karnal and in Garhwal district of U.P. Two types of their copper coins viz. Amoghbhūti and Chhatreśvara type have been discovered so far. The copper coins of first type have legend in Brāhmī script of pre-Kushāṇa period while Kharoshṭhī is used along with the national Brāhmī script on silver coins. These coin types belong to the later half of the first century B.C. After this date we do not come across Kuṇinda coins for about two hundred and fifty years. In the third century A.D. again we come across their coins of the second type. It seems that like other tribes of the Panjab, they also came under the Kushāṇa domination but threw off their yoke along with the Yaudheyas, declaring themselves independent. A.S. Altekar has advocated that the Yaudheyas Kunindas and Ārjunāyanas made a federation and jointly defeated the Kushāṇas.[32] But any concrete evidence on the point is still lacking.[33] The absence of the name of the Kuṇindas among the autonomous tribes mentioned in the Allahabad pillar inscription points to the fact that they had ceased to exist as an independent political power sometime before Samudragupta. What exaetly brought their end can not be ascerained at present.

The Ārjunāyanas

The Arjunayanas are referred to in Sanskrit literature for the first time in the work of Pāṇini who includes them in *Rājanyādi* class.[34] Varāhamihira groups them with the Sàrsvatas and Matsyas.[35] Their coins have been found in the territory lying between Agra, Alwar and Delhi. This is exactly the region contiguous to Matsya and we may be sure to locate them here. Their copper coins have been discovered as far south as Mathura.[36] The Allahabad pillar inscription mentions them along with the Mālavas and the Yaudheyas.

Not much is known about this people. From their coins of c. B.C. 100, it may be surmised that they were a flourishing republican tribe before the advent of the Kushāṇas and lost their independence to the latter. They seem to have regained their freedom along with the Yaudheyas, as they occupy the same position in the Allahabad pillar inscription as the Mālavas, the Yaudheyas and other tribes of this area. The absence of their coinage in the post-Kushāṇa period cannot be explained satisfactorily in the present state of our knowledge. Altekar's theory of Yaudheya-Kuṇinda-Ārjunāyana federation and joint coinge is just a conjecture.[37] However, it is likely that they joined hands with the Yaudheyas in overthrowing the foreign rule of the Kushāṇas.

The Mālavas

The earliest reference to the Mālavas in Indian literature is to be found in the *Mahābhāshya* of Patañjali,[38] who wrote in the second century B.C. They are also mentioned in the *Mahābhārata*[39] along with the Śibis, Trigartas and Ambashṭhas. Varāhamihira placed them in the north.[40] They find mention in the *Rāmāyaṇa* also.[41] They have been regarded as identical with the people called Malloi by the Greek historians of Alexander's campaign in India. This would mean that in the fourth century B.C. the Mālavas were in the Panjab and occupied the territory below the confluence of the Jhelum and Chenab extending towards the Ravi.

The Mālavas had offered very stiff resistance to Alexander in B.C. 326, but had suffered a defeat after some initial success. They then migrated eastwards due to the pressure of invading foreigners, the Bactrian-Greeks, Śakas and Parthians and ultimately settled in parts of Jaipur district. They were not left undisturbed for long, even here, as they were defeated by Ushavadāta, the son-in-law of Nahapāna. They had occupied Avanti for some time and had given to this region their name—Mālava, which was remembered long afterwards.[42] But they lost it to the Western Kshatrapa house of Chashṭana as both eastern and western Malwa (Ākara and Avantī) are mentioned in the Girnar inscription of Rudradāman I as forming part of his empire.[43] The Mālavas continued their struggle and were able to throw off the yoke of the Śakas at the very first opportunity sometime before A.D. 225 as is clear from the Nandasa *Yūpa* inscription.[44] The legend *Mālavānām jaya* on their coins of third century A.D. also points to the fact that they had achieved some important victory, which in all probability was over the Western Kshatrapas. The era of their prosperity continued upto the rise of Samudragupta, who forced them along with other tribes to accept his suzerainty sometime in the middle of fourth century A.D.

The Nāgas

From Panjab and Rajasthan, we may turn to the Gaṅgā-Yamunā valley. The mention of as many as eight rulers of Āryāvarta in the Allahabad pillar inscription, indicates that the Gangetic plain was divided into several petty states, many of which were ruled over by kings of the Nāga lineage. The *Vāyū* and *Brahmāṇḍa Purāṇas* mention nine Naga kings of Champāvatī and seven of Mathura immediately before the Guptas[45] The *Vishṇu Purāṇa*, however, assigns nine Nāga kings to the three states—Padmāvatī, Kāntipurī and Mathura.[46]

K.P. Jayaswal identified the Nāgas of Kāntipurī with the Bhāraśivas of Vākāṭaka inscriptions and regarded them as the imperial Hindu rulers of north India, who ousted the Kushāṇas from Āryavarta.[47] He has identified Kāntipurī with modern Kantit in Mirzapur district of U.P. and the coins with names

Nava, Vīrasena, Hayanāga, Trayanāga, Barhiṇanāga, Charjanāga and Bhavanāga as the coins of Bhāraśiva rulers.[48] None of these coins have been found from Kantit and even the reading of the names is doubtful. A.S. Altekar has clearly demonstrated the untenability of this theory.[49] The Bhāraśivas of the Vākāṭaka grants may be regarded as the Nāgas of Padmāvatī whose coins bear the symbols of bull and trident indicating their Śaiva affiliation. Altekar has given very sound reasons for identifying Bhāraśiva king Bhavanāga with the ruler of the same name whose coins have been discovered at Padam-Pawaya (Padmāvatī). Rapson suggested the possibility of a federation of nine Nāga kings of the *Purāṇas* instead of assigning them to one single Nāga dynasty.[50] There is every possibility that the two houses at Mathura and Padmāvatī were related to each other but we do not know the exact nature of their relationship. Neither the *Purāṇas* nor the coins help us in this regard. The coins of ten Nāga rulers Bhīmanāga, Vibhunāga, Prabhākaranāga, Skandanāga, Bṛihaspatināga, Vyāghranāga, Vasunāga, Devanāga, Bhavanāga, and Gaṇapatināga have been found at Padam-Pawaya. Another Nāga ruler Nāgasena of Padmāvatī is mentioned by Bāṇabhaṭṭa in the *Harshacharita*. A Nāgasena is mentioned in Harisheṇa's *Praśasti* also and is enumerated among the kings of Āryāvarta uprooted by Samudragupta. Some of these might have ruled over Padmāvatī, and some at Mathura. The coins of Gaṇapatināga are found in large numbers at Mathura, while only a few at Padmāvatī. The coins of Vīrasena have been found all over U.P. His inscription has been found at Jankhat.[51] He was probably a Nāga ruler of Mathura. Achyuta—more correctly Achyutanandi of the Allahabad pillar inscription, whose coins have been discovered from Ahichchhtra was probably a Nāga ruler.

Of the political history of the Nāgas we know very little. Some light is thrown on one Nāga dynasty, namely the Bhāraśivas, who are mentioned with a laudation in the copper plate grants of the Vākāṭakas of Central Deccan, where we are told that a daughter of Bhavanāga was married to the Vākāṭaka prince Gautamīputra, son of Pravarasena I. The Vākāṭaka records also speak eloquently about the achievements of the Bhāraśiva Nāgas. They tell us that Bhāraśivas had performed ten Horse-sacrifices, and had been consecrated to the throne by the pure waters of the Ganges obtained by the prowess of their arms.[52]

The mention of ten *Aśvamedhas* reminds us of the Daśāśvamedha *ghāṭ* at Varanasi. In the light of this statement it can be legitimately inferred that the Bhāraśivas had wrested the region around Varanasi from the Kushāṇas and celebrated their victory by performing as many as ten horse-sacrifices. The Vākāṭaka inscriptions seem to record with a sense ef pride that Rudrasena I was a daughter's son of the Bhāraśiva king Bhavanāga.[53]

According to the *Purāṇic* evidence another Nāga dynasty was ruling at Vidiśā. The following rulers of this dynasty are mentioned.[54] The founder was Śesha. He was succeeded by his son Bhogī, who is credited with exalting the Nāga lineage. After him there ruled Sadāchandra. Then came Chandrāṁśa who is regarded as powerful as the Kshaharāta ruler Nahapāna. Next came Dhanadharman, Vaṅgara and Bhūtinanda, who was perhaps the last of the line.

The Maghas

Inscriptions on stone, coins and sealings descovered from Kosam (ancient Kauśāmbī), Bhita and Fatehpur all in the south-eastern part of the Yamunā valley, furnish the names of some rulers with the title of Mahārāja. As the names of three of them end in Magha, we shall designate them as kings of Magha dynasty. In the *Purāṇas* we find mention of nine kings called Meghas, who are said to have ruled over Kosala.[55] One is tempted to identify these Meghas of Kosala with the Maghas of the inscriptions and coins but certain facts contradict such an identification. While the Meghas of the *Purāṇas* are definitely stated to have ruled over Kosala, the Magha kingdom seems to have stretched from the vicinity of Prayāga upto Fatehpur in U.P. along the course of the Yamuna, and thus covered a part of the ancient state of Vatsa. We can not confuse two distinct political and geographical units—Vatsa and Kosala as one and the same

The inscriptions of the Maghas have been found at Kosam, Ginja, and Bandhogarh and belong to the following rulers—Bhīmasena, Praushṭhaśrī, Bhadramagha, Bhaṭṭadeva, Bhadrabala, Śivamagha (Kautsīputra), Śivamagha (Gautamīputra), Rudramagha, Vaiśravaṇa and Bhīmavarman. We have also got some clay sealings of Bhīmasena from Bhita and Rajghat (Varanasi), of Kautsīputra from Bhita and of Rudramagha from Rajghat.

Their coins have been found in a big hoard at Fatehpur,[56] and recently another large hoard of 3000 coins has been discovered near Kosam.[57] The inscriptions mentioned above supply us with dates ranging from 52 to 90. However, it is not very easy to settle the chronology of the Maghas, as different scholars have referred these dates to different eras. R.B. Daya Ram Sahni thought the Maghas used the Gupta era[58] N.G. Majumdar[59] and Krishna Deva[60] assigned these dates to the Kalachuri-Chedi era, while Marshall,[61] Sten Konow,[62] Mirashi[63] and Altekar[64] regard them as dates in the Śaka Era. From the style of dating in these inscriptions, namely the mention of the season, the fortnight and the day, which is quite at variance with the style of the dates expressed in the Gupta and Kalachuri eras, where the year, the luni-solar month and the lunar day are given. Moreover, if we assign these dates to any of these two eras—Gupta and Kalachuri, that will make these kings contemporary with the Gupta emperors; and it would look incongruous that the Maghas make no mention of the Guptas who must have exercised suzerainty over this region.

The earliest ruler of the Magha dynasty was Bhīmasena for whom we have the date 52 from his Bandhogarh inscription. We may therefore suggest that by A.D. 130 Bhīmasena had succeeded in carving out a small principality for himself in the hill tracts of Baghelkhand beyond the easy reach of the Kushāṇas. He assumed the title of Mahārāja and struck copper coins. He was succeeded by his son Kautsīputra Praushṭhaśrī for whom we have the dates 86, 87 and 88.[65] Curiously enough we find almost at this time another Magha ruler at Kauśāmbī, namely Bhadramagha whose inscriptions contain the dates 81, 86 and 87. We may solve this difficulty by suggesting that Bhadramagha emerging from Bandhogarh region asserted his authority over the Kauśāmbī region and ruled over it in his own right, whereas Praushṭhaśrī and his son Bhaṭṭadeva continued to rule over the ancestral realm in Bandhogarh.[66] We have for him the date 90 = A.D. 168. A brother of Praushṭhaśrī, named Kautsīputra Śivamagha was ruling from Kauśāmbī, after Bhadramagha. We have another ruler Gautamīputra Śivamagha known to us from a Bhita sealing, who might have ruled after Kautsīputra Śivamagha. The next ruler was Vaiśravaṇa who was the son of *Mahāsenāpati* Bhadrabala. Under Vaiśravaṇa both Kauśāmbī and the Bandhogarh region came under the control of one ruler, since we find the inscriptions of Vaiśravaṇa both at Bandhogarh and Kosam, which give us the date 107=A.D. 185. The next known ruler is Bhīmavarman, whose Kosam inscription supplies the date 139= A.D. 217. Another ruler Rudramagha is known from the Rajghat sealing, but no details are available for him. Similarly the coin hoards from Fatehpur and Kosam have supplied the names of Śatamagha, Vijayamagha, Yajñamagha and Puramagha. Though there can hardly be any doubt in their being the members of the Magha dynasty as the find-spots of their coins and their names ending in Magha clearly indicate, but it is not possible to ascertain their mutual relationship and chronology in the present state of our knowledge. However, counting from the last known date of Bhīmavarman i.e. A.D. 217, and assigning 125 years for the rule of these five chiefs, we shall arrive at the time when Samudragupta was expanding the Gupta dominions by his military genius. In all probability it was Samudragupta who served the last blow to the Magha power by defeating Rudramagha who may be identified with Rudradeva of the Allahabad pillar inscription, who was one of the eight kings of Āryāvarta forcibly uprooted by this great Gupta monarch.

Western India

The Śakas

Western India including Gujarat, Kathiawar, Ujjain and parts of the lower Indus valley was dominated by the Śakas from the second century B. C. upto practically the close of the fourth century A.D., when they were finally uprooted by Chandragupta II and their kingdom was incorporated in the Gupta empire. They are known to historians as Scythians who were settled in eastern Iran before their invasion of India. A large number of Śaka coins discovered in this area together with the inscriptions enlighten us about their history. Though there are some controversial points in the Śaka history, we can draw a fairly accurate picture of their rule with the help of the above mentioned source material.

Kanishka is said to have extended his sway over western India in the end of first century A.D. and to have appointed his

Kshatrapas or viceroys in this region. The Kushāṇa rule over western India was however shortlived. The second Kshaharāta ruler Nahapāna declared himself independent as is evident from his titles *Mahākshatrapa* and *Rājan*. His son-in-law Rishabhdatta extended the realm by achieving victories over powerful neighbours like the Mālavas. Nahapāna's power was shattered by the powerful Sātavāhana monarch Gautamīputra Sātakarṇi. In the beginning of the second century A.D., Chashṭana laid the foundation of another Śaka dynasty, with Ujjain as its capital. Chashṭana's grandson Rudradaman I turned the tables against the Sātavāhanas and inflicted two defeats on Gautamīputra Sātakarṇi. The exploits of Rudradāman I are narrated in his Girnar inscription dated Śaka 72 = A.D. 150.[67] According to the *Geography* of Ptolemy, Ujjain had become a famous seat of learning and was the seat of government of the Śakas. Rudradāman I achieved great glory both by means of his extensive conquest as well as good administration. He established matrimonial relations with a number of Hindu ruling houses, specially the Sātavāhanas, the Ikshvākus and probably also the Lichchhavis.[68] The rule of Rudradāman I came to an end in c.A.D. 170 when the Western Kshatrapas were at the zenith of their power. We need hardly go into the details of the history of this dynasty and may take only the events of outstanding importance and interest. By A.D. 181, the Ābhiras had obtained much influence at the Kshatrapa court. Some of them were serving as generals.[69] An Ābhira general Īśvaradatta, deposed Rudrasiṁha I in A.D. 188 and himself ascended the throne. However, Rudrasiṁha I soon outsted Īśvaradatta and regained the throne in c. A.D. 190 and ruled as a *Mahākshatrapa* up to A.D. 197. During these years, the Sātavāhana ruler Yajñaśrī wrested Koṅkaṇa from the Kshatrapas. The Mālavas in the Udaipur-Ajmer region, also became restive. In A.D. 200 Rudrasena I came to the throne and ruled for 22 years. During his rule the Western Kshatrapas remained strong. It was probably his daughter who was married to Vīrapurushadatta, the Ikshvāku king. His sister Prabhudāmā was married perhaps to a ruler of Vaiśālī.[70] Shortly after his death, the Mālavas asserted their independence under their king Soma,[71] sometime before A.D. 226. No information is available for the period A.D. 230 to 275. This period perhaps saw the rise of an independent Śaka house in eastern Mālava between Eran and Sanchi where inscriptions of a king named Śrīdharavarman Śaka have been found. This must have further weakened the Western Kshatrapas. Herzfeld thinks that a Kshatrapa of Avanti was an ally of the Sassanian emperor Varahra II (A.D. 276-293).[72]

A change took place in the dynastic succession in A.D. 304 which brought an end to the house of Chashṭana. A ruler named Rudrasiṁha II son of *Svāmī* Jīvadāman got control of the kingdom in A.D. 304 and was succeeded by his son Yaśodāman who ruled upto A.D. 322. From A.D. 322 to 348 there is a blank in their history. In A.D. 348, we find Rudrasena III on the throne who ruled for thirty years. The last ruler of this house was Rudrasiṁha III whose rule and the Western Kshatrapa dynasty came to an end sometime about A.D. 388, when the Western Kshatrapa dominions were conquered by Chandragupta II.

EASTERN INDIA

An idea of the political map of eastern India, on the eve of the rise of the Guptas can be formed on the basis of Kālidāsa's account of Raghu's conquests in the fourth canto of the *Raghuvaṁśa,* verses 32-39, the Allahabad stone pillar inscription of Samudragupta, and to some extent on the *Purāṇic accounts of the dynasties of the Kali age* (*vaṁśānucharita*). Kālidāsa describes his hero, Raghu leading a vast army to the eastern region, overthrowing and uprooting many kings in the course of his victorious march. The first definite mention of a political power in the east which submitted to Raghu is that of the Sumhas, who have been identified as the people of Rāḍhā i.e. the districts of Burdwan, Midnapur and parts of Murshidabad. To the east of the Sumhas were the Vaṅgas who can be easily located as they are stated to have been ruling over the territory situated between the various streams of the Ganges, in the districts of 24-Parganas and Khulna. After subding the Vaṅgas, Raghu crossed the river Kasai, and passing Utkala, which may roughly be equated with the present day districts of Mayurbhanj and Keonjhar, reached Kaliṅga. Towards the close of his account of Raghu's conquests, Kālidāsa mentions the eastern-most kingdom of Kāmarūpa with its capital at Prāgjyotishapura, modern Guwahatti.

The Purāṇas mention Kālatoyakas which in all likelihood is a variant of Kāratoyakas or the people living in the valley of

Karatoyā which flows through the districts of Dinajpur, Rangpur and Bogra—all in Bangladesh.

The Allahabad pillar inscription of Samudragupta, presents a slightly different picture. It mentions Samataṭa (the Vaṅga of Kālidāsa), Ḍavāka (Nogong District of Assam) and Kāmarūpa as frontier states. The account of the kingdoms in the south-eastern region, enumerated in the Allahabad pillar inscription will be given in the chapter on Samudragupta. Here we shall briefly notice the northern parts of Orissa comprising the present day districts of Mayurbhanj and Keonjhar.

The writers on the history of Orissa have generally held the 3rd century A.D. as a complete blank. However, the veil of darkness has been gradually lifted by the discovery of new inscriptions. T. N. Ramchandran has published in *Artibus Asiae* No. XIV, an interesting *tempere* painting discovered on a rock-shelter locally known as Rāvanachhāyā, in village Sitabhinji, in the Keonjhar district of Orissa. It is a painting of a royal procession, with painted inscription below giving the name of the king as Mahārāja Śrī Dīsabhañja. According to Ramchandran[73], the characters of this inscription belong to the fourth century A.D. This places the rule of the well-known Bhanja family, over a part of Orissa in the 4th century. Though the authenticity of the date of this painting has been questioned by D. C. Sircar[74], the discovery of a very interesting inscription in characters approximately of the 3rd-4th century A.D. from the village Asanpat, in the Keonjhar district of Orissa has thrown very interesting and important light on this period of Orissa's history.[75] This inscription is engraved on the pedestal of a stone image of Śiva, discovered in the vicinity of the village of Asanpat which is situated deep in the interior, inhabited by the tribals.

From this inscription we learn that a Nāga dynasty was ruling over the region of Keonjhar, and a king of this dynasty Mahārāja Mānabhañja had added to his glory in a hundred clashes in war with the Devaputras, who are obviously the Kushāṇa rulers. It will not be too much to suggest that the Nāgas of Keonjhar region had joined hands with the Bhāraśiva Nāgas in the struggle for the overthrow of the Kushāṇa rule in India, and had shared the success of their allies. His son and successor Mahārāja Śatrubhañja is said to have made gifts of lacs of cows in tra, Gayā, Kṛimila, Daṇḍavardhana, Puṇḍravardhana,

Vardhamāna, Gorhāṭī, Tāmralipti and both the Toshālīs. This indicates that the military exploits of this ruler covered a far flung area. After gaining victories in these places, he must have made these pious gifts in the time-honoured Indian fashion. These Bhañja rulers seem to have amicable relations with the early Guptas, and that is why there is no mention of a clash between Samudragupta and the rulers of this part of Orissa.

THE DECCAN

With the death of Śrī Yajñaśrī Sātakarṇi towards the close of the second century A.D. begins the disintegration of the mighty Sātavāhana empire. A number of small kingdoms rose on its ruins. The founders of these kingdoms were their erstwhile feudatories and provincial governors, who became independent rulers. The most prominent amongst these were the Vākāṭakas in the central Deccan, Ikshvākus in Āndhra and the Pallavas in the down south of the peninsula.

WESTERN DECCAN

The Ābhīras:

The Ābhīras are mentioned in the *Mahābhārata* where they are said to have plundered the Yādava womenfolk returning from Dvārakā under the protection of the *Mahābhārata* hero Arjuna. The same text places them along with the Śūdras in the sandy parts of Rajsthan where the river Sarasvatī loses itself into sands. They had settled in certain parts of western, central and southern India. During the second century of the Christian era we find them serving as high military officers under the Śakas of Western India. There is mention of an Ābhīra general Rudrabhūti who served under Rudrasiṁha I in A.D. 181. Shortly after this an Ābhīra named Iśvaradatta seized the Western Kshatrapa throne between the years A.D. 188-191 and ruled for some time. An Ābhīra king Māṭharīputra Īśvarasena, son of Ābhīra Śivadatta, is credited with the establishment of the Kalachuri-Chedi era commencing in A.D. 248-49.[76] An inscription from Nasik, dated in his 9th regnal year records donation of one thousand and five hundred *Kārshāpaṇas* for providing medicines to the bhikshus of Govardhana.[77] This proves his jurisdiction over northern

Maharashtra. This is quite in conformity with the statement of the *Mahābhārata* which places them amongst the *Aparāntas*.[78] The Ābhīras are assigned a rule of 67 years and their number is given as 10 in the *Purāṇas*.[79] However, V.V. Mirashi is of the opinion that the Ābhīras ruled for 167 years.[80] He seems to be right because in case we regard Īśvarasena as the founder of the Kalachuri era, the Ābhīra rule will extend upto A.D. 415, and they can easily be regarded as the people mentioned in the Allahabad pillar inscription of Samudragupta.

Central Deccan

The Vākāṭakas:

The Vākāṭakas ruled in the central and western Deccan, almost contemporaneously with the Guptas. Their origin is shrouded in mystry and their chronology is far from settled. It is probable that like other contemporary powers of the Deccan, these Brahmanas of Vishṇuvṛiddha *gotra*[81] held important administrative posts under the Sātavāhanas, and continued in that position for sometime even after the latter's decline, until an enterprising scion of the family carved out a small prinicipality and became an independent ruler. His name was Vindhyaśakti. Curiously enough the *Purāṇas* do mention a ruler of this name at the end of the account of the rulers of Vidiśā.[82] It will not, however, be safe to infer that the founder of the Vākāṭaka house first built his power in eastern Mālava. The Vākāṭakas essentially belong to Vidarbha. Vindhyaśakti was succeeded by his son Pravarasena I, who is generally identified with Pravīra of the *Purāṇas*, and who raised his family to the pinnacle of glory and power. Though no detailed account of his conquests is available but it can be easily inferred from his performance of as many as four horse-sacrifices and other important Vedic rites like the *Vājapeya*, that he extended his territories by conquest, and assumed the title of *Samrāṭ* indicative of his sovereign power. He is the only ruler of this dynasty to have adopted this title. He is credited by the *Purāṇas* with a long rule of sixty years,[83] and is said to have had four sons, two of whom, Gautamīputra and Sarvasena, are known to us from the inscriptions. Gautamīputra seems to have died young, so that the interest of his son Rudrasena had to be protected by his maternal grandfather, the powerful Nāga king Bhavanāga, who is invariably mentioned in the records of his maternal grandson's descendants. In the division of the empire which took place after the death of Pravarasena I, Rudrasena seems to have got the eastern part of the Vākāṭaka kingdom. The portion consisting of the Vatsagulma region (modern Akola district and the adjecent area upto Ajanta) was obtained by Sarvasena. K.P. Jayaswal and some other scholars have identified Rudrasena I with the Rudradeva of the Allahabad pillar inscription, who was uprooted by Samudragupta, but such a view is quite unwarranted.[84] Rudrasena I was not uprooted. His kingdom was inherited by his son Pṛithivīsheṇa and the Vākāṭaka dynasty continued to rule. The most important event of his reign was the matrimonial alliance with the imperial Guptas. Pṛithivīsheṇa's son Rudrasena II was married to the Gupta princess Prabhāvatīguptā, the daughter of Chandragupta II. This brought the two ruling houses close to each other and had far reaching political significance. The rule of Rudrasena II was very short. At the time of his death all his sons were minors, and his queen Prabhāvatīguptā acted as the regent and managed the affairs of the state with the help of her father and under his guidance. The Guptas exercised considerable control and influence over the Vākāṭaka court during this period. It is clearly evident from the Vākāṭaka inscriptions of this period in which the Gupta genealogy is recorded to trace Prabhāvatī's descent and the only Vākāṭaka ruler to be mentioned is her late husband Rudrasena II.[85]

Pravarasena II, the son of Rudrasena II and Prabhāvatīguptā on attaining majority came to the throne. He was a youth of scholarly taste and is credited with the composition of the Prākṛit poetical work, *Setubandha*. Though almost a dozen records of his time have come to light nothing is known of his military achievements if any. He established matrimonial relationship with the Kadambas of Kuntala by marrying his son, the crown-prince Narendrasena to Ajjhitabhaṭṭārikā, a daughter of the Kadamba king. During his rule the Gupta influence over the Vākāṭakas continued. He was succeeded by his son Narendrasena and the Gupta-Vākāṭaka relations started deteriorating from his time onwards. The Nalas had started giving them trouble and at one time the Nala king Bhavadattavarman occupied some parts of their territory. But Narendrasena's son Pṛithivīsheṇa II restored the fallen fortunes of his dynasty. He not only recovered the lost territory, but carried the war into the enemy's home, & burnt the Nala capital Pushkarī. Prithivīsheṇa is the last known ruler of this branch.

We have already noted above that there was a division of the empire after the death of Pravarasena I. The younger son of this ruler, namely Sarvasena founded the Vatsagulma (Basim) branch in c.A.D. 330. He was succeeded by his son Vindhyasena who had a long reign of about fifty years. The other rulers of this branch were Pravarasena II, Narendrasena, Devasena, Harisheṇa etc. They kept themselves entangled in the politics of the Deccan only. This dynasty was at the zenith of its prestige at the time of Harisheṇa's death in c.A.D. 510. But within the next forty years it was completely eclipsed by the rising powers of the Chālukyas and the Rāshṭrakūṭas.

As remarked in the very beginning, the chronology of the Vākāṭakas is a ticklish question. They do not use a well known era in their inscriptions and date them in their regnal years. Jayaswal's view that the Vākāṭakas founded the Kalachuri-Chedi era of A.D. 248-49 has absolutely no basis.[86] We have to determine their chronology with the help of synchronisms. We know for certain that Rudrasena II married Prabhāvatīguptā, the daughter of Chandragupta II and Kuberanāgā. This marriage in all probability took place sometime before Chandragupta II conquered the Western Śaka dominions, which were intact upto c.A.D. 380. Rudrasena II, therefore, must have come to the throne sometime after this date. Since he ruled for sometime during his father-in-law's life time, he must have ascended the throne before A.D. 414. Another helpful piece of information is contained in the statement in the Vākāṭaka copper plate grants with regard to Pṛithivīsheṇa I that the treasury, army and other equipment of the Vākāṭakas had been augmenting for a hundred years. Assuming that Rudrasena II died c.A.D. 400[87] it may be inferred that Vindhyaśakti, the first ruler of the dynasty might have laid its foundations in c.A.D. 300.

Eastern Deccan

The Ikshvākus

As the Sātavāhana hold on the outlying provinces became

weak, the erstwhile feudatories and governors assumed independence in their respective principalities.[88] Inscriptions discovered at Nagarjunakonda, Amaravati and Jagayyapet have brought to light the rise of a family named Ikshvākus, which had its capital at Vijayapurī in the Nagarjunakonda region. It has been suggested[89] that they are identical with the Śrīpārvatīya Āndhrabhṛityas mentioned in the *Purāṇas*. The founder of the line Śāntamūla I is said to have performed *Aśvamedha*, *Vājapeya* and other Vedic sacrifices. His son and successor were Māṭharīputra Vīrapurūshadatta who came to throne in c. A.D. 275. According to his latest regnal date he ruled for twenty years. He strengthened his position by means of matrimonial alliances. One of his queens was the daughter of a king of Ujjain, probably, Kṣatrapa Rudrasena II (c. A.D. 254-74). His own daughter was married to a king of Banavasi, in north Kanara district. The next king was Vāśishṭhīputra Ehuvula Śāntamūla II, who ruled for eleven years. The dynasty was shortlived. It came under the sway of the Pallavas of Kanchi in the beginning of the fourth century. They, however, continued for sometime more as local rulers.

The Bṛihatphalāyanas

Not much is known of this family, except for a single ruler named Jayavarman who issued a copper plate grant from Kudura in his tenth regnal year.[90] K. Gopalachari suggests that his ancestors were local chiefs under Ikshvākus and carved out an independent principality after their decline,[91] and ruled over Guntur district to the south of river Krishna. D. C. Sircar has assigned him to the end of third century A.D.[92] Probably the Bṛihatphalāyanas were also subdued by the Pallavas along with the Ikshvākus.

The Vaiṅgeyakas[93]

This dynasty of the kings of the Śālaṅkāyana *gotra* had its headquarters at Veṅgī, modern Peddavegi. They seem to have risen to power in the first half of the fourth century A.D. at the expense of the Pallavas. Their first ruler known to us is Devavarman. The expression *Bappā-bhaṭṭāraka-pādabhakta* in his Ellore grant gives an idea that he was not an independent ruler, but a feudatory. He was probably succeeded by Hastivarman, known from Peddavegi plates. He has rightly been identified with Hastivarman of Veṅgī mentioned in the API. Thus he was a contemporary of Samudragupta and ruled in the middle of the fourth century A.D. He was defeated by Samudragupta but was restored to his position. The Kollair plates[94] of Nandivarman II give the names of three successors of Hastivarman viz. his son Nandivarman I, grandson Chaṇḍavarman and great-grandson Nandivarman II. Another king of this dynasty known to us is Skandavarman whose exact place is not known. Gopalachari takes him as a brother and successor of Nandivarman I[95] while D. C. Sircar conjectures that he is a brother of Nandivarman II.[96] They seem to have continued to rule upto the end of the fifth century A.D., when they were overpowered by the Vishṇukuṇḍins.[97]

South India

The Chuṭus

Just as the Ikshvākus rose in Guntur region, the Chuṭus rose to power in the Kuntala region after the fall of the Sātavāhanas. Jayaswal regards them as a younger branch of the imperial Sātavāhanas.[98] Their coins have been discovered in the north Kanara and Chitradurga districts and some inscriptions have been found in Kanheri, Banavasi and Malevalli.[99] Not much is known about them except for the name of one of their kings, Hārītīputra Vishṇukaḍa Chuṭukulānanda Sātakarṇi, and his daughter's son Hārītīputra Śivaskandavarman. The Chuṭus were supplanted by the Kadambas.

The Pallavas

The Pallavas first became known to modern historians on the discovery of their copper plate inscriptions, found mostly in the region situated between the rivers Pennar in the north and Vellar in the south, and called Toṇḍamaṇḍalam. Scholars have widely differed with regard to their nationality. J. Dubreuil regarded them as Pahlavas descended from Suviśākha, a minister of Rudradāman I, in Surāshṭra. B.V. Krishnarao agrees with him and has described them as immigrants from Koṅkaṇa and Ānarta.[100] K. P. Jayaswal connects them with the Vākāṭakas as both have the same *gotra*—Bhāradvāja. S. Krishnaswami Aiyangar equates Pallavas with Toṇḍaiyar meaning the people of

Toṇḍamaṇḍalam. R. Sathianathiar also holds that Toṇḍamaṇḍalam is the original home of the Pallavas.[101] They governed this part as governors of the Sātavāhanas and became independent sometime about A.D. 250. Between this date and the invasion of Samudragupta we may relate the following facts of their history. The founder of the house was Vīrakorchavarman who according to the Velurpalaijam inscription is said to have obtained 'the insignia of royalty' together with the hand of a Nāga princess.[102] A grant of land in Dhānyakaṭa (Amaravati in Guntur district) was issued by *Yuvamahārāja* Śivaskandavarma.[103] The next king Skandavarma is described as a *Dharmamahārāja* and the performer of the Vedic rites like *Agnishṭoma*, *Vājapeya* and *Aśvamedha* which means that he achieved conquests and extended his kingdom. The next ruler is Vishṇugopa I who was defeated by Samudragupta. His capital was still the city of Kanchi as stated in the Allahabad pillar inscription.

The Cholas, The Pāṇḍyas, and The Cheras

In the extreme south of Indian peninsula these three ancient powers, the Cholas, the Pāṇḍyas and the Cheras had their independent rule, even before the 3rd century B.C. when we find their mention as independent neighbours in the inscriptions of the great Mauryan emperor Aśoka. They kept themselves busy with their own affairs, only rising to power one after the other and fighting amongst themselves. They played no active part at all in the politics of the rest of India.

References

1. The latest view is that of Ghirshman. *JA*, CCXXXIV, 59.
2. Herzfeld, *Kushāṇo-Sassanian Coins*, *MASI*, No. 38, 32ff.
3. *Ibid.*
4. Herzfeld, *Paikuli Inscription*, 35-51.
5. Majumdar, R.C., *CA*, 52-53.
6. *Ibid.*, 53.
7. *EHI*, 290.
8. Altekar, A.S., *VGA*, 18-19; Majumdar, R.C., *CA*, 52.
9. Cunningham, A., *Later Indo-Scythians*, 122.
10. Banerjea, J.N., *CHI*, II, 252-53.

11. Banerji, R.D., *JASB, NS,* IV, 93.
12. Martin, M.F.C., *JRASB* (*L*), III, *NS* XLVII, 24-26.
13. *Ibid.*, 31.
14. *Ibid.*, 31-32; Majumdar, R.C., *CA*, 57.
15. Herzfeld, *Kushāṇo-Sassanian Coins, MASI*, No. 38, 36.
16. *Bṛihadāraṇyakopanishad*, III. 3.1 and III.7.1; *Mahābhāshya*, IV. 2.108 & 131; *Bṛihatsaṁhitā*, XIV. 22.
17. Przyluski, *JA*, 1926, 13; *Ibid.*, 1929, 315-317.
18. Tarn, W.W., *The Greeks in Bactria and India*, 171.
19. Pāṇini, IV. 1.176 and V. 3.117.
20. *Mahābhārata, Droṇa Parva*, 18.16.
21. *Brahmāṇḍa, Vāyu, Brahma, Matsya, Vishṇu, Agni, Garuḍa* and *Bhāgavata Purāṇa.*
22. Jayaswal, K.P., *HP*, 57; Altekar, A.S., *JNSI*, XI, 50; Dasgupta, K.K., *THAI*, 199.
23. *Mahābhārata*, II, 32.4-6; see also Birbal Sahni, *The Technique of Casting Coins in Ancient India.*
24. Cf. *Sarv - kshatr=āvishkṛita - vīra - śabda-jāt=otsek=āvidheyānāṁ, Yaudheyānām EI*, VIII, 42ff.
25. Altekar, A.S., *VGA*, 28-33. We have no evidence that the Yaudheyas were the first to overthrow the Kushāṇa rule as surmised by Dr. Altekar. It seems that Bhāraśiva Nāgas in U.P. also ousted the Kushāṇas simultaneously, if not earlier, from the Ganges valley.
26. The legend has been variously interpreted as, 'Of the ministers of victory of the Yaudheyas', 'Of the Yaudheyas who possess a magical formula for victory', 'Of the war council of the Yaudheyas' etc. cf. Hoernle, A.F.R., *JASB*, 1884, 139; Agrawal, Jagannath, *M.S. Randhawa Felicitation Volume*, 54.
27. *CII*, III, (1981), 213.
28. *Mahābhārata*, II, 23.13-14.
29. *Rāmāyaṇa*, IV. 33.14.
30. *Bṛihatsaṁhitā*, XIV. 30-33.
31. Dasgupta, K.K., *THAI*, 89.
32. Altekar, A.S., *VGA*, 31-32.
33. Dasgupta, K.K. has questioned the theory of A.S. Altekar, *THAI*, 106-07.
34. Pāṇini, IV. 2.53 and IV. 1.110.
35. *Bṛihatsaṁhitā*, XVI. 22 and XIV. 25.
36. Dasgupta, K.K., *THAI*, 17-19.
37. Altekar, A.S., *VGA*, 31-32.
38. IV. 1.168; II. 104.11.
39. *Sabhā Parva*, 32.7.
40. *Bṛihatsaṁhitā*, XIV. 27.
41. IV. 35.10 and IV. 36.15.
42. *Abhidhānachintāmaṇi*, IV. 22.
43. Dasgupta, K.K., *THAI*, 136; *EI*, VIII.
44. *EI*, XXVII, 252ff.
45. *DKA*, 53.

46. *Ibid.*, fn. 2.
47. Jayaswal, K.P., *HI*, 5ff.
48. *Ibid.*, 28.
49. *JNSI*, V, 111-134; also *NIA*, VI, 119 and *IC*, XII, 119.
50. *JRAS*, 1897, 421.
51. *EI*, XI, 85.
52. *CII*, III, (1888), 241.
53. *CII*, V, The copper plate grants of Pravarasena II and Pṛithivishеṇa II.
54. *DKA*, 48 & 72.
55. *Ibid.*, 51.
56. Moti Chandra, *JNSI*, II, 96ff.
57. Shastri, Ajay Mitra, *Itihāsa*, IV, 37-54; see also his presidential address to the Epigraphy Section of the *IHC*, 1978.
58. *EI*, XVIII, 159.
59. *Ibid.*. XXIV, 146.
60. *Ibid.*, 253.
61. *ASI. AR*, 1911-12, 417.
62. *EI*, XXIII, 247.
63. *Ibid.*, XXVI, 30C-02.
64. *VGA*, 41; see also *Bhārata Kaumudī*. II, 157-58.
65. *Op. cit.*, XXXI, 178ff.
66. S. Chattopadhyaya thinks that Bhīmasena and Praushṭhaśrī had no connection with Bhadramagha; *EHNI*, 141-42.
67. *EI*, VIII, 36.
68. *AIU*, II, 185.
69. *Cf.* Rudrabhūti mentioned in the Gunda inscription, *EI*, XVI, 235.
70. *Cf. ASI. AR*, 1913-14, 136.
71. Nandsa *Yūpa* inscription, *EI*, XXVII, 252ff.
72. *Paikuli Inscription*, but A.S. Altekar thinks that he was not a Western Kshatrapa of Ujjain, *VGA*, 53, fn. 1.
73. *JNSI*, XIII, 69ff.
74. *IHQ*, XXVIII, 228, fn. 6.
75. It has been published by Anirudh Das in *OHRJ*, XIII, 1-8 & Plate.
76. *Cf. ABORI*, XXVII, 1ff.
77. *EI*, VIII, 88.
78. *Sabhā Parva*, 51.
79. *DKA*, 46.
80. *CII*, IV, xxvi.
81. The *gotra* of the Vākāṭakas is known from their inscriptions. *Cf. CII*, III, 236 & *SI*, 407.
82. *DKA*, 50.
83. *Ibid.*
84. For details see infra Chapter VI.
85. *Cf.* Poona and Riddhapur copper plate inscriptions of Prabhāvatīguptā.
86. *HI*, 108-111; *JIH*, XIV, 184ff.

87. *CA*, III, 180.

88. *EI*, XX, 1; *ibid.*, XXI, 60.

89. Jayaswal, K.P., *HI*, 171 and *DKA*, 45-46; Gopalachari, *EHAC*, 175-76.

90. *EI*, VI, 315-16.

91. Gopalachari, *EHAC*, 158.

92. *CHI*, II, 336.

93. Usually the title Śālaṅkāyana has been used for this dynasty. K. Gopalachari points out that Śālaṅkāyana was their *gotra* and not dynastic name. Hence we have preferred the term Vaiṅgeyaka i.e. the kings of Veṅgī. See *EHAC*, 163-64.

94. *IA*, V, 175-76.

95. Gopalachari, K., *EHAC*, 179.

96. *VGA*, 69.

97. Sircar, D.C., *VGA*, 70. The Ānandas of the Guntur district have been assigned by Gopalachari to the 6th and 7th centuries A.D. and thus fall outside the scope of this work. See, *EHAC*, 185.

98. Jayaswal, K.P., *HI*, 165.

99. Rapson, *CCAD*, *ASWI*, V, 86; *IA*, XIV, 331.

100. *HEDA*, 173.

101. *CA*, III, 257.

102. *SII*. II, 507.

103. *EI*, VI, 86.

CHAPTER III

THE PREDECESSORS OF THE GUPTAS IN MAGADHA

THE THEORY OF THE Muruṇḍa rule in the Gangetic plain with capital sometimes located at Pāṭaliputra and sometimes at Kanauja, has been assiduously built up on the basis of evidence that will not stand a moment's scrutiny, and yet writer after writer has subscribed to it in spite of some very cogent dissent.[1] In 1896 Sylvain Levi, contributed a paper on the Muruṇḍas to the *Melanges Charles de Harlez*,[2] in which he wrote that certain Chinese envoys to the country of Fu-Nan got an account of the king of a country in India, from the envoys sent by the king of Fu-Nan to India in the third century A.D. The Chinese gave the name of this Indian king as Meou-loun, whom Sylvain Levi takes to be identical with Muruṇḍa. Another fact, generally not mentioned in this connection, is that this Indian king sent Yueh-chi horses to the king of Fu-Nan.[3] Levi is said to have identified the Muruṇḍas with the Maroundai mentioned in *Ptolemy's Geography*, where they have been placed "on the left bank of the Ganges, south of the Gogra, down to the top of the delta."[4] Levi finds further support from the Jain accounts which designate the Muruṇḍarāja as ruler of Kānyakubja and as residing at Pāṭaliputra." It has been thus sought to prove that in the third century of the Christian era, that part of the Gangetic plain which includes Magadha, was ruled over by a foreign people called Muruṇḍa.

Let us now examine these arguments one by one. First of all we must not lose sight of the fact that the information of the Chinese sources relied upon by Levi is second hand information, as they got it from the envoys of the king of Fu-Nan who had 'recently' returned from India; and therefore there is every likelihood of certain inaccuracies creeping in. Since there is mention of the Yueh-chi horses having been sent by this Indian king, it is very likely that it were the horses from Bactria (Vāhlīka) or

Kamboja—the regions which are famous for the best breed of horses. Therefore this 'Indian king' might have been the ruler of a kingdom to the west of the Indus. Secondly, there is very insufficient phonetic resemblance between the word Muruṇḍa and Meou-loun. The Chinese account places the capital of the Meou-loun 7000 *li* from the mouth of the Ganges. In other words it was about 3200 miles from the Gangetic delta and therefore it can never be Pāṭaliputra, which is not even half as much distant. The distance given by the Chinese may suit some place in Lampāka i.e. Jalalabad in Afghanistan.

Next coming to Ptolemy's account, we find that he has mentioned the following cities of the Muruṇḍa realm. together with their exact location as follows:

Boraita	142°.20′	29°
Korygaza	143°.30′	27°.15′
Kondota	145°	26°
Kelydna	146°	25°.30′
Aganagora	146°.30′	22°.30′
Talarga	146°.40′	21°.40′

Not only none of these cities can be identified, but none of them lies within the limits of India, the easternmost longitude for India being 96°. Hence we cannot locate the Muruṇḍas in the Gangetic plain at all on the authority of Ptolemy's account.[5]

Coming to the Jain accounts, which are very late in date, the *Siṁhāsanadvātriṁśikā* is a collection of romantic tales and should not be taken into consideration in sober historical discussion. Pāṭaliputra is indeed mentioned in a number of Jain works, but we have to consider its exact bearing on the present question. Take for instance the *Prabhāvakacharita* of Prabhāchandra Sūri. In its Chapter V, entitled *Pādaliptasūricharita*, we are told that Āchārya Pādalipta having resided at Mathurā for some days, went to Pāṭaliputra where resides the king named Muruṇḍa.[6] The same work further on mentions the visit of the Āchārya to Mānakheta where Kṛishṇa was ruling.[7] He paid homage at the feet of Āchārya Pādalipta. This king Kṛishṇa of Mānakheta is evidently the Rāshṭrakūta monarch Kṛishṇa I (A.D. 758-773) or Kṛishṇa II (A.D. 878-914). Therefore, the Muruṇḍarāja who was contemporary of the Rāshṭrakūṭa Kṛishṇa cannot by any stretch of imagination be taken as a king of Magadha ruling in the second or third century of the Christian era. As a matter of fact these Jain accounts have no more historical value than the works of fiction and we should not try to deduce important historical conclusions from these, as their information is not only inaccurate but also imaginary. The *Tiloyapaṇṇatti*, a Jain work on cosmography, places the Muruṇḍas in 246 B.C.[8] Lastly we must note the view of Hemachandrāchārya, who equates the Muruṇḍas with the Lampākas i.e. the people living in Lamghan in Afghanistan. That seems to be the correct identification, for the API of Samudragupta associates them with the Śakas and Kushāṇas, if at all they were an entity different from the Śakas.

The evidence of the *Purāṇas* has been similarly misunderstood. Thirteen Muruṇḍa kings are no doubt mentioned in the *Purāṇas* and assigned a total rule of 200 years,[9] which even the great Kushāṇas did not enjoy. Moreover, they are placed amongst the various local dynasties, and are never mentioned either in succession to the Āndharas in Magadha, or along with the Nāgas before the rise of the Guptas. The *Purāṇas*, on the other hand, mention one Viśvasphaṇi[10] as the king of Magadha in the third century A.D., who is said to be very valiant and the one who established other kings namely Kaivartas, Pañchakas or Madrakas, Pulindas and Brāhmaṇas in various countries. The name of the Muruṇḍas occurs nowhere in this account and Viśvasphaṇi by no stretch of imagination can be connected with the Muruṇḍas who are mentioned separately. It is, therefore, utterly unwarranted to regard them as the rulers of Magadha at any time. It is really amazing that though not even a single coin or an inscription of a Muruṇḍa king has so far been discovered from any place in the Gangetic plain, the existence of their rule over this region has been repeatedly asserted.[11] It is difficult to imagine that a dynasty of powerful rulers who received envoys from distant lands never issued a single coin and there was no state or private activity such as benefactions of land, installation of images and building of religious edifices that were worth recording in inscriptions on stone, etc. In the absence of any definite evidence, reliance is being placed on information derived from pseudo-historical writings of little historical value. That a queen of the Uchchakalpa king Jayanātha is named Muruṇḍadevī or Muruṇḍasvāminī does not prove the survival of a Muruṇḍa kingdom even in the last quarter of the 5th century A.D. It can only refer to some foreign people living outside India at this late period. There is no reason why we should not agree with Sten Konow that Muruṇḍa is only a word of the Śaka language meaning 'lord' or master, the same as Sanskrit *svāmī* which forms an integral part of the names of many of the Western Kshatrapas.[12]

The Rulers Mentioned in the Kaumudīmahotsava

K.P. Jayaswal has expressed the view that when the Bhāraśiva Nāgas were liberating the Gangetic region from the foreign yoke of the Kushāṇas, an orthodox Kshatriya family was ruling over Magadha. The family according to Jayaswal, has been called as the *Magadhakula* in a Sanskrit play named *Kaumudīmahotsava* and as *Kotakula* in the API.[13] Since Jayaswal drew far reaching historical conclusions from the play *Kaumudīmahotsava*,[14] it seems necessary to discuss it in some detail. The plot of this play may be briefly summarised as follows: King Sundaravarmā of Pāṭaliputra had no male issue and adopted one Chaṇḍasena as his heir. Later on Sundaravarmā got a son, who is named as Kalyāṇavarmā in the play. After the birth of this natural heir to the throne the relations between Sundaravarmā and his adopted son Chaṇḍasena became very strained, so much so, that Chaṇḍasena established relationship with the non-Aryan Lichchhavis, and with their aid attacked Pāṭaliputra. In the battle that followed Sundaravarmā was killed and Chaṇḍasena got possession of Pāṭaliputra. The rightful heir to the throne, Kalyāṇavarmā, was escorted to a remote place of safety by his father's faithful minister Mantragupta, who then started creating disaffection against Chaṇḍasena amongst the neighbouring tribes of Śabaras and Pulindas, and they rebelled against Chaṇḍasena. Simultaneously Mantragupta attacked Pāṭaliputra, killed Chaṇḍasena and restored the throne of Pāṭaliputra to its legitimate heir Kalyāṇavarmā. Jayaswal has identified Chaṇḍasena of the play with Chandragupta I, the founder of the Gupta imperial power, and the Kalyāṇavarmā of the play with the *Kotakulaja* (scion of the Kota family) who was captured by the armies of Samudragupta.[15] However, it has been clearly demonstrated by several writers that neither Chaṇḍasena of the play is identical with Chandragupta

I of the Gupta dynasty nor are Sundaravarmā and Kalyāṇa-varmā historical figures, much less, members of the Kota family.[16]

The statements of the play are at variance with established historical facts and militate against the proposed identification of Chandragupta I with Chaṇḍasena of the play. It is specifically stated in the play that the accursed Chaṇḍasena had been killed along with his progeny and his family uprooted.[17] Both these statements are not at all applicable to the founder of the Gupta empire. Chandragupta I, whom we know to have lived to an old age and peacefully passed on the sceptre and crown to his son Samudragupta. The second part of the statement is even more absurd. As the API speaks of the collaterals (*tulyakulaja*) of Samudragupta, it means he had brothers or step brothers. In the face of such authentic evidence it will be ridiculous to say that Chandragupta (Chaṇḍasena) had been killed along with his progeny. In the face of such discrepancies we cannot identify Chaṇḍasena of the *Kaumudīmahotsava* with Chandragupta I of the Gupta dynasty. As regards the identity of the *Kotakula* with the *Magadhakula* of the play, we must note that not even once the family of Sundaravarmā has been so designated in the play. Moreover, we have copper coins which come from eastern Panjab and bear the legend *Kota* in characters of about third century of the Christian era. We may place Kota family near the find-spots of these coins namely Sunet and Sanghol of the Ludhiana district It will thus be clear that Jayaswal's view regarding the kings mentioned in the drama *Kaumudīmahotsava* is entirely untenable.

The attempt of P.L. Gupta[18] to connect Sundaravarmā and Kalyāṇavarmā of the play with the last two kings of the Sāta-vāhana family is equally futile. There is not a single king in the long list of Sātavāhana kings having a name ending in *varman*, nor has the Sātavāhana dynasty been anywhere called as *Magadha-kula*. Gupta is also mistaken in regarding *Karṇiputra* of the play as an abbreviation of *Sātakarṇiputra*. As has been shown by Jagannath Agrawal, *Karṇiputra* of the play is a scribal error for *Karṇipatra*—the leaves of the Karṇikāra plant which had been used in making triumphal arches. The same scholar also remark-ed that there is no known instance of abbreviating Sātakarṇi as *Karṇi*.[19]

We may, therefore, conclude that the play *Kaumudīmahotsava* has nothing to do with early Gupta history and its characters must be regarded as fictitious. That also disposes of the view of Pires who proposed to identify the *Magadhakula* of the play with the Maukharīs.

Vincent Smith held the view that the Lichchhavis of Vaiśālī who had been defeated and dispossessed by Ajātaśatru, had got an opportunity to build up their power during the period of the decline of Magadha, and again obtained the possession of the old imperial capital of Pāṭaliputra.[20] K.P. Jayaswal also, has suggested that the Lichchhavis had occupied Pāṭaliputra in the beginning of the Christian era, but their occupation ended with the advance of Vanaspara, the viceroy of Kanishka, to Magadha about the close of the century.[21] But Jayaswal's surmise is based on a statement contained in the Nepal inscription of Jayadeva II[22] of the Lichchhavi dynasty of Nepal, that twenty-three generations before Jayadeva I, his ancestor Supushpa was born at the city of Pushpapura (Pāṭaliputra). This statement is of very doubtful value as it speaks only of the birth of an ancestor of the Lichchhavis of Nepal at Pāṭaliputra and not of their rule over that city.

In order to solve this puzzle of the predecessors of the imperial Guptas in Magadha, we may turn to the *Purāṇas*, which as is well known tell us that the sovereignty of the earth passed to the Āndhras after the last Kāṇva king Suśarmā had been overthrown in 28 B.C. The Āndhras as an imperial power are usually believed to have ruled upto A.D. 228 or 230. However we cannot be sure how long the Āndhras were able to exercise any effective control over their northern conquests. It is even likely that the Sātavāhana victor of Suśarma did not annex any part of Magadha to his dominions, for we find that even the greatest of the Sātavāhana rulers, Gautamīputra Sātakarni is styled as (*Dakshiṇāpatha-pati*) the 'lord of the Deccan', and no part of northern India figures in the long list of his possessions recounted in the inscription of his mother queen Balaśrī.[23] The *Purāṇas* too do not give us a clear picture of the situation in Magadha. While they mention some of the erstwhile feudatories of the Sātavāhanas, like the Śrīpārvatīya Āndhras of the south and Ābhīras of the west, as also the Śakas of Surāshṭra, they are silent about the north, unless we take it that the fourteen Tushāras of the Purāṇic accounts are the Kushāṇas.[24] However, the total number of Kushāṇa rulers of any importance does not exceed half a dozen. Moreover, it is not at all certain that any part of Bihar had been annexed to the Kushāṇa empire. Scholars are in sharp disagreement on this issue.[25] Thus there is at present an impenetrable haze around the political situation in Magadha during the period immediately preceding the rise of the Guptas.

References

1. P.L. Gupta has virtually demolished this theory in his article in *JNSI*, XXXVI, 25ff.
2. *Deux peuples Meconnus*, 176-85 of the said volume.
3. Jayaswal. K.P., *HI*, 94.
4. Allan, J., *CCGD*, xxix; This was first pointed out by Wilford who regarded the Muruṇḍas as a tribe of the Hūṇas and identified them with the Marundae of Ptolemy, *As. Res*. IX, 113.
5. J.W. McCrindle, who translated and edited Ptolemy's account, has very aptly remarked," The theory that these Muruṇḍas on being expelled from the valleys of the Kophes by the invasion of the Yetha, had crossed the Indus and advanced southwards in to India till they established themselves on the Ganges, in the kingdom mentioned by Ptolemy, is, utterly untenable, since the sovereign to whom the Muruṇḍa of the north sent their gifts was Samudragupta, who reigned subsequent to the time of Ptolemy, and they could not have left their ancestral seats before he wrote." *Ancient India as Described by Ptolemy*, 213. This clearly proves the untenability of the Muruṇḍa rule in the Gangetic plains.
6. *Prabhāvakacharita* of Prabhāchandra Sūri, ed. Muni Jina Vijaya, *Singhi Jain Series*, V, 44, page 29.
7. *Ibid.*, V, 113, p. 32, In verse 94 he is said to have visited king Bhīma of Lāṭa country, who is evidently a Chaulukya king of that name.
8. *Tiloyapaṇṇatti* ed. A.N. Upadhya and H.L. Jain, 340-42.
9. *DKA*, 47.
10. *Ibid.*, 52.
11. *CHB*, I, Pt. I, 789. We find a remarkable self-contradiction here, at page 791, where it is said, "The Lichchhavis seem to have come into power in Vaiśālī in the third century A.D."
12. The attempt to prove Muruṇḍa rule over Bihar seems to be so desperate, that even the seal of the queen Prabhudāmā has been pressed into service, though the seal does not even remotely suggest any connection with the Muruṇḍas of the Gangetic valley. It giveṣ only the name of her father Rājā Mahākshatrapa Svāmi Rudrasiṁha and that of her brother, Rājā Mahākshatrapa Svāmi Rudrasena, besides her own name. *ASI. AR*, 1913-14, 130.
13. *HI*, 113.
14. Ed. M.R. Kavi, 1929.

15. *ABORI*, XII, 50-56; *JBORS*, XIX, 113f; Jayaswal's theory has been endorsed by Dashrath Sharma, *JBORS*, 1936, 276-82 and by Edward Pires, *The Maukharis*, 17ff. and 23-41.

16. *Cf.* Jagannath Agrawal, *Thomas Festschrift*, 115-120; Winternitz, *S.K. Aiyangar Commemoration Volume*, 359-62; Sircar, D.C., *JAHRS*, VI, 139; K.C. Chattopadhyaya, *IHQ*, XIV, 582.

17. *Dishṭyā tāvat=sānubandhaḥ nihataḥ* Chaṇḍasena-hatakaḥ /

18. *IC*, XI, 137ff.

19. *PIHC*, 1948, 94-95.

20. *EHI*, 295-96.

21. *HI*, 113.

22. *IA*, IX, 178.

23. *Cf.* Nasik cave inscription, *EI*, VIII, 60ff.

24. For the relevant Puranic data see *DKA*, 45.

25. While A.S. Altekar has argued in favour of the inclusion of Bihar in the Kushāṇa empire (*JNSI*, XII, 121ff.), P.L. Gupta is vehemently opposed to this view, (*IHQ*, XXIX, 205ff).

CHAPTER IV

THE GUPTAS AS A MINOR POWER

THE ORIGINAL HOME OF THE GUPTAS

NO DEFINITE INFORMATION is available regarding the locality where the Guptas started building up their political power. Allan had suggested that the territory of the founder of the Gupta dynasty lay around Pāṭaliputra, which might have been his capital.[1] It has been generally held that they originally possessed Magadha.[2] D.C. Ganguly has tried to establish, on the basis of I-tsing's account of the travels of the former Chinese pilgrims, that the original home of the Guptas should be located in the Murshidabad district of Bengal.[3] He refers to a statement in the itinerary of the Korean pilgrim Hwui-lun, that "more than forty *yojanas* to the east of the Nalanda temple going down the Ganges, one arrives at the temple of Mi-li-kia-si-kia-po-no" where a former king Che-li-ki-to (identified with Śrī Gupta) built a temple for the convenience of the Chinese pilgrims. Taking one *yojana* as equal to 5-5/7 miles, Ganguly calculated that this place where Śrī Gupta built the 'China temple' must be about 228 miles to the east of Nalanda, and must therefore be located in the Murshidabad district of Bengal, which should be regarded as the original home of the Guptas. R.C. Majumdar has agreed with Ganguly in a general way. In his opinion Mi-li-kia-si-kia-po-no is to be identified with the Mṛigasthāpanā *stūpa* of Varendra, an illustration of which is given in a Cambridge manuscript, dated A.D. 1015. Majumdar writes that, "Foucher has pointed out that Mṛigasthāpanā is the Indian original represented by I-tsing's Mi-li-kia-si-kia-po-no, although Chavannes doubtfully restored it as Mṛigaśikhāvana. It would therefore follow that the temple of China was near the Mṛigasthāpanā stūpa in Varendra."[4]

However, the only conclusion which Majumdar has drawn from this piece of evidence is that Varendra was included in the possessions of Śrī Gupta. He has clearly stated that it does not prove that the original home of the Guptas was situated in Varendra.[5] Since the Gupta monarch Mahārāja Śrī Gupta is said to have built the China temple near Mi-li-kia-si-kia-po-no, its identification is very crucial for deciding the whole question. Jagannath Agrawal[6] and B.P. Sinha[7], identify Mṛigaśikhāvana with the famous Buddhist place of pilgrimage Mṛigadāya or the Deer Park near Sarnath, and locate the China Temple in its proximity. Majumdar has criticised their views on the ground that these are based on the faulty translation of I-tsing's account by S. Beal. He considers Chavannes's translation in French as authentic and reliable. We shall, therefore, take that account as quoted by Majumdar himself as the basis, and shall go through its relevant portions. "To the west of the temple of Great intelligence (Mahābodhi) is the temple of the state of Kapiśā. When the monks of the north come to India, they also live in this temple which is named Guṇacharita. More than two *yojanas* to the north-east of the Mahābodhi temple is the monastery called Kiu-lou-kia. Recently king Ādityasena has constructed a new temple by its side. The monks of southern countries, when they come here, mostly live in this temple. All the countries thus have their own temples through which the monks keep themselves in touch with their native lands. The Chinese alone have no such place of residence, which renders our travels painful and difficult. More than forty *yojanas* to the east of the Nalanda temple, going down the Gaṅgā, one arrives at the temple Mi-li-kia-si-kia-po-no (Mṛigaśikhāvana). Not far from this was an ancient temple, of which only the brick foundations remain. It is called the temple of China. According to tradition handed down by old men from ancient times, the temple was constructed in old days for the monks of China by the great king (*mahārāja*) Śrī Gupta." This is followed by the following: "More than seven *yojanas* to the north-east of the Mahābodhi temple is the Nalanda temple. It was built in old times by king Śrī Śakrāditya."[8]

In the account quoted above, we should note that after the mention of Ādityasena's temple at Mahābodhi, Nalanda is abruptly introduced, and Mṛigaśikhāvana with the ruined China temple is described as situated more than forty *yojanas* to its east. Then in the next para, it is said that "more than seven *yojanas* to the north-east of the Mahābodhi temple is the Nalanda temple." It is here for the first time that the proper location of Nalanda has been given. Here it is relevant to observe that the account of any place to the east of Nalanda should have followed and not preceded the description of Nalanda. We can, therefore, legitimately doubt whether Mṛigaśikhāvana was really forty *yojanas* to the east of Nalanda? It appears to us that the traveller had not yet reached Nalanda. He was at some place other than Nalanda, which is correctly said to be situated more than seven *yojanas* or forty miles to the north-east of Mahābodhi. Which this place was, we cannot say, but we feel sure that it was not Nalanda but some place to its west. This doubt is confirmed by the following passage from Beal, "Deeply he reverenced the sacred spots on the Vulture Peak, and the Cock-foot mount, gladly he advanced to the Jetavana and the Deer Park, and then taking a circuit rested in the Nalanda college and worshipped at the Bo tree."[9] This passage makes it clear that the Chinese traveller first arrived at Rājagṛiha. Both the Gṛidhrakūṭa (Vulture Peak) and the Kukkuṭapādagiri (Cock-foot Mount) are sacred spots near Rājagṛiha. From here he went to Śrāvastī where the Park of prince Jeta was situated. From here the pilgrim betook himself to the Deer Park i.e. Mṛigadāya near Sarnath, and it was from Sarnath that he went to Nalanda. There is a ring of genuineness in this account as is indicated by the words 'taking a circuit'. So we are entitled to conclude from this passage that the pilgrim first went from Rājagṛiha to Śrāvastī and Sarnath and then to Nalanda. Therefore it is quite irrelevant to suggest that Mṛigaśikhāvana was forty *yojanas* to the east of Nalanda.

As regards the Mṛigasthāpana *stūpa* of the Cambridge manuscript which was situated in the Varendra, we must say, in spite of what Foucher might have held, that it is not the exact phonetic equivalent of the Chinese Mi-li-kia-si-kia-po-no, while Mṛigaśikhāvana is nearer. Moreover, the Chinese pilgrim who travelled thousands of miles to visit the holy spots hallowed by their association with the Buddha, must not have omitted one of the four most important places of Buddhist pilgrimage i.e. Sarnath and wended his way to a little known spot in Varendra. For this consideration alone, we must identify the place as the famous Deer Park at Sarnath, where the Chinese pilgrims must have come from year to year, which fact induced Mahārāja Gupta to build a temple for the convenience of the Chinese pilgrims. The grant of as many as 24 villages, could have been made only by a ruler who had jurisdiction over this region. Hence we may infer that Sarnath lay within the realm of Śrī Gupta; and in view of the fact that we do not know of any other part of India so closely associated with the very founder of the Gupta dynasty, we may legitimately conclude that from the very beginning the Guptas controlled the eastern region of U.P. which we may regard as their original home.

From the mention of Prayāga[10] at the head of the early possessions of the Guptas, it is tempting to suggest that it might have been the original seat of the Guptas. However, we are prevented from taking such a view by the solid archaeological evidence from Bhita,[11] which affords definite proof of the rule of the Maghas only at a distance of eight miles from Prayāga. Moreover, the inscriptions of the Magha kings have been found from Kosam, which is only 38 miles from Allahabad. It does not, therefore, appears to be likely, that the Guptas from the very start possessed Prayāga.

The Caste of the Guptas

There is no specific mention of the caste of the imperial Gupta rulers, either in their own records or elsewhere. This has naturally given room to a lot of speculation on this point.

A.S. Altekar regards them as *Vaiśyas*[12] on the ground that according to the ancient Indian texts on law, the name-ending *Gupta* had been prescribed for a member of the *Vaiśya* caste. However, we find that this injunction was more often disregarded than followed. We have names of celebrated Brahmans ending in *gupta* as well as in *varman*, though according to the rule it should end in *Śarman* only. Wellknown examples of the names of Brahmanas ending in *gupta* are those of Brahmagupta, the author of the famous astronomical text *Khaṇḍakhādya* and Vishṇugupta the author of the *Arthaśāstra*. The names of Brahmans ending in *varman*, occur in the dynasty of Kadamba kings of Vanavāsī, e.g. Kākutsthavarman, Śāntivarman, etc.[13]

The late K.P. Jayaswal tried to prove that the Gupta kings

were Jāts.[14] He observed that though the Gupta kings do not disclose their caste, the Gupta princess Prabhāvatīguptā, daughter of Chandragupta II, mentions her *gotra* as Dhāraṇa, in her Poona and Riddhapur copper plate grants. Since it is not the *gotra* of her husband, Rudrasena II Vākāṭaka, which was Vishṇuvṛiddha, Dhāraṇa must be the *gotra* of her paternal house—the Guptas. Next he brought in the statement in the play *Kaumudīmahotsava*, where Chaṇḍasena whom Jayaswal identified with Chandragupta I, is described as a Kāraskara. He then quoted *Baudhāyana Dharmasūtra* where Kāraskara is coupled with Madras, Āraṭṭas, etc. and concluded that these were the Jāt communities of the Punjab and so the Guptas must be Jāṭs. This opinion of Jayaswal was endorsed by Dashrath Sharma who said that there are at present in Rajasthan, Jāts of Dhāraṇa *gotra*.[15] So far as the argument based on the epithet Kāraskara is concerned, it has no value whatsoever because it has been conclusively proved that the play *Kaumudīmahotsava* has no bearing on the early Gupta history, and Chaṇḍasena of the play cannot be identified with Chandragupta I, the founder of the imperial Gupta power.[16] We need not, therefore, bother about the suggested equation of Kāraskara and modern name Kakkar, which incidently is a sub-caste of the Kshatriyas. The Madras too were not Jāts but Kshatriyas, as is evident from their relationship with the Pāṇḍavas of the *Mahābhārata*.

Coming to the argument based on Dhāraṇa *gotra*, there is definite evidence that in the Gupta times, there were Brāhmans of this *gotra*. In the Kurud plates of king Narendra, the donee Bhaśrutasvāmi, to whom a grant of land was made, was a Brahman of Dhāraṇa *gotra*.[17] Still more important is the fact that Dhāraṇa is not the *gotra* even of Prabhāvatīguptā. On the other hand, it is the *gotra*, of the Nāga family to which her mother Kuberanāgā belonged. The correct reading in the Riddhapur copper plate seems to be *Dhāraṇasagotra-Nāga-kul=otpannāyām Kuberanāgā-devyām=utpannā*. Thus it was the *gotra* of the family of her parents. In the Kuruspal inscription of Someśvaradeva,[18] who belonged to a Nāga family, we find that the name of one of his queens is Dhāraṇa Mahādevī. She seems to have been named after the *gotra* name of her Nāga lineage. There are several instances of personal names derived from *gotra* name, such as Kauṭsi of the Kutsa, *gotra* Vātsī of the *gotra* Vatsa etc. So the name Dhāraṇā for a princess of Nāga family of Dhāraṇa *gotra* is quite in order. We may, therefore, safely conclude that Dhāraṇa is neither the *gotra* of Rudrasena II's chief queen Prabhāvatīguptā nor that of her paternal family, the imperial Guptas, but it is the *gotra* of her mother Kuberanāgā's paternal Nāga family.

So far we have arrived at negative results only. In order to find out the caste of the Guptas, we may examine some of their matrimonial alliances. No doubt, in royal families caste is not a major consideration. We find Indian kings marrying princesses of foreign descent. A daughter of Rudradāman was married to a Sātavāhana monarch. The Sātavāhanas were Brahmans. Emperor Samudragupta himself accepted 'presents of maidens' offered by the Kushāṇas, Śakas and Muruṇḍas. These examples notwithstanding, we are inclined to attach some significance to the matrimonial alliances of the Guptas. The hand of Chandragupta II's daughter Prabhāvatīguptā was accepted by the Brahman king of Vishṇuvṛiddha *gotra*, Rudrasena II. The Kadamba king Kākutsthavarman gave a daughter to a Gupta king, and this fact is mentioned with a feeling of pride in his Talgund stone pillar inscription.[19] The Kadambas were Brahmans of the Mānavya gotra. Therefore, in view of these matrimonial alliances of the Guptas with orthodox Brahman dynasties, we may infer that the Guptas belonged to the Brahman caste. The dynasty is called *Guptavaṁśa* after the name of its progenitor Mahārāja Gupta, and not because they were Vaiśyas.

Mahārāja Gupta

The first ruler invariably mentioned in the Gupta records, is Mahārāja Śrī Gupta, who was evidently the founder of this dynasty.[20] Some scholars believe that the name of this ruler was Śrīgupta, as Gupta alone does not form a proper name. Smith initially held this view.[21] But both Fleet[22] and Allan[23] have pointed out that the name was merely Gupta with *Śrī* attached to it as an honorific title. It has further been said that whenever *Śrī* was used as an integral part of the name another *Śrī* was added before it. For example, Śrī Śrīmatī.[24] Later Smith also agreed that the name was simply Gupta.[25] Fleet's view is now generally accepted.[26] B.Ch. Chhabra has recently drawn attention to the fact that Gupta is one of the thousand names of the god Vishṇu,[27] and can, therefore, alone be used as a proper name.

The title Mahārāja with the names of the first two rulers, Gupta and his son Ghaṭotkacha has given rise to another controversy. Scholars like R. D. Banerji stress that this title is indicative of subordination and the first two Gupta rulers were feudatories of the great Kushāṇas.[28] Jayaswal,[29] Chattopadhyaya[30] and Maity[31] also hold the same opinion. This view has little to recommend itself and we see no reason to believe that the title Mahārāja proves that the first two Gupta kings were subordinate of the Kushāṇas. Aśoka, the great, had the simple title of Rājan. The Vākāṭakas, Bhāraśivas, Maghas and the Nāgās were subordinate to none but were content with the title of Mahārāja only. Samudragupta himself used the simple title of Rājā on his tiger-slayer type of coins.[32] The Vākāṭaka queen Prabhāvatīguptā used the title Mahārāja with the names of Chandragupta I and Samudragupta.[33] Similarly Vainyagupta has also been called Mahārāja in his Gunaighar copper plate grant,[34] though in the fragmentary Nalanda clay sealing he bears the title *Mahārājādhirāja*. We know fully well that none of these rulers held a subordinate position at any time. Moreover, there is no evidence of any paramount power to which the Guptas bore allegiance. The Kushāṇas had been expelled by the Bhāraśivas and the Yaudheyas. The Vākāṭakas never became supreme in the Gaṅgā-Yamunā region, and the Nāgas held only small principalities, which were not in any way superior to that of the Guptas. It seems most likely that after the decline of the Kushāṇas several small states came into existence in northern India. In these circumstances, Mahārāja Gupta also carved out, an independent kingdom for himself in eastern U.P., which included Sāketa and some territory to its east up to Sarnath. The Purāṅic statement that the Guptas ruled over Prayāga, Sāketa and Magadha shows that Mahārāja Gupta's descendants (*vaṁśajāḥ*) had enlarged the ancestral kingdom.

No information is available about Mahārāja Gupta's achievements from the Gupta inscriptions. However, we learn from the Chinese pilgrim I-tsing, that an Indian monarch Che-li-ki-to built a temple at Mṛigaśikhāvana for the residence of the Chinese pilgrims and granted 24 villages towards its recurring expenditure. Allan has rightly identified the king Che-li-ki-to of I-tsing's account with Mahārāja Gupta, the progenitor of the Gupta dynasty.[35] Fleet did not agree with this view for two reasons.[36] Firstly, there is a discrepancy in the name, which is Śrī-Gupta in I-tsing's record but is simply Gupta in the inscriptions. Secondly, the king who built the temple for the Chinese pilgrims flourished five hundred years before I-tsing's time i.e. A.D. 175, which in Fleet's view is too early a date for Mahārāja Gupta. Allan has successfully met both these objections of Fleet. He explains that the Chinese writers frequently used *Śrī* as an honorific, so that we are left with the name Gupta, and as regards the date, the statement of I-tsing is vague and as suggested by Chavannes who translated the original Chinese account, should not be taken literally. We can place Gupta in the later half of the third century A.D. in c. A.D. 275, which would be four hundred years before I-tsing's time. Allan's reasoning is convincing and we may, therefore, conclude that the Indian king who ministered to the convenience of the Chinese pilgrims was Gupta, the founder of the Gupta dynasty.[37] Mahārāja Gupta appears to be a ruler of liberal religious views who made no distinction between Buddhist and Brahmanical institutions in making benefactions, and thus affords the first glimpse of the policy of religious toleration, so assiduously followed by his successors.

No coin or inscription of Mahārāja Gupta has been found so far. The seal bearing the legend *Gutasya*, published by Rapson[38] and another published by Jagannath Agrawal with the legend *Śrī-rguptasya*,[39] cannot be attributed to this ruler as in neither of these, the name is accompanied by a royal title. A gold and a silver coin attributed to this ruler are not really his according to V.A. Smith.[40]

As the early Gupta chronology cannot be determined definitely, scholars have assigned different dates to the first two rulers. R.K. Mookerji places Gupta between A.D. 240 and 280;[41] while Vincent Smith puts him from A.D. 275 to 300.[42] Allan considers Smith's dating as approximately correct. Smith appears to be right.

Mahārāja Ghaṭotkacha

Mahārāja Gupta was succeeded by his son Ghaṭotkacha, whom we know only from the inscriptions of Samudragupta and his successors. The clay sealing[43] and the gold coin in the Leningrad Museum as well as the one published by Ajit Ghosh, with the legend *Ghaṭo* on the obverse and *Kramāditya* on the reverse, are now unanimously considered to belong to a later member of the Gupta dynasty whose full name is Ghaṭotkacha-gupta, who was a son or a younger brother of Kumāragupta I and who was ruling in eastern Mālava in the year 116, according to the Tumain inscription.[44]

It has been suggested that, "It is probably a foreign name Sanskritised."[45] However, it is a very ancient name. One of the heroes of the *Mahābhārata*—the son of Bhīma from Hiḍimbā, was named Ghaṭotkacha. It is just possible that this name was given to him after he had proved to be a youth of martial vigour and adventurous spirit. His formidable physical strength appears to have elicited the praise of his neighbours and induced them to enter into a matrimonial alliance with him. This resulted in far reaching consequences for the political fortune of the Gupta house. Ghaṭotkacha seems to have successfully negotiated with the neighbouring Lichchhavi people, for obtaining the hand of their princess Kumāradevī for his son Chandragupta. The date of this fruitful alliance has been put as A.D. 308 by Vincent Smith, and he may be correct in making this estimate. Chandragupta must have been a youth of about 25 years at the time of his marriage. We shall show below that Chandragupta was the founder of the Gupta era, the epoch of which has been determined as A.D. 318-19. That may be the date both of his accession and of his assumption of the imperial title of *Mahārājādhirāja*. Ghaṭotkacha's reign may be considered as having ended sometime about February 26, A.D. 318, and the first year of his son Chandragupta's reign may be calculated from that date.

References

1. *CCGD*, xiv.
2. *Cf.* Smith, V.A., *EHI*, 295.

3. *IHQ*, XIV, 532-35.
4. *HB*, 69.
5. *Ibid.*, 70.
6. *IHQ*, 1946, 28-33.
7. *JBRS*, XXXVII, 138ff.
8. *RPHI*, 76f.
9. *JRAS*, 1881, 557.
10. *DKA*, 53.
11. *ASI. AR*, 1911-12.
12. *Bayana Hoard*, x-xi; cf. *Manu*, II. 32.
13. Talgunda Stone Pillar Inscription, *EI*, VIII, 31ff.
14. *HI*, 114-16.
15. *JBORS*, 1934, 225.
16. Jagannath, *Festschrift Thomas*, 115-20; Winternitz, *S.K. Aiyangar Commemoration Volume*, 359-62; Sircar, D.C., *JAHRS*, VI, 139; Chatopadhyaya, K.C., *IHQ*, XIV, 582; Rao, S., *IC*, IX, 100.
17. *EI*, XXXI, 26. This inscription is engraved in Box-headed Gupta Brahmī of 4th-5th centuries A.D.
18. *El*, X, 32ff.
19. *Ibid.*, VIII, 31ff.
20. The Supia inscription of the time of Skandagupta begins the Gupta genealogy with Ghaṭotkacha. But it is a private record and the mistake is clearly due to ignorance of its writer, who omits the name even of Chandragupta I.

As for the Vākāṭaka records of Prabhāvatīguptā (Poona and Riddhapur copper plate inscriptions) D.C. Sircar has rightly observed that, "the Gupta genealogy in the Vākāṭaka records is carelessly drawn" (*SI*, 412, fn. 4). In these two inscriptions Chandragupta II has been given the epithet of *sarvarāj=ochchhettā*, whereas no official record of the Guptas calls him as such.

21. *JASB*, LIII, 119.
22. Fleet, *CII*, III, (1888), 8, fn. 3.
23. *CCGD*, xiv.
24. *Op. cit.*, 215.
25. *EHI*, 296, fn. 1.
26. Some scholars like S.K. Maity still stick to the view that his name was Śrīgupta, (*Imperial Guptas and Their Times*, 19), though without much justification.
27. *JNSI*, IX, 137-39.
28. *AIG*, 2.
29. *HI*, 117ff.
30. *EHNI*, 170ff.
31. *Imperial Guptas and Their Times*, 20.
32. *Coinage*, 71-72.
33. *EI*, XV, 41 and *JPASB*, XX, 110.
34. *IHQ*, VI, 45.
35. *CCGD.*, xv.
36. *CII*, III, (1888), 8, fn. 3.
37. As regards his date, we can arrive at it approximately. Assuming

that Chandragupta I ascended the throne in A.D. 318-19, we can place Gupta some 40 years before that date, i.e. c.A.D. 278-79, which is quite close to Allan's estimate of c.A.D. 275.

38. *JRAS*, 1905, 814.

39. *JNSI*, XXVII, 98ff. Allan has mentioned a similar seal in the possession of Dr. Hoernle, see *CCGD*, xiv.

40. *JASB*, 1884, 119, fn. B.P. Sinha has stated that Cunningham had said that a coin of Śrī-Gupta was in his cabinet. *CHB*, I, ii, 2.

41. *GE*, 11.

42. *IA*, 1902, 257.

43. The sealing was published by T. Bloch, *ASI. AR*, 1903-04, 102. For Ghaṭotkachagupta's rule over eastern Mālava see *EI*, XXVI, 115.

44. For the gold coin in Ajit Ghosh's possession, see *JNSI*, XXII, 260.

45. *IA*, XIV, 179.

CHAPTER V

FOUNDATION OF THE IMPERIAL RULE

GHAṬOTKACHA WAS SUCCEEDED by his son Chandragupta, who was destined to achieve the singular distinction of raising his family to the status of an imperial power. Soon after his accession, he assumed the title of *Mahārājādhirāja* which is symbolic of suzerain power. The story of the rise of Chandragupta to this exalted position might have remained an unknown mystry, but for the discovery of his gold coins which are known to numismatists as the Chandragupta-Kumāradevī type. On the obverse of this type of coins are the portraits of Chandragupta and his queen Kumāradevī with the names of both inscribed in Gupta Brāhmī, and on the reverse is a goddess seated on a lion below which is the legend *Lichchhavayaḥ*. These coins have been found in the hoards discovered from Mathura, Ayodhya, Lucknow, Sitapur, Tanada (Faizabad district), Ghazipur, Varanasi, Bayana (Bharatpur), and Hajipur (Bihar). With remarakable ingenuity Vincent Smith interpreted the significance of this coin type and concluded as follows, "It seems probable that at the time of this fateful union the Lichchhavis were masters or overlords of the ancient imperial city, and that Chandragupta, by means of his matrimonial alliance, succeeded to the power previously held by his wife's relatives ... Certain it is that Chandragupta was raised by his Lichchhavi connection from the rank of a local chief, as enjoyed by his father and grandfather, to such dignity that he felt justified in assuming the lofty title of sovereign of Mahārājas usually associated with a claim to the rank of lord paramount."[1]

However, Allan has not concurred with this view. He thinks that Pāṭaliputra was held by the Guptas even in the time of the first ruler of the family, Mahārāja Gupta, and further that Chandragupta extended his ancestral domain by conquest. He goes on to say that, "The adjoining kingdom of Vaiśālī was one of his earliest conquests, and that his marriage with Kumāradevī was one of the terms of the treaty of peace. Too much emphasis should not be laid on the pride of the Guptas in their Lichchhavi blood, but it was probably due rather to the ancient lineage of the Lichchhavis than to any material advantages gained by this alliance."[2] Allan thinks that Chandragupta-Kumāradevī type of coins were struck by Samudragupta in memory of his parents and maternal relations.[3]

We are not inclined to accept in toto this opinion of Allan. As we have discussed above, I-tsing's account only points to the jurisdiction of the Guptas over eastern U.P. upto and including Sarnath. There is no evidence that Mahārāja Gupta had control over Pāṭaliputra. The idea of the conquest of Vaiśālī by Chandragupta is not at all tenable. If the Lichchhavis had lost their kingdom to Chandragupta *in war*, why should their name occur on these coins of Chandragupta?[4] A. S. Altekar has given a very convincing interpretation of this coin type,[5] and we shall go into detail in this question. Allan gave the following reasons for his view:

a. The common most coins of Samudragupta are those which belong to the standard type, and these are 'a close copy' of the later coins of the Kushāṇas, the only alterations being that the peaked Kushāṇa head-dress is replaced by a close fitting cap, and the trident of the former yields place to a *Garuḍa* standard on its Gupta prototype. The reverse is even more slavishly copied as both the throne of the goddess and the Śaka symbol have been retained.

b. The Chandragupta-Kumāradevi type shows greater originality in as much as there is the addition of the figure of the queen on the obverse and a lion replaces the throne on the reverse.

c. Samudragupta's standard type has no proto-type in the coinage of his father. Therefore it is bound to be his earliest type. As it is closest to his Kushāṇa original, we have to account for his return to a relatively slavish imitation of Kushāṇa type after the comparative originality of his father's coins.[6]

d. The earliest reverse of the lion-slayer type of Chandragupta II bears a goddess seated on a lion holding a cornucopiae, and closely resembles the reverse of the coins of Chandragupta-Kumāradevi type. This suggests that the latter immediately preceded the former.[7]

e. Chandragupta I reigned for a comparatively long period, and it is unlikely that as he was a *Mahārājādhirāja*, he was content to issue a 'joint' coinage throughout his reign. There is no parallel for a joint coinagc and it is contrary to all numismatic laws for a series to open with such a remarkable development from its proto-type.[8]

f. It is not necessary to expect that Chandragupta I must have struck coins on assuming the imperial title of *Mahārājādhirāja*. Some of the greatest of Hindu rulers, like Harshavardhana, do not appear to have struck coins at all.

Allan's reasoning though apparently formidable to refute, suffers from some inherent weaknesses. Firstly there is no compelling reason as to why we should regard the standard type of Samudragupta as his earliest type. There is definite evidence which points to the contrary. The legend on this type is, *Samara śata-vitata-vijayo-jita-ripur = ajito-divaṃ-jayati*, i. e. 'The unconquered one who has conquered his enemies (and) has continuously attained victories in a hundred battles, wins heaven." It means that the standard type coins were struck when Samudragupta was already the victor of many a battle. It is very likely that these coins belong to the period when the wars in the north and south described in the Allahabad pillar inscription were already over. We can be, therefore sure, that the standard type was not the earliest issue of Samudragupta's coinage. The argument of comparative originality of the Chandragupta-Kumāradevī type and the 'slavish imitation' in the standard type loses much of its force.

As regards the originality of the Chandragupta-Kumāradevī type, Altekar has adequately explained its genesis.[9] From the Allahabad pillar inscription of Samudragupta we know that Kumāradevī, the chief queen of Chandragupta I, was a Lichchhavi princess. It appears most likely that as a result of this marriage the territory of the Lichchhavis was merged into the Gupta kingdom, and thus Kumāradevī had made a substantial contribution to the rise in the fortunes of the Guptas. As pointed out by A.S. Altekar, the Lichchhavis appear to have insisted on getting some recognition of this contribution and the new coin which bears the name of the Lichchhavi people, is not only symbolic of their contribution but it also constitutes a proof of the conferment of a constitutional right on their princess who was recognised as a full-fledged partner in the new empire as queen regnant by right. We need hardly look for any provision in Hindu law for a daughter to inherit her father's possessions, because the present case may be regarded as one of mutual negotiation and agreement. Altekar has convincingly supported this by pointing to an actual precedent in British history. At the time of the death of James II, the king of England, his daughter Mary who had married William of Orange, was the constitutional heir to the throne; but her husband refused to come to England merely as a royal spouse. He wanted to share the royal position with the queen consort. A section of the English Parliament was anxious that even if William III was given the constitutional status of a British ruler, Mary should have the status not of the queen consort but of the queen reigning by her own right and that her portrait should appear by her husband's side on the coinage.[10] A similar political situation existed in India when the Lichchhavi territory was to merge into the Gupta kingdom after the marriage of the Lichchhavi princess with Chandragupta I. They appear to have insisted to get some apparent recognition of their contribution to the coming up of the new empire, and the result was the joint coinage. As regards the goddess seated on a lion, she may be the tutelary deity of the Lichchhavis whose name appears below. It is no innovation of the mint masters, nor an indication of any originality. There are earlier examples available in the coinage of Huvishka and Kanishka III.[11]

Allan considers it surprising that Chandragupta I, who ruled as a powerful emperor for a long time was content to issue joint coinage throughout his reign, to which he finds no parallel. This has again been adequately explained by Altekar who says that we have an exact parallel in the history of England, "William III continued the joint type of coinage till the death of queen Mary II in 1694, after which he issued for the first time coinage in his own name bearing only his portrait."[12] We maintain that the position of Chandragupta I was somewhat akin to that of William III. Both were willing partners to an agreement which was faithfully followed by both. It is no wonder, therefore, that just like the king of England, Chandragupta too issued only one type of coinage which was symbolic of the Gupta-Lichchhavi union. Altekar has further pointed out that, "It appears that

Kumāradevī survived her husband and so the coinage continued to be joint throughout the reign of Chandragupta I."[13] Allan's objection that there is no parallel for a joint coinage, thus falls to the ground.

S.R. Goyal has also given reasons to prove that Chandragupta-Kumāradevī type is earlier than the standard type. He points out that *Garuḍadhvaja* which occurs on the standard and Archer types of Samudragupta's coins, does not appear on the Chandragupta-Kumāradevī type. Further, the legends on the standard type and on most other coins of Samudragupta are metrical. Had the Chandragupta-Kumāradevī type been later than the standard type, the legend on the former also must have been metrical.[14] It is also relevant to consider that, had the Chandragupta-Kumāradevī type been a memorial issue, the name of the commemorator must have been placed on these coins. Altekar has drawn attention to the fact that memorial medals struck by the Indo-Bactrian kings Agathocles, Antimachos and Eukratides have on the reverse the name of the commemorator.[15]

Finally we may refer to the very cogent remark of Jayaswal that, "No Hindu would ever think of celebrating the marriage of his father and mother."[16] We can, therefore, conclude that the Chandragupta-Kumāradevī type of gold coins were struck by Chandragupta I himself, to fulfil the terms of agreement with the Lichchhavis whose princess was the heiress to her parent's dominion.

Before closing this topic we may take note of a few observations that have been made by other scholars from time to time. S.V. Sohoni thinks that the obverse does not depict the marriage of Chandragupta and Kumāradevī, but it shows the king taking leave of the queen while proceeding on a military campaign.[17] There is hardly anything to commend this suggestion. Had it been so, we should have had on this coin a legend like *Samaraśata-vitata-vijayo* . . . or *jayaty=jita-rāja-jetā* or some similar phrase indicative of his prowess and capability to achieve victory. V.S. Agrawala suggested that this coin was issued by the Lichchhavis.[18] It is highly improbable that after the negotiations with the Guptas culminating in the marriage of Kumāradevī with Chandragupta, there was any political authority left with the Lichchhavis. There is a very interesting suggestion however by V.S. Pathak, who says that the royal couple has been shown in the *vaivāhika* (nuptial) pose, where the bride is to the right of her husband.[19] But that does not lead us to the definite conclusion that the mint-master has depicted the scene of the marriage of the royal couple. We have other instances in the Gupta coinage where the queen occupies a place on the right of her husband. On the king and queen type of Chandragupta II, the queen is sitting to the right of the king.[20] In our opinion these coins simply depict the couple, as joint rulers.

EXTENT OF THE KINGDOM OF CHANDRAGUPTA

Chandragupta's matrimonial relationship with the Lichchhavis not only enhanced his prestige but also resulted in some material gains which justified his assumption of the higher title of *Mahārājādhiraja* as compared with the lesser title of Mahāraja used by his father and grandfather. We may infer that he must have ruled over more extensive territory than his forefathers but we have no direct evidence of the extent of his kingdom. However, some idea can be formed of his empire from the passage found in the *Purāṇas* and the description of Samudragupta's conquests in the Allahabad pillar inscription.

The two passages in the *Vāyu* and *Vishṇu Purāṇas*,[21] include Prayāga, Sāketa and Magadha in the territory ruled by the Guptas. It is a controversial question as to which particular time in Gupta history does it refer to. Moreover, the account in different *Purāṇas* seems to differ. While the verse given in the *Vāyu Purāṇa* runs as:

Anu Gaṅgā Prayāgaṁ cha Sāketaṁ Magadhāṃstathā
Etān janapadān sarvān bhokshyante Guptavaṁśajāḥ

This verse has been partly misinterpreted and misunderstood. The correct reading of the very first word is *anu-Gaṅgaṁ* as given by *Vāyu-Cj* of Pargiter's foot note. The grammarian Kaiyyaṭa, while commenting on *Mahābhāshya* (II.1.2) gives several examples of cities situated on rivers namely, *anu-Gaṅgaṁ Hastināpuraṃ* (Hastinapura on the Ganges), *Anu-Gaṅgaṁ Vārāṇasī* (Vārāṇasī on the Ganges), *anu-Śoṇaṃ Pāṭaliputraṃ* (Pāṭaliputra on Son). Therefore, the reading *anu-Gaṅgā* is incorrect and its translation 'along the Ganges' is misleading. Moreover, how it could be applied to all the territories, as Sāketa is obviously not situated along the river Ganges. So this verse should be taken to state that 'The descendants of Gupta shall enjoy Prayāga on the Ganges, Sāketa and Magadha'.

The corresponding passage in the *Vishṇu Purāṇa* runs thus: *anu-Gaṅgā Prayāgaṁ Māgadhā Guptāś=cha bhokshyanti,* where as the *Bhāgavata* reads the same as: *anu-Gaṅgam=ā Prayāgam guptāṃ bhokshyati medinīṃ,* meaning, 'He will enjoy the protected earth along the Ganges upto Prayāga.'' This is palpably absurd, as it turns the proper noun Gupta into an adjective and leaves the sentence without a subject. Such readings are due to the carelessness or even ignorance of the scribes and should not be bothered about. The reading of the *Vishṇu Purāṇa* also seems to be due to scribal error. It is not absolutely necessary to take Māgadhā as a separate people. We can take the word as qualifying Guptas, and translate 'Guptas of Magadha'. Again we may look at the reading of the *Vishṇu Purāṇa,* which has *Māgadhān,* another absurdity. The upshot of this digression is that we should not stick to the very letter of the variant readings, but like a sensible editor accept the more probable text: *Anu-Gaṅgaṁ Prayāgaṁ cha Sāketaṁ Magadhaṁstathā etān janapadān sarvān bhokshyante Guptavaṁśajāḥ.*

Some scholars have taken it as representing the Gupta dominions after the time of Skandagupta, which is totally untenable, as it leaves out Bengal which formed an integral part of the Gupta kingdom till the very end. For obvious reasons this can not also be a reference to the time of Samudragupta and his successors upto Skandagupta. Obviously, therefore, the Purāṇic verse refers to the extent of the Gupta empire in the time of Chandragupta I.

Harisheṇa's Allahabad *praśasti* also leads us to the same conclusion. According to this record, in the north, Samudragupta uprooted the Nāga kings of Ahichhatra and Mathura in U.P. for the first time. This shows that Chandragupta's territory could not have extended to the west of Prayāga. In the south Mahākośala was the first state conquered by Samudragupta as also the forest kings to its west. This considerably limits the area under the Gupta rule before his time. In the east, southern Bengal was definitely not included in Chandragupta's kingdom as Samataṭa is mentioned among *pratyanta* states even in the

Allahabad pillar inscription. As for Bengal, it is very difficult to include it in Chandragupta's kingdom as Bankura district was ruled by Chandravarman king of Pushkaraṇa near Susunia. It may be stated on the basis of the account given in the Mehrauli pillar inscription that Chandragupta Vikramāditya conquered Vaṅga (southern Bengal) for the first time.[22] The absence of its name in the *Purāṇas* also indicates the fact that Bengal was not included in the Gupta kingdom till the time of Chandragupta II.

Thus we can conclude that the Purāṇic verse discussed above, gives us a more or less accurate idea of the extent of Chandragupta I's empire as consisting of Oudh, Prayāga and Bihar—a territory large enough to earn for its ruler the prestigious title of *Mahārājādhirāja*.

APPENDIX

THE GUPTA ERA

J.F. Fleet while editing the inscriptions of the Guptas, their feudatories and successors for the *CII*, III, found that the inscriptions of the Gupta kings themselves bore dates which ran in continuous succession—82, 93, 96, 106, 129, 136, 138, 141, 146 and he concluded that they belong to one definite era. However he could not find convincing evidence for the view that this era was founded by a Gupta king, or was named as Gupta era. He dismissed the expression *Gupta-prakāle* or *Guptasya-kāle* occuring in the Junagadh rock inscription of Skandagupta as no clear indication of the era being associated with the name of the Gupta dynasty or dating from the time of the establishment of the dynasty; nor did he attach any importance to the occurrence of the phrase *Gupta-nṛipa-rājya-bhuktau*, in the copper plate grants of the Gupta feudatories, the Parivrājaka kings of Dāhāla. He went on to conclude that since there was no evidence of the association of the name of any Gupta king with the era, we must look for the circumstances leading to its foundation elsewhere. Since there was a reference to a Gupta-Lichchhavi alliance in some of the Gupta inscriptions, he hit upon the idea that the Guptas had borrowed the era of their Lichchhavi relations of Nepal, which had been founded in A.D. 319-320.

However, we are more happily placed than Fleet, regarding the availability of evidence. We are now in possession of a good number of inscriptions from which it is abundantly clear that the era was known as the era of the Guptas. Firstly, the date 61 in the Mathura stone pillar inscription is recorded as *Guptakālā nuvartamāna*—'following the era of the Guptas'. Again, in the Sarnath Buddha image inscriptions of the reign of Kumāragupta and Budhagupta, the wording of the inscriptions runs as follows

Varsha-śate Guptānāṁ sa-chatuḥ-paṁchāśad-uttare.[23]

and

Guptā[nā]ṁ samatikkrānte sapta-paṁchāśad-uttare [1]
śate samānāṁ pṛithiv [*īm*] *Budhagupte praśāsati* [11][24]

Such an explicit statement is an irrefutable evidence that the era was founded by the Gupta kings. Records of the later period prove the same. For instance, in the Ganjam copper plate of Śaśāṅkadeva, the date is given in the following words: *Gauptābda varsha-śatatraye* i.e. in the year 300 of the Gupta era.[25] Further in the Arang copper plate of Bhīmasena II, we get the words *Guptānāṁ saṁvatsara.*[26] In view of this clear and overwhelming evidence, it can no longer be doubted that the era used in the Gupta inscriptions is the one that was founded by a member of this royal family.

The next question is, who founded this era? As already noted above, Fleet had attributed it to the Lichchhavi ruler Jayadeva of Nepal. He had argued that the last known date for Kumāragupta was 129 from his Mankuwar Buddha image inscription. Now if we suggest that this has been counted from the accession of Chandragupta I, it will give an average of $32\frac{1}{4}$ years for four successive generations of the Gupta dynasty, which is too long a period for any Indian dynasty. Consequently, he concluded that Chandragupta I could not be the founder of the era. But George Bühler has shown that we get an average of $37\frac{2}{3}$ years for the Chaulukyas of Gujrat and an average of 33-3/4 for the Eastern Chalukyas. Therefore an average of $32\frac{1}{4}$ years is not an extraordinary long period for the Guptas. Bühler rightly concluded that, "As Gupta and Ghaṭotkacha would not have been *Śaka-kartṛis,* Chandragupta the first *Mahārājādhirāja* must have been its originator. The historical event which led to the establishment of the era was of course the *abhisheka* (coronation) of Chandragupta I."[27]

The next problem to be solved was the epoch of this era which we have shown, may be safely designated as the Gupta era. For solving this problem, we have some definite help from the statement of Alberuni, that the era of Guptas was founded 241 years after the epoch of the Śaka era. As the Śaka era is still in use, its epoch A.D. 77-78 is definitely known to us and we can fix the epoch of the Gupta era in 77—78+241=318–19. However, further remarks of Alberuni, that "As regards the *Guptakāla* people say that the Guptas were a wicked and powerful people, and that when they ceased to exist, this date was used as the epoch of an era."[28] From this statement it can be inferred that A.D. 318-19 was the date of the extinction of the Gupta dynasty. This opened a flood-gate of theories for the epoch of the Gupta era.

As very pertinently remarked by Fleet, in order to determine the epoch of the Gupta era what was needed was a date in an inscription of the Guptas in an era other than their own. Fleet himself was lucky to discover such an inscription. The Mandasor inscription[29] having the dates 493 and 529 in the Mālava *saṁvat* also mentions that Kumāragupta was ruling over this earth in the Mālava year 493. Although the epoch of the Mālava era itself is nowhere mentioned, Fleet determined it by a very intelligent process. He said that the date 493 definitely falls within the reign of Kumāragupta I i.e. between G.S. 96 and 129. Let us suppose, Fleet argued, that the date 493 falls in the middle of Kumāragupta's reign, i.e. in the Gupta year $\left(\frac{96+129}{2}\right) = 113$. In other words, the Mālava year 493 may be equated with Gupta year 113 i.e. 113+78+241 = A.D. 432. This would give us 493—432 = 61 B.C., as the approximate epoch of the Mālava era. Luckily this approximate epoch is very close to the epoch of the famous Vikrama *saṁvat* which begins in 57 B.C. Since we can not postulate the establishment of two important eras within a period of four years only, and in view of the fact that our equation M.S. 493 = G.S. 113 is only approximate, we can very reasonably conclude that the Mālava era is identical with the Vikrama era, and that by adding 241 to the epoch of the Śaka era, we can arrive at the epoch of the Gupta era.

In order to determine the epoch very precisely, Fleet examined the astronomical data of a number of inscriptions and came to the conclusion that the Gupta years being current years, and the Śaka year being expired year, we should add 242 instead of 241 to the epoch of the Śaka year. However, R.G. Bhandarkar, did not agree with this part of Fleet's finding and emphasised that the Hindus' invariable way of dating being in expired years, we should add 241 to a Śaka year in order to arrive at the corresponding Gupta year; and thus fixed the epoch of the Gupta era in A.D. 318-19.[30] He demonstrated the accuracy of this date by fresh calculations. This view has been endorsed by George

Bühler,[31] and it is the prevalent and correct view, though some dissentient voices have been raised from time to time, but none of these views is tenable.

R. Shama Shastri has suggested the years A.D. 200-01.[32] M.G. Pai has proposed A.D. 272-73 as the epoch of the Gupta era.[33] D.N. Mukherji[34] thinks it is identical with the Vikrama *Saṁvat* and places it in 57 B.C. However, it can be very easily established that all these theories are untenable. The Ganjam copper plate of Śaśāṅkarājadeva is dated in the Gupta year 300. Śaśāṅka was a contemporary of the emperor Harshavardhana, who ruled from A.D. 606 to 647. Now let us refer the date 300 Gupta era, which we have for Śaśāṅka to the various epochs. With the generally accepted epoch of A.D. 318-319, we shall get for Śaśāṅka the date A.D. 618-19. With the epoch suggested by Pai we get A.D. 591-92 and with the epoch proposed by Mukherji, we get A.D. 247. So according to these epochs proposed by Pai and Mukherji Śaśāṅka cannot be a contemporary of Harsha but flourished long before him. These epochs thus have to be rejected,[35] as also the epoch of A.D. 284-85 proposed by R.P. Sundararaman.[36]

References

1. *EHI*, 295-96.
2. *CCGD*, xix; cf. *JNSI*, V, 40.
3. *Ibid.*, LXVIII, para 73.
4. *JRASBL*, III (1937), *NS*, XLVII, 105-111.
5. A.S. Altekar's observation almost clinches the issue. He says, "Samudragupta would not have taken pride in calling himself a *Lichchhavi-dauhitra*, if the power of his maternal grandfather had been crushed on the battle field before his mother's marriage." *Bayana Hoard*, XLIII, fn. 1.
6. *CCGD*, LXVI.
7. *Ibid.*, LXVII.
8. *Ibid.*, LXVIII.
9. *JRASBL*, III, *NS*, XLVII, 105-111.
10. *Ibid.*, 107.
11. *JASB*, 1933, *NS*, 7; *JNSI*. XII, 121; CCPM, I, 1, plate XX, X.
12. *Op. cit.*, 107.
13. *Bayana Hoard*, XLIII.
14. *HIG*, 115; cf. Maity, S.K., *JNSI*, XVIII, 187ff.
15. *Bayana Hoard*, XLVI.
16. *HI*, 91, fn. 1.
17. *JNSI*, XIX. 148. This view radically differs from his earlier interpretation given in *JNSI*, V, 37-42.

18. *Ibid.*, XVII, 117-19.
19. *Ibid.*, XIX, 135.
20. *Coinage.*, 138, Pl. ix. 6.
21. *DKA*, 53-54.
22. For identification of king Chandra of the Mehrauli pillar inscription with Chandragupta II, see *infra*, Chapter VIII, Appendix II.
23. Chhabra & Gai (ed.), *CII*, III, (1981), 321.
24. *Ibid.*, 333.
25. *EI*, VI, 143.
26. *Ibid.*, IX, 342ff.
27. *VOJ*, V, 215-229. It has been suggested that the Gupta era was started by Mahārāja Gupta (*IHQ*, 1942, 73n.), However, considering his compartively inferior title, we prefer to agree with Bühler that Mahārāja Gupta would not have been the founder of an era—*Śakakartṛi*, as he puts it. As regards Samudragupta, evidence of the Nalanda and Gaya copper plates is absolutely useless, as both of these are spurious. Moreover, if we reckon the era from the accession of Samudragupta, it will give him a very long reign of about 55 years, as the earliest known date of Chandragupta II is the Gupta year 61, which according to D.C. Sircar is the fifth regnal year of Chandragupta II. Therefore, it leaves clear 56 years for Samudragupta, which is a rather inordinately long period in the Gupta dynasty.
28. Quoted by J.F. Fleet, *CII*, III, (1888), 24.
29. This inscription was first published by Fleet in 1886 in *IA*, XV, 194ff.
30. Bhandarkar, R.G., *Collected Works*, III, 388.
31. *VOJ*, V, 315-29.
32. *MASR*, 1923.
33. *JIH*, 1932 175-189; *Ibid.*, 1933, 215-240.
34. *MR*, June 1932, 650-54; *Ibid.*, July, 1932, 28-33; *IHQ*, 1932, 85-92.
35. These were criticised long ago by Karunakana Gupta. *IC*, III, 47ff.
36. *JIH*, 1937, 132.

CHAPTER VI

EXPANSION AND CONSOLIDATION UNDER SAMUDRAGUPTA

It appears that as Chandragupta I became old, he decided in accordance with the injunctions of the *Smṛitis* to relinquish the responsibility of governing the state, and pass on this burden to his son Samudragupta, who was in every way a worthy successor. From the Eran stone fragmentary inscription of Samudragupta we know that his father was highly pleased with him on account of his devotion, righteous conduct and valour, and honoured him with the glory of the royal title, anointment to the throne and other similar honours. The scene of Samudragupta's selection as successor of his father is vividly described in the Allahabad stone pillar inscription of Samudragupta, in the following words; "Thou art indeed a noble person", having said this he (Chandragupta I) "embraced him, with the hair of his body standing erect and indicating his innermost feelings; when the courtiers were puffed up (with joy) (and) while the collaterals looked at him with melancholy faces, he was thus addressed by his father who surveyed him with an eye which penetrated into the true realities and which was (just now) unsteady on account of affection and heavy with tears, 'do thou protect this earth' thus." These words of considered pronouncement clearly establish the fact that Chandragupta I was thoroughly pleased with his son Samudragupta on account of his manifold qualities and was fully convinced that it was he alone who deserved to succeed him.

The late K. P. Jayaswal's view that the verse depicts the scene when Chandragupta I after his defeat at the hands of Kalyāṇavarmā, the hero of the play *Kaumudīmahotsava*, was lying on his death bed and was commissioning his son Samudragupta to recover the lost empire from the enemies, can be easily set aside. Apart from the fact that we have conclusively proved in the previous Chapter, that the play *Kaumudīmahotsava* has no bearing whatsoever on the early history of the Guptas, the suggestion of the learned doctor is untenable on other grounds also. We are told in verse 4 of the Allahabad pillar inscription that the faces of the collaterals of Samudragupta bore a melancholy look as soon as Chandragupta I announced that Samudragupta was to rule the earth henceforth. It has been rightly pointed out by Jagannath Agrawal[1] that in case Chandragupta I was a vanquished monarch lying on his deathbed, he had nothing to bequeath to his son Samudragupta, except an arduous task of recovering the lost dominions. Consequently there could have been no cause for any frustration, nor any reason for any feelings of malice towards Samudragupta, on the part of his collaterals. Their faces could have become melancholy only in case Samudragupta was being proclaimed as the next ruler of the empire.

The selection of Samudragupta as his father's successor is perfectly in accordance with the ancient institution of the *varṇāśramadharma*. In accordance with this, Hindu kings did voluntarily renounce the throne. We need not go to very ancient days of the *Rāmāyāṇa* to find the instances of the kings' renouncing their thrones. We can point out to the frequent mention of this practice in the writings of the great poet Kālidāsa. In his *Raghuvaṁśa*, *Śākuntalam* and *Vikramorvaśīyam*, he has repeatedly mentioned this practice.[2] An actual historical instance can be met with in the Pāla dynasty of Bengal. King Vigrahapāla handed over the authority to his son Nārāyaṇapāla and himself took to a life of penance.

Although, Samudragupta's accession to the throne was a settled fact, some modern writers are inclined to the view that he had to overcome the opposition from some of the other claimants who have been mentioned in the Allahabad pillar inscription. It has been further suggested that Samudragupta had a brother named Kācha[3] whose gold coins have been found in almost all the hoards of early Gupta coins. Further support for this view has been sought from verses 5 and 6 of the Allahabad pillar inscription of Samudragupta. Verse 5 says, "Some, tormented by valour resorted to him for protection"; and in verse 6 it has been said that, "conquered by his own arms in battles, those whose wrongs were always high."

Let us take the case of Kācha first. The coins of Kācha have on the obverse the legend *Kācho gāmavajitya karmabhir-uttamair-*

divaṁ jayati, and on the reverse the most significant epithet *Sarva-rājo-chchhettā*. According to the obverse legend Kācha claims to win the heaven by means of his excellent deeds, after having conquered the earth. This would mean that Kācha had obtained actual sovereignty of the earth and had performed many a pious deeds such as the performance of Vedic sacrifices like the *Aśvamedha* as also by giving away in charity large numbers of cows and substantial amount of gold. We must also remember that this legend is to be met with for the first time on the coinage of Samudragupta and Kācha. There is no earlier precedent either in the Gupta dynasty or any other earlier ruling family. It would therefore imply that Kācha was not summarily defeated by Samudragupta but that he had ruled for a considerable time during which he had the opportunity to perform all those excellent deeds which ensured for him a place in heaven. But there is no evidence at all for Kācha having achieved all this. We cannot even regard it as a vain boast for, as remarked before, there is no precedent for such a claim, and we are sure that this could suggest itself only to one who had such actual achievements to his credit. The second legend on the reverse *Sarva-rājochchhettā*—'the exterminator of all kings' is still more fatal to the existence of Kācha as a rival of Samudragupta. This grandiloquent epithet could have been assumed only by one who had actually exterminated all kings. But we find from the Allahabad pillar inscription that at the time of the accession of Samudragupta there was a large number of small states in northern India alone which had to be conquered. Had Kācha exterminated them there would have been no mention of them in the conquests of Samudragupta, and vice versa if Kācha followed Samudragupta, there would have been no kings left for him to conquer and to style himself as *sarva-rājochchhettā*. We must also keep in view the fact that no other Gupta emperor laid a claim to such a grand achievement. These epithets on the coins of Kācha, therefore, lead to the inevitable conclusion that he must be regarded as identical with Samudragupta.

As regards the statements contained in verses 5 and 6 of the Allahabad pillar inscription of Samudragupta, the *Kechit* of verse 5 who were tormented by the valour of Samudragupta, were obviously the hostile kings like Achyuta and Nāgasena, who were defeated but pardoned. Verse 6 speaks not of one battle but of a number of battles. These must have been fought against the many kings mentioned later on in this very epigraph. They cannot by any means be connected with Kācha or another rival claimant for whosc overthrow one single battle would have been enough as for aught we know that the entire resources of the state were in the hands of Samudragupta. We may, therefore, conclude that Samudragupta's succession to the throne was undisputed and there was no war of succession.

However, there was a lot of fighting to be done by Samudragupta both in order to secure his inherited kingdom and to expand it further. We have seen that Chandragupta I was the first ruler in the Gupta dynasty to style himself as *Mahārājādhirāja*. Besides having under his direct control the kingdoms of Bihar and Eastern U.P., he must have asserted some sort of suzerainty over the neighbouring kingdoms of the Nāgas. At his death, the Nāga rulers, of which two-Achyuta and Nagasena are mentioned by name in the Allahabad record, took the earliest opportunity to throw off the Gupta yoke. Of these two Achyuta was the ruler of Ahichhatrā where his coins have been found and Nāgasena was most probably the ruler of Mathura. Samudragupta swiftly put down their rebellion and as these kings expressed repentence and sought forgiveness, Samudragupta reinstated them.[4]

Another ruler who made a bid for independence was a scion of the Kota family. But he was perhaps a small fry, as Samudragupta himself stayed in his capital and sent his army which brought him in chains to the Gupta capital. Coins bearing the legend Kota and a crude figure of Śiva and bull have been found at various places in Panjab, such as Sunet and Sanghol in the Ludhiana district.[5]

Having asserted his authority in the North, Samudragupta now launched upon his plan of unification of India, and marched towards the South. His minister of foreign affairs and a military officer of high rank, Harisheṇa, the author of the Allahabad pillar inscription, mentions the following kings of the Deccan who were conquered by Samudragupta, but were reinstated—their territories having been restored to them: i. Mahendra of Kosala; ii. Vyāghrarāja of Mahākāntāra; iii. Maṇṭarāja of Kurāla; iv. Mahendragiri of Pishṭapura; v. Svāmidatta of Koṭṭūra; vi. Damana of Eraṇḍapalla; vii. Vishṇugopa of

Kāñchī; viii. Nīlarāja of Avamukta; ix. Hastivarmā of Veṅgī; x. Ugrasena of Pālakka, xi. Kubera of Devarāshṭra; and xii. Dhanañjaya of Kusthalapura.

As there is a considerable difference of opinion amongst the modern scholars regarding the identification of several of these kings and their kingdoms, we propose to take up this problem in some detail. By Kosala, Harisheṇa obviously means Dakshiṇa Kośala or Mahākośala, which roughly corresponds to the present day districts of Raipur and Bilaspur in Madhya Pradesh, and a part of the district of Sambalpur in Orissa.

Vyāghrarāja of Mahākāntāra: Mahākāntāra which literally means a great wilderness, was at one time believed to represent a wild tract of Central India including the erstwhile Jaso state;[6] and Vyāghrarāja was identified with Vyāghradeva of Nachna-ki-Talai and Ganj inscriptions, who was a feudatory of the Vākāṭaka king Pṛithivīsheṇa. But this identification is untenable for two reasons. Firstly Jaso and the adjacent territories are situated in northern India or Āryāvarta, whereas king Vyāghra subdued by Samudragupta is specifically stated to be a ruler of Dakshiṇāpatha i.e. the Deccan. Secondly, so far as we know, Samudragupta avoided a clash with the Vākāṭakas. We can therefore reject this identification. G. Ramdas has identified Mahākāntāra with the erstwhile Agency tracts of Jhadkhand in the Ganjam district of Orissa.[7] He says that Jhadkhand means in Oriya a forest region, and also points out that the *Zamindar* of Jeypore is called a ruler of Jhadkhand. He was thus sure that Mahākāntāra is Jeypore and the region in its vicinity. J. Dubreuil locates it near Sonpur along the course of river Tel, a tributary of the Mahanadi.[8] According to K.P. Jayaswal Mahākāntāra is the same as Kāntāraka of the *Mahābhārata*, (*Sabhā Parva*, 31, 13), and it corresponds to the modern territories of Bastar and Kanker.[9] The same view is held by R. Sathianathier.[10] We also consider this to be the most satisfactory identification. There are dense forests in this region. Moreover the road from Kosala leading to the South would naturally pass through Kanker and Bastar, unless we suppose that instead of following the direct road, Samudragupta swerved to the east and thus arrived in the vicinity of Sonepur.

Maṇṭarāja of Kurāla: J. F. Fleet thought that Kaurālaka of the inscription was a mistake for Kairālaka, and the country intended was Kerala on the western coast. This suggestion had been obviously the result of a very unfamiliar name like Kurāla or perhaps Korāla.[11] L. D. Barnet would connect it with Korada.[12] S. K. Aiyangar thought it should be located near present day Khurda in the Cuttack district of Orissa. Kielhorn while editing the Aihole inscription of Pulakeśin II remarked that Kaurāla (Kuṇāla) mentioned in its verse 28, must be the same as Kurāla, which is represented by the region of the Kollar lake between the rivers Godavari and Kistna.[13] This view has been accepted by Jayaswal.[14] But as pointed out by H.C. Raychaudhuri, the territory around Kollar lake must have been included in Veṅgi, the kingdom of Hastivarman. R. Sathianathier, proposes to identify it with Cherla in Nagpur Taluk of East Godavari district.[15] This is again ruled out as the Nagpur Taluk must have formed part of Hastivarmā's territory. According to G. Ramdas, it must be the plain country to the north-east of the Mahendra hill, since it is mentioned immediately after Mahākāntāra.[16] B. V. Krishnarao identifies it with Kulūla mentioned in the Mahendragiri pillar inscription of Chola king Rājendra Chola I, which is situated to the south of the Maikal range and is included in the Chanda district of Madhya Pradesh.[17] However, that would take it too far to the north. The solution to this knotty problem seems to have been provided by the recent discovery of a copper plate grant of Mahārāja Narendra of the Śarbhapurīya dynasty of South Kosala. It mentions a territorial division—Maṇṭarājabhukti, which obviously seems to take its name from the ruler of that name who may be the same as Maṇṭarāja of Samudragupta's inscription. Therefore the kingdom named Kurāla must have been located in the vicinity of South Kosala.

Mahendragiri of Pishṭapura: There has been some controversy regarding the correct name of the ruler of Pishṭapura. Fleet thought that a name ending in *giri* could not be the name of a king, as such a name ending is associated with a sect of recluses—the Dasanāmī Gosāins. He, therefore, took the king's name as simply Mahendra and connected *giri* with the following place name Koṭṭūra, translating it as Koṭṭūra on the hill.[18] However, D. R. Bhandarkar pointed out that this division of the text was grammatically incorrect and impossible.[19] Moreover, V.S. Ramchandramurti has pointed out that several rulers of the Telugu country actually had names ending in *giri* or its synonym *adri*.[20] Thus there is nothing improbable in Mahendragiri being a royal name. Pishṭapura is modern Pithapuram, 12 miles from Kakinad in the East Godavari district of Andhra Pradesh. This is the earliest epigraphic mention of Pishṭapura. In the Ragolu plates of the king Vāsishṭhiputra Śaktivarman, it is described as a city in the Kaliṅga territory.[21] It is also mentioned in the inscriptions of Anantavarman king of Kaliṅga.[22] Early in the seventh century, sometimes before A.D. 634-635, the Chālukya monarch Pulakeśin II conquered Pishṭapura and annexed it to his dominions.[23]

Svāmidatta of Koṭṭūra: G. Ramdas has observed that Koṭṭūra is a very common Dravaḍian place-name. In the district of Ganjam there are about a dozen villages called Koṭṭūra, eight in the Vishakhapatnam and about half a dozen in Godavari.[24] According to Subramaniam, Koṭṭūra which is eleven miles from Parlakimedi in the Ganjam district, is to be identified with the one of our inscription.[25]

Damana of Eraṇḍapalla: The identification of Eraṇḍapalla is very crucial for determining the extent of Samudragupta's campaign in the south. Fleet identified it with Erandol, in the East Khandesh district of Maharashtra.[26] This identification seemed to receive some support from the fact that there were some ancient remains at Erandol which could be assigned to the Gupta period. However, Dubreuil did not agree with this view and proposed to identify it with Erandapali near Śrīkakulam (Chicacole).[27] He relies on the evidence of the Siddhantam plates issued from Kaliṅganagara by the Gaṅga king Devendravarman, which mention a place named Eraṇḍapallī.[28] G. Ramdas differs both with Fleet and Dubreuil. He suggests either Yendipalli in the Golgonda Taluk of Vishakhapatnam district or Endipalli in the Ellora Taluka of West Godavari district. He says, "The old kingdom of which Erandapalli was the capital must have extended from about the northern boundary of the Golgonda Taluk to about Ellore."[29] An Eradavishaya is mentioned in the Nagdam plates of the Gaṅga king Vajrahasta,[30] dated Śaka year 979. This grant was issued from Kaliṅganagara. However, whereas Eradavishaya is spelt with a dental *d*, the name in the Allahabad pillar inscription has cerebral conjunct instead. Jayaswal says that, "Eraṇḍapallī was a town in Kaliṅga, in the district of

Ganjam, in the neighbourhood of Kaliṅganagara (Mukhaliṅgam)." He further remarks, "This district must have been under Svāmidatta of Pishṭapura, and Damana of Eraṇḍapallī must have been a *rājā* or ruler of the status of a district officer."[31] This view is however quite unwarranted. The view of G. Ramdas that, "The old kingdom of which Eraṇḍapallī was the capital must have extended from about the northern boundary of Golgonda Taluka to about Ellore,"[32] appears to be the most acceptable.

Vishṇugopa of Kāñchī: Fortunately we possess some information about Vishṇugopa. He belongs to the well known Pallava dynasty of the south, and was the younger brother of Siṁhavarman, (c. A.D. 332-44), and son of Skandavarman II (c. A.D. 297-332). During the rule of his elder brother he was *Yuvamahārāja*, and he issued a grant.[33] His full name was Vishṇugopavarman. He was a *Yuvarāja* during his brother Siṁhavarman's rule, and then acted as regent of his nephew Skandavarman III. Samudragupta's invasion might have taken place during the period of his regency. The capital of the Pallavas was Kāñchī, the present day Kanchipuram in Tamil Nadu.

Nīlarāja of Avamukta: The identity of Avamukta is rather difficult to establish. H. C. Raychaudhuri suggested that an old sea-port named Nilapalli near Yanam in the Godavari district, reminds one of some connection with king Nīlarāja. He also refers to the temple of Avamukteśa in the Anantapur district of Andhra Pradesh. But Avimukteśa is a name of Śiva and Avimuktakshetra is generally applied to the region of Varanasi. Jayaswal invited attention to Ava and Pithuṇḍa mentioned in the Hathigumpha inscription of Khāravela,[34] and suggested that Pithuṇḍa may be the same as Pitundra mentioned by Ptolemy on the eastern coast. B. V. Krishnarao suggests that Ava may be the same as Arvarnoi of Ptolemy and may stand for Hiraṇyarāshṭra in the Kuddapah and Kurnool districts of Andhra Pradesh.[35]

Hastivarman of Veṅgī: Veṅgī has been unanimously identified with Peddavegi in the Krishna district of Andhra Pradesh. This kingdom included the entire coastal region between the rivers Godavari and Krishna, and extended in the west up to the Ghats. It was the heart of the Andhra country and a great meeting place of roads from Kaliṅga, Draviḍa, Karṇāṭa,

Mahārāshṭra and Kośala. This country played an important part in the spread of Indian culture beyond the seas in the islands of the Pacific Ocean. Hastivarmā belongs to the Śālaṅkāyana (Vaiṅgeyakas) dynasty of Veṅgī and is credited with several victories.[36] The Śālaṅkāyanas held Veṅgī for three generations. It passed on to the Pallavas for a brief interval, and was taken from them by the Vishṇukuṇḍins.

Ugrasena of Pālakka: Vincent Smith at first identified it with Palakkadu, that is the Palghat division of south Malabar, but later on he changed his view, and agreed with V. Venkanya that it should be located in Nellore district.[37] The suggestion to identify it with Policut was rejected by Hultzsch.[38] G. Ramdas refers to Pākanāḍu or Paṅkanādu or Pakāināḍu mentioned in the inscriptions of Rājarāja Chola. He proposes to identify it with Pakkai situated between Udaygiri and Venkatagiri in the Nellore district. J. Dubreuil regards it the same as Palakkada mentioned in several inscriptions of the Pallavas.[39] For instance, the Uruvapalli grant of *Yuvamahārāja* Vishṇugopavarman was issued from Palakkada,[40] which was perhaps a seat of Pallava viceroyalty. It seems to have been placed in the time of Samudragupta, under a Pallava prince whose correct name was Ugravarmā.[41]

Kubera of Devarāshṭra: Fleet identified Devarāshṭra with Maharashtra.[42] This identification was pronounced to be quite wrong by Dubreuil, who located it in the Yellamanchili Taluk of Vishakhapatnam district of Andhra Pradesh. He relied on the mention of Devarāshṭra as a *Vishaya* or district in the Elmanchi Kaliṅgadeśa, mentioned in the Kasimkot plates of the Chālukya king Bhīma I.[43] This is further supported by the evidence of the Srungavarapukota plates of Anantavarman,[44] issued from Pishṭapura, where his grand-father, Guṇavarman is described as *Devarāshṭrādhipati.* G. Ramdas objects to this identification on the ground that Vishakhapatnam district must have been included in the kingdom of Pishṭapura, and we can not have "an independent state within another independent state."[45] However, it appears that these southern kingdoms were very small in extent. Some of them were smaller than a modern district. The coastal region between the mouths of the Mahanadi and Godavari was divided into three kingdoms—Koṭṭūra of Svāmidatta in Ganjam district, Devarāshṭra of Kubera in the

Vishakhapatnam district and Pishṭapura of Mahendragiri in the East Godavari district. Y. R. Gupte has adduced some fresh evidence in support of the identification with Maharashtra. He says, "There is still a village called Devarāshṭre in the Khanpur Taluk of the Satara district. Curiously, the holiest object there—a *liṅgam* of Śiva, is named Samudreśvara." In his opinion this preserves the memory of Samudragupta's association with the place.[46] However, the evidence for locating Devarāshṭra on the eastern coast is overwhelming.

Dhanañjaya of Kusthalapura: V.A. Smith regarded Kusthalapura as a variant for Kuśāsthalapura, which is one of the names of the holy city of Dvaraka.[47] But the identifications of Eraṇḍapallī and Devarāshṭra as established above make it clear that Samudragupta's campaign was confined to eastern Deccan and he never reached so far west as Surashṭra. Barnet is of the view that Kuttalur, near Polur in the North Arcot district of Andhra Pradesh, represents the ancient kingdom of Kusthalapura. According to B. V. Krishnarao, however, the modern town of Kolorupak or Kollipak situated on the river Aleru, a tributary of Musi which flows into the Krishna is the ancient Kusthalapura, which is a variant of Kuśāsthalapura, meaning the city of Kuśa's abode.[48] He further says that the chieftains of Kot (ancient Dhānyakaṭaka) trace their descent from a Dhanañjaya who might have been the king defeated by Samudragupta. His realm lay in western Andhra, between the rivers Godavari on the north and Krishna on the south.

The foregoing survey of the kingdoms of the Deccan enables us to determine the extent of Samudragupta's conquest in the south. It was at one time believed on the basis of the identifications of Devarāshṭra with Maharashtra and of Eraṇḍapalla with Erandol as proposed by Fleet, that Samudragupta advanced along the eastern coast of the Deccan as far as Kāñchī, and thence turning westwards subdued Maharashtra and returned home via Khandesh,[49] thus covering both eastern and western Deccan. However, the new identifications of Devarāshṭra and Eraṇḍapalla proposed by Dubreuil and others, place these states on the eastern coast in Kaliṅga, and consequently Samudragupta's advance has to be limited to Kāñchī which appears to be the southern-most state subdued by him.[50] Some scholars are, however, not prepared to credit Samudragupta with any substantial success even in this region. Dubreuil, for instance, holds the view that Samudragupta advanced as far as the river Krishna but was opposed by a confedracy of the kings of the eastern Deccan and was forced to return home without meeting with any success.[51] B.V. Krishnarao, has expressed a similar opinion. He says, "It is thus obvious that Harisheṇa did not record the string of names in any topographical order, or with reference to their geographical situation, but in a haphazard fashion. The object seems to be to suggest that all these kings and princes formed a formidable coalition and gathered together somewhere in the Deccan to resist and repulse the common enemy. It is not clear where the allied armies met the Gupta invader. Jayaswal's suggestion that the battle was fought on the plains near Collar lake is improbable. No pitched battle was fought. Instead of encountering the enemy who appeared formidable he seems to have abandoned the idea of a conquest and retreated to his kingdom leaving the great kingdoms of the South utterly unscathed. His expedition ended as an unsuccessful military pageant."[52]

However, this opinion of Dubreuil and Krishnarao is based on a completely faulty understanding of the expression *sarva-Dakshiṇāpatha - rāja - grahaṇa-moksh = ānugraha-janita-pratāp = onmiśra-māhābhāgyasya* i.e. "whose magnanimity was mingled with his glory produced by his kind favour of setting at liberty after capturing all the kings of the Deccan." Both these scholars infer from this statement that Harisheṇa, the author of the inscription, has used this kind of phraseology to cover up Samudra gupta's inability to achieve a victory over these kings. But their inference is utterly incorrect and untenable when examined in the light of ancient Indian political ideas. Kauṭilya speaks of three types of conquerors, viz. the righteous conqueror (*dharmavijayī*), the coveteous conqueror (*lobhavijayī*), and the demonaic conqueror (*asuravijayī*); and defines each of them as follows: The righteous conqueror is one who restores the defeated enemy to his original position, taking away neither his kingdom nor his riches, and remaining satisfied with mere acknowledgement of his suzerainty. The coveteous conqueror is one who takes away the possessions of the defeated enemy but spares his life. Lastly, the demonaic conqueror is he who annexes the territory of the defeated foe and also puts him to death. Here, Samudragupta acting like the praiseworthy type of the righteous conqueror restored to the defeated kings of the South, their respective kingdoms and was content with having established his overlordship over them. That such political ideology was prevalent in the Gupta times, is evident from Kālidāsa's statement in his *Raghuvaṁśa*, that 'the righteous victorious monarch (Raghu) only took away the royal glory of the lord of Mahendra who had been captured and (then) released, but not his kingdom.'[53] We cannot therefore, agree with Dubreuil or Krishnarao, and take away from Samudragupta the credit for having brought the eastern Deccan under his sway. There is no evidence what so ever of the formation of a confederacy by the southern kings to oppose Samudragupta. As a matter of fact the idea of a confederacy even in the face of a grave external danger is opposed to the genius of ancient political thought. Kings of Northern India, like Pṛithivīrāja III, Jayachandra of Kannauj and the Chaulukyas of Gujrat fought singly with the Muslim invader Shihab-ud-Din Ghori, and never joined hands to meet the common national menace. That Harisheṇa has not mentioned the rulers of the south in the order of the geographical location of their kingdoms, is no proof of their entering into an alliance. On the other hand, according to the tenets of Indian polity, a neighbouring state was regarded as a potential enemy.

It is very likely that Samudragupta had to cut short his plan of the conquest of the Deccan. Certain unexpected events in the north seem to have forced his immediate return home. Though he had put down the earlier rebellions of feudatory kings like Achyuta and Nāgasena, the hostile elements in the north appear to have again conspired to throw off Samudragupta's yoke, and this necessitated his hasty return to the North, leaving his task in the South only half accomplished.

We are informed by Harisheṇa, that the following eight kings of Āryāvarta were forcibly uprooted by Samudragupta: Rudradeva, Matila, Nāgadatta, Chandravarman, Gaṇapatināga, Nāgasena, Achyutanandi,[54] and Balavarman. There were some more also whose names have not been mentioned. Perhaps they were less important. The mention of so many kings in Āryāvarta indicates that at this time Northern India was divided into many small states, and a majority amongst these belonged to the Nāgas, who had liberated the valleys of Ganges and Yamunā from the Kushāṇas, before the rise of the Guptas. It is not unlikely, therefore, that these Nāga rulers joined hands in order to preserve their recently acquired kingship and offered united opposition. However, it is not possible to agree with Jayaswal that it was a war against the Vākāṭaka empire and Rudradeva is none else but Rudrasena I of the Vākāṭaka dynasty. This identification had been first suggested by K.N. Dikshit.[55] However, it is absolutely untenable. Firstly, the Vākāṭaka state was essentially a southern (*Dakshiṇāpatha*) state, whereas Rudradeva is specifically mentioned in the list of the kings of Āryāvarta. Secondly, Rudradeva is one of those defeated kings who were forcibly uprooted i.e. they were defeated and their kingdoms annexed. This cannot be said of Rudrasena Vākāṭaka, as we know from the Balaghat plates of Prithivīsheṇa II, that the Vākāṭaka kingdom had been prospering for a hundred years.[56] This clearly speaks of an uninterrupted continuity of the Vākāṭaka kingdom in a prosperous condition. The use of the title of Mahārāja with the name of Rudrasena I in the Vākāṭaka inscriptions as compared to the title of *Smrāṭ* applied to Pravarasena I, is no proof of his defeat at the hands of Samudragupta. All the Vākāṭaka monarchs including Narendrasena who is credited with overlordship over Kuntala, Mekala and Mālava are styled as Mahārājas. Only Pravarasena I is called *Samrāṭ* on account of his having performed the *Vājapeya* sacrifice.[57] So, the identification of Rudradeva with Rudrasena is untenable and is generally rejected.[58] The suggestion[59] to identify him with one of the Western Kshatrapa rulers—Rudradāman II or Rudrasena III, is equally unsatisfactory. There is no possibility of Samudragupta coming into clash with these rulers of far off Ujjain, without having first overthrown the Śaka ruler Śridharavarman of Eran and the Nāgas of Vidiśā.

Mātila: The next ruler of Harisheṇa's list, Mātila has been identified with Māttila of the terracotta seal discovered from Bulandshahr in U.P.[60] But as pointed out by Allan, the absence of any honorific on the seal "suggests that it is a private seal and not one of a royal personage."[61] Moreover, the seal cannot be assigned to the fourth century A.D. Jagannath Agrawal assigns it to the sixth century A.D. on palaeographic grounds. In his opinion the medial *i* is so much elongated that it cannot be earlier than the sixth century A.D.[62] Mātila, therefore, must remain unidentified.

Nāgadatta: He is not otherwise known from coins or any inscription. But obviously he appears to have been the ruler of one of the Nāga principalities of northern India.

Gaṇapatināga: Copper coins bearing the legend Gaṇapati have been discovered at Padmāvatī, Vidiśā and Mathura. Smith pointed out that "although the coins of Gaṇapati which have been found in thousands do not bear the word Nāga, there can be no doubt that they were issued by a member of the Nāga dynasty. Their practical identity in type and style with the coins which bear the names of the Mahārājas Skandanāga, Bṛihaspatināga and Devanāga, leaves no room for scepticism."[63] As regards the kingdom over which he ruled, D.R. Bhandarkar had suggested Vidiśā,[64] but Mathura appears to have a better claim since Altekar found hundreds of Gaṇapati's coins there, while only a few were discovered at Vidiśā.[65]

Nāgasena: Bāṇa has mentioned a Nāgasena born in the Nāga dynasty who met with his doom in Padmāvatī, as his secret plan was divulged by a Sārikā bird.[66] As other examples given by Bāṇa are historical, this one may also be a historical fact. We may, therefore, regard Nāgasena as the ruler of Padmāvatī, modern Padampawaya on the confluence of the rivers Sindhu and Para in Madhya Pradesh.

Chandravarman: He may be identified with Chandravarmā of the Susunia rock inscription,[67] in the Bankura district of West Bengal. He is described as the lord of Pushkaraṇa, which has now been correctly identified with the modern village of Pokhran situated 25 miles to the north-east of Susunia.

Achyutanandi: In the *Purāṇas* the names of some Nāga kings end in *Nandi.* We have, therefore, following Jayaswal and Basak taken Achyutanandi as one name instead of two. Copper coins bearing the legend *Achyu* have been found in considerable numbers from the ancient site of Ahichhatrā near Ramnagar in the Bareilly district of U.P. These coins resemble other Nāga coins in fabric. It is, therefore, highly likely that Achyutanandi who was defeated by Samudragupta was the Nāga ruler of Ahichhatrā.

Balavarman: K.N. Dikshit had identified him with Balavarmā an ancestor of king Bhāskaravarmā of Kāmarūpa (Assam) who flourished eight generations before Bhāskaravarmā, the contemporary of Harshavardhana. Allowing an average of 20 years to one generation, we shall have to place Balavarmā, 160 years before Bhāskaravarmā i.e. c.A.D. 446. He could not, therefore, have been a contemporary of Samudragupta. V.V. Mirashi has proposed to assign Balavarmā to the Magha dynasty of Kauśāmbī (Kosam).[68] Alternatively we may regard him as a successor of Rājan Mahākshatrapa Śridharavarman Śaka who is known from his inscriptions to have ruled over the Eran-Sanchi region.[69] Since soon after this we find Samudragupta's rule over this region as attested by his inscription found at Eran,[70] it is reasonable to infer that this Śaka dynasty had been overthrown by Samudragupta, and king Balavarmā uprooted by him belonged to this Śaka dynasty. This victory over the Śakas of Eran, brought the whole of eastern Mālava under the direct rule of Samudragupta.

The conquest of Āryāvarta having thus been more or less completed Samudragupta now turned his attention to the hilly and forest covered terrain to the south-east of the Gaṅgā-Yamuna plain extending towards south Kośala, which had earlier come under Samudragupta's hegemony. Harisheṇa tells us that all the kings of the forest region (*āṭavikarājyas*) were reduced to subservience. The identification of these forest kingdoms is rendered certain and easy by a statement in the Khoh plates of Mahārāja Saṁkshobha, dated Gupta year 209, that the ancestral kingdom of the Parivrājaka kings named Dahāla, was situated within the eighteen forest kingdoms,[71] which may thus be located in Bundelkhand. These continuous victories of Samudragupta, created an awe-inspiring impression on the princely and republican states on the borders of the Gupta realm and they all strove to win his good will by paying tributes of all sorts, carrying out his commands, and even by personal visits to his capital.

Starting from the East, Harisheṇa first mentions Samataṭa. In literature the earliest mention of this country is to be found in the *Bṛihatsaṁhitā* of Varāhamihira.[72] Fleet has explained the name as "the country of which the rivers have flat and level banks of equal height on both sides, and it denotes lower Bengal."[73] Smith remarks, "the name Samataṭa is thus descriptive of a marked difference between the appearance presented by the country in the swamps of deltaic Bengal and that presented by the drier regions of Bihar and North-Western Provinces."[74] From the Ashrafpur plates[75] as well as from the account of I-tsing[76] we learn that during the seventh century Samataṭa was ruled over by kings of the Khaḍaga dynasty and its capital was Karmmānta, modern Kamta, 12 miles west of Kommilla.[77] Under these kings, Samataṭa included the districts of Tippera, Noakhali, Barisal, Faridpur and the eastern half of Dacca. Second kingdom in the east was Ḍavāka, which corresponds to the Kapili valley of the Nowgong district of Assam. In this valley there is a place named Doboka.[78] The next state was Kāmarūpa which is evidently Assam or more particularly that part of it which constitutes the modern district of Kamrup. The territory called Nepāla is easy to identify, as it still retains its ancient name.

The next princely state was that of Karttṛipura, which it is rather difficult to locate. Its identification with Kartarpur in the Jalandhar district of Panjab has been often repeated,[79] but it is entirely wrong. Kartarpur in the Jalandhar district, and now a place of Sikh pilgrimage did not even exist in the fourth century A.D. It was founded by the fifth Sikh Guru, Śri Arjan Dev in some waste lands granted to him by the Mughal prince Salim. Smith had very pertinently remarked that, "It may have lain in the Western Himalayas and have corresponded roughly to the modern Almora, Garhwal and Kumaon. The enumeration of the frontier kingdoms seems to proceed in regular geographical order beginning with Samataṭa and proceeding northwards through Davāka to Nepal and thence westwards to Karttṛipura."[80] Smith's view receives confirmation from the information supplied by C.F. Oldham,[81] who refers to a Garhwal tradition about Kaṭūriā Rājputs and their possible connection with the villages of Katyar and Katarmal. In his opinion the Garhwal and Kumaon districts of U.P. represent the Karttṛipura state of our inscription. We have some further information from Sanskrit inscriptions which also points to the probable location of Karttṛipura in this region. The Pāṇḍukeśvara copper plate of Lalitāśūradeva[82] and Taleśvara inscription of Dyutivarmā,[83] mention a city named Kārttikeyapura, which has been located by D.R. Bhandarkar near the modern village of Baijnath in the Almora district of U.P.[84] However, Dashrath Sharma has argued in favour of Karor or Karur, in Multan district of Pakistan.[85]

He says, that according to Alberuni an Eastern Indian king Vikramāditya defeated a Śaka ruler at Karor, and questions as to why there should be an encounter between the Gupta ruler and that of Baijnath. He further remarks, "When Purushapura changes to Peshawar or Pashaur, and Lābhapura to Lahore, Karttṛipura should as naturally be in due course Karur or Karor." But Harisheṇa has mentioned the Śakas and Kushāṇas separately, and not in the list of the frontier states. Moreover, there does not appear to have been any fighting between Samudragupta and any of the bordering (*Pratyanta*) states. So Alberuni's statement is inapplicable here. Moreover, it is a far cry from Nepal to Multan in Pakistan. We must agree with Smith and Oldham and locate Karttṛipura in the Almora and Garhwal districts of U.P.

The foregoing survey of the frontier kingdoms completes the eastern and northern boundaries of Samudragupta's empire. We are next taken to the west, where we find a string of states beginning from the southern parts of Rajasthan, and extending through Haryana and Panjab, it goes right upto the river Chenab in Pakistan. Here are mentioned the tribal republics of the Mālavas, Ārjunāyanas, Yaudheyas and Madrakas. Next come the Ābhīras, Prārjunas, Sanakānīkas, Kākas and Kharaparikas.

The Mālavas, though at one time settled in the Lyallpur and Montgomery districts of Pakistan, were at this time settled in the Jaipur district of Rajasthan. Their capital, most probably, was Kārkoṭanagara, modern Nagar about five miles to the east of Karkot hills in the south-east of Jaipur. Here Carllyle found six thousand ancient coins, all of which except 40 or 50 belonged to the Mālavas.[86] These coins bear the legend *Mālavānām Jaya* in characters of the second or third century A.D. Other find-spots of their coins are Ajmer, Tonk and Chittor. Allan thinks that the rivers Betwa and Yamuna formed the eastern boundary of the Mālava state.[87]

The Ārjunāyanas are a very ancient tribe. They are mentioned by Pāṇini.[88] Varāhamihira groups them with Sārasvatas and Matsyas.[89] According to Allan the lands of the Ārjunāyanas lay within the triangle Delhi-Jaipur-Agra.[90] This area partly covers Matsya and partly its contiguous area.

The Yaudheyas are also a very ancient and warlike people. They are mentioned by Pāṇini amongst the communities which lived by the profession of arms (*āyudhajīvi-saṁgha*).[91] Their coins have been found at Behat (Saharanpur district), Sonepat, Sirsa, Hansi and Panipat (Haryana) and at Chakrata in Dehradun district of U.P. Their coin moulds have been discovered from Khokhrakot near Rohtak and Sunet and Sanghol in the Ludhiana district. A stone inscription of a Yaudheya chief was discovered at Vijaygadh in the Bharatpur district of Rajasthan. They are mentioned as very powerful and warrior people in the Girnar rock inscription of Rudradāman. As stated in Chapter II above,[92] they had won a decisive victory upon the Kushāṇas and wrested from them the territory between the rivers Yamuna and Sutlej. Samudragupta's victorious arms almost all over India, seem to have induced the brave Yaudheyas to accept his overlordship and to agree to pay tribute.

The next people mentioned by Harisheṇa are the Madrakas, who are generally placed in the region between the rivers Ravi and Chenab in Pakistan. The territory from the river Satluj upto the Ravi must have formed the sphere of influence partly of the Yaudheyas and partly of the Madrakas. We have now reached perhaps the north-western limit of Samudragupta's empire.

Next are mentioned, the Ābhīras. Though their earliest mention is to be found in Patañjali's *Mahābhāshya*,[93] it is from the *Purāṇas* that we get some concrete facts about them. The *Vishṇu Purāṇa* groups them with the well known western people such as the Aparāntas, Saurāshṭras, Śūras and Arbudas.[94] The *Matsya*, *Vāyu* and *Brahmāṇḍa Purāṇas* speak of them as belonging to the lineage of the servants of the Āndhras.[95] In the *Bṛihatsaṁhitā*[96] and the *Mahābhārata* also they are placed with the Aparāntas (the people of the Western coast). The author of the *Periplus of the Erythraean Sea* mentions Abiria on the western coast. Epigraphic evidence also connects them with western India. An Ābhīra general named Rudrabhūti is mentioned in the Gunda inscription[98] of the reign of Rudrasiṁha I, who constructed an artisan well in the year 103 = A.D. 181. An Ābhīra king Īśvarasena son of Śivadatta figures as a ruler in a Nasik inscription.[99] It shows that the Ābhīras were ruling over the Nasik district in the third century A.D. It has been suggested that an Ābhīra king sent an embassy to the Sassanian monarch Narseh (A.D. 293-302) to congratulate him on his victory over Varhran.[100] Thus there is overwhelming evidence for placing the Ābhīras, at the time of the rise of Samudragupta in the West, and Smith's view placing them in the region called Abirwara, situated between Jhansi and Vidiśā must be abandoned.

Of the remaining four republics of this list, the Kākas seem to have given their name to the Buddhist establishment at Sanchi, which is called as Kākanādaboṭa.[101] It must have been a small state in the neighbourhood of Vidiśā. A Sanakānīka chief is mentioned in the Udayagiri inscription of the year 82 as the donor.[102] But it cannot be stated definitely, whether he belonged to the neighbourhood of Vidiśā or had come there at the call of his overlord Chandragupta II, who had set out on a campaign of conquest. The Prārjunas may be the same people as Prārjunakas mentioned in the *Arthaśāstra* of Kauṭilya, but there is no clue as to the location of their state. Smith placed them in the Narasimhapur district of Madhya Pradesh,[103] but D.R. Bhandarkar has suggested Narsinghgarh in the same state.[104]

The Kharaparikas were tentatively placed by Smith in the Seoni and Mandla districts of Madhya Pradesh (then known as Central Provinces).[105] In the Battisgarh stone inscription dated V.S. 1385, there is a mention of Kharapara armies.[106] Rai Bahadur Hira Lal has identified these Kharaparas with the Kharaparika tribe of Samudragupta's inscription, and he has located them in Damoh district of Madhya Pradesh.[107] A similar view has been expressed by S. L. Katare who regards the Kharaparas as 'freebooters' inhabiting the Chedi region. They were enlisted by Muhammad-bin-Tughlaq into his service and 'organised into a fighting force'.[108] However, Dashrath Sharma does not regard the Kharaparas mentioned in the Battisgarh inscription as an indigenous Indian tribe who can be identified with the Kharaparikas of Samudragupta's inscription. In his opinion they were foreigners—probably Mongols. He points out to the mention of one Kharapara Khan in the *Hammiramadamardan*, and also to the attack of Kharaparas on the Sultan of Delhi when Vāgbhaṭa Chāhamāna had attacked Ranthambhor. He further says that the word has become a synonym for Muslim in Dingal.[109] As there is a very big gap of time between the Gupta emperor Samudragupta and the Muslim Kharaparas of Muhammad-bin-Tughlaq, the identification is out of question. One is tempted to find some connection between the Kharaparikas and the Gardabhilas of the *Purāṇas*, as Khara and Gardabha have same meaning in Sanskrit, but that does not carry us any further since we do not know much about the Gardabhilas either.

Beyond these monarchical and non-monarchical 'frontier' states, there were in the North-Western Panjab, beyond the river Chenab, a few remnants of the Kushāṇas. These are known to us from the coins which bear such names as Śīlada, Śāka and Gaḍahara or Gaḍakhara. These people, though they are not specifically mentioned by Harisheṇa, had also come under Samudragupta's sway as is indicated by the occurrence of that emperor's name on one of their coins. Beyond these small states, the Kushāṇas were still in power to the west of the river Indus in Gandhāra, in the Kabul valley and in Bactria. It is most probably to this region that we have to assign the rule of Daivaputra-Shāhi-Shāhānusahi. There is considerable difference of opinion amongst the scholars, as to whether this expression represents one or three different ruling powers. Allan preferred to take Daivaputra, Shāhi and Shāhānushāhi as three powers each representing one separate state. Alternatively he was prepared to regard Shāhi-Shāhānushāhi as one single unit.[110] D.R. Bhandarkar argued longago that it is one single compound designating some later great Kushāṇa king, as Daivaputra being a *taddhita* form means 'a descendant of Devaputra', and it can not stand by itself. Moreover, it never occurs alone without the addition of Shāhi or Shāhānushāhi or their Indian equivalents—*Mahārāja* or *Rājātirāja,* both in the inscriptions and on the coins.[111] Therefore, the title Daivaputra-Shāhi-Shāhānushāhi must have been used for a powerful Kushāṇa ruler to the west of the Indus. He may be taken to be the Kidāra (the Ki-to-lo of the *Wei-Shu*) who is said to have left Bactria under the pressure of the White Hūṇas and set up his rule in Gandhāra and the Kabul valley c.A.D. 350. At first he acknowledged the suzerainty of Shapur II, and even helped him in his war against the Romans. In all probability he is the monarch who sought an alliance with Samudragupta, as a result of which he was able to inflict a defeat on his erstwhile Sassanian overlord in A.D. 367-68.[112] Kālidāsa speaks of the victory of his hero Raghu over the Pārasīkas.[113] It may be an echo of the victory which Samudragupta shared with his ally Kidāra against the Sassanian emperor Shapur II.

Next to the Daivaputra-Shāhi-Shāhānushāhi, are mentioned Śaka-Muruṇḍas. Scholars generally take this compound as representing two political powers, though according to Sten Konow, Muruṇḍa is not the name of a separate tribe, but is merely a common noun, meaning 'lord', in the language of the Śakas.[114] It was used as a title not only by the Śakas but also by the Kushāṇas. In the Zeda inscription, Kanishka is called *muroḍa*.[115] Konow further equates Śaka-Muruṇḍa with *Sai-Wang* of the Chinese writers and says that it simply means Śaka king or Śaka prince. It is noteworthy that several Western Kshatrapa rulers have the Sanskrit word *svāmī* prefixed to their name, which according to Sten Konow is only the Sanskrit equivalent of *Muruṇḍa*. However, other scholars like Fleet, Allan, R. D. Banerji, K. P. Jayaswal regard the Muruṇḍas as a separate people.[116] The *Purāṇas* mention the rule of 13 Muruṇḍa kings separately.[117] A very late Jain writer Āchārya Hemachandra, defines the Muruṇḍas in his *Abhidhānachintāmaṇi* as the people of Lampāka i.e. Jalalabad in Afghanistan. These however are very late references, and it is not impossible that in course of time, a section of the Śakas had come to be known simply Muruṇḍa, instead of the original name Śaka-Muruṇḍa.

Our next problem is, where to locate the Śakas? According to Smith they are the Western Kshatrapas who ruled over western Mālava and Surashṭra upto c. A.D. 388. Smith rightly remarks, "Samudragupta whose direct conquests had reached the borders of Mālava must necessarily have been in communication with the Śaka Satrapas of the West."[118] D. R. Bhandarkar, however, thinks that Śrīdharavarman Śaka of the Kanakhera inscription or his successor is intended here.[119] But, the region between Eran and Sanchi over which Śrīdharavarman appears, from his inscriptions, to have ruled, had been annexed by Samudragupta, to his empire. This is clearly established by his stone inscription found at Eran.[120] Allan does not exclude the possibility of the Western Kshatrapas being intended here, but prefers to take them as the Śakas of the North whose coins have the Ordoxsho reverse and formed the proto-type of Samudragupta's early coinage.[121] But these coins have on them the name Śāka and not Śaka, who were in some way related to the Kushāṇas. It is, therefore, far more likely that the Western Kshatrapas are meant in this context.

As regards the Muruṇḍas, we have already shown that they cannot be placed anywhere in the Gangetic plains.[122] We may, therefore, either agree with Sten Konow that they are the same as Western Kshatrapas whose name begin with *svāmī*, or we should take cue from the *Abhidhānachintāmaṇi* of the Jain Āchārya Hemachandra and place them in ancient Lampāka, the territory around Jalalabad in Afghanistan.

The statement in line 23 of the Allahabad pillar inscription regarding the foreign powers with whom Samudragupta established diplomatic relations is rounded off by the mention of Ceylon and "the dwellers of all the islands." The friendly relations with Ceylon were established as a result of the Ceylonese king Meghavarṇa, seeking Samudragupta's permission to build a monastery at Bodh Gaya for the convenience of Ceylonese pilgrims to the hallowed spot were the Buddha obtained enlightenment under the Bodhi tree. According to Smith, Meghavarṇa "despatched a mission to Samudragupta laden with the gems for which Ceylon has always been renowned, besides other valuable gifts."[123] The required permission was granted and Meghavarṇa built a splendid monastery close to the sacred Bodhi tree. At the time of Hiuen Tsang's visit to Bodh Gaya, a thousand monks were living in this monastery.

The reference to the islands of further India, is no vain boast either. Epigraphic and art evidence from Cambodia, Java and Sumatra clearly shows the penetration of Gupta influence to these lands and speaks of an intimate intercourse between India and these island kingdoms.[124] We have the testimony of Fa-hien that Tāmralipti in Vaṅga which was in the possession of the Guptas, was a busy port, for active sea borne communication with Śrī Lanka and the islands of the Pacific ocean. The wide use of the Sanskrit language for secular records, in Champā (Vietnam), Sumatra, Java and Borneo, must have been due to their intimate relations with India of the Gupta times, when Sanskrit had universally replaced Prākṛit in all spheres in Bhāratavarsha.

The line 24 of the Allahabad pillar inscription, gives an elaborate idea of the nature of diplomatic relations established by Samudragupta with the Kushāṇas, Śakas, Muruṇḍas and the islanders. They are said to have rendered service, to the great monarch, in various ways. The great military achievements of

Samudragupta must have inspired an awe amongst these foreign potentates, making them eager to enter into subordinate alliances with him. Of the various methods of service adopted by these people, the first was *ātmanivedana*, which means that these must have presented themselves in the court of Samudragupta and sought a personal audience with the emperor, seeking his good will. Secondly, they are said to have made *kanyopāyanadāna*, which has generally been translated as 'offering of maidens as presents.'[125] S. V. Sohoni has given an entirely different interpretation of this term. He says, "The expression, *kanyopāyanadāna*, means that the marriages in the feudatory families could be contracted after obtaining the sanction of the suzerain—and not that the daughters in the feudatory families had to be married to the imperial ruler."[126] This view of Sohoni is absolutely untenable and far fetched as the expression can in no way be translated to give such a sense. It can either be taken as *Kanyāś=cha upāyanāni cha teshāṁ dānaṁ* i.e. 'maidens and presents—the offering of these', or *Kanyā eva upāyanāni teshāṁ dānaṁ* i.e. 'the maidens as presents—offering of these.'[127] Therefore it is clear that these foreigners presented gifts and maidens (or gifts of maidens) to Samudragupta, in order to please the Indian emperor. Thirdly they sought a guarantee for the safe and undisturbed enjoyment of their own territories by means of charters bearing the Gupta royal seals with Garuḍa emblem, (*Garutma-daṅka-sva-vishaya-bhukti śāsana-yāchanā*), i.e. by means of permanent treaties of friendship. We have thus obtained a vivid idea of the constituents of Samudragupta's empire viz. the directly governed areas in the north, the feudatory states owing allegience to the imperial authority in eastern Deccan, the friendly frontier states who were rulers of the Indian soil in the East, North and North-West, and the foreign powers both in India and beyond its frontiers.

HORSE SACRIFICE—THE SYMBOL OF SOVEREIGN POWER

To mark the successful completion of his conquests of North and South India, Samudragupta performed the *Aśvamedha* sacrifice, in the true spirit of a *chakravartin* in accordance with the Vedic injunctions. To mark this outstanding event he issued a special variety of gold coins with the legend *Aśvamedhaprākramaḥ* (possessing the valour to perform the horse-sacrifice) on one side and *Rājādhirājaḥ pṛithivīm avitvā divaṁ jayatyāhṛitavājimedhaḥ* (the overlord of kings, who has performed the Horse-sacrifice, having protected the earth, conquers the heaven) on the other. Some coins bear the legend *Rājādhirājaḥ pṛithivīm avitvā divaṁ jayatyaprativāryavīryaḥ* (the overlord of kings, of irresistible valour, having protected the earth, wins heaven). We also find a reference to this achievement of his in the copper plate grants of his grand-daughter Prabhāvatīguptā, the Vākāṭaka queen, where Samudragupta has been described as *anekaśvamedhayāji* (the performer of many horse sacrifices).[128] This has given rise to some speculation and a group of scholars think that he performed more than one *Aśvamedha*.[129] In support of their theory, they point to the two different legends found on his *Aśvamedha* type of coins, as noted above. However, that is not a sound interpretation of the statement. In the inscriptions of his successors Samudragupta is simply described as the performer of the horse-sacrifice which was very elaborate.[130] They never mention the epithet 'the performer of many horse-sacrifices', found in the records of Prabhāvatīguptā, which may be either an exaggeration or it may be a scribal error.

The epithet *Chirotsannāśvamedhāharttā* of Samudragupta, occurring in the inscriptions of his successors has been usually interpreted, as indicative of the revival of an old Vedic rite the performance of which had not been witnessed for a long time. Fleet had translated the term as, "the restorer of the *Aśvamedha* sacrifice that had been long in abeyance."[131] It has been adopted by many scholars.[132] However, there are several instances of the performance of *Aśvamedha* sacrifice before Samudragupta's time. Leaving aside Pushyamitra Śuṅga's performance of two horse sacrifices, mentioned in the Ayodhya inscription of Dhanadeva, we have evidence of the performance of this rite by several kings shortly before the time of Samudragupta. The Bhāraśiva Nāgas performed as many as ten horse-sacrifices just before Samudragupta's time. The Vākāṭaka emperor Pravarasena I also performed four horse sacrifices. Similarly, in the South Ikshvāku king Śāntamūla, the Pallava Dharmamahārāja Śivaskandavarman and Vijayadevavarman, king of Veṅgi, performed the same celebrated rite not long before Samudragupta. Even the ruler of a small principality Yugaśaila in the Dehradun district of U.P., performed this sacrifice and the bricks of the fire-altar of this rite have come to light in the excavations at Jagatgram. These can be assigned to the late third or early fourth century of the Christian era. Eminent scholars have, however, attempted to explain away these performances. H.C. Raychaudhuri opined that it is probable that the court-poet of the Guptas knew little about these monarchs.[133] S.K. Aiyangar,[134] D.R. Bhandarkar,[135] V.C. Pandey[136] have suggested that Samudragupta performed a full-fledged *Aśvamedha* sacrifice of the epic style which indeed was in abeyance for a long time. V.C. Pandey further gives a very ingenious explanation. In line 4 of the Allahabad pillar inscription, he proposes to read *go-pravitata* instead of *pravitata* read by Fleet and Sircar, and takes it as a variant of *govitata*, a form of *Aśvamedha* said to have been performed by *Sārvabhaum* and *Chakravartī* Bharata.[137] Thus, argues he, that Samudragupta performed *govitata Aśvamedha* in a big way, which had long been in abeyance. However, there are certain difficulties in accepting the learned scholar's rendering. We have examined the estampage of this inscription with the help of Jagannath Agrawal, and failed to trace any sign of the letter *go*. Instead we noticed that the word just preceding *pravitata* is *sphuṭodhva* [*ṁ*] *sita*, which means "clearly devastated or ruined". Now, such an adjective is most inappropriate with a term like *govitata* and hence Pandey's emendation cannot be tenable. To us the correct meaning of the term, seems to be 'who performed the horse-sacrifice which is a long protracted rite', as pointed out by V.S. Pathak[138] and Jagannath Agrawal.[139]

The absence of the mention of horse sacrifice in the Allahabad pillar inscription leads to the obvious conclusion that the horse-sacrifice had not been performed before the inscription was put up. Samudragupta would appear to be a very poor statesman, if he had not planned to perform an *Aśvamedha*, and did not perform it immediately after his victories in the South and the North. We may, however, regard the *Prayāga-praśasti* as a fore-runner of that grand ceremony, for we know that 'the panegyrics of the sacrificer' formed an essential part of the *Aśvamedha*. These were sung by lute-players including a *Rājanya* who sings to the lute three songs made by himself, "such war he waged, such battles he won".[140] This is what we actually find in Harisheṇa's panegyric. It may be taken as an indication of the coming event of the performance of the great horse sacrifice.

Samudragupta and the Foreign Powers

Western frontier of Samudragupta's empire in the light of Gaḍahara coins: As we have noted above, Samudragupta was able to establish a vast empire after brilliant campaigns of conquest in the North and the South. Perceiving his military success all the Indian frontier states (*pratyanta nṛipati*) acknowledged his supremacy while the republican and the tribal kingdoms came under his hegemony. The foreigners too entered into subordinate alliances of friendship, as is clear from the testimony of the Allahabad pillar inscription. Here we shall briefly review Samudragupta's relations with foreign powers and the extent of his empire in the West in the light thereof.

After the extermination of the kings of the Gangetic valley and annexation of their kingdoms, the direct rule of Samudragupta extended upto Mathura region. The republican tribes to the west of Mathura submitted to him either as a result of military pressure or through his diplomatic skill. These republican states continued, as autonomous but not sovereign states, and paid tributes of all sorts and presented themselves personally in his court. They were gradually absorbed in the Gupta empire by the political pressure of its mighty rulers, as we do not find any record nor any mention of any of them towards the end of the Gupta rule. The grip of Samudragupta's rule was so tight and his awe so great that even the Śāka, Shīlada and Gaḍahara rulers of the Central and Western Punjab also felt its pressure and sought their welfare not only in accepting his suzerainty but surrendering all insignia of their sovereignty to this mighty ruler. The testimony for this may be seen in a gold coin[141] of the Gaḍaharas, which bears on its obverse the name Samudra written under the arm of the king and the name Gaḍahara outside the spear. We have similar situation in the coinage of some of the native states of India, during the British rule, where the portrait of the king of England appears on the obverse, and simply the name of the state on the reverse. The existence of these coins of the Gaḍaharas, points to the fact that the western boundaries of the Gupta empire in the time of Samudragupta touched the waters of river Chenab for all practical purposes.[142]

Samudragupta and the Śakas:

Among the foreign powers, Samudragupta's relations with the Śakas are of vital importance. We see that this important ruling house of foreign extraction in western India was left untouched by this mighty Gupta conqueror. There can be hardly any doubt that the Śakas mentioned in the Allahabad pillar inscription in the list of foreigners, who sought Samudragupta's friendship by personal attendance at his court, giving presents of maidens, and asking for charters bearing the Garuḍa seal for the enjoyment of their own territory, include the Śaka Kshatrapas of Surāshṭra. From the statement in the Allahabad pillar inscription it is clear that the alliance of friendship between the Gupta emperor and the Śakas was not based on equality. It is highly probable, even if we make an allowance for exaggeration on the part of Harisheṇa, the writer of the inscription, that the Śakas along with the Kushāṇas and other rulers, were overawed by the colossal military might of Samudragupta and thought it politic to establish friendly diplomatic relations with him by these means. On the other hand, Samudragupta also realised his limitations and thought it better to consolidate his position in the newly conquered areas at home, rather than venture fresh conquests in the far off lands of Surāshṭra and the regions beyond the Indus.

There seems to have been more than one Śaka principality in India in the beginning of the fourth century A.D. The Śakas of Ujjain and Surāshṭra are well known to us from their inscriptions and coins. We now know of another independent Śaka kingdom comprising the Vidiśā-Eran region. Two inscriptions, one discovered from the village Kanakhera[143] near Sanchi, and the other from the ancient town of Eran,[144] mention a Śaka ruler Śrīdharavarman, and are dated in his thirteenth and twenty-seventh regnal years respectively. As both the inscriptions have been dated in the years of his own rule, it is evident that Śrīdharavarman was an independent king. This is also evident from the use of the titles *Rājan* and *Mahākshatrapa* for him in these inscriptions. On palaeographic grounds the inscriptions of this ruler point to the latter half of the third or the beginning of the fourth century A.D. as the period of his rule. In the Kanakhera inscription he has been called the son of Śaka Nanda. This also points to the existence of Śaka rule in Eastern Mālava, before the time of Śrīdharavarman.

It is not possible to say whether Śrīdharavarman was the last ruler of his house or had any successors. K.D. Bajpai, discovered, during the course of excavations at Eran, a seal with the legend *Rājño Īśvaramitra-putrasya rājño Siṁhaśrīsenasya* (of king Siṁhasrisena son of king Īśvaramitra). The seal may be assigned, on palaeographic considerations to the early fourth century A.D. It has the 'hill and river' symbols which are so common on the Kshatrapa currency. From the style of the legend and the similarity of symbols Bajpai feels sure that king Siṁhaśrīsena is a Śaka ruler, but he is not prepared to identify him with Svāmi Siṁhasena of the Kshatrapa line who ruled about A.D. 382. He further remarks, "it is also not possible to say in the present state of our knowledge, if Īśvaramitra and his son Siṁhasena had any relationship with king Śrīdharavarmā."[145] However, from the different name endings on the seal and the inscriptions from Kanakhera and Eran, we are not inclined to suggest that the seal belongs to the rulers of the line of Śridharavarman. We would rather suggest that it came to Eran from outside with some official correspondence with the Government of Eran, and even if Siṁhaśrīsena is not a member of the Kshatrapa house of Mālava and Surāshṭra, he cannot be a successor of Śrīdharavarmā, who must have been overthrown by Samudragupta, whose Eran stone inscription proves his rule over this region.[146]

Samudragupta and the Vākāṭakas:

The conspicuous absence of the mention of the Vākāṭakas in the Allahabad pillar inscription of Samudragupta has led scholars like K.N. Dikshit,[147] K.P. Jayaswal,[148] R.N. Dandekar,[149] R.K. Mookerji,[150] S.R. Goyal[151] to surmise that Rudradeva mentioned by Harisheṇa among the eight rulers of Āryāvarta is no other than Rudrasena I, the Vākāṭaka king. It is further presumed that a battle took place between the two at Eran, in which the latter was defeated and killed.[152] It is also held that after this war the Vākāṭakas were forced to enter into a subordinate alliance with the Guptas as a result of which they lost their possessions in Bundelkhand and parts of Malwa. In support of this theory, it is argued that South Kośala and Āndhra were under Pravarasena I and thus must have been under the rule of Rudrasena I also. Therefore, it was not possible for Samudragupta to conquer these areas without measuring swords with the Vākāṭakas. Secondly, Vyāghrarāja of Mahākāntāra was a feudatory of the Vākāṭaka king Pṛithivīsheṇa I and this must have brought the Vākāṭakas in the battle-field against Samudragupta. It is further surmised that Rudrasena I being a Bhāraśiva *dauhitra* inherited the territories of Mahārāja Bhavanāga to the north of Vindhyas and thus can be enumerated amongst the kings of Āryāvarta. Eran also is, supposed to be under Rudrasena I. After defeating him, Samudragupta occupied this area. Lastly, it is pointed out that whereas Pravarasena I, the grandfather of Rudrasena I had the higher title of *Samrāṭ*, Rudrasena I is given the title Mahārāja which is indicative of his lower status and subordinate position.

But none of these arguments cuts much ice when examined seriously. Rudradeva of the Allahabad pillar inscription cannot be identified with Rudrasena I for the following reasons. Besides the difference in the name, Rudradeva was one of the kings of Āryāvarta while the empire of the Vākāṭakas lay in the Dakshiṇāpatha. The sovereignty of the Vākāṭaka king over Vyāghradeva of the Nachna and Ganj inscriptions does not change the complexion of the Vākāṭaka empire from that of Dakshiṇāpatha to that of Āryāvarta. Even a northern emperor can have control over some territory in the South and vice versa. Secondly, Rudradeva was one of the eight kings of Āryāvarta who were forcibly uprooted and their kingdoms were annexed by Samudragupta, whereas the empire of the Vākāṭakas was in continuous and prosperous existence after Rudrasena I for a period of one hundred years upto the time of Pṛithivīsheṇa II.[153] Thus Rudrasena I was not only in possession of his own territories but passed them on to his successor in a prosperous state. It is therefore absolutely incorrect to say that he was killed at Eran, as asserted by Jayaswal.[154] A.S. Altekar has pointed out that it is highly unlikely that Harisheṇa has grouped the name of a powerful emperor Rudrasena I with those of half a dozen of non-entities, when he has so eloquently given full imperial titles of the Kushāṇa sovereigns who had merely acknowledged Samudragupta's supremacy.[155] Had there been a clash with the Vākāṭakas, the story of Samudragupta's sensational victory over the Vākāṭakas would have been described in most glorious terms. South Kośala was certainly not under Pravarasena, for we find that it was ruled by a king named Mahendra. Nor is there any proof that Pravarasena's sovereignty extended over any part of Āndhra country. It is also a gratutious assumption that Rudrasena I inherited the territories of his maternal grandfather in Bundelkhand. Moreover, it is now held for certain, that it is Pṛithivisheṇa II, who is the overlord of Vyāghra of Nachna and Ganj inscriptions. Lastly, the title of Mahārāja given to Rudrasena I in the Vākāṭaka copper plate grants does not show his subordinate position. It has been explained cogently that Pravarasena has been styled as *samrāṭ* because of his performance of the *Vājapeya* sacrifice. It has been laid down in the *Śatapatha Brāhmaṇa* that a king becomes a *samrāṭ* by virtue of his having performed the *Vājapeya* sacrifice. All the other kings of the Vākāṭaka dynasty bear the title of Mahārāja.

Considering all these facts, the only possible conclusion one can draw is that at the time when the Guptas were supreme in the North, the Vākāṭakas held the same position in the Deccan. Samudragupta being a shrewd statesman deliberately avoided a clash with the Vākāṭakas. There seems to have been a silent understanding between the two, without a formal treaty, not to interfere with the affairs of each other. These relations of friendship were cemented by a matrimonial relationship by Samudragupta's equally great son and successor Chandragupta Vikramāditya, who gave his daughter Prabhāvatiguptā to the Vākāṭaka monarch Rudrasena II.

Samudragupta's Personality

The inscriptions and coins of Samudragupta enable us to get a vivid impression of his manifold personality. His imagination had been fired by the noble impulse of making India strong and impregnable to foreign invasion by effecting the unification of the political fragments into which the country had been divided since the break up of Pushyamitra Śuṅga's empire. He undertook his *digvijaya* to achieve the fulfilment of this lofty ideal. He, therefore, adopted the attitude of a righteous conqueror (*dharmavijayī*) who wants neither wealth nor territory but only royal glory or *śrī* as Kālidāsa has termed it. However, when diplomatic methods failed he did not hesitate to use his military might as he did in the case of the kings of Āryāvarta, who had been pardoned once but had rebelled a second time. Otherwise he stood for peaceful friendly relations both at home and abroad. To the independence loving republican people within India, he allowed the greatest measure of autonomy within the framework of the empire. While to the Indian kings on the frontiers he extended the hand of friendship and valued their goodwill, he strove to maintain friendly relations with the foreign powers of the Śakas and Kushāṇas, by giving them written assurance of their territorial integrity. He further strengthened the friendly ties by accepting the hands of the maidens from these foreign houses. He was perhaps following in the footsteps of his equally illustrious forerunner in the building up of a strong Indian empire, Chandragupta Maurya, who had married the daughter of the Greek invader Selukus Nikator whose armies had been routed. The crowning glory of Samudragupta's policy of pacification was the restoration of many royal houses which had lost their kingdoms and were faced with extinction.

He was a hero of many a battle, always in the thick of the fight, as is evident from Harisheṇa's description of his body as adorned with hundreds of scars of the healed up wounds which he had received from multiple weapons. According to the Eran inscription, his enemies became terrified even in dreams on remembering his super human feats on the battle field. On his coins he has been rightly described as a 'hero of irresistible valour', as one possessing the 'prowess of a tiger' and as one 'who had continuously won victory in a hundred battles.

Samudragupta was not only a great warrior, conqueror and statesman, he was a man of taste, taking deep interest in the finer side of life and cultivating the fine arts. The Allahabad pillar inscription rightly speaks of his skill in music as we have actual proof of it in the lyrist type of his coins where he is shown playing upon a lute. He was also a great poet, whose writings gave inspiration even to learned authors. His poetry was replete with pithy sayings which were worthy of study. It is very much to be regretted that none of his literary compositions have come down to us.

While his acts in war were superhuman, Samudragupta was intensely human in his behaviour. His heart was full of compassion for the poor, the miserable and the hapless. One could touch his heart by merely showing devotion and submission towards him.

Samudragupta was hailed as the ideal Hindu emperor of his age and was deemed equal to the gods Kubera, Varuṇa, Indra and Yama by virtue of his great riches, his beneficient activities, his royal splendour and stern justice. The reign of this great conqueror whom V.A. Smith has compared with Napoleon came to an end in A.D. 375.

Appendix I

CAN KĀCHA BE IDENTIFIED WITH BHASMA OF THE ĀRYA-MAÑJUŚRĪMŪLAKALPA

Ever since the discovery of some standard type of gold coins of the early Gupta period bearing the name Kācha under the left arm of the king's figure, there has arisen a most intricate problem of the Gupta history—namely the identity of Kācha of these coins. There is no mention of any king of this name in the Gupta genealogies contained in their inscriptions, nor do we hear of him from any other source. Hence the identity of Kācha has remained a much debated topic, and perhaps no scholar who has dealt with the Gupta period has left this topic untouched. This has resulted in different identifications of Kācha—with Ghaṭotkacha, the father of Chandragupta I,[156] with a foreign invader,[157] with a brother of Samudragupta, who died in the war of independence with Kushāṇas,[158] with the Kācha of Ajanta cave inscription,[159] with Rāmagupta,[160] with a rebel brother of Samudragupta who contested for the throne,[161] and finally with Samudragupta himself.[162]

K.P. Jayaswal in his *Imperial History of India*[163] has identified Kācha with Bhasma, a rebel brother of Samudragupta. He has placed reliance on some verses of *Āryamañjuśrīmūlakalpa*, a Buddhist work of the 8th or 9th century A.D. He has been ardently followed by P.L. Gupta[164] and S.R. Goyal[165] both of whom have taken Kācha as identical with Bhasma and have placed him between Chandragupta I and Samudragupta taking him as the latter's rebellious younger brother. They have entirely agreed with Jayaswal's interpretation of the verses 700-707 of the *Āryamañjuśrīmūlakalpa*. Recently L.P. Pandey published a paper identifying Kācha with Bhasma[166]. He has gone to the extent of taking the account of the *Āryamañjuśrīmūlakalpa verbatim* and has assigned to Kācha a long rule and attributed to him the conquest of Western and Northern India. In view of the conflicting identifications it appears to be worthwhile to examine the contents of the *Āryamañjuśrīmūlakalpa* afresh and see if this work has any bearing at all on the Kācha problem.

The verses in question, found in the portion dealing with the local history of Gauḍa run as follows:

Tasyādhareṇa nṛipatis-tu Samudrākhyo nāma kīrtitaḥ//700//

triṇi divasāni durmedh-aḥ rājyaṁ prāpsyati durmatiḥ/
tasyāpyanujo vikhyātaḥ Bhasmhākhyo nāma nāmataḥ//701//

prabhuḥ prāṇātipātasaṃyuktaḥ mahāsāvadyakāriṇaḥ/
nirghṛiṇī apramattaścha svaśarīre tu yatnataḥ//702//

paralokārthinenāsau balisatvadihaiva tu/
akalyāṇamitramāgamya pāpaṁ karṃa kṛitaṁ bahu//703//

dvijairākrāntatadrājyaṁ tārkikaiḥ kṛipaṇaistathā/
vividhākāra-bhogāṁścha mānushā pitarāstathā//704//

vividhāṁ sampadāṁ so-api prāptavān nṛipatistathā/
so-anupūrveṇa gatvāsau paśchimāṁ diśi bhūpatiḥ//705//

kaśmīradvāraparyantaṁ uttarāṁ diśimāśṛitaḥ/
tatrāpi-jitasaṅgrāmī rājyaṁ kṛitvā tu vai tadā//706//

dvādaśābdāni sarvatra māsāṁ pañchadaśastathā/
pṛīthivyāmārtarogoasau mūrchhitaścha punaḥ punaḥ//707//[167]

They have been translated by Jagannath Agrawal as follows:

(700) "Below him is recounted the king called Samudra.

(701) Evil of intellect and evil of thought, (he) will obtain the kingdom for three days.[168]

(702) His famous younger brother too, called by the name of Bhasma, the lord, embroiled in the destruction of life, (was associated with) the performers of acts which were liable to censure. (He was) cruel (but) was diligently vigilant about his own body.

(703) He who was seeking good in the next world, he did not (desist) from sacrifice of living beings, in this world; and having obtained friends who were doers of evil, he did much evil.

(704) His kingdom was infested by Brahmans who were logicians (but) were wretched. The human beings as well

as the manes (were offered) enjoyable things of various types.

(705) And the king also obtained riches of various kinds, having gone to the western direction, in due order of succession.

(706-07) He reached the northern quarter upto the gate of Kashmir. There also, having won the battle, and then having ruled (there) for twelve years and 15 (?) months, and afflicted by a disease, fell into swoons again and again."[169]

The above account provides us the following information:

1. There was a king named Samudra (of Gauḍa?) who ruled for three days (or three years).
2. Samudra had a younger brother famous by the name of Bhasma, who was heartless, wicked and of low intelligence.
3. Bhasma went upto the gate of Kashmir in the north and won a battle there. After ruling for 12 years and 15 (?) days/months he died of a fatal disease after suffering great pain.

The foregoing account of Samudra in the *Āryamañjuśrīmūlakalpa* does not provide the slightest evidence for taking him as Samudragupta, the imperial sovereign of the Gupta dynasty. This Samudra of the Buddhist work is placed amongst the local rulers of Gauḍa, and he is credited with a rule barely lasting three days (or three years), while it is a well known fact that *Mahārājādhirāja* Samudragupta was an imperial sovereign who achieved great conquests in the North and the South of India and had a long reign of about three decades. Had it been a reference to the imperial sovereign, it should have been placed with the verses 646-47 where the names of some of the imperial Gupta rulers seem to have been recorded. It seems that the Samudra mentioned in the verse 700 of the *Āryamañjuśrīmūlakalpa* was either a local ruler of Gauḍa or the Buddhist writer of the 9th century had a vague knowledge of some names of yore which he inserted here and there without caring to present authentic facts of history.

We have no evidence that Samudragupta had a brother named Bhasma, who ruled after him for more than twelve years, nor is there any basis for assuming that Bhasma rebelled against Samudragupta. The account of the *Āryamañjuśrīmūlakalpa* is absolutely silent on this point. Those who support the idea of rebel brother, they consciously or unconsciously base their assumption on the fourth verse of the Allahabad pillar inscription, where it is said that the faces of those of equal birth (*tulya-kulaja*) became melancholy on Chandragupta I's calling upon Samudragupta to 'protect the earth'. They further say that verses 5 and 6 of this inscription contain a reference to Samudragupta's war with his rebel brother Kācha. The verse 4 of the Allahabad pillar inscription no doubt refers to the disappointment of other princes on Samudragupta's nomination to the throne but it does not in any way portend a war of succession. It rather indicates that they resigned themselves to their inevitable fate and accepted the verdict with heavy hearts. As regards the statement contained in the verses 5 and 6, the *kechit* of verse 5 who were tormented by the valour of Samudragupta, were obviously hostile kings like Achyuta and Nāgasena who were defeated but pardoned. Verse 6 speaks not of one but many battles. These must have been fought against the kings mentioned later in this very epigraph. They cannot by any means be connected with Kācha or another rival claimant for whose overthrow one single battle would have been enough, as the entire resources of the state were in the hands of Samudragupta. Thus so far as the Allahabad pillar inscription is concerned it provides no evidence of war between the different contenders for the throne.

L.P. Pandey has not only identified Bhasma with Kācha but has also taken the account of the *Āryamañjuśrīmūlakalpa* as a sober fact of history and credited Kācha with the conquest of Western India i.e. Mālava upto Gujrat and northern India upto Kashmir which will imply his conquest of the Panjab *ipso facto*. Both these conclusions of Pandey are contradicted by positive and irrefutable evidence. We know that Western Kshatrapas held Mālava and Gujrat right upto c. A.D. 390. They were overthrown by Chandragupta II Vikramāditya. This is definitely established by the numismatic evidence. Western Kshatrapa's coinage continues up to A.D. 390. Similarly we know that in Punjab, the Madras had accepted Samudragupta's suzerainty. This means that right upto the river Chenab, the North-Western region was within Gupta sphere of influence and any military adventure on the part of a Gupta ruler was superfluous. There would have been some substance in the account had it spoken of the conquest of Kashmir. But it only takes Bhasma upto the gate of Kashmir, where the Guptas were already in control.

We also know from the Allahabad pillar inscription that the republican tribes of Punjab and Rajasthan were subdued by Samudragupta and there is no evidence at all that they raised a standard of revolt after his death. In such a situation it is absolutely useless to speculate, as Pandey has done, that these republics rebelled against the successor af Samudragupta and Kācha conqeured them again and went upto Kashmir. Had such been the case, it is more likely that his name would have been found on some local coins, like that of Samudragupta's on the coins of the Gaḍaharas and Śākas. Considering all these points we must reject Pandey's theory about the conquests of Kācha. As regards a reign of 12 years assigned to Kācha by Pandey, that is an impossibility. We know from the Mathura pillar inscription that Chandragupta II was ruling in the G.S. 61 or A.D. 380. As shown by D.C. Sircar it was Chandragupta's fifth regnal year. It means that he ascended throne in A.D. 375. Some period has to be assigned to Rāmagupta whose historicity has been definitely established by the discovery of the Vidiśā Jain images inscriptions. We thus have a period of about fifty years between the establishment of the Gupta imperial rule in A.D. 319 and the accession of Rāmagupta in c. A.D. 370. If we take out another twelve years out of this for the reign of Bhasma of the *Āryamañjuśrīmūlakalpa* we are left only with a period of 38 years which is absolutely inadequate for the two eventful reigns of Chandragupta I and Samudragupta.

Let us examine the contents of the *Āryamañjuśrīmūlakalpa* more closely in order to check its authenticity as a work of history. Verses 646-47 of this work tell us that 'there will be the kings Samudra, Vikrama of good fame, Mahendra the leader of the kings, followed by the *Sa* initialled. *Sa*'s name (will be) Devarāja, he will have several names. He will be the best, wise and religious king.' Now if we take *Sa* as Skandagupta then we are faced with a contradiction because Skandagupta was never known as Devarāja which was another name of Chandragupta II. From *Sa* the writer straightaway jumps to mention Bāla (Bālāditya) (?) the patron of Buddhism. After Bāla is mentioned

Kumāra and then in the end a king named *Ū*. It is clear from this account that it is neither complete nor accurate. Many names such as Purugupta and Budhagupta are missing from the list, who are otherwise known to us as the rulers of the imperial Gupta dynasty. Further the name of one king is transferred to another and it may be concluded that the Buddhist writer of this work had no accurate knowledge of history and merely wrote whatever he had heard in the form of stories. Therefore no reliance can be placed on the contents of this work for the reconstruction of history.

Finally, the legend on the coins of Kācha is almost fatal to his identification with Bhasma. It reads *Kācho gāmavajitya karmabhir-uttamair-divaṁ-jayati* i.e. 'Having conquered the earth Kācha wins heaven by (his) excellent deeds.' It is really amazing that none of the scholars identifying Kācha with Bhasma has paid even the slightest attention to the fact that Kācha of these coins is the performer of excellent deeds. Quite contrary to this Bhasma is described in the verses quoted above, as heartless, of low intelligence and a wicked person. Such a glaring discrepancy cannot be dismissed merely as due to the attitude of a Buddhist writer towards a Hindu ruler, specially when we know that the same writer has portrayed other staunch Hindu rulers like Samudra, Vikrama and Skanda in favourable light.

It is therefore quite obvious that Bhasma of the *Āryamañjuśrimūlakalpa* cannot be identified with Kācha of the gold coins nor can he be assigned a place in the Gupta genealogy either as a predecessor or as a successor of Samudragupta.

APPENDIX II

IDENTIFICATION OF CHANDRAPRAKĀŚA

The Kashmirian rhetorician Vāmana who flourished in the 8th century A.D. has quoted the following verse in his *Kāvyālaṅkārasūtravṛitti*:[170]

so = yaṁ samprati Chandragupta-tanayaḥ Chandraprakāśo yuvā/
jāto bhūpatir-āśrayaḥ kṛitadhiyāṁ dishṭyā kṛitārthaśhramaḥ//

It means, "So now, this youthful son of Chandragupta, (by name) Chandraprakāśa, has become king and the resort of men of letters, and fortunately his labours have become fruitful."

Who is this monarch Chandraprakāśa, the son of Chandragupta? Scholars have expressed different views. Vincent Smith identified him with Samudragupta. According to him, "In his youth Samudragupta must have borne the titles of both Chandraprakāśa and Bālāditya or Prakāśāditya."[171] Hoernle thought that Chandragupta must be Chandragupta II and consequently Chandraprakāśa should be regarded as another name of Kumāragupta I.[172] Numismatic evidence seems to support Hoernle's view. As pointed out by Allan, some of the epithets of Kumāragupta I found on his gold coins such as *Gupta-kul = āmalachandraḥ*, *Gupta-kula-vyoma-śaśī* and *Pṛithivītal = āmbara-śaśī* (all on horseman type) are closely akin to Chandraprakāśa in meaning. D.R. Bhandarkar preferred to identify him with Govindagupta, a son of Chandragupta II, then known from the Basarh clay sealing of his mother the chief queen Dhruvasvāminī.[173] Unfortunately, we have no coin or seal of Govindagupta which may be quoted in support of this view. K.B. Pathak was in favour of identifying him with Kumāragupta I.[174] The problem became more complicated on account of attention being invited to a statement in Paramārtha's life of Vasubandhu, to the effect that king Vikramāditya of Ayodhyā sent his son Bālāditya for instruction to the sage Vasubandhu who according to Vāmana's comment on the verse under discussion, became a minister of Chandraprakāśa. Here the knot is becoming more tight. On the one hand we find that Vasubandhu was associated with Bālāditya and his father was Vikramāditya which is a title of Skandagupta, whereas the name of Bālāditya's father is Purugupta. Further the sage Vasubandhu became the minister of a son of Chandragupta and not of a son of Skandagupta, nor that of Purugupta. Allan has rightly remarked that, "It is the verse itself that is of importance and not Vāmana's commentary, on which little reliance can be placed."[175] More recently Frauwallner has suggested that there were two Vasubandhus, an elder one the brother of Asaṅga who lived at Peshawar c.A.D. 320-380 and the younger one who was the author of *Abhidharmakośa* and it must be this Vasubandhu whom Takakusu places between A.D. 420 and 500.[176] Steering clear of this vortex of Vasubandhus we may prefer to stick to the verse itself and identify Chandraprakāśa, on the strength of the numismatic evidence, with Kumāragupta I who was the son of the famous ruler Chandragupta II Vikramāditya.

Arpendix III

SAMUDRAGUPTA AND THE AUTHORSHIP OF *KṚISHNACHARITAM*

Samudragupta besides being a military and an administrative genius was a man of high intellectual qualities. Harisheṇa, the author of the Allahabad pillar inscription has highlighted his literary talent. Samudragupta has been credited with compositions of many poetical works which could inspire even learned writers to take cue from them. He has been given the title of *Kavirāja.* Unfortunately no writing of Samudragupta has come down to us.

In 1941 Rājavaidya Jivarama Kalidasa Shastri published three leaves of a manuscript and described them as an introduction to a poetical work *Kṛishṇacharitaṁ* by *Mahārājādhirāja Paramabhāgavata Śri* Samudragupta. After a careful and critical examination of its contents, competent scholars have pronounced it to be a modern forgery.[177] It seems that taking cue from the references contained in the Allahabad pillar inscription of Samudragupta, to the latter's personal qualities, someone has cleverly, put together, in the manner of the *Kāvya,* certain incidents, characters and literary writings well known in the history of ancient India. Some of the authors and works are definitely later than the time of Samudragupta. This makes it clear that Samudragupta cannot be regarded as the author of this modern forged text.

APPENDIX IV

THE GAYA AND NALANDA COPPER PLATE GRANTS

There are two copper plates recording grants of land purported to be made by the emperor Samudragupta. The first of these was discovered at Gaya and was published by Fleet,[178] who regarded it as spurious. It is dated in the year nine. The second was discovered from Nalanda during the archaeological excavations conducted at the site of ancient university of Nalanda during 1927-28. It has been published by A. Ghosh.[179]

However, both these documents are forgeries indeed. This is evident from the following considerations. Firstly, the characters used in both the grants are of a period much later than the reign of Samudragupta. The bipartite *ya*, the looped *ka* and the elongated medial *i*, all indicate that the grants were engraved sometimes in the seventh century A.D. Secondly, the writer of both the documents has betrayed himself by putting all the adjectives qualifying Samudragupta in the genitive and then abruptly changing to the nominative construction when recording the name of Samudragupta. This makes it evident that he is copying from some genuine but later Gupta record of the time of some successor of Samudragupta where all his epithets had been put in the genitive, and since it was purported to be an order of Samudragupta, he abruptly changed to the use of nominative, without realising that it was incompatible.

Further as pointed out by D.C. Sircar, the forger stands betrayed by his using the expression *chirotsann=aśvamedhāharttuḥ* as an epithet of Samudragupta which is to be found only in the records of his successors.[180] It is not even used in Samudragupta's Allahabad pillar inscription.

A. Ghosh's remark that no late forms have been used in the Nalanda grant is incorrect for the *ya* in that record is bipartite throughout and therefore it cannot be earlier than the sixth century A.D. The data of these grants are therefore useless for any historical discussion. Further, the dates of these two inscriptions do not constitute any evidence of Samudragupta having founded the Gupta era.

APPENDIX V

SAMUDRAGUPTA II(?)

P.L. Gupta published a gold coin weighing 136 grains[181] with the name of Samudragupta on the obverse and his title *Parākrama* (*ḥ*) on the reverse. As the coins of this weight were introduced for the first time by Skandagupta, Gupta concluded that this coin cannot be assigned to the famous son of Chandragupta I but must have been issued by a king who came after Skandagupta. Since we have as many as three Kumāraguptas and two Chandraguptas in the Gupta dynasty, the existence of two Samudraguptas is not impossible. But the evidence on the point is totally insufficient to draw such a conclusion. A.S. Altekar[182] has drawn attention to an unpublished variety of Samudragupta's archer type which according to Kittoe occurred in the Bharsar hoard[183] and which had on the reverse the legend *Parākrama* instead of *Apratiratha*; but Altekar thinks that the coin now published by Gupta belongs to the post-Skandagupta period for the following reasons:

a. The weight of the clipped coin being 136 grains, its original weight must have been 144 grains. This weight standard was unknown in the reign of Samudragupta and became common only with the coming of Skandagupta.

b. The style in which Lakshmī folds her legs on the reverse, became common only during the reigns of Narasiṁhagupta and Prakāśāditya.

c. The gold is impure as is the case generally with the later Gupta coinage.

These are all weighty arguments and we are left with no choice but to assign this coin to a later period. However, in the absence of any other evidence on the point we cannot accept the idea of a second Samudragupta. It is highly probable, as Altekar has pointed out that the coin may be a forged one.[184]

References

1. *Festschrift F.W. Thomas*, 115ff.
2. For details see Agrawal Jagannath, *JIH*, XIX, 27-29,
3. Gupta, P.L., *JNSI*, IX, 33-37; *ibid.*, XII, 36. This view has been contradicted by K.C. Ojha, *JNSI*, XII, 170. The statement in the *AMMK*, verse 701, that Samudragupta had a younger brother named Bhasma who may be identified with Kācha of the gold coins according to P.L. Gupta and others, will be disposed of by these very arguments of Ojha.
4. According to K.P. Jayaswal 'a pitched battle' was fought at Kauśāmbī. *HI*, 132. This is a mere assumption.
5. Rodger, C.J., *CCCM*, 145-150; Smith, V.A., *CCIM*, I, 263; Rapson, *JRAS*, 1898, 449ff.
6. Aiyangar, S.K., *SGH*, 39; Raychaudhuri, H.C., *PHAI*, 452.
7. *IHQ*, I, 684. However, his statement that "It is mentioned immediately before the territory of Svāmidatta" is incorrect. After Mahākāntāra there is the mention of Kurāla, then comes Pishṭapura and then Svāmidatta.
8. *AHD*, 60-61.
9. *HI*, 126, fn. 2.
10. *Studies in the Ancient History of Toṇḍamaṇḍalam*, 13-19.
11. *Cf.* Dubreuil, *AHD*, 59.
12. *BSOAS*, II, 569.
13. *EI*, VI, 3, fn. 3.
14. *HI*, 127
15. *Op. cit.*, 13-19.
16. *IHQ*, I, 685.
17. *HEDA*, 366.
18. *CII*, III, (1888), 7, fn. 2.
19. *IC*, II, 761.
20. *Ibid.*, III, 230-31.
21. *EI*, XII, 1.
22. *Ibid*. XXIII, 56ff.
23. The Aihole inscription, *EI*, VI, 1; and the Timmapuram plates, *EI*, IX, 317.
24. *IHQ*, I, 681.
25. *BRAAH*, 121.
26. *JRAS*, 1898, 369.
27. *AHD*, 59-60.
28. *EI*, XIII, 214.
29. *IHQ*, I, 682f.
30. *Op. cit.*, IV, 183.
31. *HI*, 137. Jayaswal is wrong in saying 'Svāmidatta of Pishṭapura' because the latter was under Mahendragiri and Svāmidatta was the ruler of Koṭṭūra.
32. *IHQ*, I, 682f.
33. *IA*, V, 154.
34. *EI*, XX, 79.
35. *HEDA*, 364ff.

36. *Cf.* Pedda-Vegi and Kolleru copper plates, *IA*, V, 175. Hultzsch's view that Hastivarman was a Pallava (*IA*, IX, 102), is no longer tenable in the light of these inscriptions.

37. *EHI*, 301.

38. *EI*, VIII, 161.

39. *AHD*, 58.

40. *IA*, V, 50ff. Pālakka is evidently a Northerner's mistake for Palakkada.

41. *Cf. BRAAH*, 103.

42. *JRAS*, 1898, 369.

43. *Madras Report for Epigraphy*, 1909, 108-09.

44. *EI*, XIII, 56ff.

45. *IHQ*, I, 687.

46. *JBBRAS*, 1928, 88.

47. *Harivaṁśa*, 112.

48. *HEDA*, 369-70.

49. *Cf.* Smith, V.A., *EHI*, 301.

50. Saletore's attempt to locate Koṭṭūra in the Kudligi Taluka of Bellary district (*ABORI*, XXVI, 120) must remain unsuccessful. See Jagannath Agrawal's criticism in *Summaries of Papers*, *PAIOC*, 1949.

51. *AHD*, 60-61.

52. *HEDA*, 364-65 & 372-73.

53. There is a close kinship between the expression *grahaṇamoksha* of the Allahabad pillar inscription and *gṛihīta-pratimukta* of Kālidāsa (*Raghuvaṁśa*, IV. 43).

54. Since the *Purāṇas* mention several names of Nāga kings with the ending *Nandi*, e.g. Śivanandi, Yaśonandi etc., we have taken Achyutanandi as one name and not two as is usually done. R.G. Basak (*HNEI*, 22, fn. 2, & 28) and Jayaswal (*HI*, 133) have also taken it as one name.

55. *PAIOC*, 1919, CXXIV.

56. *EI*, IX, 267ff.

57. *Cf. Śatpatha Brāhmaṇa*, V.1.1.13.
Rājā vai rājasūyeneshṭvhā bhavati, samrāṭ vājapeyana |

58. *Cf.* Altekar, A.S., *IC*, IX, 99.

59. Sircar, D.C., *PIHC*, VII, 78 and *IHQ*, XXII, 65. Copper coins bearing the legend Rudra were recently discovered in U.P. These might have been issued by Rudradeva.

60. Growse, F.W., *IA*, XVIII, 289.

61. *CCGD*, XXIII.

62. Personal information from Jagannath Agrawal.

63. *JRAS*, 1897, 876-77.

64. *IHQ*, I, 251ff.

65. *VGA*, 130, fn. 3.

66. *Harshacharita*, VI. 198.

67. *EI*, XII, 317. H.P. Shastri who edited the inscription, wrongly identified Pushkaraṇa with Pokharan in Jodhpur (Rajasthan). K.P. Jayas-

wal's attempt (*HI*, 143) to place him in eastern Punjab is too far fetched to deserve credence.

68. *EI*, XXVI, 304.

69. One of his inscriptions was found from the village Kanakhera, at the foot of the Sanchi hill, and was published by R.D. Banerji in *EI*, XVI, 232. For the latest readings see, Sircar, D.C., *Sel. Ins.*, I, 180-81. The Eran inscription has been published by V.V. Mirashi in *CII*, IV, Pt. II.

70. *CII*, III, (1981), 220ff.

71. *CII*, III, (1888), 114, L. 8.

72. *Bṛihatsaṁhitā*, XIV. 6.

73. *IA*, XXII, 189.

74. *JRAS*, 1897, 878.

75. *JASB*, 1885, 49-52.

76. Watters, II, 188.

77. Bhattasali, N.K., *JASB*, 1914, 85, 87.

78. Sen, P.C., *JARS*, I; Nath, R.M., *IC*, VI, 460. The earlier identifications with Bogra, Dinajpur and Rajshahi proposed by V.A. Smith (*JRAS*, 1897, 879) or with Dhaka by Fleet (*CII*, III, 1888, 309) have to be discarded.

79. Bhandarkar, D.R., *IHQ*, I, 257; Sharma, D., *JIH*, XIV, 30; Majumdar, R.C., *CA*, 8; Sircar, D.C., *Sel. Ins.*, I, 258.

80. *JRAS*, 1897, 885.

81. *Ibid.*, 1898, 198f.

82. *IA*, XXV, 178.

83. *EI*, XIII, 115 & 118.

84. *Mālavīya Commemoration Volume*, 194-95.

85. *JIH*, 1935, 30-33.

86. *JNSI*, V, 6-7.

87. Allan, J., *CCAI*, CIV.

88. *Ashṭādhyāyī*, IV.I. 110.

89. *Bṛihatsamhitā*, XVI. 22.

90. *CCAI*, LXXXIII.

91. V.3.117.

92. Supra Chapter II.

93. I.2.72.

94. II.3.

95. *DKA*, 45.

96. XIV. 12.

97. *Sabhā Parva*, 51.

98. *IA*, X, 157ff.; *EI*, XVI, 235.

99. *EI*, VIII, 88.

100. Herzfeld, *Paikuli Inscription*, I, 43, 119.

101. *CII*, III, (1981), 250. They are mentioned in the *Mahābhārata*, VI. 9.64, where they are associated with the Vidarbhas. Law, B.C., *NIA*, I, 460.

102. *CII*, III, (1981), 244.

103. *JRAS*, 1897, 892.

104. *IHQ*, I, 250-60,

105. *JRAS*, 1897, 859ff.

106. *EI*, XII, 45.

107. *Ibid.*

108. *IHQ*, XXXVII, 81-82.

109. *IHQ*, XXXVIII, 327.

110. *Cf.* "There is some evidence to show that by the third and fourth centuries these titles were no longer those of one great suzerain, but had each become the peculiar title of the ruler of one of the smaller states into which the Kushāṇa empire had been broken up." *CCGD*, XXVII, and also, "The *Śāhānushāhi* (or perhaps the *Śāhishāhānushāhi*) is to be identified with the king of the Kushāṇas whose kingdom stretched from the Indian borders to the Oxus." *Ibid.*, XXVIII.

111. *IHQ*, I, 259.

112. *Cf.* Martin, F.C., *JRASB. L*, III (1937), *NS*, 32.

113. *Raghuvaṁśa*, IV, 60. Samudragupta might have sent help in men and material.

114. *CII*, II, i, 142.

115. *Ibid.* However, the reading *Muroḍa* by Sten Konow is disputed.

116. *CII*, III, (1888), 14; *CCGD*, XXIX; *AIG*, 24; *JBORS*, XVI, 203.

117. *DKA*, 46.

118. *JRAS*, 1897, 859ff.

119. *IHQ*, I, 250-60.

120. *CII*, III, (1981), 220ff.

121. *CCGD*, XXV.

122. See Supra Chapter III.

123. *EHI*, 303-04. *Cf.* The inscriptions of Mahānāman at Bodh Gaya, *CII*, III, 274ff.

124. *Cf.* Coomaraswamy, A.K., *HIIA*, 181.

125. *CII*, III, (1981), 218.

126. *ABORI*, LXII, 173.

127. Tr. Jagannath Agrawal.

128. *EI*, XV, 41ff.

129. Chattopadhyaya, S., *EHNI*, 197; Goyal, S.R., *HIG*, 187-88; Pandey, V.C., *ABORI*, LIII, 228-29.

130. *Cf.* Sircar, D.C., *Sel. Ins.*, I, 412, fn. 4 and Gupta, P.L., *Gup. Sam.*, 273.

131. *CII*, III, (1888), 44, 54.

132. Mookerji, R.K., *GE*, 30; Basak, R.G., *HNEI*, 36 etc.

133. *PHAI*, 484.

134. *SGH*, 44-45.

135. *IC*, I, 118.

136. *ABORI*, LIII, 228-232.

137. *Ibid.*

138. *JNSI*, XIX, 14ff.

139. *PAIOC*, Lucknow; and *Essays Presented to Sir Jadunath Sarkar*, II, 10ff.

140. *PHAI*, 153.
141. *Coinage*, 52.
142. Jayaswal, K.P., *HI*, 146-47; Dwivedi, Gautam, *PIHC*, 1973, 76.
143. *CII*, IV, 15-16.
144. *Ibid.*, 609-10.
145. *JNSI*, XXVIII, 1-4.
146. *CII*, III, (1981), 220ff.
147. *PAIOC*, I, CXXIV.
148. *HI*, 140-41.
149. *HG*, 57.
150. *GE*, 23.
151. *HIG*, 141ff.
152. *HI*, 141.
153. *Cf. Varsha - śataṁ-abhivarddhamāna-kosha-daṇḍa-sādhana- santāna-putra-pautriṇaḥ*, *CII*, III, (1888), 237.
154. *HI*, 141.
155. *VGA*, 96; *IC*, IX, 99-106.
156. Prinsep and Thomas quoted in the *Coinage*, 79; Aiyangar, S.K., *SGH*, 31.
157. Sitholey, B.S., *JNSI*, XII, 39ff.
158. Banerji, R.D., *AIG*, 9-10.
159. Buddha Prakash, *AIHC*, 80ff.
160. Bhandarkar, D.R., *Mālavīya Commemoration Volume*, 189ff. Altekar, A.S., *Coinage*, 86-87 & *JNSI*, IX, 131ff.
161. Heras, H., *ABORI*, IX, 83ff.; Jayaswal, K.P., *IHI*, 48-49; Dandekar, R.N., *HG*, 40f.; Sinha, B.P., *CHB*, I, ii, 14ff.; Gupta, P.L., *Gup. Sam.*, 243ff., & *JNSI*, XII, 36-37; Goyal, S.R., *HIG*, 191ff.; Thakur, V.K., *JNSI*, XXXIX, 108-113.
162. Fleet, J.F., *CII*, III, (1888), 27; Smith, V.A., *IA*, 1902, 59; Allan, J., *CCGD*, XXXIII; Raychaudhuri, H.C., *PHAI*, 470-71; Mirashi, V.V., *JNSI*, XX, 90; Mookerji, R.K., *GE*, 17; Chattopadhyaya, S., *EHNI*, 179.
163. *IHI*, 48-49.
164. *JNSI*, XII, 36-37 & *Gup. Sam.*, 243.
165. *HIG*, 191.
166. *Nāgarī Prachārani Patrikā*, *S*. 2034, 53-63.
167. Sankṛityāyana, Rahula, *Text of Mañjuśrīmūlakalpa*, 52, (Appendix to the *Imperial History of India* by K.P. Jayaswal).
168. One Ms. of the work has *trīṇi-varshāṇi* instead of *trīṇidivasāni.*
169. For Jayaswal's translation see *IHI*, 48.
170. III.2.2.
171. *EHI*, 347.
172. *IA*, 1911, 264.
173. *IA*, 1912, 1ff.
174. *JBBRAS*, XXIII, 185-86.
175. *CCGD*, XLIII-XLIV, fn.
176. Frauwallener, E., *On the Date of Buddhist Master of Law Vasubandhu*, Rome, 1951.

177. Agrawal, Jagannath, *ABORI*, XXVI, 313-18; Pusalkar, A.D., *JUB*, XXII, 36-44.

178. *CII*, III, (1888), 254ff.

179. *EI*, XXV, 50ff.

180. *Ibid.*, XXVI, 136.

181. *JNSI*, XVI, 102-04.

182. *Coinage*, 340-41.

183. *JASB*, 1852, 190.

184. *Op. cit.*, 341.

CHAPTER VII

THE PROBLEM OF RĀMAGUPTA

THE MODERN RESEARCHERS and historians of the Gupta dynasty were quite unaware of the existence of a Gupta emperor named Rāmagupta, till Sylvain Levi published, in 1923, some extracts of a Sanskrit play, called *Devīchandraguptam*, now lost, as quoted in the *Nāṭyadarpaṇa*, a work on Sanskrit dramaturgy, by the two Jain writers Rāmachandra and Guṇachandra, pupils of the famous Jain teacher Hemachandrācharya.[1] The *Nāṭyadarpaṇa* contains six quotations from this play and the information contained in them may be summarised as follows:

The first quotation describes a conversation between Rāmagupta and his younger brother Chandragupta, who is ready to go to the enemy's camp in the disguise of the queen. It is overheard by Dhruvasvāminī who totally misunderstands it and gathers the impression that the king is deeply in love with some other lady and for her sake, is ready to abandon his queen, who naturally feels distressed.[2]

The second quotation which is taken from the Fourth Act, informs us about Chandragupta's love affair with a lady named Mādhavasenā, and describes his ardent desire for a passionate embrace.[3] The third quotation describes Dhruvadevī's pitiable plight on her becoming aware of her husband's decision to give her away to the enemy.[4] The fourth quotation which consists of a single verse addressed by Chandragupta to Mādhavasenā is rather too open an expression of flirtation and the authors of the treatise have informed us that such vulgarity is permissible where the heroine is a courtesan.[5]

The fifth quotation is from Act II of the play. Here we are informed by the authors that the surrender of the queen to the Śaka king has been agreed to and the prince Chandragupta putting on the apparel of Dhruvadevī is desirous of going out for killing the enemy. He is thus addressed by king Rāmagupta: "Abide by my words, I dare not abandon you for my love for you is too strong. I have decided to give away the queen like a straw." But Dhruvadevī misunderstands these words. She thinks that her husband is speaking to some other lady. Rāmagupta says more about his attachment for his brother but all that is misconstrued by Dhruvadevī.[6] Here there is repetition of some matter from the first quotation.

The sixth quotation is from Act V. Here we are told in a pun that the moon i.e. Chandragupta, having destroyed the darkness i.e. his enemies, enters the mansion of the sky i.e. the palace. In the same Act further on we are told, that Chandragupta who was pretending to be insane but exerting to conceal his love-sickness and slightly afraid of the enemy, indicates his exit in order to proceed to the palace.[7]

In the same year R. Saraswati quoted three passages from the same play, as quoted by king Bhoja in his *Śṛiṅgāraprakāśa* and *Sarasvatīkaṇṭhābhāraṇa*.[8] The first of these confirms the statement that Chandragupta in female disguise went to the enemy's camp in order to kill the *Śakapati*. The second again refers to the same strategy of Chandragupta. It appears that Chandragupta's companion, the *Vidūshaka* was dissuading him from the hazardous attempt as he was all alone, but Chandragupta dispelled his fear by saying that for a brave man numbers do not matter.

The third extract is a mere repetition of the verse given in the fourth quotation of the *Nāṭyadarpaṇa*. Here the writer has by mistake, changed the name of the lady to Vasantasenā.

R. D. Banerji was the first scholar to utilise the information brought to light by Sylvain Levi and R. Saraswati, in his Manindra Chandra Nandy Lectures, delivered in 1924, and supplemented it by the information contained in a verse of the Sanjan copper plate inscription of Amoghavarsha I dated A.D. 871 and the brief reference by Bāṇa in his *Harshacharita* which has been illucidated by the commentator Śaṅkarārya. These lectures were subsequently published under the title *Age of the Imperial Guptas*. Banerji was thus the first scholar to introduce the name of Rāmagupta in the imperial Gupta dynasty.

Subsequent to the publication of the extracts from the *Nāṭyadarpaṇa*, some more matter was collected together from the *Śṛiṅgāraprakāśa* of Bhoja by V. Raghvan.[9] Some of these quotations confirmed the information obtained earlier from the *Nāṭyadarpaṇa* while some were new.

The first extract giving an example of adventure confirms the statement that Chandragupta disguised as a woman went to the enemy's camp in order to kill the Śaka lord and actually killed him.

Another extract refers to Chandragupta's pretended madness. The third illustrating courage, shows him on his way to the Śaka camp. The *Vidūshaka* asks him how was it that in the very midst of so many ministers he will go about alone? In the fourth extract again there is mention of the critical situation to which Rāmagupta's army had been reduced, and the prince Chandragupta finding no other means of rescuing it, undertaking the propitiation of a vampire, was asked by his companion the *Vidūshaka* whether it was possible for him to move at this time even one step from the midst of the custodians of the stores? At this Chandragupta begins to think of some means. At this juncture help comes quite unexpectedly. A maid-servant comes holding a packet in her hands. After greeting the prince Chandragupta she inquires about the whereabouts of the queen Dhruvasvāminī, saying that she has received these clothes and ornaments worn by the queen, as a gift, and requests the *Vidūshaka* to keep these till she is able to find out the queen. So saying she makes her exit. Upon this the *Vidūshaka* is angry and says, "am I your store-keeper?" In the meantime Chandragupta, behind the curtain puts on the woman's garb and goes out. Now, this female garb comes very helpful, in the absence of any other means, of making his exit from the camp.

That is all the information we get from the fragments quoted from the *Devīchandraguptam*. Some of these statements get remarkable confirmation from the epigraphic evidence. Besides the Sanjan copper plate inscription of the Rāshṭrakūṭa king Amoghavarsha, we have also another verse which occurs in the Cambay[10] and Sangli[11] copper plates. In the third line of this verse we are told that Sāhasāṅka, (i.e. Chandragupta Vikramāditya) resorted to a demoniac conduct with an utter disregard for purity or impurity. This obviously refers to Chandragupta's taking recourse to propitiate a vampire, as stated in one of the fragments of the *Devīchandraguptam* as quoted in the *Śṛiṅgāraprakāśa*.

All this evidence from the fragments of *Devīchandraguptam*, the copper plate grants of the Rāshṭrakūṭa kings Amoghavarsha and Govinda IV from Sanjan, Cambay and Sangli, the cryptic remark of Bāṇabhaṭṭa in his *Harshacharita*,[12] a stray verse quoted by Rājaśekhara in his *Kāvyamīmāṁsā*[13] together with the story of Rawwal and Barkamaris given in the *Mujmal-ut-Tawarikh* by the Arabic writer Abul Hasan Ali,[14] was critically examined by A. S. Altekar,[15] who concluded that Rāmagupta was a king of the imperial Gupta dynasty, who succeeded Samudragupta but ruled for a short time as he was overthrown by his younger brother Chandragupta with whom the former's relations became strained and ended in his death. This Rāmagupta was involved in a war with a Śaka king during the course of which he came within the stranglehold of the enemy, who would spare his life and allow him to retire only on condition of the surrender of his wife, Dhruvadevī.

This was such a sensational event in the ancient history of India that it was remembered for generations. The earliest reference is that by Bāṇa who has mentioned only the strategy resorted to by Chandragupta of assuming the guise of an attractive woman and killing the Śaka king. According to Bāṇa this happened in the Śaka king's own camp (*aripura*).[16] Śaṅkarārya, the commentator of the *Harshacharita* has made the reference more explicit by stating that the Śaka king was killed by Chandragupta II disguised as Dhruvadevī, the wife of Chandragupta's brother.[17] The doubts expressed regarding the historicity of this event and the objections raised are all untenable. There is nothing impossible regarding Chandragupta's thinking of such a strategy to kill the enemy. As regards the marriage with the widowed queen, apart from the *Śāstric* approval in works like the codes of Nārada[18] and *Parāśara*[19] we must not ignore the fact that Dhruvadevī must have felt absolutely disgusted with her husband,[20] who proved to be such a coward as to surrender his wife to the enemy to purchase his own safety. It was perfectly natural for her not only to entertain a feeling of gratitude and admiration but also become attracted towards such an audacious and brave young man who could risk his own life in order to save the honour of his family.

Attention has been drawn to some minor discrepancies between the account of the play *Devīchandraguptam* and a solitary verse of unknown authorship quoted by Rājaśekhara. In this verse the name of the Gupta king is Śarmagupta and not Rāmagupta. Are there not scribal errors in manuscripts handed down from ancient times. If the verse reads Śarma or Sena instead of Rāma, which suits the metre excellently well, it cannot vitiate the accuracy of the main event, i.e., being detained by the enemy and surrendering Dhruvadevī to him. Further, if the scene of the disaster is placed by Rājaśekhara's verse in the Himalayas which is not indicated in the play, can't we hold that the author of this verse had merely heard of the happening only from oral tradition and thus cannot be expected to be accurate in all the details? The facts of Chandragupta killing the enemy, seizing the throne and marrying the lady whom he rescued from the voluptuous enemy, are common to all our sources and must be taken to be correct. Even a solitary detail like the pretence of madness by Chandragupta in order to save his own life, finds an echo in quite an unexpected quarter—the commentary of Chakrapāṇidatta on the *Charakasaṁhitā*, a treatise on *Āyuraveda.* Here, while giving example of pretence, the commentator refers to the murder of his own brother by Chandragupta.[21]

All the doubts about the historicity of Rāmagupta have been dispelled by the remarkable discovery of three Jain statues from Durjanpur near Vidiśā in Madhya Pradesh, which clearly mention Rāmagupta with the title of *Mahārājādhirāja.*[22] The inscriptions on these stone images are inscribed in the Gupta Brāhmī characters of 4th-5th centuries A.D. and can neither be pushed back earlier nor placed later even in the 6th century A.D. The characters of the inscriptions cut at the very roots of all doubts and prove the existence of Rāmagupta in the early Gupta age.

Although the historicity of Rāmagupta has been proved beyond any reasonable doubt by the discovery of his own inscriptions from Durjanpur, it is necessary to answer a few objections raised from time to time, against assigning to him a place in the imperial Gupta dynasty. It has been questioned sometimes as to why his name does not figure in the genealogical lists in the official records of the Guptas. It can be very well explained. The official genealogies only give the line of succession and not a complete dynastic genealogy. Since Rāmagupta was succeeded, rather ousted, by his brother Chandragupta II, who was succeeded by his son Kumāragupta I, there was no occasion to mention the name of Rāmagupta. There is a very pertinent example in the available Gupta records themselves. In the Bhitari stone pillar inscription of Skandagupta, only his name is given as the son and successor of Kumāragupta I, whereas in the Bhitari silver seal and the Nalanda clay sealings, only Purugupta is mentioned as the son and successor of Kumāragupta I and the name of Skandagupta is left out, obviously because Kumāragupta III traced his descent through his father Narasiṁhagupta to his grandfather Purugupta and in the process the name of Skandagupta is automatically left out.

Another objection that is often raised is the absence of the gold coins of Rāmagupta. As is well-known Rāmagupta ruled for a very short time. So the number of his gold coins must not have been large enough to find a place in the hoards collected in later times; and we cannot expect to find them even in large hoards. As his rule was rather short he might not have issued any gold coins at all. Quite apart from it, we may point out that there are no gold coins even of Purugupta; but we can not deny his existence since he is mentioned in the sealings of his successors. We can cite even a modern example. Edward VIII, king of England and emperor of India, had a very short rule, after the death of his father George V. We have no coins of his brief rule, though even the copper coins of the East India Company struck as early as 1781 are still available not to speak of the coinage of Queen Victoria, Edward VII, George V and George VI which are available in plenty not only in gold and silver but also in copper. Therefore the absence of the gold coins of Rāmagupta is quite immaterial and should be ignored in view of the discovery of his own inscriptions in which he figures as a *Mahārājādhirājā*, as well as his copper coins from Eran-Vidiśā region in Madhya Pradesh, in as many as five types, specially the ones bearing the *Garuḍa* emblem.[23]

Last of all, R. C. Majumdar's argument that the story of the play is uncorroborated by independent evidence,[24] is the weakest. Bāṇa has made a cryptic reference to the murder of the Śaka lord by Chandragupta disguised as a young lady. Bāṇa's statement does not indicate that he knew the play *Devīchandraguptam*. It may also be pointed out, that it is by no means certain that the author of *Devīchandraguptam*, Viśākhadatta was prior to Bāṇa. He has been assigned to the eighth century A.D. by competent scholars.[25] Moreover, we cannot ignore the testimony of the authors of the Rāshṭrakūṭa grants of Amoghavarsha and Govinda IV who have made a comparison between these historical monarchs and the Gupta king who bore the title of Sāhasāṅka, but was guilty of several improprieties. Surely, they would not have instituted a comparison between their patrons and the Gupta monarch whose account as known to them was fictitious.

Majumdar has attached undue importance to the expression *tatparigṛīhīta* used in the official Gupta records with the name of Chandragupta II with reference to his father Samudragupta. Such expressions are the stock-in-trade of the framers of the genealogies. We can confidently conclue that there should be no reasonable doubt regarding the historicity of Rāmagupta after the discovery of the Durjanpur (Vidiśā) inscriptions.

References

1. A monograph entitled '*Deux nouveaux traites de dramaturgie Indienne*' published in *JA*, CCIII, 1923, 193-218.

2. *Nāṭyadarpaṇa*, 71.
3. *Ibid.*, 84.
4. *Ibid.*, 86.
5. *Ibid.*, 118.
6. *Ibid.*, 141-42.
7. *Ibid.*, 193-94.
8. *IA*, LII, 181f.
9. *JBHU*, II, 23ff.
10. *EI*, VII, 38.
11. *IA*, XII, 250.
12. *Cf. Aripure cha parakalatra-kāmukaṃ kāminīveshaguptaḥ Chandraguptaḥ Śakapatimśātayat. Harshacharita*, pp. 199-200.
13. *Cf. Dattvā rudhagatiḥ Khasādhipataye devīṁ Dhruvasvāminīm,*
yasmāt khaṇḍita-sāhaso nivavṛite śrī Śarmagupto nṛipaḥ |
tasminneva Himālaye giriguhākoṇa-kvaṇatkinnare,
gīyante tava Kārttikeya-nagara-strīṇāṃ gaṇaiḥ kīrtayaḥ ||
Kāvyamīmāṃsā, Ch. IX (*Arthavyāptiḥ*), p. 47.
14. Elliot & Dawson, *The History of India as Told by its Own Historians*, I, 110ff.
15. *JBORS*, XIV, 223ff. & XV, 134ff.
16. It is not a proper name. Those who identify it with Aliwal in the Ferozpur district of Punjab are entirely off the mark. It must be noted that Aliwal is a village, founded sometime during the Muslim rule and named

after Ali, a relative and follower of the Prophet Muhammad, or that of some Muslim dignitary.

17. *Cf. Śakānāmāchāryaḥ śakādhipatiḥ Chandragupta-bhrātṛijāyāṁ Dhruvadeviṁ prārthayamānaḥ,*
Chandraguptena Dhruvadevī - veshadhāriṇā strīveshajana-parivṛitena vyāpāditaḥ.

18. *Nārada*, XII. 97.

19. *Parāśara.*

20. *Cf. Lajjā-kopavishāda-bhītyaratibhiḥ kshetrīkṛitā tāmyati. Nāṭyadarpaṇa*, 86.

21. *Upetya dhīyate iti upādhiḥ chhadma ityarthaḥ, tamanubandhene tyuttarakālīnaphalena; uttara-kālam hi bhrātrādivadhena phalena jñyāte yadayamunmatta-chhdmaprachārī Chandragupta iti. Charakasaṁhitā, Vimānasthāna*, Chapter V, 248-49.

22. Chhabra & Gai (ed.), *CII*, III, (1981), 231-234.

23. For detailed discussion on the copper coins of Rāmagupta see, Gupta, P.L., *JNSI*, XII, 103ff.; Bajpai, K.D., *JNSI*, XVIII, 208ff. and *ibid.*, XXIII, 340ff.

24. *VIJ*, IV, 53-64.

25. *CHI*, III, Pt. I, 51f.

CHAPTER VIII

ADVENT OF THE GLORIOUS EPOCH CHANDRAGUPTA II VIKRAMĀDITYA

WE HAVE DISCUSSED in the previous Chapter that Samudragupta's immediate successor was Rāmagupta of the Vidiśā images inscriptions and not Chandragupta Vikramāditya as previously believed. Moreover, the statement in the Udayagiri cave inscription of Vīrasena Śāba that Chandragupta had undertaken the conquest of the whole earth, shows that he had virtually to undertake a *digvijaya* in order to consolidate his position and strengthen his hold on the empire. This is further supported by the account of his military activity given in the Mehrauli iron pillar inscription which by a consensus of opinion is now assigned to him, and by the Madasor stone inscription dated 524 M.S.

Historians of ancient India generally hold that Chandragupta II peacefully succeeded his father Samudragupta in A.D. 375[1] as he had been selected by him as his successor.[2] But this view needs a second look on account of some new evidence having come to light. There is reason to believe that neither Chandragupta II was the immediate successor of Samudragupta nor was his accession peaceful.[3] The disaster that overtook Rāmagupta had serious repercussions on the prestige of the Gupta empire, which was shaken to its very foundations. Chandragupta II Vikramāditya had, therefore, to face an uphill task to re-establish the lost glory of his house and practically to reconquer some parts of the territories which had slipped out of their hands. There had been revolts in the east and in the south where the feudatories emboldened by Rāmagupta's ignominous defeat had repudiated the overlordship of the Guptas.

The significance of the epigraphic statement[4] that Vīrasena, the foreign minister of Chandragupta II had come to Udayagiri with his master whose immediate objective was the conquest of the whole world, has not been fully appreciated nor has the account of the Mehrauli pillar inscription been examined in its proper setting, as pertaining to Chandragupta II himself. Chandragupta II, not only crushed the rebellious uprisings in the East (the Vaṅga country) and the South, but also won fresh laurels by the conquest of Avantī and Surāshṭra and ended the Śaka rule which had lasted in these parts for about three centuries. This was such an outstanding and glorious achievement that the Indian nation spontaneously added to the name of Vikramāditya the significant and proud epithet of *Śakāri*. It seems that encouraged by the ignominal episode of Rāmagupta the rulers of Bengal and adjoining areas, who had acknowledged the supremacy of Samudragupta, formed a confederacy in order to break the yoke of the Gupta suzerainty and assert their independence. It became imperative for Chandragupta to undertake a military campaign. We learn from the Mehrauli iron pillar inscription that a battle was fought in Vaṅga against a confederacy of these rebellious kings, in which Chandragupta displayed exraordinary valour and the resultant victory brought him glory. Peace was thus restored in the east. Similarly there were revolts in the South and Chandragupta II undertook another military expedition to these areas where his deeds of valour were remembered by the people long afterwards. This great victory is not only recorded in the Mehrauli pillar inscription but we may trace an echo of these events in the *Purāṇas* which speak of the extension of Gupta rule over Kośala, Oḍra, Tāmralipta and Purī on the sea board by Devarakshita or Devagupta i.e. Chandragupta II.[5]

After re-establishing his supremacy in the eastern and southern parts of the empire, Chandragupta II turned his attention to Western India where the Śaka kingdom was like a thorn in one flank of his empire. The expedition against the Śakas must have become an imperative necessity after Rāmagupta's complete discomfiture at the hands of a Śaka adversary as a consequence of which the Śakas began to be looked upon as a potential danger to be rooted out at the earliest opportunity. There must have been the additional motive of obtaining control of the highly profitable trade with the Western world. These were reasons weighty enough for undertaking the conquest of the Śaka dominions and Chandragupta set about to planning an expedition against the Śakas and made necessary preparations.

First of all he ensured the safety of his left flank by entering into a matrimonial alliance with the Vākāṭakas,[6] and eliminating any danger of an attack from the rear. The magnitude of this expedition is clearly reflected in the statement of his foreign minister Vīrasena Śāba, that he had come to Udayagiri in the company of the emperor whose object was the conquest of the entire world.[7]

No details of the expedition are available but we can be sure that the Śaka ruler, who was most probably Rudrasiṁha III, was over-thrown and his kingdom was annexed. We are able to establish the approximate time of this conquest with the help of the numismatic evidence. In the latest available date on the silver coin of the Western Kshatrapa ruler Rudrasiṁha III, discovered from Pushkar near Ajmer in Rajasthan, the unit figure is not clearly legible. The figure for the tenth place is 1 and that for the hundredth it is 3.[8] The date is therefore 31x. If x is zero the date shall be 310+78=A.D. 388; and if x is 9, the date shall become 319+78=A.D. 397. Again the earliest known date on Chandragupta II's silver coins struck on the Śaka pattern is 90 G.E. or A.D. 409.[9] Therefore we can safely place Chandragupta's conquest of the Śaka dominions between A.D. 388 and A.D. 409. This date is supported by some indirect epigraphical evidence. According to the Mehrauli pillar inscription, Chandra crossed the seven mouths of the Indus and conquered the Vālhikas.[10] In order to cross the seven mouths of the Indus he obviously passed through the newly conquered Śaka territories. It would not have been possible without overthrowing the Śaka ruler. It does not seem probable that Chandragupta II undertook the expedition of these farflung areas beyond the frontiers of his dominions at the fag end of his reign when he would have been an old man in the seventies of his life.[11] Another line of argument on this point is however not quite convincing. The Udayagiri cave inscription of the year 82[12] i. e. A.D. 401-402 records the construction of a cave temple by a Sanakānīka Mahārāja, who was a feudatory of Chandragupta II. Similarly the Sanchi railing inscription of the year 93[13] i.e. A.D. 412 records the donation of a village and 25 *dīnāras* to the *Mahāvihāra* of Kākanādaboṭa by Āmrakāradava, another officer of Chandragupta II, who had won glory in many battles. It has been generally inferred from these inscriptions that the conquest of the Śakas took place about the time these inscriptions were put up, as these persons must have visited this area along with Chandragupta II during this expedition only. But the date of the Sanchi railing inscription viz. Gupta year 93 appears to be too late to be associated with the expedition against the Śakas. We have pointed out above that already in the Gupta year 90, Chandragupta II had struck silver coins on the pattern of the Śaka coinage, which were evidently meant to replace the Śaka coinage and to be in circulation in the newly conquered dominions. It is therefore more probable that the Śaka dominions had been conquered before the dates of these inscriptions.

As already stated, after the victory in Mālava and Surārhṭra Chandragupta II carried his arms successfully in the Trans-Indus region. According to the Udayagiri cave inscription he had set out to conquer the whole world. The Mehrauli pillar inscription records his victory over the Vālhikas after crossing the seven mouths of the Indus. Different opinions have been expressed regarding the interpretation of *saptamukhāni* and the identification of Vālhikas. The *saptamukhāni* of the inscription has been taken to stand for the seven tributaries of the river Indus. However the word *mukha* does not mean a tributary. There is no instance of its usage in that sense. In Sanskrit the word *mukha* with reference to a river means the point where the river falls into the ocean. The Sanskrit lexicon *Amarakosha* assigns the meaning of exit, as it equates the word *mukha* with *niḥsaraṇa*. Kālidāsa has twice spoken of entering the ocean through the mouth of a river.[14] In English and Persian also we have the word mouth and *dahānāh* for the place where the river falls into the sea. There is definite evidence of the existence of the seven mouths of the Indus. The *Periplus* and the *Geography* of Ptolemy actually mention these mouths of the Indus along with their names.[15] As for the Vālhikas the term has often been erroneously confused with Vāhīka and taken for the Central Punjab. Vālhika here definitely stands for Bactria, ancient Persian Vagdhi and modern region of Balkh in north-eastern Afghanistan. It is, however, also possible to identify the Vālhikas with the people called Bactrionio who were occupying the south-eastern portion of Iran, as mentioned by Ptolemy. It can also be postulated that the route adopted by Chandragupta II in his military expedition against the Vālhikas lay through Surāshṭra to southern Afghanistan via

Trans-Indus region and from there he headed northwards, reached Bactria, where perhaps he had a battle with the Hūṇas on the Oxus. This view remarkably tallies with Kālidāsa's account of Raghu's conquests of the north. His description seems to be based on a historical background and he seems to have combined the conquests of Samudragupta and Chandragupta II into that of the legendary Raghu.[16]

Buddha Prakash has proposed to equate the account of the north-western conquest of Raghu with the conquest of Bactrians (Vālhikas) described in the Mehrauli pillar inscription. He concludes, "Hence it follows that Chandragupta II led an expedition in Bactriana in order to remove the menace of the Śakas, Kushāṇas and Pārasīkas root and branch."[17] The Mehrauli pillar inscription simply says that Chandra conquered the Vālhikas. Who were they? We have seen before that the Kushāṇas had moved out of Bactria c. A.D. 350 under the ever increasing pressure of the Chionites and were in the Kabul valley about this time, and the Chionites or the Hūṇas had occupied Bactria. Assuming that Kālidāsa's account of Raghu's campaign of conquest has a real historical background and that Chandragupta Vikramāditya adopted a land route for conquering the Pārasīkas, he must have come close to the south-eastern fringe of the Sassanian empire, where according to Kālidāsa he defeated the Pārasīkas. Kālidāsa's mention of the bearded heads of the Persian warriors suggests their identification with the Sassanians who bore beards. After this victory Chandragupta proceeded further northwards. Passing by Kapiśā where his soldiers enjoyed the famous wine of this region, he pressed towards the river Oxus, on the banks of which were the newly established settlements of the Hūṇas. Having subdued them with his might Chandragupta II seems to have brought his victorious march to a halt. He returned home from Bactria proper, crowned with glory and perhaps laden with riches.

To these achievements of Chandragupta II, may be added, the extension of the Gupta rule over Kośala, Oḍra, Puṇḍra and Tāmralipta as mentioned in the *Purāṇas*.[18] The Gupta suzerainty over Kośala is also indicated by the reference to the *Paramabhaṭṭāraka* in the Kursud copper plate grant of king Narendra.[19] The wars described in the previous paragraphs not only re-established the prestige and glory of the Gupta dynasty but also brought new splendour to the Gupta throne and much wealth to the state treasury. The frontiers of the empire were made immune from any danger of a foreign invasion as the Śakas, Kushāṇas and even the Hūṇas had been cut to size, the war having been carried to their very home and fought on their soil. The glory of the Guptas was at its zenith. There was, therefore, ample justification for Chandragupta II to adopt the title of Vikramāditya, 'the Sun of valour'.

The prosperity and great wealth of Chandragupta Vikramāditya is adequately reflected in his copious gold coinage. A.S. Altekar has aptly remarked, "Probably no other Hindu king issued so extensive a currency in the yellow metal as did Chandragupta Vikramāditya. The imperial mints were active throughout the reign. Even now the most common ancient gold coins that one comes across are those of this emperor."[20]

Chandragupta II issued his gold coinage in eight different types. The Standard type was issued for a short while and then discontinued. The Archer type was minted copiously and had a large number of varieties. This type has on its reverse the title *Śri-Vikramāditya*. Chandragupta II introduced several new types. One of these is the lion slayer type which has perhaps allusion to his acquisition of Surāshṭra, the home of lions in India. Another new type is the Horseman type. Chandragupta was a highly skilled horseman as is indicated by his having led a cavalry against the Sassanians, Kushāṇas and the Hūṇas. Kālidāsa while speaking of Raghu as *aśvasādhanaḥ* "having a force of cavalry" probably had in his mind the army of Chandragupta Vikramāditya, whose horses got rid of the fatigue of the journey by rolling on the banks of the Oxus.[21] The reverse legend *Ajitavikramaḥ* 'Of invincible valour' on this type beautifully sums up his achievements. Still another new type introduced by him was the Chhatra type in which a dwarf attendant is shown holding a parasol over the king's head. The legend on this coin, "Having conquered the earth Vikramāditya wins the heaven by laudable deeds" is indicative of a time of peace. His Couch type has an enigmatical legend *rūpākṛitī*, but it can yield an easily intellegible sense with a slight emendation. If we read it as *rūpakṛitī*, as suggested by Altekar, it can be rendered as 'the writer of plays' and will show that Chandragupta II like his father, was a talented writer. An altogether novel type of which only two coins have been found so far was an innovation. One of these belongs to the Bayana hoard and the other is said to be in the possession of a goldsmith of Shahganj in Jaunpur District of U.P.[22] This is his Chkra-vikrama type. On the obverse of this coin we have a deity who is identified as the *Chakra-purusha*, the personification of Vishṇu's discus, who is regarded as Vishṇu himself.[23] The male figure facing the deity is king Chandragupta Vikramāditya who is shown as receiving from the god Vishṇu, three balls which symbolise three-fold royal power—*Mantraśakti* (the power of policy making), *Utsāhaśakti* (the power of initiative and drive) and *Prabhāvaśakti* (the power of royal majesty). Chandragupta's devotion to Vishṇu is well known. He is called *parama-bhāgavata* on his coins and in the official genealogies. In the Mehrauli pillar inscription he is said to have set-up that wonderful iron flag-staff, having placed in deep faith, his belief in Vishṇu.

MATRIMONIAL ALLIANCES OF CHANDRAGUPTA II

If the time of Chandragupta Vikramāditya was important for new conquests and consolidation of the Gupta empire, it was equally important for the matrimonial alliances with the powerful ruling families of the time. The Gupta rulers seem to be well aware of the political advantage of the matrimonial alliances which played an important role in their foreign policy. It is well known how such an alliance with the Lichchhavis helped Chandragupta I to rise to imperial position. Samudragupta is also known to have received presents of maidens from the foreign rulers. An important alliance, perhaps of his time was the marriage of his son Chandragupta II with the Nāga princess Kuberanāgā, which seems to have been arranged by Samudragupta himself to pacify the defeated Nāga kings. P.L. Gupta is not inclined to attach any political importance to this marriage and he takes it as an event of Chandragupta's own reign.[24] He thinks that there is no ground to believe that this marriage took place in the time of Samudragupta. What the learned scholar has failed to grasp is that it can in no way be ascribed to the reign of Chandragupta II. It is a well established fact that Chandragupta married his daughter Prabhāvatīguptā born of Kuberanāgā to

Rudrasena II in c. A.D. 380. Even if Prabhāvatīguptā was eighteen years of age at the time of her marriage, the marriage of her parents has to be placed c. A.D. 362, which date definitely falls within the reign of Samudragupta, and comes soon after the completion of his conquests. This clearly proves that our observation about the political significance of this alliance, viz., the pacification of the defeated Nāga dynasty, is perfectly valid.

The real advantage of this alliance was derived by Chandragupta II himself, who after feeling sure that his position in northern India was secure, went ahead with his plans to proceed against the Western Kshatrapas. Taking another precaution of securing his left flank, he contracted a matrimonial alliance with the Vākāṭakas of the Deccan, by giving in marriage his daughter Prabhāvatīguptā to the Vākāṭaka crown prince Rudrasena II, the son of Pṛithivīsheṇa I. It was a remarkably strategic move on the part of Chandragupta II who foresaw that the powerful Vākāṭaka monarch of south-western Deccan could be 'of much service or diservice' to the northern invader of the dominions of the Śaka kshatrapas of Mālava and Surāshṭra.[25] Rudrasena II the son-in-law of Chandragupta II had a short reign and died in c.A.D. 390. After his death the rule of Prabhāvatīguptā as the regent queen of her minor sons continued for about twenty years. The Guptas exercised great influence on the Vākāṭaka kingdom during this time by deputing their own civil and military officers to the Vākāṭaka court.

Another matrimonial relationship with the Gupta royal house had been established by the Kadamba ruler Kākutsthavarman, who according to the Talagund stone pillar inscription[26] is said "to have caused to blossom the lotus beds in the form of the families of rulers the foremost among whom were the Guptas." The name of the Gupta emperor is not mentioned but as Kākutsthavarman ruled between A.D. 405 and 435, the Gupta king whose son married a daughter of Kākutsthavarman might have been either Chandragupta II or Kumāragupta I.

There is yet another piece of literary evidence which appears to have some important bearing on the history of Chandragupta Vikramāditya's time. It consists of some verses from a Sanskrit play the *Kuntaleśvardautyam*, now lost, some verses from which have been preserved in the *Śṛiṅgāraprakāśa* and *Sarasvatīkaṇṭhābharaṇa* of Bhoja (A.D. 1000 to 1047), the *Auchityavichāra-*

charchā of Kshemendra (A.D. 990-1065) and the *Kāvyamīmāṅsā* of Rājaśekhara (A.D. 880-920). According to the prefatory notes given by Kshemendra and Bhoja these verses relate to the deputation as a Commissioner, of the poet Kālidāsa, by his patron king Vikramāditya to the court of the lord of the Kuntala country whose name has not been mentioned. On reaching his destination Kālidāsa appears not to have been received with due honour, and as if to protest and show his annoyance he sat on the ground where upon someone requested him to take a proper seat. In order to express his annoyance Kālidāsa replied as follows:

Iha nivasati meruḥ śekharaḥ kshmādharāṇāṁ
Iha vinihitabhārāḥ sāgarāḥ sapta chānye/
Idam-ahipatibhogastambhavibhrājyamānaṁ
Dharaṇitalamihaiva sthānamasmadvidhānām//

"Here on stands Meru, the crest of (all) mountains, and the seven oceans also have set down their weight here. This surface of the earth which is resplendent with the pillar of the hood of the lord of serpents, is the place for people like me."

In spite of such an experience Kālidāsa appears to have stayed at the court of the *Kuntaleśvara* and then returned and reported to his patron Vikramāditya as follows:

Asakala-hasitatvāt-kshālitānīva kāntyā
mukalitanayanatvād-vyaktakarṇotpalāni/
pibati madhu-sugandhīnyānanāni priyāṇāṁ
tvayi vinihitabhāraḥ Kuntalānāmadhīśaḥ//

"The lord of Kuntalas, having placed the burden (of looking after the dominions) on you, sucks the mouths of his beloveds which are richly fragrant with wine, and which are resplendent with lustre (lit. which have been washed as it were with the lustre) of smiles (lit. partial laughter)".

On this the king makes the following simple comment:

Pibatu madhusugandhīnyānanāni priyāṇāṁ
mayi vinihitabhāraḥ Kuntalānāmadhīśaḥ/

"Let the lord of the Kuntalas drink the mouths of his beloveds which are richly fragrant with wine, having placed the burden (of looking after his administration) on me."

On the basis of these verses S. Krishnaswami Aiyangar concluded that the *Kuntaleśvara* referred to herein is the Vākāṭaka king Pravarasena II. However we learn from the Balaghat copper plate grant of Pṛithivīsheṇa II, that Pravarasena II's son Narendrasena was married to the daughter of the lord of Kuntala (*Kuntaleśvara*). Hence the identification of *Kuntaleśvara* with Pravarsena II becomes untenable. We may therefore agree with V.V. Mirashi that the *Kuntaleśvara* to whose court Kālidāsa went as a Commissioner of Chandragupta Vikramāditya was Devarāja of the Rāshṭrakūṭa family of Mānapura.[27]

Chandragupta as an Administrator

Having vanquished his enemies at home and abroad, and having thoroughly consolidated his empire, Chandragupta II actively set about to establish an ideally efficient system of administration. One important measure which he adopted in order to strengthen his hold on the empire was the appointment of his kith and kin as heads of the provincial administrations. We are told in the Mandasor inscription dated M.S. 524 that,

n = ādy = āpi moksham̐ samupaiti yena
sva-vam̐śya-pāśair = ava-pāśitā bhūḥ/[28]

'The earth does not even now find release, having been held in firm grip by means of the fetters (in the form) of his own kinsmen.'

Luckily some clay sealings discovered in 1903-04 during the archaeological excavations by T. Bloch at Basarh, the site where once stood the ancient famous city of Vaiśālī, which appears to have been made in Gupta time the capital of the province of *Tīrabhukti* (Tirhut). Some of these sealings belong to the members of the royal family and the others to the various administrative officers and their respective departments. One clay sealing belongs to *Mahādevī* Dhruvasvāminī, the chief queen of *Mahārājādhirāja* Chandragupta II and the mother of Mahārāja Govindagupta, who may be presumed to be the governor of *Tīrabhukti* province.[29] Another set of sealings has helped to clearly grasp the meanings of the official designation *kumārāmātya*, which had been previously rendered as 'prince's minister', or 'prince as a minister'. The correct meaning has come out in the light of the study of the following legends found on the Basarh sealings:

a. *Kumār = āmāty = ādhikaraṇasya.* "Of the office of the *Kumāramātya.*"
b. *Yuvarāja-pādīya-kumārāmāty = ādhikaraṇasya.* "Of the office of the *Kumārāmātya* serving under the heir-apparent."
c. *Yuvarāja bhaṭṭāraka-pādīya-kumārāmātyādhikaraṇasya.* "Of the office of the *Kumārāmātya* serving with the Lord heir-apparent."
d. *Śrī-paramabhaṭṭāraka- pādīya - kumārāmātyādhikaraṇasya.* "Of the office of the *Kumārāmātya* serving the illustrious Supreme Lord (i.e. the emperor)."

A careful perusal of these legends makes it at once clear that *Kumārāmātya* was not a 'minister of the prince' but it was a designation of a class of high ranking officers who served in various capacities. We find that emperor Samudragupta's minister of peace and war had the title *Kumārāmātya.* In the Damodarpur copper plate grants the officer incharge of the administration of a district was designated as *Kumārāmātya.* Above all when we come across the sealing which mentions a *Kumārāmātya* of the emperor himself, it becomes apparent that the rendering 'Prince's minister' is untenable. Another sealing informs us regarding the existence of the Department of Military Stores (*śrī-raṇa-bhāṇḍāgār = ādhikaraṇasya*). There is also a sealing of the Army office of the heir-apparent (*Yuvarāja-pādīya-balādhie karaṇasya*). It shows that the military force in the province was in the charge of the heir-apparent who was the provincial governor. One sealing tells us about the office of the officer in charge of the police (*Daṇḍaypāśik-ādhikaraṇasya*). That the government under Chandragupta Vikramāditya made arrangements of the education of the people and there was an officer in charge of this activity as well as for the preservation of the established order in the society is revealed by the following legend of a sealing: *Vinaya-sthiti-sthāpak = ādhikaraṇasya*—of the office of the officer in charge of education and the maintenance of the established norm of life. For the interpretation of this sealing we are indebted to Kālidāsa who in his *Raghuvaṁśa*[30] speaks of the king's concern for imparting education (*vinay = ādhāna*), and in the same work further tells us that for the preservation of the order the king punished the guilty.[31] Kālidāsa has used almost the same phraseology as we find on the sealing: *sthityai daṇḍayato daṇḍyān.*

Another sealing informs us about an officer named Vinayaśūra, who held the two high offices of the Chief-Chamberlain and the City-Prefect. The legend on this sealing is *Mahāpratihāra-Tara-vara-Vinayaśūrasya*. From the Allahabad pillar inscription we are already familiar with an officer called *Mahādaṇḍanāyaka*. Amongst these sealings we have the sealing of an officer named Agnigupta, who bears this designation. The exact nature of this office is not certain. He can be a judge, a magistrate or a leader of the army. However the last sense is ruled out here, as the army is called *bala* and not *daṇḍa* in these sealings. Another important sealing belongs to the office of the *Uparika* of *Tīra-bhukti*. The status of this officer can now be definitely determined with the help of the Damodarpur copper plate inscriptions, where the *Uparika* figures as governing the *bhukti* of Puṇḍra-vardhana. The connotation of this official title has been discussed by B. Ch. Chhabra in detail.[32] These sealings present a vivid picture of the administrative set up in the time of Chandragupta Vikramāditya, and we can say that his administration was as well organised as can be expected in any civilized modern state. No wonder therefore that the Chinese pilgrim Fa-hien was all praise for the government of the day. It is not unlikely that a practical manual of administration like the *Kāmandakīyanītisāra* was written by Kāmandaka at the instance of Vikramāditya. It has been suggested that Kāmandaka is the pen name of Vikramāditya's chief-minister Śikharasvāmī who has been called as Saqar by Muslim writers; and the author of a work on polity.[33]

Chandragupta as a Man of Letters

Chandragupta Vikramāditya was not only a conqueror and a great administrator but like his father Samudragupta was also a man of letters and a friend of poets. His minister of war and peace, Vīrasena was a poet, as mentioned in the Udayagiri cave inscription.[34] We learn from the poet Rājaśekhara that Chandragupta, who can be no other than Chandragupta Vikramāditya, was one of those poets (*Kāvyakāras*) whose poetic talent was adjudged by the assembly of learned at Ujjain.[35] A more specific reference has been pointed out by Ajay Mitra Shastri[36] who has quoted the following verse from the *Kuvalayamālā* of Udyotanasūri:

> *Tipurisa charia pasiddho supurisa chariena payāto loya|*
> *sa jayati Devagutto vaṁse Guttānaṁ rāyarisi||*

It means that *Rājarshi* (royal saint) Devagupta of the Gupta dynasty became famous in the world by his writings *Tripurushacharita* and *Supurushacharita.* Here the monarch Devagupta of the Gupta family is evidently Chandragupta Vikramāditya, who has been called a *rājarshi* in the Udayagiri cave inscription of his minister Vīrasena Śāba and whose name Devagupta occurs in the Vākāṭaka copper plate grants, for which the more popular name Chandragupta has been substituted in the Poona and Riddhapur grants of queen Prabhāvatīguptā. Chandragupta II seems to have written some Sanskrit plays also since on the couch type of his gold coins we have the epithet *rūpā* (*pa*) *kṛiti,* the writer of plays.

APPENDIX I

VIKRAMĀDITYA TRADITION

The assumption of the title Vikramāditya[37] by Chandragupta II, has been responsible for confusing his name with the legendary founder of the *Vikrama saṁvat* of B.C. 57 in spite of the fact that ever since the discovery, in 1884, of the Mandasor stone inscription of the Guild of silk-weavers bearing dates 493 and 529 it has been established that the era which commenced in 57 B.C. was founded by the Mālavas and dates from the time of the foundation of the Mālava republic. The identification of the legendary king Vikramāditya of Ujjaini has been discussed at length by various scholars for a long time. A considerable number of scholars of Sanskrit hold that the era commencing in 57 B.C. was founded by king Vikramāditya who defeated the Śakas; was a historical figure and ruled at Ujjaini in the first century B.C.[38] There are others who have tried to identify Vikramāditya with Gautamīputra Sātakarṇi, Yaśodharman of Daśapura, Kanishka, I Azes I, Chashṭana etc. R.G. Bhandarkar[39] held that Chandragupta II was the Vikramāditya who overthrew the Śaka rule and made Ujjain his second capital; and founded an era.

In order to establish the identity of this mighty hero who has been remembered as the liberator of India from the yoke of the Śakas, we must examine all available historical evidence and analyse it critically. The *Purāṇas* give an account of successive dynasties of India from the time of the accession of Parīkshita upto the advent of the Gupta rule. We naturally expect the writers of the *Purāṇas* to record not only the name but the glorious achievements of Vikramāditya. But they do not mention anywhere a king Vikramāditya ruling over Ujjain in the first century B.C. It is rather highly surprising that no mention of this national hero has been made in the *Purāṇas* which never fail to record the important episodes in our ancient history in spite of their cryptic style. For example, the overthrow of the Nandas by Kauṭilya and of Maurya ruler Bṛihadratha by Pushyamitra Śuṅga have been specifically mentioned in the *Purāṇas*. According to the dynastic account given in the *Purāṇas*, the Kaṇvas ruled from 78 B.C. to c. 28 B.C.. The date of the origin of Vikrama era thus falls within the period of their rule. But the *Purāṇas* do not associate the title Vikramāditya with any Kāṇva ruler, nor any ruler from any other dynasty. It clearly indicates that the prevalent tradition has no historical basis whatsoever. Not only are the *Purāṇas* silent about Vikramāditya but our ancient inscriptions too do not associate his name with an era till the 9th century of the Christian era.[40] On the other hand the era which began in 57 B.C. has been known by different names such as *Kṛita*, *Mālava* or simply as *Saṁvat*.[41]

The tradition which makes Vikramāditya as the founder of the era commencing 57 B.C. also associates with this august king, nine luminaries in the fields of literature, science and arts who adorned his court and have been termed as "the Nine Jewels". They are Dhanvantari, Kshapaṇaka, Amarasiṁha, Śaṅku, Vetālabhaṭṭa, Ghaṭakarapara, Kālidāsa, Varāhamihira and Vararuchi. A glance at these names is enough to show the utter worthlessness of this statement. It is a well established fact that Varāhamihira flourished in the sixth century of the Christian era, atleast six hundred years after the founder of the Vikrama era. Of the rest Kālidāsa cannot be placed earlier than fifth century A.D. The existence of persons like Śaṅku and Vetālabhaṭṭa itself is almost legendary. All this tends to show that king Vikramāditya of Ujjaini in the first century B.C. is a pure myth.

The identification of Vikramāditya with Sātakarṇi Sātavāhana also cannot hold good because the latter was a contemporary of the Western Kshatrapa king Rudradāman who flourished in the second century A.D. He never adopted the title of Vikramāditya. It oes not occur in his own inscriptions nor in those of his successors. Moreover he never started an era. All of his own inscriptions as well as those of his successors are dated in regnal years only. Yaśodharman of Daśapura came after the decline of the Guptas and he was ruling in circa A.D. 532—the date of the Mandasor stone slab inscription. Moreover he is not given the title of Vikramāditya in his known inscriptions. Similarly Kanishka never gets this title in his inscriptions. Instead he is called Devaputra Shāhi-Sbāhānushāhi. His accession has been variously placed in A.D. 78, 129 and 146. Lastly he is famous as the ruler of Purushapura (Peshawar) and never as a ruler of Ujjain.

We know that Chandragupta II of the Gupta dynasty adopted the title of Vikramāditya which occurs on his gold coins. His association with the city of Ujjain, which perhaps became his second capital, may be regarded as a historical fact, as with the overthrow of the Śakas Chandragupta II is likely to have consider ed it politically expedient to govern his newly acquired territories from Ujjain. To crown all, the traditional Vikramāditya is popularly called Śakāri—the enemy of the Śakas. The Śakas entered India in c. 85 B.C. and established their rule in the North-Western and Western India. They continued to hold Western India, with Ujjain as their capital, uptill c. A.D. 390 when they were uprooted by the Gupta emperor Chandragupta II. So any ruler who flourished in 57 B.C. cannot be called a *Śakāri* by any stretch of imagination, even if we thrust upon him the name Vikramāditya. It is only Chandragupta II of the Gupta dynasty, who has to his credit the complete overthrow of the Śakas, and who bears the title of Vikramāditya which appears on his gold coins. Therefore only he can be designated as Vikramāditya Śakāri, with justification.

As regards the era commencing in 57 B.C., we know that it was originally known as the Mālava era.[42] We also know that Chandragupta II because of his conquest of Avanti can be justifiably called *Mālaveśa* (Lord of Mālava). In course of time, after the lapse of some centuries after the reign of Chandragupta II people confused the name of the Mālava people who were the lord of Mālava in the first century B.C. with *Mālaveśa* Chandragupta Vikramāditya and thus grafted the name of Vikramāditya upon the era which had been known even in earlier times as the era of the Mālavas.

APPENDIX II

THE MEHRAULI IRON PILLAR INSCRIPTION

The iron pillar bearing an inscription in Brāhmī characters of the 4th or 5th century of the Christian era stands in the court-yard of mosque, now almost in ruins, which its builders the early Slave kings, named as Quwwat-ul-Islam, and which now forms a part of the archaeological remains of what was once the fort of the Chāhamāna emperor Pṛithivīrāja III. The site is now included in the village of Mehrauli, nine miles to the south of Delhi. This pillar is 23 feet 8 inches in height and is made of malleable iron of 7.66 specific gravity. It is veritably a wonder of ancient Indian metallurgical skill. It could not be even slightly damaged by a canon ball which has merely left its mark thereon. Still more notable is the fact that the pillar has not rusted in the course of its existence of about sixteen hundred years.

The inscription consists of four verses written in elegant Sanskrit. These verses constitute an eulogy of king Chandra, of whom neither genealogy nor the date have been recorded. The inscription simply tells us that king Chandra, in the course of repulsing his enemies who had combined together to give him battle in the country of Vaṅga (Southern Bengal) engraved his glorious achievement on his arm by means of the sword; and having crossed the seven mouths of the Indus, in the course of a military campaign, conquered a people called Vālhikas. It further informs us that the Southern ocean is still fragrant with the breezes of his might. The great glory of this monarch which is mere remanant of his exertions which brought about the annihilation of his enemies, does not even now leave this earth like the glow of a forest conflagration which has gone out, and like that of a king who has gone to the other world as if tired, but has remained on this earth through his fame. That lord of the earth named Chandra who had obtained the sole sovereignty of this earth by the prowess of his own arms for a long time, who bears the beauty of the countenance like that of the full moon, having placed in devotion his faith in the (god) Vishṇu, has set up this lofty *garuḍa*-flagstaff, of the venerable lord Vishṇu, on the hill named Vishṇupada.

Ever since the publication of this record, there has been going on a controversy regarding the identification of this king Chandra. J.F. Fleet[43] who finally edited this inscription, was slightly inclined to regard him as Chandragupta I, but at the same time he thought it more likely that Chandra was a younger brother of Mihirakula. The latter suggestion is almost fantastic and entirely untenable. There is not a single argument in its favour. R.G. Basak[44] and S.K. Aiyangar[45] have identified him with Chandragupta I of the Gupta dynasty. V.A. Smith[46], A.F.R. Hoernle[47], K.P. Jayaswal[48], D.C. Sircar[49], R.N. Dandekar[50] and Buddha Prakash[51] regard him as identical with Chandragupta II Vikramāditya. H.P. Shastri[52] proposed to identify him with Chandravarmā of the Susunia rock inscription. Hemchandra Raychaudhuri[53] considered some powerful Nāga king such as Chandrāṁśa or Sadāchandra mentioned in the dynastic account of the *Purāṇas* likely to be this Chandra. H.C. Seth[54] proposed the name of Chandragupta Maurya, and R.C. Majumdar[55] once suggested that Chandra is identical with Kanishka. Otto Stein[56] after examining all aspects of the problem concluded that a definite identification was not possible. Recently S.R. Goyal[57] has attempted to prove that Samudragupta of the imperial Gupta line is Chandra of the Mehrauli inscription.

Some of these theories are prima facie untenable. For example, the identification with Chandragupta Maurya is simply ridiculous. It is preposterous to suggest, as Seth had done, that the original inscription on the Mehrauli iron pillar was engraved in Mauryan Brāhmī but as it had become effaced it was re-written in the Gupta script by Chandragupta II. How can we imagine that an inscription on an iron pillar had become effaced owing to natural decay within a period of seven hundred years, while we know that the inscriptions of Aśoka on stone pillars and rocks which are softer than iron are still clearly legible even after the lapse of more than two thousand years. Chandra's conquest of Vālhikas is out of question in the case of his Mauryan namesake because Bactria was held by the Greeks not only during the reign of Chandragupta Maurya but long after him till 135 B.C.

As regards the identification with Kanishka, it is well known that he was a worshipper of the Buddha and not of Vishṇu. The conquest of Bactria becomes an absurdity in his case, since it was already in the possession of the Kushāṇas before his time. Finally, Kanishka never conquered any part of the South nor he is known to have defeated a confederacy of foes in Bengal.

Mahamahopadhyaya Har Prasad Shastri's conclusion was rather hasty. He does not seem to have given proper consideration to the contents of the Susunia inscription. Chandravarmā of this inscription was a local king of Pushkaran (*Pushkaraṇādhipati*) in the Bankura district itself. His title of Mahārāja shows that he could not have been the sole sovereign of the earth. There is no evidence of his having led a campaign to Bactria or waging war in Vaṅga nor in the South.

Hemchandra Raychaudhuri had suggested the name of Nāga kings simply because no other theory appeared to him as satisfactory. There were flaws in the proposed identification with Chandragupta I and Chandragupta II of the Gupta dynasty.

In view of the fine Sanskrit of the Mehrauli pillar inscription and its script being Gupta Brāhmī, only one of the imperial Gupta rulers can be a proper claimant for identification with Chandra. R.G. Basak and S.K. Aiyangar had argued with some justification in favour of the identification of Chandra with Chandragupta I of the Gupta dynasty, who indeed had created a sovereign rule with the prowess of his own arms and he might have been a *Vaishṇava* too. But the similarity between the two ends there and there are hard facts contradicting Chandra's identity with Chandragupta I. Firstly, we know that Chandragupta I's empire was not an extensive empire which can be described as an *ekādhirājya*. His authority in all probability was confined to Bihar and eastern U.P. only. In western U.P. and to the south-west of it there were the Nāga kingdoms of Ahichhatra, Mathura, Padmāvatī and Vidiśā. There was no possibility of his leading an expedition for the conquest of the Bactrians, before subduing the Nāgas, the republics of Yaudheyas and Madrakas as well as the foreign rulers like Śākas and Śiladas in central Punjab and the Kidarites in Gandhāra. Further, he cannot be credited with the conquest of any part of the South. We get a clear impression from the Allahabad pillar inscription that Samudragupta's was the first attempt to bring the South within the fold of a northern empire. These are weighty reasons which force us to reject any suggestion regarding Chandra's identification with Chandragupta I of the Gupta dynasty.

As regards the claim of Samudragupta, it is true that he ruled for a long time over an extensive empire which had virtually been created by the prowess of his own arms. He had also performed mighty deeds of valour in the South, the memory of which might have lingered on in the minds of men for a pretty long time. But there is one big hurdle. King Chandra of the Mehrauli pillar inscription is said to have crossed the seven mouths of the river Indus and conquered the Vālhikas. Some scholars take the expression 'seven mouths' to stand for the seven tributaries of the Indus, and they think that Chandra first overran the Punjab and then proceeded to conquer the people of Balkh. Some even suggest that Vālhīka is the same as Vāhīka, which according to the *Mahābharata*[58] is the modern central Punjab region. It has not been realised that such a view suffers from an inherent contradiction. The Vāhīkas according to the *Mahābhārata* are to be located to the east of the Indus, between that river and the Satluj, whereas Chandra is said to have conquered the Vālhikas after crossing all these rivers and not in the land where these rivers flow. Moreover, we must remember that the western-most people to acknowledge Samudragupta's suzerainty were the Madras, who were in occupation of the land between the upper courses of the Ravi and Chenab. Therefore the question of his crossing the tributaries of the Indus does not arise at all. Moreover it is absolutely incorrect to take the word *mukha* in the sense of 'feeder' and translate *sapta-mukhāni* as the 'seven tributaries'. The word *mukha* never has that sense in Sanskrit. The word *mukha* in the case of a river means the point where a river falls into the sea. We read in Kālidāsa, for example, that Raghu mastered the various branches of learning through the picking up of the alphabet just as one enters the ocean through the mouth of a river.[59] In English and Persian too the place where a river enters the ocean is called its mouth. Therefore the seven mouths of the Indus are not its seven tributaries. We have actual mention of the names of these seven mouths of the Indus in the *Geography* of Ptolemy. The mouths are also referred to in the *Periplus*, though their names have not been noted in that work. It is therefore clear that Chandra proceeded for the conquest of the Vālhikas from the lower Indus valley via Bolan pass and thence took a northernly direction towards Bactria which was held partly by the Kushāṇas and partly by the Hūṇas about this time. Samudragupta's relations with the Śakas and Kushāṇas were cordial as stated in the Allahabad pillar inscription. We cannot think of him as leading an army for the conquest of Vālhika. This could have happened only after the Rāmagupta episode which embittered those friendly ties. We can think of such a campaign only in the time of Chandragupta II. Goyal says that it was to fight with the Chionites who had attacked the dominions of the Kidārites, that Samudragupta undertook this expedition.[60] We have no evidence however that Samudragupta undertook such a far flung campaign to help the Kidārites. As we have seen above Chandra proceeded to conquer the Vālhikas after crossing the seven mouths of the Indus. In order to follow this route it would have been imperative for any Gupta ruler to have a free passage to the mouths of the Indus, to have control of Avanti and Surāshṭra, which Samudragupta never had. In his time these territories were held by the Western Kshtrapas. The Chionite avalanche was faced and successfully held by the Sassanian emperor Shapur II. As already pointed out by R.C. Majumdar, Ammianus an officer in the Roman army who fought against Shapur II in Mesopotamia, informs us that Shapur II "was engaged from A.D. 350 to 358 in fighting against certain tribes on his eastern frontier, namely the Chionites and the Kushāṇas."[61] Shapur apparently succeeded in enforcing their submission, for we find that both the Chionites and the Kushāṇas helped Shapur against the Romans in the siege of Amida, which took place in A.D. 358. However Kidāra soon asserted his independence, and we learn from the Armenian historian, Faustos of Byzantium that "the Kushāṇas inflicted two crushing defeats on the Sassanians in A.D. 367-68 and on one occasion even forced Shapur II to fly from the battlefield."[62] It is quite obvious from this statement that the Kushāṇas who were powerful enough to defeat the mighty Sassanian emperor, cannot be supposed to have sought the help of Samudragupta for which there is no evidence either. It is therefore purely gratutious assumption of Goyal to assert that the Vālhikas of the Mehrauli pillar inscription are the Chionites and Samudragupta proceeded against them and even conquered them. It is very essential to keep in mind the language of the Mehrauli inscription. It clearly tells us that the king who set up the lofty column of Vishṇu, had the name Chandra. The word *āhva* is a synonym for *name* according to the *Amarakosha* and we cannot do so much violence to language as to attempt a different translation. The identification of Chandra with Samudragupta is totally out of question.

S.R. Goyal has stressed the point that it was Samudragupta who conquered "the rest of Bengal himself" and therefore the statement of the Mehrauli pillar inscription that Chandra acquired great fame by waging war in Vāṅga is applicable to him. But the Allahabad pillar inscription shows that the states of Ḍavāka and Samataṭa were frontier states—not an integral part of the Gupta empire. Were these states recognised as independent and friendly neighbours after a bloody war? Certainly not.

Goyal further doubts about any notable military achievement of Chandragupta II in the South. It can be pointed out that the *Vishṇu Purāṇa* does speak specially of Chandragupta's rule over Kośala, Oḍra, Puṇḍra and Tāmralipta.[63] The special mention of these territories can only mean that these were fresh acquisitions of Chandragupta II. The mention of Chandra's invasion of Bactria, after crossing the seven mouths of the Indus, clinches the issue against Samudragupta, who did not have any control over the lower Indus valley nor over Surāshṭra, which could have facilitated his crossing the Indus Deltas.

We think that the account of Chandra as given in the Mehrauli pillar inscription is applicable to Chandragupta II in each and, every detail and he alone can be identified with him. Firstly Chandra is said to have deep faith in Vishṇu and we know that Chandragupta II was a devout worshipper of Vishṇu as stated in his coin legends. His Chakra-Vikrama type of gold coins specifically prove this. Chandragupta Vikramāditya enjoyed a long rule of at-least thirty three-years. This tallies with the statement of the Mehrauli inscription that Chandra ruled for a long time. It has been sometimes doubted how far the sovereign rule of Chandragupta II can be called as created by the prowess of his own arms. It is true that Samudragupta had created an extensive empire, but we must not ignore the fact that the defeat of Rāmagupta had created a crisis and the Gupta empire was on the verge of disintegration and collapse. What other meaning can be placed on the statement of the Udayagiri cave inscription that the minister of peace and war, Vīrasena Śāba, had come there in the company of the emperor 'whose purpose was the conquest of the whole earth". The same inscription further states that ' this earth had been purchased with the price of valour and its kings had been reduced to subjection". Further the Mandasor stone inscription dated M.S. 524 also tells us that "Because of his having snatched away the kingship of many kings on this earth by means of his intellect and valour; and having put this earth in firm hands (in the form) of the members of his family, she (the earth) has still not been able to free herself."[64] What more evidence is required for proving the great military achievements of Chandragupta II Vikramâditya? Taking all these facts into consideration the identity of Chandra of the Mehrauli iron pillar inscription with Chandragupta II Vikramâditya stands beyond all doubt.

References

1. The earliest known record of Chandragupta II's reign is the Mathura stone pillar inscription dated G.S. 61 i.e. A.D. 380-81. In its third line, D.R. Bhandarkar, who edited this inscription, read the regnal year as *prathame* (*EI*, XXI, 8ff.). D.C. Sircar has read it as *pañchame* (*Sel. Ins.*, I, 270). Jagannath Agrawal who read this inscription in 1933 from the original pillar opines that the word is so badly damaged that no definite reading can be given.
2. The expression *tatparigṛihīta* (accepted by him i.e. Samudragupta) has been used for Chandragupta II in the Gupta genealogies. But it may be taken as a formal expression of goodwill and respect towards his father without implying 'special selection' or 'immediate succession.'
3. Supra, Chapter VII.
4. Chhabra & Gai (ed.), *CII*, III, (1981), 256.
5. It was first pointed out by Dashrath Sharma, *IHQ*, XXX, 374-78.
6. S.R. Goyal is of the view that the alliance can hardly have any political importance for this campaign, as the two events had a gap of about two decades between them and that the Śakas were not even a second rate power at this time (*HIG*, 246). It is hard for us to agree with him as we know that Chandragupta II being a shrewd statesman must have planned every thing well in advance and moreover the Śakas were still a power in India to reckon with. Our view is strengthened by the fact that great importance was attached to this event in Indian tradition after which the title *Śakāri* is attached with the name of Vikramâditya i.e. Chhndragupta II.
7. Chhabra & Gai (ed.), *CII*, III, (1981), 256-57.
8. Rapson, *CCAD*, *WK*, coin no. 907, P. 192.

9. Allan, *CCGD*, 49-50.
10. Chhabra & Gai (ed.), *CII*, III, (1981), 259.
11. Chandragupta II must have been born in c. A.D. 335.
12. Chhabra & Gai (ed.), *CII*, III, (1981), 243-44.
13. *Ibid.*, 250.
14. *Raghuvaṁśa*, III, 28; XVII, 53.
15. Ptolemy gives the following names of the seven mouths of the Indus: i. The most western mouth is called *Sagapa*, ii. The next is *Sinthan*, iii. The third is called *Khrysoun* (the golden), iv. The fourth is called *Kariphron*, v. The fifth is called *Sapara*, vi. The sixth is called *Sabalaessa*, and vii. the seventh is called *Lonibare*. *Ancient India as Described by Ptolemy*, ed. & trans. J.W. McCrindle, 33.
16. As long ago as 1922, it was pointed out by R.G. Basak that the description of Raghu's conquests by Kālidāsa has historical basis. He tried to establish that the description fits the conquests of Chandragupta I and Samudragupta. The learned scholar had identified king Chandra of the Mehrauli pillar inscription with Chandragupta I instead of Chandragupta II. Hence the difference with us. *PAIOC*, 1922, 325-34.
17. Buddha Prakash, *SIHC*, 326. See also his paper 'The Central Asiatic Expedition of Chandragupta Vikramāditya', *JRASB. L.*, 1947, 31-39.
18. *DKA*, 54; 73-74.
19. *EI*, XXXI, 265. *cf.* Sircar, D.C., "The Kursud plate shows that South Kośala formed an integral part of the empire of the Guptas towards the close of the fifth century." *EI*, XXVIII, 83.
20. *Coinage*, 90.
21. *Raghuvaṁśa*, IV, 67.
22. *JNSI*, XXII, 261.
23. *Chakrapāṇiḥ svayaṁ Hariḥ.*
24. *Gup. Sām.*, 296.
25. Smith, V.A., *JRAS*, 1914, 324.
26. *Guptādipārtthiva—kulāmburuhasthalāni*
snehādara-praṇaya-sambhrama-kesarāṇi |
Śrīmantyaneka nṛipashṭpada-sevitāni
yo=bodhyadduhitṛi-dīdhitibhir-nṛirpārkkaḥ ||

"Who the Sun of a king caused to bloom by means of the rays in the form of his daughters, the lotus beds (in the form of) royal families such as the Guptas, whose filament consisted of love, regard, affection and reverance, and who were waited upon by a large number of bees in the form of kings." *EI*, VIII, 31. in the form of the illustrious lineages of kings the foremost of whom were the Guptas.

27. Mirashi, V.V., *Studies in Indology*, I, 10-11.
28. *EI*, XXVII, 12ff.
29. For further details see Chapter IX.
30. *Raghuvaṁśa*, I, 24.
31. *Ibid.*, I, 25.
32. *D.R. Bhandarkar Felicitation Volume* (*Āchārya Pushpāñjali*), 233.
33. *JBORS*, 1932, 37-39.
34. Chhabra & Gai (ed.), *CII*, III, 255f.

35. At page 55 of the *Kāvyamimāṅsā* we find the following statement:
Shrūyate chojjayinyāṁ kāvyakāra-parīkshā:—
Hari-chandra Chandraguptau parīkshitāviha Viśālāyāṁ //"

36. *PIHC*, 1965, 111.

37. The epithet occurs on his coins either by itself or in compounds like *Chakra-Vikrama*, *Siṁha-Vikrama*, *Ajit-Vikrama* etc.

38. Pandey, R.B., *Vikramāditya of Ujjaiyinī*, 1949.

39. *JBBRAS*, XX, 398.

40. The first inscription in which the name of Vikrama is attached with *saṁvat* is Dhiniki copper plate inscription of the *Vikrama Saṁvat* 794. Bühler, *IA*, XII, 155ff. However, this is regarded as spurious by scholars like Bhagwanlal Indraji. The next mention of the *Vikrama saṁvat* is to be found in the Dholpur inscription of Chāhamāna Chaṇḍamahīsena dated *Vikrama Saṁvat* 898, Hultzsch, *ZDMG*, XL, 39ff.

41. For example, Mandasor stone inscription of Naravarman is dated in the Mālava year 461, Badva stone pillar inscription of the Maukharis is dated *Kṛita* year 295 and Mandasor stone slab inscription of Yaśodharman of the Mālava year 589.

42. *Cf.* Mandasor inscription dated M.S. 493 and 529 and the Mandasor inscription dated M.S. 589.

43. Fleet (ed.), *CII*, III, (1888), 140, fn. 1.

44. *HNEI*, 13ff.

45. *SGH*, 14ff.

46. *JRAS*, 1897. But he changed his view in favour of Chandravarmā of Pushkarana, *EHI*, 307, fn. 1.

47. *IA*, XXI, 43-44.

48. *JBORS*, XVIII, 31ff.

49. *JRASB. L.*, V, 413ff.

50. *HG*, 27-28.

51. *SIHC*, 326.

52. *EI*, XII, 315.

53. *PHAI*, 472, fn. 2.

54. *JIH*, XXVI, 177ff.

55. *JRASB. L.*, IX, 179ff. He has since given up this view in favour of Chandragupta II, *CA* 20-21.

56. *NIA*, I, 198.

57. *HIG*, 201ff.

58. *Pañchānāṁ Sindhu-shashṭhānāṁ nadīnāṁ ye=ntarā sthitāḥ* /
tān dharmabāhyānaśuchīn Vāhīkānapi varjjayet //
Mahābhārata, VIII, 44.7.

59. *Raghuvaṁśa*, III, 28.

60. *HIG*, 207.

61. *CA*, 56.

62. *Ibid.*, 57.

63. *DKA*, 54, fn. 20.

64. *EI*, XXVII,

CHAPTER IX

GOVINDAGUPTA

THE DISCOVERY FROM BASARH, in the Muzaffarpur district of Bihar by T. Bloch, of a clay sealing of *Mahādevī* Dhruvasvāminī, the chief queen of *Mahārājādhirāja* Chandragupta II Vikramāditya, brought to light for the first time, the name of Mahārāja Govindagupta as a son of the chief queen Dhruvasvāminī. The legend on the seal is as follows:

1. *Mahārājādhirāja-śrī-Chandragupta—*
2. *patnī mahārāja-śrī-Govindagupta—*
3. *mātā mahādevī-śrī-Dhru—*
4. *va-svāminī.*[1]

A careful examination of the text of this sealing at once brings to our minds the perfectly natural question, as to why the chief queen Dhruvasvāminī has been called the mother of Mahārāja Govindagupta, and not of Kumāragupta who has, so far, been generally accepted as the eldest son and successor of *Mahārājādhirāja* Chandragupta born of the chief queen Dhruvadevī, on the basis of the Gupta genealogy as given in the inscriptions and the official seals of the dynasty. From the use of the expression *tatpād=ānudhyāta* with his name with reference to his father, it has been stressed that Kumāragupta must have been the immediate successor of Chandragupta II. From the use of the title Mahārāja with the name of Govindagupta on the Vaiśālī sealing it can be inferred that he was the governor of *Tīrabhukti* during the reign of Chandragupta II Vikramāditya, and the seal was prepared when *Mahādevī* Dhruvasvāminī was staying with him at Vaiśālī. It was therefore natural, that she should have been called the mother of Govindagupta who was the governor of Vaiśālī. However when we study the sealing in the light of some more sealings discovered from the same place, this answer does not appear to be satisfactory. We have from Basarh, the sealings of several officers serving under the *Yuvarāja* (heir-apparent). We have, for instance, the sealings of the office of the *Kumārāmātya* attached to the heir-apparent[2] and also of the War Office of the lord heir-apparent.[3] The presence of these sealings at Vaiśālī suggests that the governor of the province of Vaiśālī was also the heir-apparent, and that was why his mother, the chief queen Dhruvasvāminī, was styled as the mother of Govindagupta.

D.R. Bhandarkar had long ago suggested that Govindagupta must have enjoyed a special status such as that of a *Yuvarāja*.[4] Bhandarkar further suggested that Govindagupta may be "the young son of Chandragupta" referred to as Chandraprakāśa in the verse quoted by Vāmana, in his *Kāvyālaṅkārasūtra-vṛitti*.[5] Since Chandraprakāśa of the verse was said to have assumed royal authority, Bhandarkar suggested that Govindagupta must have ruled before Kumāragupta I, sometimes between A.D. 412-13 and A.D. 415-16. So far as Govindagupta's appointment as the governor of Vaiśālī is concerned, S. Krishnaswami Aiyangar had expressed a similar opinion[6], but he had rather gone too far in suggesting that in reality it was Kumāragupta I who had been appointed the governor of Vaiśālī, but since he had to be away from the headquarters, Govindagupta had been named as the acting governor and since the latter was too young, the administration was being run by the queen Dhruvasvāminī.

Some very welcome light has been thrown on this problem by the discovery in 1923[7] of the Mandasor stone slab inscription dated in the Mālava year 524[8] = A.D. 467. This inscription contains a very important statement regarding Govindagupta. It says that Chandragupta begot a son named Govindagupta whose virtues and whose majesty were well known like those of Govinda i.e. Lord Kṛishṇa, and who resembled the gods as well as the *asuras*. The record further informs us that even the Lord of the gods i.e. Indra started entertaining apprehension when the vanquished kings whose glory had vanished, embraced Govindagupta's lotus-like feet.[9] On the basis of this information Jagannath Agrawal[10] put forward the theory that Govindagupta having first been a *Yuvarāja* and governor of the province of Vaiśālī, ascended the throne after the death of his father Chandragupta II sometimes in A.D. 413-14. Agrawal has argued that Govindagupta, at whose feet a number of kings, who had been subdued, paid homage and who had a commander-in-chief of his own, and of whose might and glory even the Lord of the gods (Indra) became jealous, must have been a ruler of imperial status. He could not have been a mere governor, for the simple reason that in a feudatory state like that of Daśapura which had its own ruler named Prabhākara, there is absolutely no place for a governor exercising supervisory powers over and above the local king. There is not a single precedent for such an arrangement in the whole history of the Guptas. There were either the directly held territories (*rāja-vishaya*) ruled through governors like Parṇadatta and Śarvanāga in the time of Skandagupta or there were the feudatory kings like the Parivrājaka kings in Ḍahāla, the Varmans in Daśapura and the Maitrakas in Valabhī. Before assigning the status of a governor to Govindagupta in Daśapura, we should seriously think whether there is any other instance of such an administrative arrangement in the Gupta period itself. Have we got any evidence of a Gupta governor placed over the Parivrājaka or the Maitraka kings? D.C. Sircar[11] pointed out that in the Chammak copper plate of the Vākāṭaka monarch Pravarasena II, we find that the grant was made at the request of Koṇḍarāja son of Śatrughṇarāja. But what does that prove? Neither Koṇḍarāja nor Śatrughṇarāja have any titles like Mahārāja to show that they were vested with a high administrative status like that of a governor. These are mere names of two individuals who had access to the king and so requested him to make a grant. They stand in no comparison with Govindagupta. It has even been ignored that the Mandasor inscription of the guild of silk-weavers mentions only the imperial sovereign Kumāragupta I and his feudatory Bandhuvarmā in the year M.S. 493 = A.D. 436. There is no mention of any intermediary Governor or even a Resident. While it may be conceded that there can be an element of poetic hyperbole in describing the great power and glory even of a district officer (*vishayapati*) like Mātṛivishṇu in the Eran boar inscription, there is a ring of genuineness in the description of Govindagupta in the Mandasor inscription dated M.S. 524. But in what capacity shall we place Govindagupta in Daśapura when this country had its own line of rulers represented by Naravarmā, Viśvavarmā and Bandhuvarmā. Moreover, we find that Naravarmā was ruling in M.S. 461 i.e. A.D. 404. He was thus a contemporary of Chandragupta II. But we do not find any reference to a

Gupta governor of Daśapura in his time. We get our next glimpse of Daśapura in the Gaṅgadhāra stone inscription of Viśvavarmā, dated M. S. 480 i.e. A.D. 423, which date falls during the rule of Kumāragupta I. Here again we do not get any indication of a governor appointed by Kumāragupta I. Thus during three generations of the Varman rule over Daśapura, there is not the slightest indication of any governor appointed by the Gupta sovereign power. Therefore, the conclusion is irresistible that Govindagupta has been given a place in the Mandasor inscription of the M.S. 524 like that of his father Chandragupta II, because Prabhākara the ruler of Daśapura regarded him as the sovereign who enjoyed imperial jurisdiction over Daśapura.[12]

Govindagupta enjoyed a very short reign between G.S. 93 and G.S. 96 or A.D. 412-13 and A.D. 415-16, and this probably accounts for the absence of his coins. Much emphasis is laid by some scholars on the use of the expression *tatpād=ānudhyāta* with the name of Kumāragupta I with reference to his father Chandragupta II. It has been argued on this score that Kumāragupta I must be regarded as the immediate successor of his father Chandragupta II.[13] But that is certainly not the implication of this expression. For example, we know that the immediate successor of Kumāragupta I was his valiant son Skandagupta, and yet in the Bhitari seal of Kumāragupta III the expression *tat-pād=ānudhyāta* has been applied to Purugupta, another son of Kumāragupta I, who surely came after and not before Skandagupta.[14] It is, therefore, idle to argue that the use of this word is a clear indication of Kumāragupta I having been the immediate successor of his father.

It may therefore be concluded that the evidence of the Mandasor inscription dated Mālava year 524 definitely points out that Govindagupta, son of Chandragupta II, was an imperial Gupta ruler to whom a large number of kings paid homage; and whose armies under the command of his general, wiped out all opposing armies. We are unable to agree with the recent suggestion of D. R. Bhandarkar,[15] that Govindagupta was another name of Kumāragupta I. The Mandasor inscription mentions only one name to the exclusion of the other. The inscription of the

Guild of silk-weavers mentions only Kumāragupta I as ruling over the earth bounded by four oceans, while that of Dattabhaṭa dated M.S. 524 mentions Govindagupta only as an illustrious ruler of great might.

References

1. *ASI. AR*, 1903-04, 107. The suggestion of Bloch that Govindagupta of this sealing may be identified with Kṛishṇagupta of the Aphsad inscription is untenable for the simple reason that there is an interval of a century and a half between the two.
2. *ASI. AR*, 1903-04, 103ff.
3. *Ibid.*, 108, No. 12.
4. *IA*, XLI (1912), 3.
5. *Kāvyālaṅkārasūtrāvṛitti.*
6. *SGH*, 60.
7. This was announced by M.B. Garde, Director of Archaeology of the then Gwalior State. See *ASI. AR*, 1922-23, 187.
8. Garde, M B., *EI*, XXVII, 12ff.
9. *Cf. Tasminnṛipair=astamita-pratāpaiśśirobhirāliṅgita-pādapadme |*
vichāradolāṁ vibudhādhipo=pi śaṅkāparītaḥ samupārūroha ||
EI, XXVII, 12.
10. Agrawal, Jagannath, *IHQ*, XXII, 286ff.; and *Bhārata Kaumudī*, II 1083-88; PAIOC, 1968.
11. *IHQ*, XXIV, 72.
12. *Cf. PIHC*, 1960, 50ff.
13. *Cf. Mahārājādhirāja śrī Chandraguptastasya putrastatpādānudhyāto mahādevyāṁ Dhruvadevyāmutpanno mahārājādhirāja śrī Kumāraguptaḥ.*
14. Bhitari seal of Kumāragupta III, Chhabra & Gai (ed.), *CII*, III, (1981), 359-60.
15. *Ibid.*, 72-73.

CHAPTER X

THE EMPIRE AT ITS ZENITH—KUMĀRAGUPTA I

KUMĀRAGUPTA I, the second son of Chandragupta II Vikramāditya, born of *Mahādevī* Dhruvasvāminī, inherited the empire when it was at the zenith of its glory. The first known date of his reign as recorded in the Bilsad stone pillar inscription[1] is the G.E. 96 i.e. A.D. 415-16. His last known date is 135 which is found on his silver coins.[2] The first known date of his son and successor Skandagupta as recorded in the Junagadh Rock inscription is G.S. 136 i.e. A.D. 455.[3] Thus Kumāragupta may be said to have enjoyed a long reign of forty years from A.D. 415 to A.D. 455.

R.D. Banerji has rightly said about Kumāragupta, that, "His long reign of over forty years was by far the most prosperous period in the total rule of the Gupta dynasty. The impetus received by the Western overseas trade and influx of foreign gold into the country manifested itself in a great revival of art. It was in this reign that Gupta architecture and sculpture received its final form. The influence of art is also to be distinctly seen in the coins of the ruling emperor, which are the finest of the entire series."[4] We have ample evidence to establish the validity of the above statement. Fifteen inscriptions of his time are available, which record construction of religious monuments, donations and religious and charitable grants.[5] Such things are possible only in the time of peace and plenty. Only a strong administration could have kept the vast empire so thoroughly intact.[6] His copious coinage is available in gold, silver and copper. Of the gold coins as many as fourteen types have been found, and each type has different varieties. No other Gupta ruler before or after him issued so many types of coins and in so pure gold. Some of his coins like the Peacock type are unanimously considered as the finest specimens of art in the field of numismatics. Equally prolific were his issues in silver currency, in numbers as well as types, found not only in the Western provinces but also in the Gangetic valley. All this clearly indicates that the empire had reached its climax in the field of economic prosperity as well as in art.

Kumāragupta I inherited a vast empire from his predecessors which stretched from Bengal in the east to Gujarat and Kathiawar in the west and from the Himalayas in the north upto the Narmadā in the south. He governed it well and proved to be a very strong administrator. There was peace and prosperity throughout his extensive realm. The Mandasor inscription dated M.S. 493, beautifully depicts this happy state of affairs.[7] We are told that Kumāragupta was ruling over a dominion bound by the four oceans, and possessing mountains having lofty peaks such as Kailāśa and Sumerū. This land of abundance and plenty with exuberance of produce of farms and gardens, looked like a lady radiant with smiles. He was sagacious in the selection of his governors and viceroys for the different provinces from amongst the princes of the blood-royal, ministers and officers, as is evidenced by several inscriptions. Damodarpur copper plate inscriptions dated 124 and 128 inform us that the governor (*uparika*) appointed by Kumāragupta himself was governing the province of Puṇḍravardhana, the modern Rajshahi division of Bangladesh.[8] Ghaṭotkachagupta, a prince of royal blood, probably a son of the emperor himself, was the viceroy of Eastern Mālava as is known from the Tumain fragmentary inscription.[9] The region around Daśapura—modern Mandasor in Madhya Pradesh was ruled by Bandhuvarmā, a feudatory of Kumāragupta I.[10] The Baigram copper plate inscription tells us that the *Kumārāmātya* Kulavṛiddhi was administering the district of Pañchanagarī, modern Panchili in the Bogra district of Bangladesh.[11]

These administrative measures ensured the stability and integration of the empire and were conducive to the preservation of internal peace and order. Kumāragupta assumed the title Mahendrāditya and it is profusely used on his coins in a variety of combinations such as *Siṁha-mahendraḥ* on archer and lion-slayer types, *Ajitamahendraḥ* on horseman type, *Mahendra-gajaḥ* on elephant rider type, *Mahendra-khaḍgaḥ* on Rhinoceros type, *Aśvamedha-mahendraḥ* on Aśvamedha type, *Mahendra-kumāraḥ* on Kārtikeya type, and simple *Śrī-mahendrāditya* on Chhatra and Garuḍa types.

The Performance of the Aśvamedha

Although it is not definitely known that Kumāragupta achieved any new military conquests but his gold coins with the legend *Aśvamedha-mahendraḥ* and the portrait of the sacrificial horse do prove that Kumāragupta did perform a horse sacrifice, the time honoured rite symbolic of universal sovereignty. Perhaps there was sufficient justification for the performance of this celebrated rite in ensuring the peace and prosperity of the extensive empire and protecting it well. The sense of pride born of this achievement is beautifully reflected in a statement of the Tumain inscription which expresses the popular feeling of contentment, as follows:

Śri-Chandraguptasya Mahendrakalpaḥ,
Kumāraguptas = tanayas = samagrām
raraksha sādhvīm = iva dharmma-patnīm
vīryy-āgra-hastair = upaguhya bhūmīm //[12]

"The son of the illustrious Chandragupta, (namely) Kumāragupta, who is almost equal to Indra, has protected this earth having held her with the fore-hand of his valour, like a noble spouse held in a firm embrace."

Apart from this, Kumāragupta does appear to have extended the boundaries of the imperial influence. In the Mandasor inscription of Naravarman dated M.S. 461 i.e. A.D. 404, there is no mention of the Gupta ruler as a sovereign. So also in the Gangdhar inscription of Viśvavarman dated M.S. 480 i.e. A.D. 423 any reference to a Gupta over-lord is absent. But in the year 493 i.e. A.D. 436 when the Varman ruler Bandhuvarmā was ruling over Daśapura, we find a specific mention of the Gupta sovereign Kumāragupta in the Mandasor inscription of the Guild of Silk-weavers. This shows that Kumāragupta had extended the Gupta suzerainty over the region of Daśapura.

The Supposed Setback and the Invasion of the Kaṅkas

The use of simple title Mahārāja for Kumāragupta I in the Mankuwar image inscription dated 129,[13] has given rise to the view that the last days of his rule were troublesome and there was definitely a deterioration in the status and prestige of Kumāragupta I. Though Fleet had struck a note of caution and remarked that "the use of the subordinate title may perhaps be due to carelessness or ignorance on the part of the drafter of the inscription", his alternative suggestion that, "possibly it may indicate an actual historical fact, the reduction of Kumāragupta, towards the end of his life, to feudal rank by the Pushyamitras and the Hūṇas, whose attacks on the Gupta power are so pointedly alluded to in the Bhitari inscription of Skandagupta,"[14] has found greater favour with some of the later writers. Buddha Prakash[15] has put forward the theory that the inferior title of *mahārāja* has been used for Kumāragupta because he had lost power and prestige owing to his defeat at the hands of a section of the Kushāṇas—the Kidārites. He says that the son and successor of Kidāra was called Kuṅgkas, and sees in the latter the original of the Kaṅka mentioned in the *Bhāgavata Purāṇa*[16] and in an introductory verse of Subandhu's *Vāsavadattā*.

As for Fleet's suggestion, he himself has remarked that the use of the title *mahārāja* may be due to the writer's mistake. We have already noted above that the use of a title, higher or lower, in private records is no sure indication about the status of a ruler in all cases. The Mankuwar inscription is not an official record. This is a private record which mentions the installation of a statue of the Buddha by a monk in the year 129 in the reign of Kumāragupta. We should not expect a monk to be meticulous in the use of the political phraseology, when mentioning the name of the ruling king. Even the officials of the mint of Samudragupta have given him the simple title of Rājā on the tiger-slayer type of his gold coins.[17] How can we expect a greater accuracy from an ascetic while recording a religious or pious act? It may also be noted that the name of Kumāragupta I is mentioned with full imperial titles in the Damodarpur copper plate inscription dated G.S. 128,[18] almost close in time to the Mankuwar image inscription. The absence of inscriptions of Kumāragupta's reign after the year 129 is also sometimes cited as evidence of such a setback. We must remember that we have his silver coins dated 135, with the legend *vijitāvanir=avanipati Kumāragupto divaṁ jayati* (the lord of the earth having conquered the world wins heaven). No inscription of Chandragupta II is available between the years 61 and 82. Does that mean that there was a setback in his rule during this time? Another argument given in support of the supposed foreign invasion is the existence of some silver-plated copper coins of Kumāragupta I.[19] It has been argued that the foreign invasions had put a heavy strain on the royal treasury and to overcome this shortage silver-plated copper currency was issued. However, side by side with silver-plated copper coins we find the coins of pure silver also being minted upto A.D. 454, the last definite date of his reign. We may also note that the silver-plated copper coins are of very crude manufacture and are evidently forgeries.[20]

We may now examine Buddha Prakash's theory in some detail. He maintains that there was an alliance between the Kushāṇas and the Sassanians and to maintain the balance of power Kumāragupta I was anxious to enter into an alliance with the Chinese. Consequently he sent an embassy to the Chinese court in A.D. 428. He further says that there was a pressure of the Hūṇas which led to westward movement of the various peoples in Central Asia. One of these people were the K'ang-kiu or the Kaṅkas of Sanskrit literature.[21] As a result of these, Kidāra invaded Gandhāra and defeated Kushāṇas of that region and occupied that area in the first half of the fifth century A.D. He had a son named Kuṅgkas, who along with the Persians and Kaṅkas invaded the Gupta empire sometimes between A.D. 451 and 455. This happened simultaneously with the rebellion of the Pushyamitras. The learned scholar has marshalled facts from the Chinese, Persian and Indian sources, none of which, however, can prove his contention. So far as the embassy to China is concerned, it was sent by a king of Assam in the Kapili valley and not by Kumāragupta I.[22] Buddha Prakash does not mention the source where Kuṅgkas is mentioned as the son of Kidāra. From the numismatic evidence discussed by Martin we know that Kidāra and his two successors Piro and Varahran should be referred to the latter half of the fourth century A.D.[23] The rule of Kidāra Kushāṇas came to an end in c. A.D. 400 due to the Hūṇa occupation of this area. Therefore the question of a son of Kidāra named Ku-ṅgkas being a contemporary of Kumāragupta I does not at all arise. Kaṅkas are no doubt mentioned in Sanskrit literature but these statements are vague and do not give us an exact idea of their rule and their time. They are grouped with various foreign tribes. There is no reliable evidence to show that there was any Kushāṇa, Kaṅka or Persian invasion of India during the reign of Kumāragupta I.

Relations with the Vākāṭakas

We have noted above that a daughter of Chandragupta II Vikramāditya was married to Mahārāja Rudrasena II of the Vākāṭaka dynasty. The amicable relations between the two royal houses established through this matrimonial alliance must have proved conducive to the enhancement of the power and prestige of both. We find that Prabhāvatīguptā proudly records her descent from the Gupta lineage in both of her copper plate grants discovered from Poona and Riddhapur. While the Poona copper plate was issued when Prabhāvatī was acting as the regent on behalf of her son, *Yuvarāja* Divākarasena, she issued the Riddhapur copper plate in the nineteenth year of the reign of her son Pravarasena II. Even in his Pattan copper plates dated in his regnal year 27,[24] Pravarasena refers to his maternal-grandfather Chandragupta II, of course under the name *Mahārājādhirāja* Devagupta which seems to have been more familiar to the officers of the Vākāṭaka court.

Some recent writers have formulated the view that Kumāragupta I invaded the Deccan and came into clash with the Vākāṭakas.[25] What was only a casual remark of Hemachandra Raychaudhuri has been developed by S.R. Goyal into an established fact. Raychaudhuri had observed, "the assumption of the title *Vyāghra-bala-prākrama* 'displaying the strength and prowess of a tiger' on coins of the tiger-slayer type by Kumāra may possibly indicate that he attempted to repeat the southern venture of his grandfather and penetrated into the tiger infested forest territory beyond the Nerbudda. Expansion towards the South is also indicated by a find of 1395 coins in the Satara District. But the imperial troops must have met with a disaster."[26] Goyal has taken this statement to prove his theory of Vākāṭaka-Gupta conflict towards the end of Kumāragupta's reign. But he is mistaken at the very start of his argument, when he says that "according to the Vākāṭaka records Narendrasena had to regain the fortunes of his family."[27] We have no inscriptions of the reign of Narendrasena himself; but we do have two copper plate grants of his son Pṛithivīsheṇa II—the Balaghat plates and the Mahurjhari plates. In both of them there is no mention what so ever that he "regained the fortunes of his family." The expression *nimgna-vaṁśoddhar-tuḥ* (of him who had raised up the sunken family) has been applied to Pṛithivīsheṇa II and not to Narendrasena who has been extolled as one whose commands were honoured by the rulers of Kośala, Mekala and Mālava. In the light of this evidence we can only say that for sometime Narendrasena ruled in glory and even extended his sphere of influence, but later on he himself met with a disaster and died soon after that. The fortunes of the Vākāṭaka family had therefore to be retrieved by Narendrasena's son and successor Pṛithivīsheṇa II, whose records give him this credit. Thus it is evident that far from retrieving the fortunes of his family and avenging the defeat at the hands of the Nalas, Narendrasena left the Vākāṭaka kingdom in a very sad plight—obviously due to the attack of the Nala king Bhavadattavarman who occupied the Vākāṭaka capital Nandivardhana in the modern Nagpur District of Maharashtra. It was left to Narendrasena's son Pṛithivīsheṇa to restore the fallen fortunes of the Vākāṭakas not only by expelling the Nalas from the Vākāṭaka territories but also carrying the war to the home of the Nalas. As stated in the Podagadh inscription[28] the Nala capital named Pushkarī was devastated by an unnamed enemy who can only be Pṛithivīsheṇa II. Therefore the invasion of the Vākāṭaka territories by Bhavadattavarman and his occupation of Nandivardhana as well as subsequent rallying of the Vākāṭaka forces under Pṛithivīsheṇa were purely a Nala-Vākāṭaka clash and the Guptas had nothing to do with it.

Goyal has gone still further by postulating a Gupta-Nala alliance between Kumāragupta and Bhavadattavarman, whose visit to Prayāga—the sacred place of pilgrimage for all Hindus, as mentioned in his Riddhapur copper plate, is taken by Goyal as a proof of the Gupta-Nala *entente cordiale*. This view is entirely untenable. Firstly, as explained above the Nala-Vākāṭaka clash took place most probably during the last days of Narendrasena's rule (A.D. 450-470)[29] or the early years of Pṛithivīsheṇa's rule. Therefore Kumāragupta I whose rule definitely came to an end in A.D. 454 can never be regarded as living when the Nala ruler attacked the Vākāṭaka kingdom. Secondly, the Riddhapur copper plate does not seem to refer to a marriage of Bhavadattavarman celebrated at Prayāga. The wording in the copper plate is—*asmābhih .....Prayāga-sthitair= udaka-pūrvvakaṁ mama chāchapi* (*chāpi*) *bhaṭṭārikāyāś=cha dāṁpatyasy = āsmākam = anugrah-ārtthaṁ ... dattā.*[30] It simply means that "We have gifted (some land or village) for procuring blessings for mine as well as the queen's relationship as husband and wife". We know that it is the accepted Hindu practice that all pious acts performed by the husband are shared by the wlfe. In the light of this convention the reference to *dāmpatya* should be taken to refer to the already existing marriage and not to a newly contracted one as supposed by Goyal. In the case of a newly contracted marriage, a different phraseology such as *pariṇaya* would have been used; and in case the king Bhavadattavarman had married a Gupta princess, or a lady from amongst the Gupta nobility, the fact would have been eloquently described with a sense of pride. The gift of land made at the holy junction of the Ganges and Yamunā was just a pious act for the religious merit of the royal couple, and there is no room for the inference that a new marriage was contracted. As a matter of fact there is no evidence of a Gupta-Nala alliance against the Vākāṭakas during the reign of Kumāragupta I, which had ended in A.D. 454. The invasion of the Vākāṭaka dominions by Bhavadattavarman must have taken place late in the reign of Narendrasena who came to the throne in c. A.D. 450 according to V.V. Mirashi and A.D. 480 according to R. C. Majumdar. The fact that Pṛithivīsheṇa II had to restore the sunken fortunes of his dynasty shows that the Nala invasion of the Vākāṭaka dominions took place very late in the reign of Narendrasena.

We must also take note of Mirashi's view based on the Indore copper plate of Pravarasena II.[31] The first plate of this grant shows that it was issued from Tripuri when Pravarasena II was in residence there. From the mention of Tripurī, modern Tewar, six miles from Jabalpur, Mirashi has concluded that the Vākāṭakas under Pravarasena II pushed across the Narmada towards the north, and wrested some territory from the Guptas who were the 'Lords of the North' at this time. Mirashi has further stated that in the battle with the Vākāṭakas, Skandagupta had the command of the Gupta armies and was at one occasion so hard pressed that he had to pass a whole night on bare earth, as is expressly stated in the Bhitari stone pillar inscription.[32] In our opinion such a conclusion is hardly warranted by the evidence at our disposal. Firstly it is not definitely known that the region of the present day Jabalpur District was in the possession of the imperial Guptas in the reign of Kumāragupta I. At a much later date we find a copper plate grant of an Uchchakalpa king Jayanātha dated in the year 174 (A.D. 493) from Karitalai in the Murwara Tehsil of the Jabalpur District. Had Pravarasena conquered it from the Guptas as postulated by Mirashi, he would not have passed it into the hands of the Uchchakalpas. Further it is almost impossible to concede that verse 4 of the Bhitari stone pillar inscription at all refers to a conflict between the imperial Guptas and the Vākāṭakas. In this verse we are told that the battle during the course of which Skandagupta was forced to sleep on bare earth, was fought when Skandagupta was up in arms in order to make firm the tottering sovereignty of his dynasty. Such a crisis could have been created by a terrible invasion like that of the Hūṇas to which specific reference has been made further on in this very record. Even the war with the Pushyamitras was only an additional factor as is clearly indicated by the presence of the conjunct 'and' immediately before the word Pushyamitras. That any sanguine battle between the Vākāṭakas and the Gupta forces under Skandagupta, of which there is no mention elsewhere, took place, is most unlikely. At best it could have been a minor campaign against the Uchchakalpa kings whom we find owing allegiance to the Vākāṭakas as mentioned in their Ganj and Nachna-ki-talai stone inscriptions. That Pravarasena II was accustomed to touring, is apparent from his Tirodi grant which was issued from Naratangavari station, and the Wadegaon grant which was made from his camp at Hiraṇyā-nadī.

We may finally conclude that Kumāragupta I died leaving the empire intact. Neither did he meet with any military reverses during his life-time, nor were there any invasions or internal rebellions so long as he occupied the throne.

It has been argued on the basis of his Apratigha type of gold coins[33] that Kumāragupta I abdicated the throne in favour of one of his sons. The stories contained in the *Kathāsaritasāgara* and the *Chandragarbhaparipichchhā* have been cited in support of this theory. According to the *Kathāsaritasāgarā*, Vikramāditya, the valiant son of Mahendrāditya defeated the Mlechchhas. After this, Mahendra satisfied with the attainments of his son decided to relinquish the reins of authority and retired along with his queen to Vārānasī. No doubt these references go to support this theory but there are certain points which remain unexplained. Firstly, the scene portrayed on the *Apratigha* type of coins has not been satisfactorily explained as yet nor the circular legend has been completely deciphered. If we accept the theory of Kumāragupta's abdication, the question arises as to who issued these coins? It could not have been Kumāragupta as he must have lost all imperial rights to issue any state currency as soon as he renounced the throne. If we regard them as commemorative medals it may be asked, was the event worth commemorating? Moreover, the name of the commemorator should have been there on these coins. The story contained in the works mentioned above may be regarded as a vague reminiscence of Gupta history but cannot be acceped as actual historical fact. No attention has been given to the weight standard of these coins so far. They weigh between 120 and 123 grains, which is the lowest in the series of Kumāragupta's gold coins except for a few specimens of Archer type. Considering the fact that there was a gradual increase in the weight of Gupta gold coins till the time of Skandagupta, the *Apraigha* type of coins have to be the earliest issues of Kumāragupta I. This knocks out the very bottom of the theory of abdication, and it may be safely assumed that Kumāragupta died peacefully as an old man after a rule of four decades leaving the throne to his valiant son Skandagupta.

APPENDIX I

THE PROBLEM OF SUCCESSION AFTER THE DEATH OF KUMĀRAGUPTA I

Until A.D. 1889, Skandagupta was the only son of Kumāragupta I, known from the inscriptions and coins, who succeeded to the throne immediately after the death of his father. However, the discovery of the Bhitari silver-copper seal of Kumāragupta III,[34] a great-grandson of Kumāragupta I brought to light the name of another son of Kumāragupta I, born of his chief queen Anantadevī, namely Purugupta. As Purugupta had been given the title of *mahārājādhirāja* in this seal from Bhitari, it was obvious that he had enjoyed the imperial rule for some time. The Bhitari seal supplied two more names, that of Purugupta's son Narasiṁhagupta and the latter's son Kumāragupta, all of whom are given the title of *mahārājādhirāja* and their gold coins have also been found. This new information has given rise to a lot of speculation regarding the nature and order of succession after Kumāragupta I. Hoernle was inclined to regard Skandagupta and Purugupta as the two names of one and the same king. He even suggested that Skandagupta took the name Puragupta,[35] "later in his reign in allusion to the resistance of his fortresses to the Hūṇas."[36] However, Hoernle's view can be easily set aside. Firstly, now we know that the correct form of the name of Kumāragupta I's son in the Bhitari seal is Purugupta and not Puragupta. Therefore Hoernle's explanation 'protected by forts' is no longer valid. Secondly in all the five known inscriptions of Skandagupta, there is nowhere even a hint that he had another name also. Further all the known gold coins of Skandagupta bear this name alone. It has been very aptly pointed out by B.P. Sinha that we cannot have two names of the same king in the official records, as it would lead to utter confusion in the administration.[37]

Allan's view that the imperial Gupta line bifurcated after Kumāragupta I, though now quite obsolete may be briefly noticed, as this has also been taken by some later writers. Allan observed, "Their existence suggests that in Skandagupta's reign his brother Purugupta revolted, perhaps taking advantage of his brother's absence in the West and was able to establish a dynasty of his own. Purugupta's line is known from the Bhitari seal, so that these three (Prakāśāditya, Chandragupta III and Ghaṭotkachagupta) probably represent Skandagupta's line; it may at least be considered certain that towards the end of the fifth century, the Gupta line became divided in the inevitable Oriental fashion."[38] However, the fresh discoveries of inscriptions and new interpretations of legends on coins, considered by Allan, have made his view absolutely untenable. The discoveries of the Sarnath Buddha image inscriptions of Kumāragupta dated G. E. 154 and of Budhagupta dated G. E. 157, of the Damodarpur copper plate of Budhagupta dated G. E. 163, the Varanasi pillar inscription dated 159 and the Nalanda clay sealing of Budhagupta now clearly establish that Purugupta who has to be placed immediately after A.D. 467 was succeeded by Kumāragupta II in A.D. 473 who in his turn was followed by Budhagupta in A.D. 476 who ruled atleast up to A.D. 495 over the whole of Northern India from Eastern Malva to Northern Bengal. There can therefore be no place for a second Gupta dynasty in Northern India itself. The issue is finally decided by the evidence of the Nalanda clay sealing according to which Budhagupta is a son of Purugupta. Therefore it is absolutely certain that there was no divisions of the empire after the death of Kumāragupta I and all the kings from Skandagupta to Budhagupta ruled over the whole of the Gupta empire.

As if to butteress his theory of the split in the royal house Allan had suggested that Prakāśāditya, Chandragupta III and Ghaṭotkachagupta probably represented the line of Skandagupta.[39] This view loses all validity when examined in the light of the latest researches. Chandragupta III who was believed to exist only on the basis of gold coins assigned to him by Allan[40] vanishes into thin air as these coins have been now proved to belong to Vainyagupta.[41] As regards Ghaṭotkachagupta, the Tumain inscription dated 116 G.E. shows that he was already a governor of Eastern Mālava during the rule of Kumāragupta I in A.D. 435. In all probability he was a son of Kumāragupta I and cannot be taken to represent the line of Skandagupta. Prakāśāditya was identified with Purugupta by Hoernle[42] and

Smith[43]. Allan however doubted this identification, for he had assigned the heavy weight coins to Puruguta which he had read as Pura, with the title Vikramāditya. He argued that one king cannot be given two different titles—Vikramāditya and Prakāśāditya. However, now that the coins assigned to Purugupta by Allan have been shown to be really the issues of Budhagupta, the title Vikramāditya has to be referred to the latter and we are again left with the coins having no name but only the title Prakāśāditya. The opinion is now again veering round to the original view of Hoernle and Smith, and Prakāśāditya is believed to be a title of Purugupta, though tentatively.[44] Thus we again find that there is no evidence at all on the basis of which we may agree with Allan in regarding Prakāśāditya as a lineal descendant of Skandagupta. This discussion leaves no room for Allan's theory of the partition of the Gupta empire between Skandagupta and Purugupta. This also disposes of the theory of R.G. Basak.[45]

The most crucial point in this question of succession is R. C. Majumdar's view that there was a fratricidal war for the throne between Skandagupta and his brothers or half-brothers.[46] He pointed out that there is no mention of the name of Skandagupta's mother even in the Bhitari pillar inscription of her son, in contrast with those of Chandragupta II and Kumāragupta I, which shows that she was not a *mahādevī*; and as such her son Skandagupta had no legal claim to the throne which he must have obtained by force. Majumdar then furnishes evidence from the Bhitari stone pillar and the Girnar rock inscriptions pointing to such a conflict. Accepting the reading *yudhy=amitrān* in preference to *Pushyamitrān* in verse 4 of the Bhitari inscription he concluded as follows: "This would mean that the enemies whom Skandagupta defeated are not specifically named and only referred to in general terms. If we proceed on this assumption we may reasonably hold that calamity was brought about by a disputed succession leading to a civil war." He further pointed out that, "Verse 3 of the Junagadh inscription tells us that after his father had died Skandagupta made himself the ruler of this earth by his own prowess."[47] Finally he has referred to verse 5 of the same record which says that Skandagupta was chosen by Lakshmī (the goddess of sovereignty) of her own accord after rejecting all other sons of kings. This statement, in the opinion of Majumdar, clinches the issue in favour of a war of succession which resulted in Skandagupta's getting the throne. However, all this evidence is open to an altogether different interpretation; but before doing that we may digress a little in order to examine some suggestions which are quite relevant to the present discussion.

Relying on Fleet's text of the last *pāda* of verse 7 of the Bhitari inscription viz. *gītaiś = cha stutibhiś = cha vandaka-jano yaṁ prāpayaty = āryyatām*, which had been translated by Fleet as "whom the bards raise to distinction with their songs and praises."[48] A. L. Basham has remarked that Skandagupta's mother was "an humble Śūdrā concubine."[49] Similarly P. L. Gupta has also come to the conclusion that the omission of the name of Skandagupta's mother is not accidental but deliberate, showing thereby that he was shy of mentioning his mother's name and did not feel pride in claiming to be her son, for she was neither an *agra-mahishī* nor even a *mahishī*.[50] Both these scholars have been led astray by Fleet's faulty reading of the text of the inscription. Jagannath Agrawal had pointed long ago that this line should be read as *gītaiś = cha stutibhiś = cha vṛitta-kathane yaṁ hrepayaty = āryyatā* which he translated as, "whom his (innate) nobility causes to blush at the recounting of his exploits by means of songs and panegyrics".[51] With the correct text of the Bhitari inscription placed before us by Agrawal there remains no ground whatever for regarding Skandagupta's mother as 'humble Śūdrā concubine'. It is really surprising that these scholars have completely ignored the fact that no court poet could ever, even remotely introduce into the *praśasti* of his patron a remark so derogatory which may cast an aspersion on the mother of the emperor himself.[52] P. L. Gupta is entirely mistaken to imagine that Skandagupta felt shy to make mention of his mother. Quite contrary to this, we actually find a statement in verse 4 of the Bhitari inscription itself that after defeating his enemies, Skandagupta betook himself to his mother and broke the news of his victory to her.[53]

Let us now examine the arguments of R. C. Majumdar. As regards the omission of Skandagupta's mother's name from the genealogical portion of the Bhitari pillar inscription, it has been pointed out by Hemchandra Raychaudhuri that "there is no rule prohibiting the mention of ordinary queens in inscriptions."[54]

Even the names of non-*mahādevīs* are sometimes mentioned as in the case of Kuberanāgā, a junior queen of Chandragupta II and the mother of Prabhāvatīguptā, the Vākāṭaka queen. Her name finds mention in the Riddhapur copper plate grant as well as the Poona copper plate grant of Prabhāvatīguptā. We actually come across appreciable discrepancies in recording the genealogy of one and the same royal house in two different records. For example in the Madhuban and Banskhera copper plate grants of Harshavardhana, the name of Yaśomatī is given as the mother of Rājyavardhana, but it is left out in the case of Harsha who is simply mentioned as the younger brother (*anuja*) of Rājyavardhana. It is still more noteworthy that in both of these copper plate grants as well as in the Nalanda clay sealing of Harsha, when Yaśomatī is mentioned as the mother of Rājyavardhana she is simply styled as *Devi* whose fame was pure;[55] but when she is mentioned as the mother of Harsha, she is styled as *Parambhaṭṭārikā Mahādevī.*[56] The same queen during the same period of the rule of her son Harshavardhana has been mentioned with two different titles—one inferior and the other superior. Therefore we must make allowances for such discrepancies, and should not conclude that Skandagupta's mother was not a *mahādevī* simply because her name does not figure in the Bhitari pillar inscription.[57]

Both the Bhitari stone pillar and the Girnar rock inscriptions provide no evidence of a "disputed succession leading to civil war". Majumdar thinks that the enemies by whom the royal fortune of the Gupta dynasty was placed in a perilous situation were Skandagupta's brothers and he finds evidence for this in the mention of *amitras* (according to Divakar's reading) in verse 4 of the Bhitari inscription. However, a little careful scrutiny of this verse will make it clear that there is absolutely no such indication. The last line of this verse informs us that Skandagupta placed his left-foot on the the foot-stool that were the kings. The use of the word *kshitipa* here, is significant. His rivals could not be called kings, for as yet they were contesting for the throne and had not become kings. Moreover, with the reading Pushyamitras, which is more probable, we get a clear cut idea of the peril that faced Skandagupta after the death of his father. The Pushyamitras are described as a power which had built up a strong army and an ample treasury.

Majumdar finds further support to his view of a disputed succession in verses 3 and 5 of the Girnar rock inscriptions of Skandagupta.[58] Verse 3 says that Skandagupta brought under his control the empire extending upto the four oceans by his own strength after his father had died; and in verse 5 we are informed that the goddess of fortune chose Skandagupta of her own accord after rejecting all other princes. It is indeed true that Skandagupta brought the whole of the empire under his control by his own prowess, but the enemies over whom Skandagupta triumphed were not his own kith and kin but powerful outsiders. In the Girnar rock inscription itself, we are told in the very first verse after the salutation to Vishṇu, that Skandagupta put down with a strong hand those kings who had raised their heads in pride and arrogance.[59] Here the inscription mentions the defeated opponents as full-fledged kings and not mere princes of the blood-royal who were contending for the throne and were yet to become kings. These kings were evidently enimical outsiders. There is a still more important indication of the formidable enemy who posed a grave threat to the security of the Gupta empire. They were the Hūṇas who are mentioned in verse 8 of the Bhitari inscription and are referred to as Mlechchhas in the Girnar rock inscription. The gravity of the danger from this enemy can be very well appreciated when we remember that about the same time the Hūṇas brought about the downfall of the Sassanian power in Persia and worked havoc in the Roman empire. The war with Skandagupta was equally terrible as the poet who composed the Bhitari inscription tells us that "the earth was shaken when Skandagupta confronted the Hūṇas in battle."[60] Thus we clearly see that the danger which threatened the stability of the Gupta empire emanated from the rebellious kings within India and the barbarian invaders from outside.

As regards the statement in the Girnar rock inscription that the goddess of fortune selected Skandagupta of her own voluntary choice it is merely a poetic way of depicting the hero's outstanding merit. In a *svayaṁvara*, 'the ceremony for the selection of the husband by a princess herself', a princess has the full freedom to choose a bridegroom for herself, and naturally she chooses the most talented according to her judgment. In the Girnar rock inscription we are told that Lakshmī (the goddess of Fortune) chose Skandagupta out of many princes (*manujendra-putras*) who were not necessarily the sons of Kumāragupta. We have almost a parallel statement in the Eran pillar inscription dated 165 of the reign of Budhagupta, and also in the Eran stone Boar inscription of the reign of Toramāṇa, even with respect to a mere District Officer (*vishayapati*) Matṛivishṇu, who is said to have been "secured by the Royal Fortune like a maiden choosing her husband of her own accord."[61] Therefore the verse from the Girnar rock inscription too does not refer to any conflict for the throne. We may therefore conclude that Skandagupta ascended the throne after the death of his father "*pitari divam=upete*" in the natural course and had not to fight his way to it. He is described in the Bhitari and Girnar inscriptions as the abode of royal virtues (*nṛipati-guṇa-niketaḥ*) and the sole hero of the Gupta dynasty (*Gupta-vaṁś=āika-vīraḥ*). As such it was but natural that he should occupy the throne and inherit the empire.[62]

References

1. Chhabra & Gai (ed.), *CII*, III, (1981), 267ff.
2. V.A. Smith has read the date 136 on one silver coin. *EHI*[4], 346. The last date on his coins read by A.S. Altekar is 135. *Coinage*, 230-31. According to A.L. Basham the whereabouts of Smith's coin are unknown and it is difficult to rely on such evidence. cf. *BSOAS*, XVII, 367.
3. *Op. cit.*, 299.
4. *AIG*, 36-37.
5. For details see supra, Chapter I.
6. *CA*, 24.
7. *Cf. Chatusmudrānta - vilola - mekhalāṁ Sumerū - Kailasa-bṛihat-payo-dharāṁ* /
van-ānta-vānta-sphuṭa-pushpa-hāsinīṁ Kumāragupte pṛithivīṁ praśāsati //
Mandasor Inscription of the year 493 & 529, Chhabra & Gai (ed., 1981), *CII*, III, 326.
8. *EI*, XV, 130 & 133.
9. *IA*, XLIX, 114-15.
10. Chhabra & Gai (ed. 1981), *CII*, III, 323ff.
11. *EI*, XXI, 78.
12. Chhabra & Gai (ed. 1981), *CII*, III, 278.
13. *Ibid.*, 293.
14. Fleet (ed. 1888), *CII*, III, 46.
15. *IHQ*, XXX, 219-36. Also *SIHC*, 374-75.

16. *DKA*, 45, fn. 13.
17. *Coinage*, 71.
18. *EI*, XV, 133ff.
19. *Op. cit.*, 232-33.
20. *Ibid.*
21. *Mahābhārata*, II, 47.26; *Bhāgavata Purāṇa*, *DKA*, 45.
22. *EHI*, 316.
23. *JRASB. L*, III, *N.S.*, XLVII, 23-50.
24. *CII*, V, 60.
25. Goyal, S.R., *HIG*, 256ff.; Sinha, B.P., *DHM*, 11.
26. *PHAI*[5], 570. Curiously enough Goyal further remarks that R.C. Majumdar agrees with it (*HIG*, 257, fn. 2), whereas quite contrary to this Majumdar says," Obviously we cannot draw any definite conclusion from this or the find of 13 coins from Elichpur." *VGA*, 159. Subsequently Majumdar refuted the suggestion even more emphatically. He said, "We should not draw from them any further inference of actual conquest or even military campaign in the Deccan." *CHI*, III, Pt. I, 67.
27. *HIG*, 258.
28. *Cf. EI*, XXI, 153.
29. This is according to V.V. Mirashi's view. R.C. Majumdar places him later still in c. A.D. 480.
30. *EI*, XIX, 102.
31. At first only three plates of the Indore grant were found. The first plate was missing. The available plates were published by S.K. Bose in *EI*, XXIV, 52ff. and subsequently by V.V. Mirashi in *CII*, V, 38ff. Later on Mirashi got the first plate also and wrote an article on its basis and also published the text in his *Indological Research Papers*, I, 65ff.
32. *Cf.* Verse 4, Chhabra & Gai (ed. 1981), *CII*, III, 315.
33. For different views on the *Apratigha* coins see Altekar, A.S., *Coinage*, 207; Hoernle, *JASB*, 1883, 144; Smith, V.A., *JRAS*, 1888, 107; Allan, J. *CCGD*, 87; Mirashi, V.V., *JNSI*, XII, 68; Majumdar, R.C., *JNSI*, XII, 72; Sinha, B.P., *JNSI*, XVI, 210; Sohoni, S.V., *JNSI*, XVIII, 56 and XXIII, 345; Ghosh, A., *JNSI*, XXII, 179; Pandey, V.C., *JIH*, LI, 345 etc.
34. *JASB*, 1889, 84-105.
35. That was the form of name read by Smith and Hoernle. The correct form Purugupta was first pointed out by Jagannath Agrawal in *PIHC*, 1940.
36. Quoted by Allan, *CCGD*, li.
37. The Bhitari Silver-copper seal of Kumāragupta III is an official document.
38. *CCGD*, liv-lv.
39. *Ibid.*
40. *Ibid.*, 144; liii-liv and cxxiii. But Allan was within an ace of the correct name on *B.M.C.* No. 588, as he conceded that the first letter looked like *Va* and the second like *tya*.
41. Ganguli, D.C., *IHQ*, 1934, 195.
42. *JASB*, 1889, 93-94.

43. *IA*, 1902, 263.
44. *Coinage*, 284.
45. *EI*, XV, 118-22; *HNEI*, 78ff.
46. *JASB* (*N.S.*), XVII, 249ff. However, R.C. Majumdar's final view was expressed in the following words," It should be remembered, however, that while this is undoubtedly a probable view, it cannot be regarded as an established fact." *CA*, 26.
47. *CHI*, III, Pt. I, 70.
48. Fleet (ed. 1888), *CII*, III 54 and 56.
49. *BSOAS*, XVII, 368-69.
50. *JIH*, XL, 247.
51. *BV*, IX, 282.
52. Jagannath Agrawal has discussed this question in his paper in the Golden Jubilee Number of the *ABORI*, XLVIII-XLIX, 326.
53. *JIH*, XLIII, 221.
54. *PHAI*, 572f.
55. *Devyām=amala-yaśomatyām*, *EI*, I, 75, line 5 of the text; and *EI*, XXI, 75.
56. *Ibid.*, 76.
57. A probable explanation of these discrepencies has already been offered by Jagannath Agrawal in *ABORI*, XLVIII-XLIX, 326. In the copper-plate grants of Harshavardhana also, the writer on arriving at Rājyavardhana's name departed from the usual pattern of the genealogy and composed a verse eulogising his patron's brother. As a result of this change he missed the usual epithets to be given to Yaśomatī.
58. Cf. verses 3 & 5 of the Junagadh Rock Inscription, Chhabra & Gai (ed. 1981), *CII*, III, 299.
59. *Tad=anu jayati śaśvat śrī-parikshipta-vakshāḥ sva-bhuja-janita-vīryo rāja rājādhirājaḥ |*
 Narapati-bhujagānām māna-darpp=otphaṇānāṁ pratikṛiti-Garuḍā-jñāṁ nirvvishīṁ ch=āvākarttā ||
 Chhabra & Gai (ed. 1981), *CII*, III, 299.
60. *Hūṇair=yasya samāgatasya samare dorbhyāṁ dharā kampitā*, *Ibid.*, 315.
61. Fleet (ed. 1888), *CII*, III, 89 and 160.
62. Prof. Jagannath Agrawal has brought to my notice a Sanskrit saying from Bhāravi meaning that, 'Fortunes which are enamoured of virtues, select a sgacious person of their own free will.'

CHAPTER XI

THE GREATEST HERO OF THE DYNASTY—SKANDAGUPTA

SKANDAGUPTA WHO WAS perhaps the eldest son and the most qualified, ascended the throne after the death of Kumāragupta I, whose last known definite date G.E. 135, is found on his silver coins. The Junagadh rock inscription supplies us the Gupta year 136 when Skandagupta had firmly established his control over the entire Gupta empire after putting down all those enemies who had dared to raise their heads after the death of his father Kumāragupta I. We may therefore place Skandagupta's date of accession to the throne in G.E. 135 or A.D. 454.[1]

Soon after ascending the throne Skandagupta was confronted by a sea of troubles. The Girnar rock inscription tells us that by means of Skandagupta's commands bearing an image of Garuḍa, the heads of hostile kings raised through pride, were bent down, just as the raised up hoods of serpents are bent down at the sight of Garuḍa and their poison is taken out

From the comparison of the rebellious kings with serpents, D.R. Bhandarkar has inferred that these hostile kings belonged to a Nāga family, which was related to Skandagupta's mother.[2] However, a Nāga rebellion at this stage in the Gupta history and that too by his mother's relations is most unlikely. Most of the powerful Nāga kings like Achyutanandi, Nāgasena, Nāgadatta, Gaṇapatināga etc. had been entirely uprooted by Samudragupta, and the kingdoms of Mathura, Padmāvatī, Vidiśā and Ahichhatra had been merged in the Gupta empire. It is not likely that during the strong rule of Chandragupta II Vikramāditya and Kumāragupta Mahendrāditya the Nāgas had again built up a mighty military machine and were able to revolt. It is still more inconceivable that the rebels were Skandagupta's maternal relations, for we do find a specific statement in the Bhitari inscription that Skandagupta conveyed the news of his victory over his enemies to his mother who shed tears of joy at the grand achievement of her son. Surely these foes could not have been the relations of Skandagupta's mother.

The Pushyamitras

The enemies who had posed a serious threat to the Gupta sovereign power, and who were overcome after a very strenuous fight were the Pushymitras, who had built up a strong military power and the resources for a war. At one stage the situation became so grave that Skandagupta had to pass a whole night on bare ground.[3] The *Purāṇas* record thirteen kings of the Pushyamitra dynasty and they have been placed in the third century of the Christian era by Pargiter.[4] Some people doubt the very existence of the Pushyamitras, as they prefer to read *yudhy-amitrān* in place of Fleet's reading *Pushyamitrān*, in the fourth verse of the Bhitari inscription. But the doubt is entirely misplaced as Fleet's reading has been confirmed by a competent authority after a careful examination of the inscription *in situ*.[5] It has also been urged that an obscure power like that of the Pushyamitras could not have dared to clash with the mighty imperial Guptas. We may only point out to the very successful invasion of the Vākāṭaka empire by Bhavadattavarman of the Nala dynasty which was ruling over the tiny kingdom of Pushkarī, in the erstwhile Jeypore state in Koraput District of Orissa. Not only did the Nala king defeat the Vākāṭaka army, but occupied the Vākātaka territory in the heart of Vidarbha and made a grant of land which was issued from the Vākāṭaka capital Nandivardhana.[6] There can be, therefore, no doubt that the Pushyamitras were able at the initial stage to make the struggle so grim even for a heroic warrior like Skandagupta, who ultimately tided over the critical situation and emerged victorious. The success enhanced Skandagupta's prestige still further and we are told in the Bhitari inscription, that the people sang the songs of his glory in every nook and corner of the empire. By these military achievements Skandagupta brought under his firm control the empire which extended up to the shores of the ocean.

The Hūṇa Invasion

Skandagupta had hardly got respite from the arduous fighting with the internal enemies, when he found himself face to face with a far more formidable foe. The Epthalites or Hepthalites, a people of Hunnish race, known to Sanskrit writers as Hūṇas, having occupied Bactria and established their headquarters near Herat in Afghanistan, were moving in waves towards Persia in the west and towards India in the east. They were terrible warriors and we are told by the author of the Bhitari inscription that when Skandagupta clashed with these Hūṇas, even the earth was shaken.[7] However, Skandagupta worked such a havoc in their ranks, that they suffered a crushing defeat and took to flight, carrying with them the tales of Skandagupta's extraordinary prowess.[8] The Indian frontiers were made immune from this menace for another half a century. An echo of Skandagupta's victory over the Hūṇas is perhaps to be found in the Sanskrit collection of stories—the *Kathāsaritasāgara* of Somadeva. In the XVIII section of this work, we are told that Mahendrāditya King of Ujjain sent his son Vikramāditya to fight against the Mlechchhas who were oppressing the world. Vikramāditya defeated the barbarians and returned victorious. His father abdicated the throne and went to Varanasi along with his queen and Vikramāditya ascended the throne. Though the story can not be accepted *in toto* as historical truth, it is plausible to hold that Mahendrāditya and Vikramāditya of the *Kathāsaritasāgara* are really the Gupta monarchs Kumāragupta I and Skandagupta who are known to have adopted these titles. The Mlechchhas of course can be identified with the Hūṇas.

In our account of the Hūṇa war we have held that the Hūṇas of the Bhitari pillar inscription, and the Mlechchhas of the Junagadh rock inscription and the *Kathāsaritasāgara* are one and the same people. However, some scholars have expressed different views. S. Chattopadhyaya considers them to be a mixed horde of Persians, Greeks etc.[9] This is a view which cannot stand a minute's scrutiny. The Persians had more than enough trouble at their hands at this time and were in no way in a position even to think of an invasion of India. The Epthalites were menacingly knocking at their door. Although the Chionites—another section of the Hūṇa people had done a good deal of damage to the northern outposts of the Persian empire in about A.D. 356, the Epthalite advance which began c. A.D. 420 became a real threat to the Sassanian empire and kept it on tantrums—often inflicting crushing defeats such as that suffered by the Sassanian emperor Yazdigird in A.D. 454 and by Firoz in A.D. 480, which ultimately led to thc breaking up and ruin of the Sassanian dynasty. Thus the Persians who had to defend their own home against a relentless foe could never have even enterrained a momentary thought of invading India. As regards the Greeks, little need be said. They were nowhere of any count, either from the point of view of numbers, or of military training qualifying them as mercenaries, not to speak of having any political status. They had lost Bactria to the barbarians centuries ago.

P.L. Gupta's identification of the Mlechchhas with the Kidāra Kushāṇas[10] is equally untenable for the simple reason that the Kidārite Kushāṇas had lost all power before the reign of Skandagupta commenced. Kidāra, after whom the Bactrian Kushāṇas are called Kidārites, established an independent Kushāṇa dynasty in Gandhara in A.D. 367-68, but the attacks of the Epthalites compelled him to move westwards, leaving his son Piro to rule over Gandhara. The Sassanians under Ardashir II (A.D. 379-383) seized some territory from Piro, and Shapur III (A.D. 383-388) achieved a decisive victory over Piro, who now accepted the Sassanian overlordship. After this defeat the Kidārite power declined fast and did not last more than twenty-five years.[11] This clearly shows that the Kidārites could not by any means be the Mlechchhas who fought with Skandagupta. They had probably been themselves swept away by the Epthalites whose occupation of Bactria was complete by A.D. 425.[12] These can be absolutely no doubt that the Mlechchhas of the Junagadh rock inscription have been rightly taken to stand for the Hūṇas of the Bhitari pillar inscription by competent authorites.[13]

There is difference of opinion amongst the scholars regarding the date of the Hūṇa invasion described above. Hoernle placed it in A.D. 465.[14] Chattopadhyaya agrees with him.[15] In the opinion of R.D. Banerji Skandagupta fought a number of times against the Hūṇas, whose first invasion took place in the life-time of Kumāragupta I.[16] The views of Hoernle and Chattopadhyaya can be easily disposed off. We learn from the Junagadh rock inscription that by the year 136 of the Gupta reckoning, Skandagupta had brought the whole earth under his control and that his fame was being spread even in the barbarian lands by the enemies whose pride had been shattered down to its very roots. The Mlechchhas of this inscription are clearly the Hūṇas as has been shown above. As regards R.D. Banerji's view, there is absolutely no evidence of a series of Hūṇa invasions. Quite contrary to it, the epigraphic evidence shows that after Skandagupta's victory over the Hūṇas there was perfect peace and tranquitlity in the empire. In the Kahaum pillar inscription, Skandagupta's rule has been specifically described as *śānta*—all calm and quite. R.C. Majumdar has rightly summed up the whole episode in the following words: "The statement in his inscriptions that he thoroughly defeated them seems to be borne out by the fact that we have no evidence of the Hūṇa depredations east of Gandhara till the close of the fifth or the beginning of the sixth century A.D."[17]

We have nowhere any specific mention of the locality where the battle with the Hūṇas was fought; but there seems to be no justification for the view that the Hūṇas had overrun the Gangetic plain up to Bhitari in the Ghazipur District of Eastern U.P. In the middle of the fifth century the Hūṇas were still carrying on a see-saw struggle against the Sassanians in Persia and their hands were not free for a full scale invasion into the very heart of India. That the fighting took place in Surāshṭra or somewhere very close to it is most likely, as the province of Surāshṭra seems to have given Skandagupta some very anxious moments. We are told in the Junagadh rock inscription that Skandagupta, "having conquered the entire earth and having appointed the heads of administration in all the provinces, had to ponder for days and nights in selecting a proper governor for the province of Surāshṭra.[18] In this context we may refer to the view of Jagannath Agrawal who has suggested that the Hūṇas came by the Bolan Pass,[19] and only this province had become vulnerable. The suggestion gets further support from the fact that the Hūṇas, who were still far away from the Indian frontier, had fixed their headquarters at a place called Badghis, only a little to the north of the modern city of Herat in South-Eastern Afghanistan.[20]

The Relations with the Vākāṭakas with Reference to the Balaghat Inscription of Pṛithivīsheṇa:

A statement contained in the Balaghat copper plate inscription of Pṛithivīsheṇa II,[21] has given rise to an interesting speculation regarding the Gupta-Vākāṭaka relations during Skandagupta's reign. In this grant of Pṛithivīsheṇa II, his father Narendrasena has been described as a ruler, "whose commands were honoured by the lords of Kośala "Mekala and Mālava." On the basis of this statement R.N. Dandekar putforward the theory that there had been some military engagements "between Skandagupta and the Vākāṭakas".[22] He suggested that taking advantage of Skandagupta's troubles during the Pushaymitra and the Hūṇa invasions, Narendrasena attacked the Guptas but suffered a set back due to Skandagupta's success in these wars. He further opined that these hostilities were renewed in the last years of Skandagupta's reign and immediately after his death Narendrasena established his sovereignty in Kośala, Mekala and Mālava, with the help of his valiant son Pṛithivīsheṇa II, who has been described as one who "twice uplifted his sunken family".[23] This theory has been given new colour by S.R. Goyal[24] and B.P. Sinha[25] who support it with new arguments. We have already shown the impossibility of Goyal's theory about the Vākāṭaka-Kadmba alliance against the Gupta-Nala confederacy and the war between the two in the initial years of Skandagupta's reign or towards the end of Kumāragupta I's reign.[26] Goyal's surmise that the Pushyamitras were a subordinate ally of Narendrasena and were instigated by him to attack the Guptas and further that during this period of trouble the Varmans of Daśapura shifted their allegliance to the Vākāṭakas, is mere speculation and is not based on any evidence. No Aulikara ruler is known to have owed allegience to any Vākāṭaka monarch.

It is very significant indeed that while there is not the slightest hint to the Vākāṭaka suzerainty over Daśapura in the Mandasor stone slab inscription dated M.S. 524 i.e. A.D. 467—the last known date of Skandagupta, this inscription specifically mentions the Gupta emperors Chandragupta II and his son Govindagupta and also records that king Prabhākara who was presumably ruling over Daśapura in A.D. 467, was "the fire to the wood of the enemies of the Gupta dynasty".[27] Similarly the Mandasor inscription of the Guild of Silk-weavers which was composed in the year 529 M.S. or A.D. 472 by the command of the same guild which built the temple, does not mention the name of the Vākāṭaka Narendrasena.

To us the statement in the Balaghat plates regarding Narendrasena's sovereignty over Mālava appears to be only a vain boast, regarding a monarch who had actually suffered two severe defeats and in whose reign the fortunes of the Vākāṭaka dynasty had sunk very low. V.C. Pandey has pertinently pointed out that had there been a Gupta-Vākāṭaka conflict it was sure to find mention in the inscriptions of Skandagupta.[28]

The copious silver coinage of Skandagupta, of the Western variety, definitely points to the Gupta hold over the western parts of the Gupta empire upto the last days of Skandagupta's rule.[29]

In Kośala, the continuation of the Gupta overlordship is indicated by the fact that a daughter's son of Śarabharāja of this region fought on the side of the Guptas at Eran, as mentioned in the Eran pillar inscription of Goparāja dated 191 G.E.[30] The *Purāṇas* also confirm the continuation of the Gupta rule in Eastern India. It is stated that Guha (Skanda) will rule over Kaliṅga, Mahisha and Mahendra regions.[31] In view of all this numismatic, epigraphic and literary evidence it does not stand to reason to hold that Narendrasena had replaced the Gupta suzerainty in Kośala, Mekala and Mālava. All these regions, in our opinion, continued to form part of the empire of Skandagupta.

The Re-Organisation of the Administration

Soon after the Hūṇa invasion and the Pushyamitra upheaval had been successfully dealt with, Skandagupta found it necessary to pay immediate attention to the reorganisation of the administrative machinery of the empire which had passed through a great strain and was in need of a complete overhauling in order not only to give it a fresh look but also for making it efficient and effective. We are informed in the Junagadh rock inscription that having conquered the entire earth Skandagupta appointed governors in various provinces.[32] The same record informs us that Surāshṭra had become a problem province for Skandagupta. We learn that in order to find a competent governor for this province, Skandagupta pondered for several days and nights to pick out an officer endowed with the requisite qualities to govern well and successfully.[33] It appears that after the Hūṇa invasion the province needed a particularly faithful, honest, efficient and hardworking officer on whom the emperor may be able to rely fully. It also appears that the defence of this part of the country had also become the subject of the emperor's special concern. It is very likely that alongwith the appointment of Parṇadatta as the civilian governor, Skandagupta had appointed a very capable soldier and tried military leader named Bhaṭārka as the *senāpati* or the chief commander of the army stationed in this region.

One may very well agree with the poet of the Junagadh rock inscription when he says, that during the rule of Skandagupta there was none amongst his subjects who may be devoid of proper regard for the moral order, who may be steeped in misery or poverty, who may be addicted to vice, who may be avaricious, or who may be oppressed by heavy taxation. In these words the poet has depicted the high efficiency of the administration which was conducive to the general welfare of the people. That the government machinery was wide awake towards its duty to provide speedy relief in times of distress, is exemplified by the repairs of the dam of the Sudarśana lake in Girinagara, carried out promptly. There was therefore every justification for Skandagupta to be styled a *parahitakāri* 'the benefactor of others' on his coins.

Skandagupta's gold coinage has been struck only in three types—Archer, King and Lakshmī (or King and Queen) and Chhatra type. To these one more may be added—the horseman type represented by a single coin in the Bodlian collection. While the obverse legend on this type is entirely blurred, the *biruda* on the reverse can be read as *Kramāditya*. The coins of Skandagupta (later issues of Archer type) have been struck on the Indian standard of the *Suvarṇa* of 80 *rattis,* and obviously indicate a conscious discarding of foreign weight standard.

The valour and prowess of Skandagupta is fairly attested by his adoption of the titles *Kramāditya* and *Vikramāditya*, 'the Sun of valour', like his grandfather Chandragupta II. He had all the justification for the adoption of these titles, seeing how he tackled the menace of the Hūṇas and the Pushyamitras, and emerged as a national hero. Skandagupta was a master archer, the noise of whose bow-string struck terror in the hearts of his enemies.[34] His archer type coins and the legend *Sudhanvī* on them attest this very quality. He has been variously described as 'the sole hero of the Gupta dynasty'[35] and 'like Rāma in strength and valour',[36] in the inscriptions of his time. The Junagadh rock inscription refers to Skandagupta as one, "whom the goddess of fortune and splendour, selected as her husband of her own accord, due to his virtues, after discarding all the other sons of the king", and as 'the supreme king of kings, whose breast is embraced by the goddess of royal fortune and who has developed heroism by the strength of his arms'.[37] Skandagupta came upto the standard of all these praises bestowed upon him, by means of his prowess and military skill.

The last known date of Skandagupta is G.E. 148 (A.D. 467) from his silver coins. His rule seems to have come to an end around this time. Though Skandagupta had a short reign of about fourteen years, he can justly be called the greatest of all the Gupta rulers by all standards of judgment.

References

1. Placing reliance on the date 136 on a silver coin of Kumāragupta I published by V.A. Smith in *JASB*, 1894, 175, the date of the end of Kumāragupta's reign and the succession of Skandagupta is usually placed in A.D. 455. But since the very existence of the coin has been questioned, and since Skandagupta appears to be ruling in perfect peace in the year 136 or A.D. 455 after having put down the rebellions of erstwhile feudatory kings and having crushed the Hūṇa invaders, it appears to be more reasonable to place his accession at least an year earlier in A.D. 454. *Cf.* A.L. Basham, *BSOAS*, XVIII, 368f.

2. Chhabra & Gai (ed. 1981), *CII*, III, 80.

3. *Vichalita-kula-lakshmī-stambhanāy=odyatena*
kshititala-śayanīye yena nītā triyāmā ,
samudita-bala-koshān=Pushyamitrāṁś=cha jitvā
kshitipa-charaṇapīṭhe sthāpito vāma-pādaḥ ||

Verse 4 of the Bhitari Pillar inscription. Fleet (ed. 1888), *CII*, III, 54.

4. *DKA*, 51, 73.

5. See Jagannath Agrawal, *IHQ*, XXII, 112ff.

6. *EI*, XIX, 100ff.

7. *Hūṇair=yasya samāgatasya samare dorbhyāṁ dharā kampitā*, Chhabra & Gai (ed. 1981), *CII*, III, 315.

8. Cf. Chhabra & Gai (ed. 1981), *CII*, III, 315.

9. *EHNI*, 218-19.

10. *Gup. Sam.*, 324.

11. *Cf.* R.C. Majumdar, *CHI*, III, 116.

12. Mcgovern, W.M., *EECA*, 409. The flimsy statement of R.K. Chaudhary that the Mlechchhas are mentioned separately in the Bhitari pillar inscription (*JBRS*, 1959, 117ff) is hardly worth any notice, for this inscription does not contain any such reference.

13. Allan, J., *CCGD*, XLVI; Majumdar, R.C., *VGA*, 163; Raychaudhuri, H.C., *PHAI*, 510; Sircar, D.C., *Sel. Ins.*, I, 301; Sinha, B.P., *DHM*, 24; Thakur, U., *The Hūṇas in India*, 66ff.

14. *JRAS*, 1909, 126ff.

15. *EHNI*, 220.

16. *AIG*, 48-49.

17. *VGA*, 163-64.

18. *Cf.* Girnar rock inscription, Verses 7 to 13, Chhabra & Gai (ed. 1981), *CII*, III, 299f.

19. *PIHC*, 1958, 160-61.

20. *EECA*, 409.

21. *EI*, IX, 267.

22. *HG*, 115, 117-18.

23. *Ibid.*

24. *HIG*, 274-90.

25. *DHM*, 1 & 11.

26. Supra Chapter X.

27. *EI*, XXVIII, 12.

28. *Pra. Bha. Iti.*, 116.

29. *Coinage*, 250.

30. Fleet (ed. 1888), *CII*, III, 91ff.

31. *DKA*, 54.

32. Chhabra & Gai (ed. 1981), *CII*, III, 299, Verse 7.

33. *Ibid.* Verses 8-12, 299-300.

34. Cf. Verse 8 of the Bhitari pillar inscription, Chhabra & Gal (ed. 1981), *CII*, III, 315.

35. *Ibid.*, 315ff.

36. Supia pillar inscription, *ibid.*, 318ff.

37. *Ibid.*, 299.

CHAPTER XII

THE SUCCESSORS OF SKANDAGUPTA

BEFORE THE DISCOVERY of the Bhitari silver-copper seal, the imperial Gupta line was considered to have ended with *Mahārājādhirāja* Skandagupta, the end of whose reign was placed in A.D. 480.[1] This seal added three more names of the following Gupta emperors as successors of Kumāragupta I, viz., Purugupta, Narasiṁhagupta and Kumāragupta. This information was confirmed by the discovery of clay sealings from Nalanda during the excavations carried out there in 1927-28. These sealings belonged to *Mahārājādhirāja* Narasiṁhagupta son of Purugupta and grandson of Kumāragupta I and to another Kumāragupta who was a great-grandson of Kumāragupta I. Excavations at Sarnath during 1914-15 added further information regarding the later imperial Guptas who succeeded Skandagupta. The Buddha images installed by the mendicant Abhayamitra in the monastery at Sarnath supplied the name of the emperor Kumāragupta with his date 154, when he was ruling over this earth[2]; and two other images brought forth the information that Budhagupta was ruling over this earth in the year 157[3], thus bringing him into the line of the Gupta emperors of all India status. This fact was further confirmed by the discovery of a clay sealing of Budhagupta in which he is styled as *Mahārājādhirāja* and the son of the emperor Purugupta. Still another clay sealing came to light amongst the hoard of sealings discovered at Nalanda during 1927-28; and supplied the name of another Gupta emperor *Mahārājādhirāja* Vainyagupta. Though it is a mere fragment, but it has been rightly argued by R. C. Majumdar that the name of Vainyagupta's father was Purugupta as indicated by the presence of the sign for medial *u*.[4] In this connection the discovery of yet another inscription, in 1919, from Tumain in the Guna District of Madhya Pradesh has to be noted. This damaged record dated in the Gupta year 116 when Kumāragupta was ruling over the earth, supplies the name of a Gupta prince Ghaṭotkachagupta, who was in all likelihood, a governor of this part of Mālava[5], and has been credited with having issued the gold coin with the legend Ghaṭo. So we now have the following new names which have to be arranged in a proper genealogical and chronological order: Purugupta, Narasiṁhagupta, Kumāragupta of Bhitari silver-copper seal, Kumāragupta of the Sarnath Buddha image inscription dated 154 G.E., Budhagupta, Vainyagupta of the fragmentary Nalanda clay sealing, Ghaṭotkachagupta of the Tumain inscription and Bhānugupta of the Eran memorial stone pillar inscription dated 191 G.E.

GHAṬOTKACHAGUPTA

First we shall consider the place of Ghaṭotkachagupta in the Gupta history. We have been familiar with this name since the discovery of his clay sealing from Basarh in 1903. The seal does not contain any official title such as *yuvarāja*, nor the name of any office he might have been holding. In Bloch's opinion Ghaṭotkachagupta of the seal was identical with Mahārāja Ghaṭotkacha, the father of Chandragupta I. This view is untenable for two reasons. Firstly it does not contain his official title of Mahārāja. Secondly there is a glaring discrepancy in the name. Whereas the name of Chandragupta I's father is invariably mentioned as simply Ghaṭotkacha, without the addition of the word Gupta in all inscriptions of the Guptas, the name on this clay sealing is given as Ghaṭotkachagupta. It was not known what office had been held by Ghaṭotkachagupta in the Gupta administration till the discovery of the Tumain inscription by M.B, Garde in 1919.[6] This inscription is dated in the Gupta year 116, and mentions Kumāragupta as the Gupta emperor ruling over the earth with a firm hand. Obviously Ghaṭotkachagupta finds mention in this record as the governor of Eastern Mālawa about this time. It has further to be noted that a gold coin with the king's name as *Ghaṭo* and the marginal legend *Kramāditya* has been known from the collection in the St. Petersburg (Leningrad) Museum. It weighs 141.22 grains.[7] A second coin of this monarch has been reported by Ajit Ghosh, from his personal collection.[8] The existence of the two gold coins of Ghaṭotkacha shows that he had ruled for sometime as a king.

Putting together the information from the Vaishali (Basarh) clay sealing and the Tumain inscription we can infer that Ghaṭotkachagupta of the sealing and the Ghaṭotkachagupta of the inscription are one and the same person. However it is not possible to agree with D.R. Bhandarkar that this Ghaṭotkachagupta was, "Governor at first at Airikiṇa, *Yuvarāja* thereafter stationed at Vaiśālī, and the successor to the Gupta throne after the demise of his father Kumāragupta I."[9] Bhandarkar further presumes that, "On the demise of Kumāragupta, Ghaṭotkacha occupied the Gupta throne. But hardly had he ascended when the Nāgas raised the standard of revolt with such virulence and ruthlessness that the fortunes of the Gupta dynasty sank to the lowest level. Ghaṭotkachagupta was probably killed and his brother Skandagupta who had stood by him had to flee and sleep some nights on the bare earth."[10] All these are gratuitous assumptions. Firstly we do not know for certain that Ghaṭotkacha was a son of Kumāragupta I. The Tumain inscription which could throw light on their relationship is silent on the point. Secondly there is no evidence of his being nominated as *Yuvarāja* by Kumāragupta. The mere presence of his clay sealing—which too does not give him this designation does not entitle us to conclude that he was the heir-apparent. Thirdly there is not even an iota of evidence to show that there was a Nāga revolt at the death of Kumāragupta, in which his successor Ghaṭotkachagupta was killed. For aught we know the Nāgas had been utterly uprooted in northern India by Samudragupta, who even thought it politically prudent to arrange the marriage of his son Chandragupta II with a Nāga princess Kuberanāgā. It is absolutely unthinkable that after their complete merger in the Gupta empire during the two long reigns of Chandragupta II and Kumāragupta I, c. A.D. 375 to A.D. 455, the Nāgas could have become so powerful as to rout the Gupta armies and force Skandagupta to flee. On the contrary we find that any Nāga families which had survived were faithful to Skandagupta and enjoyed his complete confidence. The scion of a Nāga family was the governor of Antarvedī under Skandagupta.[11] Hence the suggestion that Ghaṭotkachagupta was killed at the hands of the Nāgas and Skandagupta had to take to flight at their onslaught is absolutely untenable. Of course because of the gold coins of Ghaṭotkachagupta it has to be conceded that he did assume royal authority for sometime, but when and how long are questions that remain to be answered.

Some scholars who believe that there was a war of succession between Skandagupta and his brothers Purugupta and Ghaṭotkachagupta after the death of Kumāragupta I, hold that Ghaṭotkacha declared himself independent at the time of this struggle and struck gold coins as a symbol of his royal authority.[12] We have already shown above that there was no war of succession after the death of Kumāragupta I and Skandagupta ascended the throne without any opposition. Moreover, there is no time between the last known date of Kumāragupta I (G.S. 135) and the first known date of Skandagupta (G.S. 136) to accommodate any other king.[13] The weight of the gold coins of Ghaṭotkacha shows that this king has to be placed after Skandagupta who is usually regarded to have issued coins of the *suvarṇa* standard for the first time. It is not unlikely that after the death of Skandagupta both Purugupta and Ghaṭotkachagupta strove to obtain the throne, and in this scramble the latter was successful. But after a brief rule he was either ousted or died a natural death.[14] He was succeeded by Purugupta.

Purugupta Prakāśāditya

No inscription of Purugupta has been discovered so far. His name as a *Mahārājādhirāja* and a son of the emperor Kumāragupta I born of his chief queen Anantadevī, first became known to us with the discovery of the Bhitari silver-copper seal of his grandson Kumāragupta (III). Subsequently the Nalanda clay sealings of Narasiṁhagupta, Budhagupta and Kumāragupta III substantiated the same. Allan had attributed to him the heavy weight Archer type coins from Hoey's collection, and had read the name *Pura* on the obverse and the title Vikramāditya on the reverse.[15] But now it has been conclusively established that these coins really belong to Budhagupta, and the reading Pura is incorrect.[16] Allan had at first doubtfully regarded the Horseman-lion slayer type of gold coins with the title Prakāśāditya as the issues of Purugupta,[17] and adduced convincing arguements in support of his suggestion. He remarked, "the Bharsar hoard[18] contained coins of Samudragupta, Chandragupta II, Kumāragupta I, Skandagupta and Prakāśāditya; the natural deduction would be that Prakāśāditya succeeded Skandagupta, and that the hoard was buried in his reign."[19] Allan further remarked, "the style of these coins although late and degraded in comparison with those of Kumāragupta I, compares favourably with that of Narasiṁhagupta's coins and hardly permits them to be placed much later". He further remarked, "the fineness of the gold of all the specimens likewise suggests a date previous to the coins of Narasiṁhagupta and his successors."[20] However, in spite of these weighty arguments only one single consideration outweighed with Allan. As seen above Allan had assigned the coins with the reverse legend Vikramāditya to Purugupta, he now found it inconsistent to attribute Prakāśāditya coins also to Purugupta. He concluded, therefore, that, "It is highly improbable that Purugupta was called both Vikramāditya and Prakāśāditya so that we must attribute these coins to some king probably a Gupta whose name is not yet known, and who must be placed about the end of the fifth century A.D."[21] But now that the coins with the reverse legend Vikramāditya have been proved to be the issues of Budhagupta, the objection fades away in the light thrown by S. K. Saraswati;[22] and we can attribute the Prakāśāditya coins to Purugupta with assurance.

The correction made by S. K. Saraswati from 'Pura' to Budha rectifies another historical error which had crept into Gupta history. J. Takakusu drew attention to a statement of Paramārtha in his Life of Vasubandhu, that king Vikramāditya of Ayodhyā became a patron of Buddhism through the influence of Vasubandhu and sent his queen and the crown prince Bālāditya to study under him. When Bālāditya became king he invited Vasubandhu to Ayodhyā.[23] Takakusu, took Vikramāditya to be Skandagupta Vikramāditya. He did not notice the discrepancy that Bālāditya was not the son of Skandagupta, but a nephew. The father of Bālāditya, if we accept his identity with Narasiṁhagupta, was Purugupta, whose title as shown above was certainly not Vikramāditya, but most probably Prakāśāditya. Paramārtha's account therefore has no bearing what-so-ever on this part of Gupta history.

Purugupta's reign came to an end most probably before G.E.

154 i.e. A.D. 473, since we find from the Sarnath Buddha image inscription that another king Kumāragupta was ruling over the earth in that year.[24]

Purugupta had a number of sons, though for a long time only one namely Narasiṁhagupta was known from the Bhitari silver-copper seal. Subsequently, the Nalanda clay sealing revealed the name of Budhagupta. The publication of the fragmentary Nalanda clay sealing of Vainyagupta also seems to indicate that he was also a son of Purugupta.[25] It is possible that Kumāragupta of the Sarnath Buddha image inscription dated 154 was also a son of Purugupta, as his date is so close to the time of Purugupta.

Kumāragupta II

His name came to light for the first time with the discovery of the Sarnath Buddha image inscription of G.E. 154. Previous to that Kumāragupta of the Bhitari silver seal was called Kumāragupta II.[26] However this view is no longer tenable and has been discarded.

Only one epigraph of his reign is known at present, the Sarnath image inscription mentioned above. Accidently, this is also the date of composition of the Mandasor inscription of the Guild of Silk-weavers, namely A.D. 472-73.

Kumāragupta II bore the title Kramāditya which is found on the gold coins of Archer type and weigh between 139.5 and 143 grains.[27] During his rule the Buddhist monastery at Sarnath appears to have been in a highly flourishing condition. Pious monks like Abhayamitra were enhancing its splendour by installing the images of the Buddha of a very high aesthetic merit. It can be safely inferred that the Gupta empire was enjoying peace and prosperity and the country had emerged unscathed from the Hūṇa invasion which took place during the rule of Skandagupta.

The absence of the silver coins of Kumāragupta II cannot be taken as an indication of the loss of Gujarat to the Guptas, as opined by B.P. Sinha.[28] We learn from the Bhamodra Mohotta copper-plate of the Maitraka ruler Droṇasiṁha dated Gupta-Valabhī year 183 i.e. A.D. 502, that the sovereignty of the

Guptas was still recognised in these parts.[29] Therefore the question of the loss of Gujarat does not arise at all. Moreover Kumāragupta II had a short reign. Even his gold coinage is not copious. The absence of the silver coinage should not be taken as an indication of any territorial loss. His rule came to an end in c. A.D. 476, the year in which we find Budhagupta ruling over the Gupta empire.

BUDHAGUPTA

Budhagupta, a son of Purugupta, appears to have peacefully obtained the throne after Kumāragupta II. His earliest known date is G.E. 157 which we get from the Sarnath Buddha image inscription. Before the discovery of these duplicate epigraphs, the only known inscription of Budhagupta was the Eran stone pillar inscription which records the setting up of this pillar as a flag-staff of Vishṇu (*garuḍa-dhvaja*) by two brothers Mahārāja Matṛivishṇu and his younger brother Dhanyavishṇu.[30] In spite of the fact that the inscription contained a mention of a governor named Suraśmichandra, who was governing the entire country lying between the river Yamunā and Narmadā, it was not realised that Budhagupta was a ruler of imperial status. He was designated by Fleet as the ruler of Eastern Malwa only.

In 1915, five copper plates of Gupta emperors were discovered in Damodarpur village in West Dinajpur District of West Bengal. Two of these belonged to the reign of Budhagupta. One of these is dated 163[31] while in the other the date is lost.[32] In both these copper plates Budhagupta has been given the epithets of *Parma-daivata*, *Paramabhaṭṭāraka* and *Mahārājādhīrāja*. Another inscription discovered on a stone pillar from Rajghat in 1940-41 also belongs to the reign of *Mahārājādhirāja* Budhagupta.[33] Yet another copper plate inscription dated 159, obviously of the Gupta era, was discovered in 1927.[34] Although it does not mention the name of Budhagupta as the reigning emperor but the date coupled with the mention in line 16 of the fact that one-sixth of the religious merit of this donation accrued to the *Paramabhaṭṭāraka*, clearly shows that the ruling authority in the region was the emperor Budhagupta whose title *Paramabhaṭṭāraka* and name we get in the Damodarpur copper plates referred to before. The newly discovered Buddha image inscription from Mathurā, and dated in Budhagupta's reign, shows that his authority extended as far north as Mathurā.[34a] All this evidence proves beyond the possibility of any doubt that Budhagupta's authority extended over those parts of northern India, which were ruled over by the Gupta emperors previously; and that the Gupta empire had suffered no loss of territory as yet. It is purely a gratuitous assumption of D.R. Bhandarkar, that, "like Ghaṭotkachagupta before Skandagupta, the three brothers Vainyagupta, Kumāragupta and Budhagupta, after the demise of their father, came to the throne one after another, in quick succession, everyone of them being foiled in his attempt to stay the flood of the Hūṇa immigration into India."[35] There is absolutely no evidence of the Hūṇa menace to the Gupta empire upto A.D. 494-95. In A.D. 473 when Kumāragupta II was ruling we find the religious gifts of high merit being made at Sarnath and there is mention of the erection of a *garuḍadhvaja* at Eran in Eastern Mālava in A.D. 484 when Budhagupta was ruling. Moreover, we know that the Hūṇas were themselves engaged in a serious conflict with the Sassanian rulers of Persia and could not have been in a position to undertake an invasion of India before having settled the scores with king Feroze of Persia, whom they could defeat as late as A.D. 484. The Epthalites could have made a move towards India only after that year; and we can be sure that right upto A.D. 484 India enjoyed peace under Budhagupta. This is also confirmed by the uninterrupted religious activity in Buddhist as well as Brahmanical institutions. Life was proceeding normally and we get the impression of peaceful times. In Puṇḍravardhana, the far eastern part of the empire, pious house-holders were purchasing land from the government for building temples or for settling Brahman families. In the monastery built on the spot where the Buddha delivered his first sermon, at Sarnath, the exquisitely sculptured images of the Buddha were installed; and in Eastern Mālava a fine *garuḍadhvaja* was erected by the administrator of the district, at Airikina, the modern Eran, in the Sagar District of Madhya Pradesh.

Some indication of the loosening of the imperial authority has been sensed in the existence of the land grants made during Budhagupta's rule, where any reference to the emperor has been omitted. Two land-grants recorded on copper plates dated 158 issued by a Mahārāja Lakshmaṇa whose jurisdiction appears to have extended over some territory in the neighbourhood of Allahabad, do not make mention of the sovereignty of the Gupta emperor. However, this cannot be regarded as an evidence of the defiance of Budhagupta's authority because the Sarnath inscription dated G.E. 157 proves Budhagupta's rule in the Gangetic valley, and the Eran inscription dated 165 is proof enough of his authority over whole of the region between the Yamunā and Narmadā rivers. Similarly the grants made by Mahārāja Subandhu from Māhishmatī cannot be indicative of the loss of Gupta authority, because even the territories beyond Māhishmatī continued to owe allegiance to the Guptas as is shown by the Bhamodra Mohatta copper-plate of the Maitraka ruler Mahārāja Droṇasiṁha dated G.E. 188. We may therefore conclude that Budhagupta kept under control the entire Gupta empire extending over Northern Bengal, Uttar Pradesh and westwards up to the Paśchim Payodhi (the Arabian Sea), and ensured peace and prosperity for the people. He was thus fully justified in adopting the title Vikramāditya—a symbol of political eminence—which occurs on his gold coins discovered in 1948[36] and also on the gold coin of Hoey's collection wrongly attributed by Allan to Purugupta before but rightly pointed out to be of Budhagupta by S. K. Saraswati.[37] Coins No. 550 and 551 in the *British Museum CCGD*, weighing 142.7 grains and without the king's name on the obverse but with the legend Śri-Vikrama on the reverse are to be attributed to Budhagupta.[38]

Budhagupta issued silver coins of the Madhyadeśa type having the bust of the king on the obverse.[39] Five of these bear the date 175, while on the sixth it has been read as 180;[40] but this reading is doubtful.[41]

A verse in the Sanskrit prose romance Vāsavadattā by Subandhu makes a wistful reference to Vikramāditya, showing that the great prose writer had enjoyed the patronage of this king. As Subandhu is generally believed to have preceeded Bāṇa, he can very well be placed towards the close of the fifth century or the beginning of the sixth century of the Christian era. It, therefore, seems very likely that Subandhu had enjoyed the patronage of Budhagupta who had the title Vikramāditya as shown above. The verse in the *Vāsvadattā* runs as follows:

Sā rasavattā vihatā navakā vilasanti charati no kaṃ kaḥ,
sarasīva kīrttiśashaṁ gatavati bhuvi Vikramāditye.

"When Vikramāditya has been left on this earth only in renown, that appreciation (of literature) has been killed. The novices are flourishing. Who does not attack whom? Just like a pool left only in name with the waters having dried up, the cranes do no longer sport, and the heron (too) does not move about."

The king Vikramāditya of this verse is most probably Budhagupta who patronised Subandhu, the author of *Vāsvadattā*, who laments the death of his patron and is finding the new situation unfavourable and intolerable.

Budhagupta seems to have died shortly after A.D. 494 or in A.D. 499 if we accept the date of his silver coin as 180. Eastern Mālwa seems to have been lost to the Gupta empire soon after his death. The Hūṇas appeared again on the Indian soil, and this time had a better luck than in the time of Skandagupta who had repelled their attack and achieved a resounding victory. In the Eran stone pillar inscription dated G.E. 165, the officer named Mātṛivishṇu who was incharge of the district of Airikiṇa together with his younger brother Dhanyavishṇu installed a flag-staff of Vishṇu. At this time Suraśmichandra was governing the land between the rivers Yamunā and Narmadā and the reigning emperor was Budhagupta. We have another inscription from the same locality, engraved on a stone image of god Varāha, recording the construction of a stone temple of this deity by Dhanyavishṇu alone. This inscription is not dated in the Gupta era like the one on the *garuḍadhvaja* mentioned above, and in place of the Gupta emperor Budhagupta we find the name of an alien ruler *Mahārājādhirāja* Toramāṇa who is obviously the father of the Hūṇa emperor Mihirakula. This evidently means that the *Vishaya* of Eran had passed into the hands of foreigners just within one generation, after Mahārāja Mātṛivishṇu whose younger brother Dhanyavishṇu built the stone temple of god Varāha sometimes after A.D. 484.

When did Toramāṇa conquer this part of the Gupta empire and who was the ruling Gupta emperor at that time? Though these are difficult questions to answer because of the lack of direct evidence on the point, we shall take them up in the next Chapter.

It looks very likely that Budhagupta ruled upto c. A.D. 500. He was succeeded in all likclihood by Vainyagupta who was most probably another son of Purugupta.

References

1. John Allan, *CCGD*, xlix. E.B. Havel in his *History of Aryan Rule in India*, and V.A. Smith in the *Early History of India*[3] had expressed similar view. J.F. Fleet in the *CII*, III, did not regard Budhagupta and Bhānugupta as members of the Imperial Gupta dynasty and designated them as rulers of Eastern Malva.

2. Chhabra & Gai (ed.), *CII*, III (1981), 321.
3. *Ibid.*, 333.
4. *IHQ*, XIV, 67.
5. Chhabra & Gai (ed.), *CII*, III (1981), 278.
6. *EI*, XXVI, 115-18.
7. *Coinage*, 354.
8. *JNSI*, XXII, 260.
9. Chhabra & Gai (ed.), *CII*, III (1981), 80.
10. *Ibid.*, 81.
11. Indore Copper plate of Skandagupta dated 146, *CII*, III(1981), 308.
12. Sinha, B.P., *DHM*, 6ff.; Gupta, P.L., *Gup. Sām.*, 178ff.; Goyal, S.R., *HIG*, 311ff.
13. *BSOAS*, XVII, 367ff.
14. For detailed discussion on the place of Ghaṭotkachagupta in the Gupta history see *PURB* (*Arts*), XVII, I, 141-46.
15. *CCGD*, 135.
16. It was first pointed out by S.K. Saraswati, *IC*, I, 692.
17. *CCGD.*, 135.
18. JASB, 1852, 390-400.
19. *CCGD.*, li-lii.
20. *Ibid.*
21. *Ibid.*
22. *IC*, I, 692.
23. *JRAS*, 1905, 49.
24. Chhabra & Gai (ed.), *CII*, III (1981), 321.
25. *IHQ*, XIV, 67.
26. Panna Lal, *Hindustan Review*, 1918; Majumdar, R.C., *IA*, 1918, 61-67.
27. Allan, J., *CCGD.*, 140. However, the coins which Allan terms as class II of this type, must now be assigned to Kumāragupta III, as they are heavier in weight but have a greater percentage of alloy.
28. *JBRS*, XXXIV, 18-26.

29. *EI*, XVI, 17ff.
30. *CII*, III (1981), 339ff.
31. *Ibid.*, 335ff.
32. *Ibid.*, 342.
33. *Ibid.*, 334.
34. *EI*, XX, 59ff.
34a. *JESI*, IX, 6.
35. *CII*, III (1981), 85.
36. *JNSI*, XII, 112.
37. *IC*, I, 692.
38. *Coinage*, 276.
39. *Ibid.*, 279.
40. *IA*, XVIII, 227.
41. *Coinage*, 279; Majumdar, R.C., *CHI*, III, 87. According to him "the date may be anything between 180 and 189".

CHAPTER XIII

THE FINAL PHASE

THE CLOSE OF BUDHAGUPTA'S reign circa A.D. 500, marks the culmination of the imperial authority of the Guptas. Of course the empire continued to exist, as we shall see for another fifty years or so, but the hey-day of the glory of the Guptas was now a thing of the past. It was about this time that two new dynasties of kings appear on the scene almost simultaneously. These are the Maukharīs, whose progenitor was Harivarmā and the Later Guptas of Magadha whose founder was Kṛishṇagupta. Apparently, to begin with, both these houses were not independent sovereign powers; and both of them owed allegiance—may be nominal—to the imperial Gupta monarch. During this period of their subordinate position which can be said to have lasted upto circa A.D. 550, the mutual relations between these two houses, the Maukharis and the descendants of Kṛishṇagupta were cordial, and there were even two matrimonial alliances between them. A Gupta princess Harshaguptā was the queen of the Maukhari king Ādityavarman and Upaguptā was married to the Maukhari king Īśānavarmā, but the scramble for the imperial position made them hostile to each other as we shall see later.

VAINYAGUPTA AND BHĀNUGUPTA

From the Nalanda clay sealing of Narasiṁhagupta as well as from the Bhitari silver seal we know that Purugupta had a son Narasiṁhagupta, who issued gold coins with *Nara* written on the obverse and the *birud* Bālāditya on the reverse. In these sealings he is described as *tatpādānudhyāta* with reference to his father Purugupta, but this expression is merely a formal statement showing the respect and regard of a descendant for the ancestor. It does not by any means indicate immediate succession. In the present case too we have the name of another Gupta king, who in our opinion is nearer in time to Budhagupta and might have come to the throne immediately after the latter in c. A.D. 500. The name of this king—*Mahārājādhirāja* Vainyagupta—is supplied by the fragmentary Nalanda clay sealing, the Gunaighar copper plate dated 188 and some gold coins. Unfortunately, the available fragment of the seal does not furnish the names of the father or grandfather of Vainyagupta, but in the presence of a mark for medial *u*, R. C. Majumdar is inclined to regard this vowel mark as indicative of the name Purugupta.[1] A Mahārāja Vainyagupta became known by the discovery of the Gunaighar copper plate inscription dated 188 G.E. i.e. A.D. 507 which records the grant of land to a Buddhist monastery established at Guṇaikagrahāra, the present day Gunaighar.[2] Although the name of the father and grandfather of Mahārāja Vainyagupta is not mentioned in this copper plate, its date is so close to the end of Budhagupta's rule, that it does not seem impossible to take him as identical with *Mahārājādhirāja* Vainyagupta of the Nalanda clay sealing. R.C. Majumdar at first did not agree with this identification[3] but in his latest work he has veered round to the view favouring this identification.[4] Moreover, Vainyagupta is a very rare name and it is rather difficult to visualise two Gupta kings ruling almost about the same time having the same name. As regards the title of *mahārāja* given to Vainyagupta of the Gunaighar copper plate, we find the careless use of the title even in official records in many cases. D.C. Ganguli has pointed out that, "The Pratihāra Vatsarāja, Nāgabhaṭa and Bhoja are imperial rulers. The Barah copper, plate of Bhoja dated *Saṁvat* 893, which is a royal grant, designates Vatsarāja, Nāgabhaṭa, Rāmabhadra and Bhoja as Mahārājas".[5] There still remains another hurdle in the way of this identification. The Mahārāja Vainyagupta of the Gunaighar grant is a devotee of Śiva (*Bhagavān-Mahādeva-pādānudhyāto*) whereas the *Mahārājādhiraja* Vainyagupta of the Nalanda sealing is a *paramabhāgavata*, i.e. a devout worshipper of Vishṇu. This discrepancy has been explained by N. N. Dasgupta who says, "Vaidyadeva of Kāmarūpa is represented in the Kamauli inscription, as both *parama-māheśvara* and *parama-vaishṇava*."[6] Although it may look quite unusual that the same king professed devotion to

Śiva in one part of his realm and to Vishṇu in another part, still there is no way out in this impasse but to acquiesce in the identity of the two.[7] We may therefore conclude that *Mahārājādhirāja* Vainyagupta was a son of Purugupta and was ruling over the whole of the Gupta empire in the year 188 or A.D. 507. He must have ascended the imperial throne sometime about A.D. 500 when Budhagupta's rule appears to have ended.

Here we must consider the implications of the Eran stone Boar inscription of Dhanyavishṇu dated in the year 1 of *Mahārājādhirāja* Toramāṇa and the memorial stone pillar inscription of Goparāja dated G.E. 191 commemorating the death of Mahārāja Goparāja in battle and mentioning a Gupta ruler Bhānugupta whose heroic deeds have been equated with those of the epic hero Arjuna. The mention of Toramāṇa as the ruling sovereign in the inscription of Dhanyavishṇu who along with his elder brother Matṛivishṇu, the officer-in-charge of the district of Eran had professed allegiance to the Gupta emperor Budhagupta in A.D. 484, clearly shows that the district of Eran or perhaps a substantial portion of Eastern Mālwa had been lost to the Gupta empire and had passed into the hands of the Hūṇas under Toramāṇa, the father of Mihirakula. We have also to consider against whom did Bhānugupta fight the battle at Eran and in what capacity?

There is definite evidence to show that Vainyagupta was a sovereign ruler. He is styled as a *mahārājādhirāja* in the Nalanda clay sealing fragment. The gold coins issued by him are known.[8] There can therefore be no doubt about his having ruled as an emperor. As for Bhānugupta we have no inscription of his own, nor do we have any coins issued by him. Therefore in the opinion of some eminent scholars he is not to be regarded as a sovereign ruler who fought against the Hūṇas on his own. But we cannot ignore the fact stated about him in the Eran inscription dated A.D. 510. Bhānugupta has been in this brief record called *rājāmahān* who had Mahārājas like Goparāja as his allies. We may therefore have to regard him as a Gupta emperor and accommodate him in the succession list; and in order to do so we may suggest the following course of events:

Vainyagupta seems to have died soon after A.D. 507 and was succeeded by Bhānugupta, who might have been his brother or half-brother. As generally accepted, it appears that the battle fought by Bhānugupta, referred to in the Eran memorial stone pillar inscription dated G.E. 191, was against the Hūṇa king Toramāṇa.[9] On account of the lack of clear evidence it is not possible to know the outcome of this war. R. C. Majumdar has observed that, "We do not know whether he (Bhānugupta) defended the province against the Hūṇa attack or made an attempt to recover it from Hūṇa possession."[10] It is certain in the light of the Eran stone pillar inscription of G.E. 165 and the Eran Stone Boar inscription of the first year of Toramāṇa's reign that the territory of Eran was lost to the Guptas soon after the death of Budhagupta and passed into the hands of the Hūṇas. Toramāṇa was not destined to enjoy his rule over Eran region for long. He lost much of his power and prestige, having suffered a crushing defeat at the hands of the Aulikara emperor Prakāśadharmā, who not only routed the army of Toramāṇa but also captured the ladies of his harem and put an end to his imperial status depriving him of the title of 'Overlord of Kings', sometime before Mālava year 572 i.e. A.D. 515.[11] It is therefore very likely that when Toramāṇa was on the run after suffering defeat at the hands of Prakāśadharmā the Guptas regained their control over Eran region as we find a reference to 'the enjoyment of sovereignty by the Gupta kings' upto G.E. 209 i.e. A.D. 528 in the inscriptions of the Parivrājaka kings, whose territory was not very far from Eran District.

Although no coins or inscriptions of Bhānugupta have been discovered so far, but the statements made about him in the Eran memorial pillar inscription dated G.E. 191 clearly show that he was an imperial ruler. He is described as a great king (*rājā-mahān*) which is only a different way of calling him a *mahārājā-dhirāja.* Further his valorous deeds are compared to those of Arjuna, the heroic Pāṇḍava. In view of these facts there should be little hesitation in regarding him a sovereign king, who ascended the imperial Gupta throne in circa A.D. 509. He does not seem to have ruled for a long time and his reign most probably ended sometime before A.D. 520.

R. C. Majumdar's suggestion regarding the division of the empire between Vainyagupta and Bhānugupta does not appear to be tangible. The clay sealings of the latest imperial Gupta kings, beginning with Vainyagupta onwards, that is Narasiṁhagupta Kumāragupta III and Vishṇugupta have been found at Nalanda, showing that the imperial capital of Pāṭaliputra was still in the hands of all these rulers. The question of any partition does not therefore arise. It is also to be remembered that some districts of Madhya Pradesh such as Gwalior and Sagar along with some undeterminable parts of western U.P. had passed into the hands of the Hūṇas in the beginning of the sixth century A.D.

Narasiṁhagupta Bālāditya

Though Narasiṁhagupta Bālāditya had been known since 1847 when Prinsep obtained his gold coin with the legend Narasiṁhagupta on the obverse and Vālāditya on the reverse, his exact position in the Gupta dynasty first became known with the discovery of the Bhitari silver-copper seal in 1889. From this seal we know that he was a son of Purugupta[12] and a grandson of Kumāragupta I. Narasiṁhagupta's clay sealings have also been discovered from the ruins at Nalanda[13] and this makes it highly probable that he is identical with king Bālāditya, who built a very lofty and magnificent temple of the Buddha at Nalanda as stated in the stone slab inscription of the reign of emperor Yaśovarmadeva.[14] This inscription contains a highly eulogistic reference to king Bālāditya. It states, "The great king Bālāditya, who possessed irresistible valour, having conquered all the enemies and having enjoyed (the sovereignty) of the whole of the earth, raised this great, white and wonderful temple of the son of Śuddhodana (i.e. Buddha) as if with the desire to surpass the Kailāśa." There can be no element of exaggeration in this statement as Bālāditya flourished long before the time of this inscription.

We must therefore conclude that Narasiṁhagupta Bālāditya was a powerful emperor who had put down all his enemies and was ruling in glory. The story told in Hiuen Tsang's life that king Bālāditya took refuge in an island when the foreign invader Mihirakula invaded the former's territory appears to lack conviction. The story seems to be based on mere folk-tale which had been given to the Chinese pilgrim by ill-informed Indians. Moreover, the statement of the pilgrim that Mihirakula flourished some centuries before the time of the pilgrim's visit, makes it totally fantastic, as we know that hardly even one century had passed between the visit of Hiuen Tsang (A.D. 629) and the time of Mihirakula (c. A.D. 530). This glaring inaccuracy regarding the time factor makes the account altogether unreliable and nothing more than a folk-tale. The Hūṇas had recently suffered a crushing defeat at the hands of the Aulikara ruler Prakāśadharmā, who looted the entire camp of Toramāṇa. Mihirakula had himself bowed down his forehead before the successor of Prakāśadharmā i.e. Yaśodharman Vishṇuvardhana.

On the basis of the gold coinage, A. S. Altekar has postulated the existence of two Narasiṁhagupta Bālādityas.[15] He thinks that class I of Allan's coins which has a higher percentage of pure gold—71%—and show finer workmanship belongs to Narasiṁhagupta I whereas class II which shows crude workmanship and has a gold content of 54% only, belongs to Narasiṁhagupta Bālāditya II. However, we have now an almost uninterrupted order of succession from Kumāragupta I down to Vishṇugupta (A.D. 543) from the various clay sealings and inscriptions and it is veritably impossible to accommodate another ruler in this compact order of succession.

KUMĀRAGUPTA III

Narasiṁhagupta was succeeded by his son Kumāragupta III, whose silver-copper seal was discovered from Bhitari in 1889 and supplied for the first time the names of his father Narasiṁhagupta and grandfather Purugupta. A clay sealing of Kumāragupta III reiterating the same genealogy as the Bhitari silver-copper seal was discovered from Nalanda.

No copper-plate recording a grant has been found attached to the Bhitari seal, but its very existence proves that Kumāragupta III made some handsome grant either to an individual or to the temple at Bhitari where a statue of Vishṇu had been installed and a stone-pillar erected by his grand-uncle Skandagupta. The shrine at Bhitari seems to have had special significance for the Gupta emperors since the days of Kumāragupta I, whose name is inscribed on some bricks discovered during the excavations carried out near Skandagupta's stone pillar.

The gold coins of the Archer type, but of crude fabric and of less purity of gold which Allan designated as class II of the Archer type coins of Kumāragupta II,[16] belong in all probability to Kumāragupta III. There are some clear indications that the coins of class II do not belong to Kumāragupta II. Not only these coins are ruder in fabric but they also contain a greater amount of alloy. Further whereas the reverse legend on the coins of class I is simply *Kramāditya*, it is *Śrī-Kramāditya* on those of class II. Thirdly the coins of class II of Allan have the letter *go* between the king's feet, while there is no such letter on the coins of class I. Therefore the coins of class II appear to belong to a different king who in all likelihood is Kumāragupta III.

Though the decrease of purity of gold in his coins may indicate a period of economic strain during the rule of Kumāragupta III, there seems to be no slackening of the royal patronage to the religious institutions as Kumāragupta III definitely made some munificent donations of land by means of a copper plate charter, now lost. He might have suffered a temporary eclipse of power as a result of Yaśodharmā's victorious campaign who claims to have extended his sway upto the river Brahmaputra.[17]

Kumāragupta III was succeeded by his son Vishṇugupta whose identity and exact position in Gupta dynasty remained uncertain till the publication of the fragment of his clay sealing discovered at Nalanda during the excavations of 1927-28.[18]

VISHṆUGUPTA

Gold coins bearing the name Vishṇu written vertically on the obverse and the title Chandrāditya on the reverse had been found in the Kalighat hoard, discovered in 1783. These have been described by Allan,[19] who has rightly attributed them to a Gupta emperor contradicting Hoernle's view who proposed to assign them to Yaśodharman Vishṇuvardhana. Since the publication of his fragmentary Nalanda clay sealing, the position of Vishṇugupta as a member of the imperial Gupta dynasty has been assured, and it is now almost certain that the coins found in the Kalighat hoard belong to this Gupta emperor. Unfortunately on account of the fragmentary nature of the sealing we get only the name of his father Kumāragupta and his grandfather

Narasiṁhagupta. These two names however are sufficient to warrant the conclusion that Vishṇugupta is an imperial Gupta ruler and a son of Kumāragupta III. It is now possible to regard the fifth Damodarpur copper plate dated G.E. 224 in which the first part of the emperor's name is damaged, as belonging to the reign of Vishṇugupta. We thus obtain a date A.D. 543 for Vishṇugupta. This copper plate shows that the Gupta empire still extended from Magadha upto Northern Bengal which was being governed by a prince of the blood royal—*Mahārājaputra* Devabhaṭṭāraka.

In the present state of our knowledge, Vishṇugupta appears to be the last imperial ruler of the Gupta dynasty. About this time we find that the house of the Maukharis whose feudatory status is indicated by the title *Mahārāja* which was borne by all the kings up to Īśvaravarmā, had now attained an independent position and its king Iśānavarmā whose achievements are detailed in the Haraha inscription dated 611 or A.D. 554, bears the title *Mahārājādhirāja*. His contemporary and rival the Later Gupta king Kumāragupta was out to contest for the imperial position in northern India; and according to the Aphsad inscription even gained a victory over Iśānavarmā. These two royal houses of the Maukharis and the Later Guptas were really responsible for the final collapse of the imperial Gupta line and shared between themselves those territories of the Gangetic plain which formed the heart of the Gupta empire ruled over by Samudragupta and his successors. The western half covering practically the whole of Uttar Pradesh and some western districts of Bihar, formed the Maukhari empire, while Magadha and Gauḍa were held by the descendants of Kṛishṇagupta. It were thus the Maukharis and the Later Guptas who gradually built up their military power, and dismembered the great Gupta empire which had been mauled but not destroyed by the ravages of the Hūṇas and the *digvijaya* of the Aulikara Yaśodharman Vishṇuvardhana.

THE HŪṆAS

We have referred to the terrible conflict of Skandagupta with a barbarian (*mlechchha*) people called the Hūṇas;[20] and have also spoken of the invasion of Central India by Toramāṇa shortly after the reign of Budhagupta and the story of the clash between Toramāna's son Mihirakula and the Gupta emperor Narasiṁhagupta Bālāditya and the Aulikara emperor Yaśodharman. It is therefore necessary to give some information about the Hūṇas and the part they have played in the Gupta history.

Although the Hūṇas are mentioned as a barbarian people in the *Mahābhārata* and the *Purāṇas*, but we do not get from these works any definite information of historical value and interest. In the story of the conflict between the two ancient Indian sages Vasishṭha and Viśvāmitra, as given in the *Mahābhārata*, we find that the Hūṇas are said to have been produced from the froth which came out of the mouth of Vasishṭha's cow. This shows that the epic and Purāṇic accounts are merely mythological and of little use for historical investigations. Kalhaṇa in his *Rājataraṅgiṇi* has given in detail the atrocities perpetrated by Mihirakula whom he counts amongst the kings of Kashmir, but he does not distinctly designate him as a Hūṇa. Moreover, Kalhaṇa places him sometime in the seventh century B.C. which means that Kalhaṇa's own information was very vague and based on heresay. We get some accurate information about the Hūṇas from Kālidāsa, who in his *Raghuvaṁśa* places them on the banks of the river Oxus where they were defeated by Raghu. Taking Kālidāsa to be a contemporary of Chandragupta II, we can conclude that the Hūṇas had occupied Bactria in the last quarter of the fourth century A.D. Varāhamihira mentions them in his *Bṛihatsaṁhitā* (XIV, 27) and also refers to a particular group amongst them namely the White Hūṇas. He mentions Sita-Hūṇa in *Bṛihatsaṁhitā*, XI, 61 and Śveta-Hūṇa in XIV, 37. It is this section of the Hūṇas which concerns us here, but we may also speak about the Hūṇas in general, though very briefly. For their early history we have to depend mainly on the Chinese sources. The barbarian tribes living to the west and north of the Chinese frontier were called as Hiung-nu. Closely connected with this tribe were Juan-Juan and the Chionites. Between A.D. 150 and 400 the various Hunnish tribes moved westward and occupied Northern Turkestan. It was from here that they moved westwards to Europe where under their leader Attila, who has become a symbol for fire and sword, they brought about the crash of the Roman Empire. One branch of these Hunnish people, namely the

Chionites gave much trouble to the Persians. Another group of the Hunnish people known as Epthalites or Hepthalites, whose exact affinities are not definitely known, became a great menace for the Sassanian empire in Persia and the Gupta empire in India, The Greek and Roman historians simply call them Huns. However the Chinese writers make a distinction between the Huns proper, and the Epthalites. They call the Huns as Hiung-nu and the Epthalites as *Ye-ti-i-li-do*. According to Procopious, "they alone among the Hunnish people have white skin and regular features." The Śveta-Hūṇas of the *Bṛihatsaṁhitā* are evidently the White Huns of European writers.

The Epthalites appear to have left their original home and to have moved westwards and subjugated the city states of Karashahar, Kucha, Kashgar and Khotan. Next they overran Sogdiana. About A.D. 350 the Epthalites moved into Bactria and under their pressure the Kushāṇas moved southwards into Gandhāra. Between A.D. 366 and 376 the Epthalites were completely in possession of Bactria. In the last quarter of the fourth century A.D. they overthrew the later Kushāṇas known as Kidārites after their chief and leader Kidāra, and occupied Gandhāra. They were soon on their way to India and about A.D. 454 they crossed the Indian frontier. Their advance was halted by the valiant Gupta hero Skandagupta, who inflicted upon them a crushing defeat after fighting a terrible battle. After the victory of Skandagupta, India became safe from their devastating inroads and enjoyed peace for half a century.

It is worth our while to take stock of the fortunes of the Epthalites in their struggle against the Sassanian kings of Persia. It was sometimes about A.D. 427, when Varhran V, popularly called Bahram Ghor was ruling over Persia, that the Epthalites invaded Persia. Varhran fled in panic but his ministers managed to persuade the barbarian hordes to leave, by offering huge bribe. The Epthalites accepted the money and were peacefully returning when they were ambushed by Varhran and defeated. The Epthalites renewed their invasion during the reign of Yazdigird and defeated him in A.D. 454. Now commenced a see-saw struggle between the Sassanians and the Epthalites, which ultimately ended in a decisive victory for the Hūṇas who inflicted a very severe defeat on the Persian king Piroz or Feroze in A.D. 484. The Hūṇas now turned their covetous eyes towards the smiling plains of the Indus and Gangetic valleys; and under the leadership of a chief named Toramāṇa they soon crossed the Indian frontier and lodged themselves in north-western Punjab as is indicated by the stone inscription discovered from Khewra (Kura of earlier editors) in the Salt Range in the District of Jhelum, which mentions a *Rājādhirāja* Toramāṇa who is given the titles of *Shāha* and *Jaūbla*, ruling over this region.[21]

After the death of the powerful Gupta ruler Budhagupta in India, Toramāṇa found the opportunity to attack the Gupta empire, and like a skilled military leader, he made a fianking attack on Eran in East Malva. Toramāṇa avoided to proceed through the Antarvedi, which he must have found strongly fortified. His conquest of Eran is indicated by the mention of his name as the ruling *Mahārājādhirāja* in the Eran Stone Boar inscription recording the building of a temple of god Varāha by a Brahaman named Dhanyavishṇu. Since this man along with his elder brother Mātṛivishṇu had erected a flagstaff in the temple of god Vishṇu in this very temple complex in Eran it is evident that the transfer of political authority in Eran had taken place within a very short period after the setting up of the pillar in honour of Vishṇu in the year 165 of the Gupta era i.e. in A.D. 484. We can safely conclude that circa A.D. 500 the province of Eran was lost to the Guptas. The victory of Toramāṇa at Eran seems to have overawed some of the small feudatory states in the west to hasten to acknowldege Toramāṇa as their overlord. In the Sanjeli copper plate a certain Mahārāja Bhūta describes himself as enjoying the favour of *Mahārājādhirāja* Toramāṇa in the *vishaya* of Śivabhāgapura.[22]

There has been considerable difference of opinion regarding the nationality of Toramāṇa and his identity with Toramāṇa of the Eran inscrption.[23] George Bühler who edited the Khewra (Kura) inscription observed, "I am not able to assert that the Toramāṇa of our inscription is identical either with the Toramāṇa of the Eran inscription or with Toramāṇa of Kashmir who is mentioned by Kalhaṇa and who has left behind so many coins inscribed with Gupta characters. The fact that Toramāṇa bears the title or surname *Shāha* or *Shāhi* and receives the epithet Jaūvla, which may be a tribal name or a *birdua*, is, it seems to me, sufficient to prevent the identification with other Toramāṇas who are not characterised in this manner."[24]

Sir Aurel Stein[25] and K.P. Jayaswal[26] regarded him a Kushāṇa. But Sten Konow has given convincing proof to show that Toramāṇa was a Hūṇa.[27] He points out that the coins of some Hepthalite kings described by Herzfeld bear the legend *Soho Zobol*; and concludes that, "the collection of these two titles in Hepthalite legends and in the Kura inscription shows that our Toramāṇa was in all probability a Hūṇa," K.G. Shankar also discussed this problem and held that Toramāṇa was either a Kshatriya or a Parthian.[28] Shankar's argument have been refuted by Jagannath Agrawal who holds that both Toramāna and his son Mihirakula are Hūṅas.[29] The issue has been finally clinched by the discovery of the Risthal stone inscription of Prakāśadharmā, dated *Mālava Samvat* 572 i.e. A.D. 515. In this inscription Toramāṇa has been specifically called a Hūṇa king—*Hūṇādhipa.*[30]

Toramāṇa's rule over Eran and his sovereignty over some small states in western India appears to have been short lived. As already stated he was signally defeated by the Aulikara ruler Prakāśadharmā whose Risthal inscription has recently come to light. We are told in this inscription that Prakāśadharmā having conquered Toramāṇa in the fore front of the battle by means of force, captured the ladies of his harem and presented them to the temple of Śiva as *devadāsīs.*[31] As the Risthal inscription is dated in the *Mālava* year 572, the defeat of Toramāṇa must have taken place before A.D. 515. About this very time we hear of another great battle having been fought at Eran, in which the Gupta monarch Bhānugupta's ally Goparāja was killed in a fierce battle and his wife became a *sati.*[32] It appears that Bhānugupta had come to fight against the Hūṇas. Though the outcome of this battle is not clear from this inscription, the Hūṇa emperor Toramāṇa appears to have been forced out of Central India about this time and retreated to Gwalior, where Toramāṅa's son Mihirakula is known to have ruled for fifteen years, according to the Gwalior inscription of his reign.[33]

Mihirakula was certainly a powerful and proud ruler who is, said "to have never reduced his head to the abject and wretched state of making an obeisance before anyone except the god Śiva."[34] The Alexanderian Greek, Cosmos Indicopleustes has supplied some valuable information in his work the *Christian Topography*, which he probably started writing in A.D. 535 and completed in A.D. 547. He writes, "Higher up in India, that is farther to the north, are the White Huns. The one called Gollas, when going to war takes with him, it is said no fewer than two thousand elephants and a great force of cavalry. He is the lord of India and oppressing the people forces them to pay tribute. The river Phison separates all the countries of India from the country of the Hūṇas."[35] We are informed by Cosmos himself that, "the river Phison is the same as the river Indus."[36] Gollas of Cosmos is evidently Mihirakula, also written as Mihiragula on his coins of the Standing King type.

Another interesting piece of information about the Hūṇa king of Gandhāra and Udyāna in the first quarter of the sixth century A.D. is available in the account of the Chinese ambassador, Sung-yun, although he does not mention Mihirakula by name. The account as quoted by Hiuen Tsang in his *Si-yu-ki* tells us that, "The disposition of this king was cruel and vindicative, and he practised the most barbaric atrocities. He did not believe in the law of Buddha but loved to worship demons. Entirely self-reliant on his own strength, he had entered on a war with the country of Ki-pin, disputing the boundaries of their kingdom, and his troops had been already engaged in it for three years. The king has 700 war elephants. The king continually abode with his troops on the frontier and never returned to his kingdom."[37] From both these accounts which are almost contemporary it can be definitely concluded that between A.D. 520 and 535 Mihirakula's seat of government was to the west of the Indus in Gandhāra and Udyāna, and he was at war with Kashmir.

Kalhaṇa's information about Mihirakula was entirely based on traditional information handed down orally and it contradicts established historical facts. According to Kalhaṇa Mihirakula was the son of king Vāsula of the Gonanda dynasty and ruled over Kashmir c. 705 B.C. Both these statements are palpably wrong. The Hūṇa king Mihirakula, according to the Gwalior inscription dated in his regnal year 15, was the son of Toramāṇa; and according to the Mandasor stone pillar inscription of Yaśodharman, he was defeated by the latter, sometimes before A.D. 532. Therefore we can not place much reliance upon the account as given in the *Rājataraṅgiṇi*. Of course the stories of Mihirakula's callous nature and his atrocious behaviour as narrated by Kalhaṇa,[38] are based on popular tradition handed down to Kalhaṇa's own time.

Hiuen Tsang's account of Mihirakula too is based on oral tradition as current in the days of the Chinese pilgrim's visit between A.D. 629 and A.D. 649. It is also not entirely reliable. While giving an account of the city of Śākala, modern Sialkot in Pakistan Punjab, he tells us, "Some centuries ago Mihirakula established his authority in this town and ruled over India. He subdued all the neighbouring provinces without exception." Then he goes on to narrate at length Mihirakula's persecution of Buddhism, till he tells us about the defeat of the Hūṇa emperor at the hands of Bālāditya, in the following words:" Bālādityarāja, king of Magadha, profoundly honoured the law of Buddha. When he heard of cruel persecution and atrocities of Mihirakula he strictly guarded the frontiers of his kingdom and refused to pay tribute. When Mihirakula invaded his dominions, Bālāditya took refuge with his army in an island. Mihirakula left the main part of his army incharge of his younger brother, embarked on boats and landed with a part of his troops on the island. He was, however, ambushed by the troops of Bālāditya, in a narrow pass and was taken prisoner. Bālāditya resolved to kill Mihirakula, but released him on the intercession of his mother. Mihirakula found on his return that his brother had gone back and occupied the throne. He, therefore, sought and obtained an asylum in Kashmir. Then he stirred up a rebellion there, killed the king and placed himself on the throne of Kashmir. He next killed the king of Gandhāra, exterminated the royal family, destroyed the *stūpas* and *saṁghārāmas*, plundered the wealth of the country and returned. But within an year he died."

It is impossible to believe this story of Hiuen Tsang, as it is palpably full of so many inaccuracies. Firstly, Mihirakula flourished not some centuries but hardly one century before the arrival of Hiuen Tsang in India. We know that he was defeated by Yaśodharman shortly before A.D. 532. Secondly, there is no evidence to show that Śākala was ever a seat of Mihirakula's government. On the contrary we have some proof that Gwalior was the place of his residence in the fifteenth year of his reign. Thirdly, it is altogether absurd to think that after Toramāṇa's disastrous defeat it would have been possible to exact tribute from the Gupta emperor Narasiṁhagupta Bālāditya about whom the Nalanda inscription of the reign of Yaśovarmadeva eloquently tells us that, "the great king Bālāditya of irresistible valour, having conquered all his enemies, and having enjoyed the entire globe of this earth, built this great temple of the Buddha." Surely such a monarch could not have paid tribute to Mihirakula. Lastly, Gandhāra must have been conquered and occupied by the Hūṇas soon after their victory over the Sassanian king Feroze in A.D. 484 and it is unthinkable that Toramāṇa had occupied Khewra in the Salt Range of the Punjab, without having first conquered Gandhāra. It is therefore absurd to believe that Mihirakula first occupied Kashmir and then conquered Gandhāra. Cosmos clearly states that Mihirakula was at war with Ki-pin, at the time he was writing—c. A.D. 535.

Hiuen Tsang's story apparently looks like one of the many such anecdotes told to foreigners by the Indians about whom the learned Arab scholar, Al-Beruni has remarked that "the Indians do not possess accurate knowledge of their history, and "when pressed for information take to story telling."

We may briefly recapitulate the definitely ascertained facts about the Hūṇas, regarding their dominion in India. After defeating the Persian king Feroze in A.D. 484 the Epthalites advanced towards India, under the leadership of Toramāṇa, whom we find safely entrenched in the Salt Range in the Jhelum District of Punjab (Pakistan). Having consolidated his position he advanced towards the interior of India but instead of entering the Gangetic plain, he made a flanking move and keeping to the west of the Yamuna he attacked the Gupta territory between the Kālindī and Narmadā. We find him occupying the Airikiṇa *Vishaya*[40] and extending his influence further westwards in the Panch Mahal area in eastern Gujrat. This was challanged by a hitherto unknown house of the Aulikara dynasty, recently brought to light through the discovery of the Risthal stone inscription.[41] Its ruler Prakāśadharmā inflicted a crushing defeat on Toramāṇa and sacked and plundered his camp, taking captive the ladies of Toramāṇa's harem. About the same time, the Guptas must have reconquered Eran. As usual with the ancient Indian kings neither Prakśadharmā nor the Guptas pressed their victories to advantage and allowed Toramāṇa to retire to Gwalior where we find his son Mihirakula ruling atleast for 15 years, but he too was defeated by the successor of Prakāśadharmā, namely Yaśodharman sometime before A.D. 532. After this defeat the Hūṇas appear to have lost their Indian dominion.

Although Hiuen Tsang and Kalhaṇa have painted black and frightful picture of Mihirakula, the only known inscription of his time discovered inside the fort at Gwalior, speaks of him in highly favourable light. Mihirakula is described here as the 'remover of affliction'. He is also described as incessantly engaged in the worship of Paśupati i.e. Śiva.[42] Mihirakula's ardent devotion to Śiva is refered to in Yaśodharmā's Mandasor stone pillar inscription, which states that Mihirakula had never reduced his forehead to the abject state of obeisance before anyone except the god Sthānu i.e. Śiva. The legend *Jayatu vṛishaḥ* on his coins also points to his devotion to Śiva.

However, the arrogant independence of Mihirakula was not to be tolerated by a mighty conqueror like Yaśodharmā who humbled the pride of the Hūṇa ruler and forced him to retire to Gandhāra beyond the river Indus, which became the boundary line between the Hūṇa dominions and India proper, as definitely stated by Cosmos.

REFERENCES

1. *IHQ*, XXIV, 67.
2. *IHQ*, VI, 53ff.; *Sel. Ins.*, 331.
3. *IHQ*, IX (1933), 989.
4. *CHI*, III, 88.
5. *IHQ*, IX, 784-88.
6. *IC*, V, 297.
7. For the opposite view see D.R. Bhandarkar, *CII*, III (New Ed. 1981), 85.
8. *Coinage*, 281; Ganguli, D.C., *IHQ*, 1934, 195.
9. B.P. Sinha's view (*DHM*, 6 3) that Vainyagupta was a son of Narasiṁhagupta and was won over by Toramāṇa and instigated to become independent lacks plausibility in the absence of any definite evidence.
10. *CA*, 34.
11. Vide Risthal stone inscription, Mirashi, V.V., *Studies in Ancient Indian History*, 27.
12. Parmārtha's account as given in his Life of Vasubandhu makes Bālāditya a son of king Vikramāditya of Ayodhya who sent his son Bālāditya to the great teacher Vasubandhu for instruction, has to be rejected as faulty and therefore irrelevant.
13. *MASI*, No. 66.
14. *EI*, XX, 37ff.
15. *Coinage*, 266-67.
16. *CCGD*, 141; also *JBRS*, XXXIV, 20-22.

17. *Cf.* Mandasor Pillar Inscription, Fleet, J.F., *CII*, III (1888), 142ff.
18. Krishan Deva, *EI*, XXVI, 235.
19. *CCGD*, 145.
20. Vide *BPI*, *Hūṇair-yasya samāgatasya samare dorbhyāṁ dharā kampita* |
21. *EI*, I, 238ff.
22. Mirashi, V.V., *Indological Research Papers*, Vol. I, 88.
23. Fleet, J.F., *CII*, III, (1888), 159.
24. *EI*, I, 239.
25. *IA*, 1905, 73ff.
26. *JBORS*, XVIII, 203.
27. *IHQ*, XII, 532.
28. *NIA*, IV, 36.
29. *NIA*, V, 249. The suggested identification of Toramāṇa with Torarāya mentioned in the *Kuvalayamalā*, has been rightly rejected by K.P. Mitra in *IHQ*, XXXII, 353-59.
30. Verse 16 of this inscription contains this significant statement:

Ā Taramāṇa nṛipater=nṛipa-mauli-ratna-jyotsnā-pratāna-śabalī-kṛita-pāda-pīṭhām |
Hūṇ-ādhipasya bhuvi yena gataḥ pratishṭhām
nīto yudhā=vitathatām-Adhirāja-śabdah ||

"The title 'Overlord of kings' of the Hūṇa emperor, which had got well established on this earth, from the time of king Toramāṇa whose foot-stool was rendered variegated by the offshoots of lustre of the jewels in the crowns of kings, was rendered meaningless by means of war."

Agrawal, Jagannath, *Researches in Indian Epigraphy & Numismatics*, 92-94.

31. Verse 18; Mirashi, V.V., *Studies in Ancient Indian History*, 27ff.
32. Chhabra & Gai (Ed.), *CII*, III (1981), 352.
33. Fleet, J.F., *CII*, III, (1888), 161ff.
34. Vide the following statement of the Stone Pillar inscription of Yaśodharmā:

Sthāṇor-anyatra yena praṇati-kṛipaṇatāṁ prāpitaṁ n-ottamāṅgam |
CII, III (1888), 147.

35. *Christian Topography*, English Translation by J.W. McCrindle, 371-72.
36. *Ibid.*, 366.
37. Beal, S., *Buddhist Records of the Western World*, 1ff.; See also Chavannes, "*Voyage de Song-Yun dans l'Udyana et le Gandhara*", *Bulletin de l'Ecole d'Extreme Orient*, 1903.
38. *Rājataraṅgiṇi*, I, 289-293. Kalhaṇa's account of Mihirakula's expedition against Siṁhala and his conquest of Chola, Karnāṭa and Lāṭa is nothing more than a fairy tale.
39. *Cf. Vasatām cha girivare=smin rājñaḥ . . . . pādānām.* Fleet, J.F., *CII*, III, (1888), 162ff. These words of the Gwalior inscription of Mihirakula show that he was residing at Gwalior after the defeat of his father Toramāṇa.

40. Vide Eran stone Boar inscription, Fleet, J. F., *CII*, III, 158ff.

41. Mirashi, V.V., *op. cit.*

42. In the inscription the adjective *abhaṅga* is used for Mihirakula with reference to Paśupati. D.C. Sircar has explained *abhaṅga* as *Pūjāvyāpāre virāma-rahitaḥ*, (non-stop in worship) in *Sel. Ins.*, 401, f.n. 3.

CHAPTER XIV

THE FEUDATORIES OF THE GUPTAS

THE AULIKARAS OF MALWA

Epigraphical discoveries of the late nineteenth century brought to light two ruling houses of kings in Malwa, who call themselves Aulikaras. In 1883, J. F. Fleet received from Col. W. Muir, Political Agent at Kota, the photograph of an inscription engraved on a stone tablet which had been noticed in the village named Gangadhar in the present Jhalawar District of Rajasthan. The inscription mentioned a ruling king named Viśvavarmā as also his father Naravarmā who was also a king. In 1884, Fleet's copyists discovered another stone slab built into the wall of a flight of steps at the Mahādev Ghat at Mandasor, the head-quarters of district of the same name, in Madhya Pradesh.[1] This inscription after eulogising king Viśvavarmā with attributes similar to those found in the Gangadhar record supplied a brief eulogy of the latter's son Bandhuvarmā. This inscription composed by a poet Vatsabhaṭṭi became famous because on the basis of this record Fleet identified Mālava reckoning mentioned in line 19 of this record with the famous Vikrama era commencing in B.C. 57. and succeeded in determining the epoch of the Gupta era. The inscription was published by him in 1886 in the *Indian Antiquary* and subsequently included in the *CII*, III published in 1888. Fleet designated the kings mentioned in these two inscriptions as the 'rulers of Malwa'. In 1912 another stone was discovered in a field of the village Todi just close to Mandasor, which belongs to the reign of Naravarmā, and gives the date 461 of Mālava era for his reign. This inscription supplied for the first time a fuller genealogy of this family, It was founded by Jayavarmā whose son Siṁhavarmā was the father of Naravarmā. Thus we have an unbroken succession of five kings from Jayavarmā to Bandhuvarmā who ruled at Daśapura, modern Mandasor. The discovery of the Bihar Kotra stone inscription of Naravarmā dated 474 (A.D. 417) added an interesting piece of information. In the first line of this inscription, Naravarmā is called an Olikara, which is an inaccurate form of Aulikara, which was first met with in the stone slab inscription of Yaśodharman Vishṇuvardhana, dated Mālava year 589.

In 1883 Fleet saw the eye copy of a fragmentary inscription which Arthur Sulivan had sent to General Cunningham in 1879. Fleet sent his copyists to prepare an estampage of this inscription and during the search for this record they discovered another magnificent monolith column with the complete inscription of Yaśodharman. It was first published by Fleet in 1885 in the *Indian Antiquary* and then edited by him in the *CII*, III. Although all the three inscriptions of Yaśodharmā were discovered from Mandasor and although the family is called as *Aulikaralāñchhanaḥ*, his exact relationship with the house of Jayavarmā and better known by the name of Bandhuvarmā since the discovery of the inscription of the Silk-weavers' Guild dated M.S.529, could not be definitely ascertained. In 1923, M.B. Garde, discovered from Mandasor another stone inscription dated M.S. 524. This inscription mentions a king named Prabhākara whom it describes as a great bulwark of the Gupta dynasty. The discovery of two inscriptions of Mahārāja Gauri, one from Mandasor and the other from Chhoti Sadri in the Chittorgarh District of Rajasthan[2], have brought about a new problem regarding the sovereign rule of Ādityavarddhana mentioned in Mahārāja Gauri's inscription from Mandasor. Most important of all is the recent discovery of the Risthal stone slab inscription of Prakāśadharmā dated M.S. 572, which not only enables us to trace the history of the ruling Aulikara house to which the great conqueror Yaśodharmā belonged but also enlightens us about a hitherto unknown and a resounding victory of Yaśodharmā's predecessor Prakāśadharmā over the Hūṇa emperor Toramāṇa.

These inscriptions have brought to light two royal houses of Mālava, both of which called themselves as Aulikaras. The first to become known to modern historians is the line of kings who ruled at Daśapura from the very start. Their inscriptions mentioned above furnish the names of the following kings in order of succession: Jayavarmā, Siṁhavarmā, Naravarmā, Viśvavarmā and Bandhuvarmā. King Prabhākara known from the Mandasor inscription of M.S. 524 belongs most probably to this house, though in the absence of any positive evidence it is difficult to ascertain his relationship to Bandhuvarmā who was ruling in M.S. 493 i.e. A.D. 436. We do not know who ruled over Daśapura after A.D. 436 up to A.D. 467, when Prabhākara was occupying the throne.

In the Mandasor inscription of the Guild of Silk-weavers dated M.S. 529, we have a significant statement in verse 36 that, "much time has passed (since the building of the Sun temple in M.S. 493) and other kings are ruling."[4] Apparently it points to some dynastic change at Daśapura. Is it that Prabhākra, who is described as a very close and faithful ally of the imperial Guptas, was not a lineal descendant of Bandhuvarmā, but had been installed at Daśapura with the material assistance of the imperial Gupta power? We also find that in the year M.S. 547 one Mahārāja Gauri of the Mānavāyani family ruling over Daśapura as a governor or feudatory ruler under the suzerain Ādityavarddhana. This again points to a dynastic change. A definite point is reached in the history of Daśapura when we find that it had passed into the hands of a different Aulikara house sometimes about M.S. 572, when Prakāśadharmā, the victor of Toramāṇa, constructed a magnificent temple of Śiva named after the king's own name as Prakāśeśvara.

Regarding the history of the Aulikaras of Daśapura, we get the earliest details from the Mandasor inscription of Naravarmā. In this record Jayavarmā, the grandfather of Naravarmā is simply described as a king. No conquests or achievements of his have been described. Jayavarmā's son was Siṁhavarmā, who also has been called simply a *Kshitīśa* or king. His son was Naravarmā who too has been termed as a king—*Pārtthiva*; and given an epithet *Siṁhavikrāntagāmī* i.e. moving with the stride of a lion. D.R. Bhandarkar is mistaken in regarding Naravarmā as a feudatory of Chandragupta II on the basis of this epithet of the former. Bhandarkar takes *Siṁhavikrānta-gāmī* in the sense of "a follower of *Siṁha-Vikrānta*",[5] and says, "Siṁhavikrānta is obviously the same as Siṁhavikrama, which we know from Gupta coins, was a title of Chandragupta II." But the word *siṁha-vikrānta* and *siṁhavikrama* do not have the same meaning.[6] Therefore we can not regard Naravarmā as a feudatory of Chandragupta II on the basis of this inscription. Moreover, we do not find any reference to Chandragupta II's sovereignty over Daśapura in the Gangadhara inscription of Viśvavarmā nor in the Mandasor inscription of the Guild of Silk-weavers. In the Bihar Kotra stone inscription too, there is no mention of any sovereign of Naravarmā, though he is given the title of Mahārāja only.

Naravarmā's son and successor, Viśvavarmā, is mentioned in the Gangadhar stone inscription dated M.S. 480 when he was ruling. The inscription describes his prowess and glory in glowing terms. He is said to have excelled the lord of gods, Indra, in valour. Even the oceans are said to have bowed before his armies, at whose march the earth sank down. When that exalted one amongst the kings was ruling, there was none addicted to unrighteous act or to vices; and there was none who may be bereft of happiness. It is a picture of a strong and efficient rule which was conducive to the welfare of the subjects.

Viśvavarmā was succeeded by his son Bandhuvarmā who is profusely showered with praise by the poet Vatsabhaṭṭi in the Mandasor stone inscription dated M.S. 529. It was during his rule over Daśapura, that a magnificent temple of the god Sun was built at Daśapura by the Guild of Silk-weavers in the Mālava year 493, when Kumāragupta was ruling over the earth bounded by the four oceans. The mention of the name of Kumāragupta clearly shows that the Guptas had extended their sway over Daśapura.

For some time after Bandhuvarmā, we are left in the dark about the history of Daśapura. Vatsabhaṭṭi has made a very pregnant remark that 'other kings' were ruling over Daśapura between A.D. 436 and A.D. 472. We now know from the Mandasor inscription dated M.S. 524, that king Prabhākara, who was 'a destroyer of the enemies of the Gupta house' was ruling over Daśapura in A.D. 467. So it can be inferred that upto the last known date of Skandagupta, the rulers of Daśapura were extremely friendly towards the Guptas. For aught we know Vatsabhaṭṭi may also be right and the house of the Aulikaras founded by Jayavarmā might have been replaced. As stated above two inscriptions have come to light, one from Mandasor and the other from Chhoti Sadri. The former supplies the name of a suzerain ruler Ādityavarddhana who is said to have set up his rule at the lovely city of Daśapura after conquering the army of his enemy in battle. The latter inscription from Chhoti Sadri supplies us the genealogy of a family of feudatory rulers, the last of whom was Mahārāja Gauri who was governing this part of Mālava in M.S. 547 (A.D. 490). It is possible that king Ādityavarddhana whose feudatory Mahārāja Gauri excavated a tank at Daśapura, was connected with *Mahārājādhirāja* Dravyavarddhana of Avanti from whom Varāhamihira learnt the science of omens and portents, and thus must have flourished about A.D. 500. However, the rule of Varddhanas of Avanti did not last long as we find a new line of kings—the Aulikaras of the Risthal inscription ruling over Daśapura.

The Risthal stone slab inscription discovered in 1983 has brought to light a new Aulikara dynasty. The founder of this line of valiant heroes was Drumavarddhana, who bore the title of *Senāpati.* It appears that like Pushyamitra Śuṅga, Drumavarddhana also started his career as commander-in-chief of the army of some king, and by dint of his personal prowess he rose to the position of a king.

He begot a son named Jayavarddhana who possessed a large fighting force. His son was Ajitavarddhana whose commands were honoured by the opponent kings. He was constantly engaged in the performance of Soma sacrifices. His son was Vibhīshaṇavarddhana, who removed the darkness of the worlds by means of his noble deeds. His son was Rājayavarddhana, who extended the ancestral domains. His son was Prakāśadharmā on whom the royal fortunes was conferred by his father, who had been much pleased by the virtue of the former.

Prakāśadharmā more than justified his father's choice, by achieving a brilliant victory over the Hūṇas which tremendously enhanced the prestige of the Aulikaras. He inflicted a crushing defeat on the Hūṇa emperor Toramāṇa, sacked his camp, carried away the ladies of the Hūṇa emperor's harem and sent them as maid-servants to the temple of Śiva at Daśapura. Of the tusks of the enemy's elephants killed in battle, he caused to be made splendid chairs which he presented to the ascetics. He also constructed a splendid tank at Risthal, which he named after his grandfather as Vibhīshaṇasara. A temple dedicated to Brahmā was also built by him at Daśapura. Prakāśadharmā had in his service a minister named Bhagavaddosha, whose ancestors had enjoyed this position since the days of his grandfather Shashṭhidatta, a scion of Naigama family. The post of the minister had become hereditary in this family and we find Nirddosha, the grandson of Bhagavaddosha serving under Yaśodharman Vishṇuvardhana;[8] who in all probability was the son and immediate successor of Prakāśadharmā.

Although two inscriptions of Yaśodharman had been long ago discovered at Mandasor which provided detailed information about his conquests, we did not have definite information regarding his ancestory. Even the victory pillar inscription at Mandasor made the vague statement that he was born in a praiseworthy family. The second inscription from Mandasor itself, only furnished us with the fact that his family had the appellation Aulikara; and on this basis he has so far been associated with the house of Jayavarman. However the discovery of the Risthal inscription has established it for the first time that he belonged to a different Aulikara family which had been ruling from Risthal or its neighbourhood for several generations. We may adduce the following reasons for regarding Yaśodharmā as a successor of Prakāśadharmā. Firstly we find that both these rulers had their capital at Daśapura. Secondly, the author of Yaśodharmā's pillar inscription, the poet Vāsula son of Kakka was also the author of the Risthal epigraph of Prakāśadharmā. Not only the name is common but the very wording of the last verse is almost identical.[9] Thirdly the ministers of both the kings are members of the same Naigama family. Shashṭhidatta who was the grandfather of Bhagavaddosha, the minister of Prakāśadharmā, calls himself as one whose good name had become famous on account of his serving at the feet of those kings who were the founders of the family of the lord (Yaśodharmā). So it is crystal clear that both Prakāśadharmā and Yaśodharmā belonged to the same Aulikara family.

From the two Mandasor inscriptions we get a graphic account of the prestige, prowess and the conquests of Yaśodharmā. We can also form a vivid idea of his imperial jurisdiction. We are told in the stone slab inscription that, "having brought under his control many great kings of the east as well as of the north, he adopted the titles of *Rājādhirāja* and Parmeśvara.' From the stone pillar inscription we learn that the feudatories from the vicinity of the river Brahmaputra and from the Mahendra mountain in the east, up to the Himalayas in the north and the

Paśchima Payodhi (Arabian Sea) in the west, came to the seat of his government to pay homage. This is a picture of Yaśodharmā's extensive jurisdiction practically over the whole of northern India. Some scholars have doubted the veracity of this claim particularly in view of the fact that we find the imperial Gupta rulers like Kumāragupta III and Vishṇugupta still ruling over the territory from Bhitari in Eastern U.P. to Puṇḍravardhana in northern Bengal. While some element of exaggeration in the claim of Yaśodharmā may be conceded, the whole of it can not be regarded as a vain boast. It may be suggested that as stated in the stone slab inscription, Yaśodharmā had achieved the position of a supreme ruler both by means of war as well as by diplomacy.

Yaśodharmā's crowning glory was his subjugation of the Hūṇa emperor Mihirakula, who is said to be so powerful as to have never bowed before anyone except the god Śiva. We may take it as certain that Yaśodharman had succeeded in completely crushing the Hūṇa power which had already received a heavy blow at the hands of Prakāśadharmā. It is therefore quite probable that Mihirakula had been forced by Yaśodharmā to retire beyond the Indus, where the Alexanderine writer Cosmos found him in c. A.D. 535. We are in complete agreement with V. V. Mirashi in giving the entire credit for Mihirakula's defeat to Yaśodharmā who was as great a national hero as Skandagupta Vikramāditya.

[The Aulikaras of Risthal and Yaśodharmā were not Gupta feudatories]

The Maitrakas of Valabhī

A large number of copper plate grants discovered from various places in Surāshtra and adjacent .regions in Gujrat, reveals to us a line of rulers who call themselves Maitrakas and had their capital at Valabhī, the present day Vallabhipur in the Bhaunagar District of Gujrat. The founder of this royal house was Bhaṭārka, who has been given the title of *Senāpati* in the records of his successors. We have no records of his own. For a long time there prevailed a misunderstanding regarding Bhaṭārka's relationship with the Maitrakas. It was generally believed that Bhaṭārka rose to power after defeating the Maitrakas.[10] It was Hultzsch who first pointed out the mistake and established that Bhaṭārka himself belonged to the Maitraka family.[11] Another misunderstanding about the Maitrakas was that they were foreigners and a Sun worshipping people and closely connected with the Hūṇas.[12] While Mihira and Mitra both mean the Sun, the derivative Maitraka is never used in Sanskrit literature in the sense of a Sun-worshipper.[13] What is still more important is the fact that the Maitraka rulers with the exception of one king, were not the worshippers of the god Sun. Out of twenty-one kings of this dynasty as many as nineteen were devoted worshippers of Śiva. Only Dharapaṭṭa, the fifth in descent from Bhaṭārka was a *param-Ādityabhakta*—a great devotee of the Sun. In the face of this definite evidence it is preposterous to suggest that the Maitrakas were a Sun-worshipping people.

The real explanation of the word Maitraka is as follows:

Mitra was one of the pupils of Lakulīśa, who is regarded as an incarnation of Śiva. A follower of this religious preceptor is called a Maitraka. Being the followers of Mitra the family came to be known as Maitraka.

We have no definite information as to how did Bhaṭārka gain political power. His title of *Senāpati* shows that probably like Pushyamitra Śuṅga he was also a commander-in-chief of the army of some great ruler. As Bhaṭārka's second son Droṇasiṁha is known to be ruling in the year 183 (A.D. 502), we can place Bhaṭārka circa A.D. 462 by assigning twenty years each to Bhaṭārka and his eldest son Dharasena I. At this time Skandagupta was still ruling over Surāshtra. We may therefore suggest that Skandagupta who had exercised so much vigilance in the selection of the governor for this province, had also felt the urgency of posting a capable military officer in this vulnerable region and had appointed Bhaṭārka as *Senāpati*, who was later on put incharge of entire administration, civil as well as military. Bhṭārka's authority was thus established in Surāshṭra. We have already seen in several cases that senior administrative posts in the Gupta administration had become hereditary. Bhaṭārka's son Dharasena became the governor of Surāshṭra like his father but still with the title *Senāpati*. Dharasena's younger brother Droṇasiṁha became the governor after his elder brother and made a grant of land recorded in his Bhamodra Mohotta copper plate dated 183 or A.D. 502.[14] In this inscription Droṇasiṁha expressly acknowledges his allegiance to his overlord whose name is not mentioned but who is designated as "the sole owner of the entire circumference of the earth and the highest Lord". This is very clear from this statement that the Maitrakas still professed allegiance to the imperial authority and had not declared themselves as independent. The records of the successors of Droṇasiṁha further confirm this fact by recording that 'the installation in the royalty by besprinkling' of Mahārāja Droṇasiṁha was personally performed by 'the supreme lord who was the master of the circumference of the whole world'. This ceremony of the anointment of Droṇasiṁha must have taken place sometimes before A.D. 502, since we find him using the title Mahārāja in his Bhamodra Mohotta copper plate, instead of that of *Senāpati* borne by two of his predecessors. It is therefore clear that Droṇasiṁha had become a feudatory ruler before A.D. 502 and his relations with his overlord were very cordial. We are not faced with any difficulty in finding out the name of the paramount ruler to whom Droṇasiṁha owed allegiance. The only ruler in northern India in c. A.D. 500 who can rightly claim this honour must be a Gupta emperor and he was in all probabilty either Budhagupta or Vainyagupta.[15] He cannot be the Hūṇa ruler Toramāṇa, as suggested by some, because the Maitrakas continued to use the Gupta era in dating their records. The Hūṇas and their feudatories like Mahārāja Bhūta used the regnal years in their inscriptions. Therefore, it can be definitely stated that the Maitrakas did not part company with the Guptas in bitterness but assumed independence only when the Guptas had themselves collpased.

Mahārāja Droṇasiṁha was succeeded by Dhruvasena I whose copper plate grants supply dates from G.S. 206 to G.S. 226 which means he ruled from 525 to 545. Dhruvasena seems to have kept the semblance of allegiance to his Gupta overlord since there is the old style reference to a supreme lord in all his grants. Perhaps he was the last of the Maitrakas to show this courtesy. Of his immediate successor Dharapaṭa we have no records. The next ruler Mahārāja Guhasena however made several grants of land from which we get dates ranging from 237 to 248 i.e. A.D. 556 to 567. He is the first Maitraka ruler who does not express his allegiance to any overlord. The imperial

Guptas had collapsed by this time and naturally the Maitrakas ceased to make any reference to their sovereignty.

Parivrājaka Mahārājas

In the Allahabad stone pillar inscription of Samudragupta, he is said to have reduced to servitude all the kings of the forest region, which has been identified with Bundelkhand on the basis of the mention of 18 forest kingdoms in the Khoh copper plate grant[15] of the Parivrājaka Mahārāja Saṁkshobha, dated Gupta year 209. It may therefore be inferred that the Parivrājaka kings had become the feudatories of the Guptas sometimes circa A.D. 350. The copper plate grants of two kings Hastin and Saṁkshobha which have been discovered from various places in the erstwhile Jaso and Nagod states in Madhya Pradesh, supply us with the following genealogy of the dynasty. The progenitor of the dynasty was the royal ascetic Suśarman of Bhāradvāja *gotra*. Born in his family was Mahārāja Devāḍhya, whose son was Mahārāja Prabhañjana from whom was born Mahārāja Dāmodara. His son was Mahārāja Hastin, from whom was born Mahārāja Saṁkshobha.

We have no records of the time of first four rulers, and whatever we know about them is derived from the copper plates of Mahārāja Hastin and Mahārāja Saṁkshobha. These grants explicitly mention the prevalence of the rule of the Gupta kings which indirectly points to the sovereignty of the Guptas over the Parivrājaka kings.

The founder of the dynasty Suśarman, who is compared with the great sage Kapila, belonged to the Bhāradvāja *gotra* of Brahmans and though a king his way of life was that of a sage. Of the next three kings Devāḍhya, Prabhañjana and Dāmodara, no particulars are given, but we get some details about the son of Dāmodara namely Mahārāja Hastin who in his copper plate charters is described as a donor of thousands of cows and of land. He is credited with victories in a hundred battles and is said to be devoted to gods and Brahmans. His charitable disposition is clearly established by his many grants of land to Brahman families. The dates given in his copper plate inscriptions range from 156 to 198, thus giving him a long rule of forty-two years. He was a contemporary of Mahārāja Śarvanātha of the family of the kings of Uchchakalpa, whose kingdom was contiguous to that of his own, as is indicated by the Bhumra pillar inscription.[17] Of his son and successor Saṁkshobha we have two copper plate grants, one from Betul which is dated 199 and the other from Khoh dated 209. Saṁkshobha appears to have been an ideal Hindu ruler who was constantly engaged in establishing the law of castes and *Āśramas*. He is described as a great devotee of Vishṇu—*Parama-bhāgavata.* His Khoh grant opens with an invocation of the god Vāsudeva. This is a departure from the time of Hastin whose grants open with salutation to Śiva—Mahādeva. The reference to the enjoyment of sovereignty by the Gupta kings in the Khoh grant dated 209 is important in as much as it shows that in the year A.D. 528, a Gupta emperor was still recognised as the sovereign. This ruler might have been Narasiṁhagupta Bālāditya. The copper plate grants of the Parivrājakas therefore are an important evidence for the continuation of the imperial Gupta power up to A.D. 528. The Parivrājaka dynasty might have come to an end with Saṁkshobha for we have no record of this dynasty after him.

KINGS OF UCHCHAKALPA

Quite close to the territory of the Parivrājaka Mahārājas, there ruled another line of feudatory rulers who issued their charters of grants of land from a place called Uchchakalpa which was most probably their capital. It is identical with the modern city of Nagod, in the Satna District of Madhya Pradesh. It was locally called Uchahara up to recent times, when Nagod was a princely state.

From the copper plate grants which were issued from Uchchakalpa and which have been discovered during the last one hundred years or so we get the following list of succession of the kings of Uchchakalpa. Mahārāja Oghadeva, Mahārāja Kumāradeva, Mahārāja Jayasvāmī, Mahārāja Vyāghradeva, Mahārāja Jayanātha and Mahārāja Śarvanātha. Only of the last two kings, the charters of grants of land have come to light which have supplied us the succession list given above. In order to form some idea of their jurisdiction, it seems necessary to give a brief account of the find spots of the two copper plate charters of Jayanātha, written in the Central Indian variety of the Gupta alphabet. The one dated 177 has been found from the valley near the village Khoh in the Satna District of Madhya Pradesh. The other dated 174 was discovered from the village Karitalai, 23 miles from Murwada, the headquarters of the Tehsil of the same name in the Jabalpur District. Three copper plates of the reign of Mahārāja Śarvanātha, bearing dates 193, 197 and 214 and one undated have been found at the village Khoh already mentioned; and one copper plate of Mahārāja Śarvanātha dated 191 was discovered at village Sohawal in the Satna District of Madhya Pradesh.[18] Two inscriptions on stone slabs have been found, one at Nachne-ki-talai,[19] a hamlet seven miles from the town of Jaso in the Satna District and the other at Ganj[20] near Ajaigarh in Panna District of Madhya Pradesh. Both these inscriptions record that a certain Vyāghra who appears as a feudatory of the Vākāṭaka king Pṛithivīsheṇa [II] performed some charitable act for the religious merit of his parents.

There has been some difference of opinion among scholars, as to the era to which the dates in the grants of the Uchchakalpa kings have to be referred. Some scholars prefer to regard these dates as pertaining to the Kalachurī era of A.D. 248-49, whereas others refer them to the Gupta era. However, V.V. Mirashi has convincingly shown that these dates cannot be referred to the Kalachurī era as that goes against the known fact that Mahārāja Hastin of the Parivrājaka dynasty was a contemporary of Mahārāja Śarvanātha of the Uchchakalpa dynasty. The two kings are mentioned in the Bhumra stone pillar inscription.[21] The known dates for Mahārāja Hastin are 156 to 198 of the Gupta era i.e. A.D. 475 to 517. The known dates of his contemporary Śarvanātha are 193 to 214. If we refer these dates to the Kalchuri era of A.D. 248-49, we get for Śarvanātha the dates A.D. 441 to 462, when he cannot be a contemporary of Mahārāja Hastin. But if we refer his dates to the Gupta era we get for Śarvanātha, the dates A.D. 512 to 534, when he becomes a contemporary of Mahārāja Hastin. Thus it is clear that the dates in these copper plate grants are to be referred to the Gupta era. It is also to be noted that these copper plates are engraved in the Central Indian variety of the Gupta script and not in the

Box-headed variety which is generally used in the Vākāṭaka inscriptions. The Vākāṭaka sovereignty over this dynasty as indicated by the Ganj and Nachne-ki-talai inscriptions, was therefore a transient phenomenon. The successors of Vyāghra, appear again to have switched over their loyalty to the Guptas.

REFERENCES

1. This stone is now preserved in the Gujri Mahal Museum at Gwalior.
2. *EI*, XXX, 223ff.
3. First published by K.V. Ramesh & S.P. Tewari, *JESI*, X, 96ff.; an improved version by V.V. Mirashi, *Studies in Ancient Indian History*; correction of readings and translation by Jagannath Agrawal, *Researches in Indian Epigraphy and Numismatics*, 91.
4. *Bahunā samatītena kālen=ānyaiś=cha pārtthivaiḥ |*
vyaśiryyat=aika-deśo=sya bhavanasya tato=dhunā ||
Chhbra & Gai (ed.), *CII*, III, (1981), 327.
5. *Ibid*., 66-67.
6. According to Prof. Jagannath Agrawal, the expression *siṁha-vikrāntagāmī* means "one who moves with the stride of a lion." We may compare with this expression, Kālidāsa's line *tato mṛigendrasya mṛigendra-gāmī* in *Raghuvaṁśa*, II, 30, where *mṛigendragāmī* means 'having the gait of a lion'. In order to obtain the sense of 'follower' we need a word like *anugāmī*. *Vikrānta* as a noun means hero; but as an adjective it means 'powerful'. It is derived from the root *kramu* (*pāda vikshepe*). So the meaning stride is the only proper one, when it is accompanied by the word *gāmī*, (explained by Jagannath Agrawal.)
7. V.V. Mirashi does not agree with this view. But his explanation of the mention of Kumāragupta's name that it "was probably intended to mark the time of their migration as the Gupta kings were famous in those days" is far from satisfactory. *Studies in Ancient Indian History*, 104-05.
8. Vide Mandasor stone slab inscription dated M.S. 589. J.F. Fleet, (ed. 1888), *CII*, III, 150ff.
9. *Iti tushṭūshayā tasya nṛipateḥ puṇya-karmaṇaḥ |*
Vāsulen=oparachitāḥ ślokāḥ Kakkasya sūnunā || Mandasor Pillar inscription. The only difference is that the Risthal inscription has *pūrvv=eyaṃ* instead of *ślokāḥ* and *Kakkasūnunā* in place of *Kakkasya sūnunā*.
10. *Cf*. Fleet, J.F., *CII*, III, ed. 1888 167.
11. *EI*, III, 319.
12. Bhagwanlal Indraji had stated that, "though these Maitrakas are mentioned in no other record from Surāshtra, there seems a reason to identify the Maitrakas with the Mihiras." *JASB*, 1909, 184. (Quoted by D.R. Bhandarkar). For similar opinion see Fleet, J.F., *IA*, 1886, 361; Ray, N.R., *IHQ*, 1928, 457; Bhandarkar, D.R., *JASB*, 1909, 183.

13. *Cf.* Jagannath Agrawal, *IC*, V, 408.
14. *EI*, XVI, 18f.
15. The last known date for Budhagupta is 180 and for Vainyagupta we have 188 from the Gunaighar copper-plate inscription.
16. Fleet, J.F., (ed. 1888), *CII*, III, 112.
17. *Ibid.*, 110.
18. *EI*, XIX, 129; for other inscription see Fleet, J.F., (ed. 1888), *CII*, III, 117-135.
19. *Ibid.* 233.
20. *EI*, XVII, 13.
21. Fleet, J.F., *Op. cit.* The stone has been called a *bala-yashṭi* in the inscription, which means a memorial stone set up in memory of a departed relative. We have other examples, Supia stone pillar is a *yashṭi.* Some *yashṭis* were set up during the reign of Chashṭana, Mirashi, V.V., *Inscriptions & Coins of the Sātavāhanas and Western Kshatrapas*, 118-19.

EPILOGUE

DISINTEGRATION AND COLLAPSE

BEFORE CLOSING our survey of the glorious epoch of the Gupta rule which is regarded as the golden age of Indian history, we have to answer one question. It is amazing how this splendid edifice of the Gupta empire which had been built up by the heroic efforts of mighty conquerors like Samudragupta and further expanded and fortified by the dazzling personality of Chandragupta II Vikramāditya who planted the Gupta flag on the banks of the river Oxus, the northern-most boundary of ancient Bhāratavarsha, and who rebuilt and enhanced its prestige even after the debacle of Rāmagupta, an empire which had been successfully protected from the terrible avalanche of the barbarian Hūṇas whose pride had been completely humbled by that sole hero of the Gupta dynasty—Skandagupta, tumbled down within a span of half a century after the death of Budhagupta. We have to examine this amazing phenomenon in depth and find out the causes responsible for this catastrophe.

In order to find a satisfactory answer to this question, we shall study some of the trends which mark the course of events in Gupta history after the death of Skandagupta. The mystery of the crash, will then, unfold itself.

Firstly it may be noted that after Skandagupta whose reign came to a close circa A.D. 467, the succession to the throne did not proceed in the usual and time honoured manner, from the father to his eldest son. Probably Skandagupta died issueless and consequently the throne passed on to his half-brother Purugupta, who had several sons, two of whom namely Budhagupta and Narasiṁhagupta are known from the Nalanda clay sealing of the former and the latter from his Nalanda clay sealing and the Bhitari copper-silver seal. Two more kings—Kumāragupta of the Sarnath Buddha image inscription dated G.S. 154 and Vainyagupta known from his Gunaighar copper plate inscription dated G.S. 188 and the fragmentary Nalanda clay sealing were most probably the sons of Purugupta since their dates run consecutively. The great king Bhānugupta known from the Eran memorial pillar inscription dated G.S. 191 was also in all probability a son of Purugupta. Purugupta must have come to the throne after A.D. 467 and was followed by Kumāragupta II for whom we have the date G.E. 154. Then comes Budhagupta whose known dates run from G.S. 157 to G.S. 178/180. Next we have Vainyagupta whose available date is 188 followed by Bhānugupta who fought a battle at Eran in G.S. 191. Last of all comes Narasiṁhagupta for whom we have no date.

This order of succession from brother to brother must have resulted in excluding from accession to the throne, the eldest son of the deceased king in favour of a brother of the deceased. This went on happening for five generations continuously from Kumāragupta II to Narasiṁhagupta. This departure from the general practice of the law of primo-geniture must have led to a sense of frustration amongst the princes and in consequence discontent, which ultimately must have resulted in wranglings and scramble for the throne. In such a situation the feudatories, whose support must have been sought by the various claimants played a crucial role in the matter of succession. The feudatories thus came to get great importance, which must have made them over-bearing. So long as the imperial sceptre was in strong hands the integrity of the empire remained unimpaired, but when the rulers became weak, the feudatories threw off their alligiance. Consequently the empire was fragmented into several principalities.

When this was the state of affairs in the imperial house, there appeared on the scene a new and unforeseen danger to the security of the Gupta rule. A line of Aulikara kings, founded by Drumavarddhana had been gradually building its strength and by the time of its king Prakāśadharmā, it achieved a sovereign status. Prakāśadharmā became so powerful that he challenged the Hūṇas and inflicted a crushing defeat on Toramāṇa and deprived him of his imperial title.[1] Prakāśadharmā's successor Yaśodharmā further strengthened his position and undertook a *digvijaya*, the traditional Indian 'conquest of the quarters', and subjugated "many great kings of the East and several of the North."[2] He also claims that feudatories from the vicinity of the river Brahmaputra and from the Mahendra mountain (Eastern

Ghats) and from the Himalayas to the Western ocean, paid homage at his feet.[3] While it is not possible to accept this claim in its entirety, this much at least must be conceded that the armies of the Aulikara hero had marched over the length and breadth of northern India and he received the submission of many rulers.

We must however note that Yaśodharman's military campaign did not result in the collapse of the Gupta empire, because epigraphic evidence clearly points out that the Gupta king Kumāragupta III was still issuing grants in Bhitari in Ghazipur District of U.P. and made some donation to the university of Nālandā in Magadha, and even his son Vishṇugupta whose fragmentary clay sealing has been found at Nalanda still exercised sovereign power over Puṇḍravardhana in northern Bengal as is apparent from the Damodarpur copper plate dated G.S. 224 or A.D. 543.[4] We have therefore to take Yaśodharman's claim made in A.D. 532, with the modification that the Gupta emperors were still exercising imperial authority over considerable areas in northern India. The Gupta empire might have received some jolt as a result of Yaśodharman's campaign but the Gupta emperors still occupied the imperial throne.

The substantial loss of territory and imperial authority of the Guptas was caused by their own erstwhile feudatories—the Maukharis and the house of Kṛishṇagupta. Considerable light has been thrown on the history of the Maukharis by the discovery of the Haraha stone inscription dated *Saṁvat* 611.[5] It supplies the names of four Maukhari rulers—Harivarmā, Ādityavarmā, Īśvaravarmā and Iśānavarmā. From the Asirgadh seal of Maukhari Śarvavarmā and the Nalanda clay sealing of Maukhari Avantivarmā, we know that the first three rulers had the title of Mahārāja only. This means that they were feudatory rulers owing allegiance to some sovereign power. The fourth ruler of the family namely Iśānavarmā is styled as a *Mahārājādhirāja*, which means that he was an independent and sovereign ruler. While he had achieved this position by means of his widespread conquests which have been detailed in the Haraha inscription, it may also be inferred that he had also overthrown the overlordship of the Guptas.

Just like the Haraha inscription, the Aphsad inscription of Ādityasena,[6] has brought to light the existence of another ruling house which was feudatory to begin with but became sovereign at about the same time, as the Maukharis. This is the house of Kṛishṇagupta, generally called as the Later Guptas of Magadha. The fourth ruler of this house was Kumāragupta who was a contemporary of the Maukhari Iśānavarmā and was a contestant for the imperial position in northern India. Being a contemporary of Iśānavarmā, Kumāragupta can be easily assigned to the middle of the sixth century A.D. He too may be taken to have repudiated the imperial Gupta overlordship and declared himself independent, after which he entered into a contest for supremacy with the Maukhari Iśānavarmā.

Thus these two powers, the Maukharis and the line of Kṛishṇagupta, snatched from the hands of the Guptas considerable territory in U.P. and Bihar and hastened the crash of the Gupta empire. Another new political power came in existence almost about this time. It was that of the Pushyabhūtis in the Śrikaṇṭha *janapada* or modern Haryana. Its early rulers from Naravardhana to Ādityavardhana were Mahārājas. It was Prabhākaravardhana who assumed the title of *Mahārājādhirāja*, in the middle of the sixth century A.D.

The story in the far eastern parts of the empire was not much different. Samataṭa or south-eastern Bengal was a frontier state in the time of Samudragupta, but it was conquered and annexed by Chandragupta II after the great battle mentioned in the Mehrauli pillar inscription. We find Vainyagupta ruling over a part of it in A.D. 507. But shortly after this date Mahārāja Vijayasena who owed allegiance to Vainyagupta figures as a feudatory of *Mahārājādhirāja* Gopachandra in the Vardhamāna *bhukti*.[7] The Faridpur copper plates also show that in this region an independent kingdom had come into existence under *Mahārājādhirāja* Dharmāditya.[8]

The Ghugrahaṭṭi[9] copper plate tells us about king Samāchāradeva in this very region. His gold coins of *Rājalīlā* type were discovered on the river Arunkhali in the Jessore District of Bangladesh and a sealing was found at Nalanda.[10] The copper plate and the coins indicate his jurisdiction over the Faridpur-Jessore region. He appears to have succeeded Dharmāditya. This was yet another defection from the imperial Gupta authority.

So we find that right from the mouths of the Ganges in the east up to the Yamuna in the west, the Gupta empire was being parcelled out into small independent kingdoms. The centrifugal tendencies were at full play and the empire was crumbling to bits.

It has been generally believed that the Hūṇa invasions under Toramāṇa and his son Mihirakula were the primary cause of the downfall of the Guptas. While there is no doubt that Toramāṇa penetrated into Central India as far as Eran, and brought under his overlordship some parts of Gujrat, but the new evidence that has come to light with the discovery of the Risthal stone slab inscription, proves beyond doubt that Toramāṇa's success was shortlived and confined to a small part of the Gupta empire. We are told in this inscription that Toramāṇa was signally defeated by the Aulikara emperor Prakāśadharmā sometimes before M.S. 572 or A.D. 515. The Hūṇas now were on the run and we find that Mihirakula had retired to Gwalior. He had even done homage to Prakāśadharmā's successor, the Aulikara emperor Yaśodharman. The Hūṇas were thus only a contributory factor to the decline of the Gupta imperial power and not an important cause of it. R.C. Majumdar has rightly observed, "In spite of their initial success the Hūṇas were effectively checked. They had no doubt caused damages and devastations on a large scale, and dealt a great blow to the prestige of the empire, but except for a very short period, they did not count as an important factor in Indian politics, and the Gupta empire successfully outlived that period."[11]

The last known ruler of the imperial Gupta line is Vishṇugupta, to whose reign belongs most probably, the Damodarpur copper plate dated G.E. 224. This date may be regarded as practically marking the end of the imperial Gupta rule. In the Jain works, the *Harivaṁśa Purāṇa* and *Tiloyapaṇṇatti*, the total duration of the Gupta rule is given as 231 years. Counting from the epoch of the Gupta era i.e. A.D. 318-19. this brings us to A.D. 550 as the closing date for the imperial Gupta rule which is very near to A.D. 543, the date of Damodarpur copper plate inscription.

In the west, the Maitrakas who were in control of Surāshṭra and Gujrat, realising the weak position of the imperial Gupta power, ceased after sometime to keep even the semblance of allegiance and became independent *de facto*. Thus collapsed one of the greatest, the most brilliant in achievements and most efficient in administration, of all the empires that ancient India had created.

Although the empire perished in the middle of the sixth century A.D., its name lingered on in some remote parts of India, just as has been said in the Mehrauli iron pillar inscription of Chandra, "The great heat of the forest conflagration continues even after the fire has been extinguished." The Sumandal copper plate inscription of king Pṛithivīvigraha who was the ruler of Kaliṅga, refers to the sovereignty of the Guptas in the year 250 i.e. A.D. 569-70. This was perhaps the last flicker of an extinguishing lamp.

References

1. Mirashi, V.V., *Studies in Ancient Indian History*, 27ff.
2. Mandasor stone slab inscription, Fleet, J.F., *CII*, III, (1888), 153, line 6.
3. *Ibid.*
4. Vide Damodarpur copper plate dated 224, *CII*, III, (1981 ed.), 361f.
5. *EI*, XIV, 110ff.
6. Fleet, J, F, (ed. 1888), *CII*, III, 200ff.
7. *EI*, XXIII, 159.
8. *IA*, 1910, 95 and 200ff.
9. *EI*, XVIII, 74ff.
10. *MASI*, No. 66, 31-32.
11. *CHI*, III, 106-07.

BIBLIOGRAPHY

ORIGINAL SOURCES

SANSKRIT LITERATURE

EPICS:

Mahābhārata: Text, Gita Press Gorakhpur, V.S. 2013. Tr. (Hindi), Gita Press Gorakhpur. Critical Edition, Bhandarkar Oriental Research Institute, Poona. Eng. Tr., M.N. Dutt, Calcutta, 1895-1905.

Rāmāyaṇa of Vālamiki: Text, N.S. Press, Bombay. Text, Ed. Siva Ram Sharma, Chowkhamba Vidyabhawan, Varanasi, 1975. Eng. Tr., R.T.H. Griffith, Benaras, 1915.

PURĀṆAS:

Bhāgavata Purāṇa: 2 Vols. Gita Press, Gorakhpur.

Brahmāṇḍa Purāṇa: Motilal Banarsidass, Delhi.

Harivaṁśa Purāṇa: Ed. R. Kinjawadekar, Poona, 1936.

Mārkaṇḍeya Purāṇa: Eng. Tr., F.E. Pargitar, Calcutta, 1904.

Vāyu Purāṇa: Venkateśvara Press, Bombay, 1913.

Vishṇu Purāṇa: Eng. Tr., H.H. Wilson, London, 1864-70.

Pargitar, F.E.: *Purāṇa Text of the Dynasties of Kali Age*, Oxford, 1913. *Ancient Indian Historical Tradition*, Delhi, 1972.

DHARMAŚĀSTRA

Bṛihaspati Smṛiti : Ed. K.V. Rangaswami Aiyangar, Baroda, 1941. Eng. Tr., J. Jolly, *Sacred Books of the East*, Oxford, 1889.

Nārada Smṛiti: Sacred Books of the East, Oxford, 1889.

Yājñavalkya Smṛiti: Text, Bombay, 1909. Eng. Tr., J.R. Gharpure, Bombay, 1936.

Historical Works

Bāṇa: *Harsha-Charit*, N.S. Press, Bombay, 1946. Eng. Tr., E.B. Cowell & F.W. Thomas, London, 1897.

Daṇḍin: *Daśakumāracharita*, Eng. Tr., A.W. Reyder, Chicago, 1927.

Kalhaṇa: *Rājataraṅgiṇi*, Text, Stein, M.A., Bombay, 1892. Eng. Tr., Stein, M.A., 2 Vols., Delhi, 1961. Text, Vishva Bandhu, Hoshiarpur.

Shastri, Jivaram: *Kṛishṇacharita* aṭtributed to Harisheṇa Kālidās.

Polity

Kāmandakīyanītisāra Ed. T. Ganapati Sastri, Trivendrum, 1912.

Lexicons

Amarasiṁha *Amarakośa*, N.S. Press, Bombay.

Astronomy

Varāhamihira *Brihatsamhita*, V. Subramanya Sastri & M. Ramakrishan Bhat, 2 Vols., Bangalore, 1947.

Poetics & Dramaturgy

Bhoja *Sarasvatī-kaṇṭhābharaṇa*, N.S. Press, Bombay, 1934.
Śṛiṅgāraprakāśa, Ed. G.R. Josyer, Mysore, 1955.
Kshemendra *Auchityavichāracharchā*, N.S. Press, Bombay.
Rājaśekhara *Kāvyamīmāṁsā*, Baroda, 1934.
Rāma Chandra & Guṇa Chandra *Nāṭyadarpaṇa*, Baroda, 1929.
Vāmana *Kāvyālaṅkāra-sūtra-vṛitti*, Bombay, 1926.

Drama, Poetry & Fable

Agrawala, V.S. & Moti Chandra (Ed.) *Śṛiṅgārahāṭa* or *Chaturabhāni*, Bombay.

Kālidāsa *Abhijñāna Śākuntalam*, Ed. M.R. Kale, Bombay; *Mālavikāgnimitram*, N.S. Press, Bombay. *Meghadūta*, N.S. Press, Bombay, 1953. *Kumārasambhava*, N.S. Press, Bombay, 1946. *Raghuvaṁśa*, N.S. Press, Bombay. *Ritusaṁhāra*, N.S. Press, Bombay, 1922. *Vikramorvaśīyām*, Ed. S.P. Pandit, Bombay, 1901.

Somadeva: *Kathāsaritasāgara*, N.S. Press, Bombay. Eng. Tr., C.H. Tawney & N.M. Penzer, London, 1924-1928.

Subandhu: *Vāsavadattā*.

Vijjikā (?): *Kaumudīmahotsava*, M.R. Kavi, Madras, 1929.

BUDDHIST & JAIN LITERATURE

Abhidhāna-chintāmaṇi of Hemachandra Acharya, Ed. Hargovindas Bechardas & Muni Jina Vijaya, 2 Vols., Bhavnagar, 1914-19.

Āryamañjuśrī-mūlakalpa Ed. K.P. Jayaswal, Ed. T. Ganapati Sastri, Trivandrum, 1925.

Prabhāvaka-charita

Prabandha-chintāmaṇi of Merutuṅga, Ed. Muni Jina Vijaya, Santiniketan, 1933.

Tiloyapaṇṇatti of Yati Vṛishbhācharya Ed. A.N. Upadhyaya & H.L. Jain, Sholapur, 1956.

Chandragarbhaparipichchhā

FOREIGN WRITINGS

Beal, Samuel: *Si-yu-ki, Buddhist Records of the Western World* (*Hiuen tsang's account of his travels in India*), 2 Vols. London 1906. Motilal Banarsidass Delhi.

Giles, H.A.: *The Travels of Fa-hien*, Cambridge, 1923.

Legge, J.H.: *Record of the Buddhist Kingdoms, Being an Account of the Chinese Monk Fa-hien*, Oxford, 1886.

Sachau, E.C.: *Kitab-ul-Hind*, Eng. Tr., *Alberuni's India*, London, 1914.

Takakusu, J.A.: *Record of the Buddhistic Religion as Practised in India and the Malay Archipelago by I-tsing*, Oxford 1896.

Watters, T.: *On Yuan-chwang's Travels in India*, 2 Vols., London, 1904-1905.

INSCRIPTIONS:

Agrawal, Jagannath: *Recent Researches in Indian Epigraphy & Numismatics*, New Delhi, 1986. *Inscriptions of the Imperial Guptas*, (Manuscript).

Agrawala, P.K.: *Imperial Gupta Epigraphs*, Varanasi, 1983.

Bhandarkar, D.R.: *Corpus Inscriptionum, Indicarum* III, Ed.Chhabra, B. Ch. & Gai, G.S., Delhi, 1981.

List of Inscriptions of Northern India, Appendix, *EI*, XIX-XXIII.

Fleet, J.F.: *Inscriptions of the Early Gupta Kings & Their Successors, Corpus Inscriptionum Indicarum*, III, Calcutta, 1888.

Herzfeld: *Paikuli: Monument & Inscription*, 2 Vols., Berlin, 1924.

Mirashi, V.V.: *Inscriptions of the Vākāṭakas, Corpus Inscriptionum Indicarum*, V, Ootacamund, 1963. *The History and Inscriptions of the Sātavāhanas and the Western Kshatrapas*, Bombay, 1981.

Sircar, D.C.: *Select Inscriptions*, Vol. I, Calcutta, 1942. Vol. II, Delhi, 1983. *Indian Epigraphy*, Delhi 1965. *Indian Epigraphical Glossary*, Delhi, 1966.

Thaplyal, K.K.: *Studies in Ancient Seals*, Lucknow, 1972.

LIST OF GUPTA INSCRIPTIONS:

1. Allahabad Stone pillar inscription of Samudragupta, Chhabra & Gai (ed.), *CII*, III, 203.
2. Eran Stone inscription of Samudragupta, Chhabra & Gai (ed.), *CII*, III, 220.
3. Nalanda copper plate of Samudragupta, Chhabra & Gai (ed.), *CII*, III, 224.
4. Gaya copper plate inscription of Samudragupta, Chhabra, & Gai, (ed.) *CII*, III, 228.
5. Vidiśā (Durjanpur) Jain image inscriptions of Rāmagupta, Chhabra & Gai (ed.), *CII*, III, 231.
6. Mathura stone pillar inscription of Chandragupta II dated 61, Chhabra & Gai (ed.), *CII*, III, 234.
7. Udayagiri cave inscription of Chandragupta II, year 82 Chhabra & Gai (ed.), *CII*, III, 242.
8. Udayagiri cave inscription of Vīrasena Śāba, Chhabra & Gai (ed.), *CII*, III, 255.
9. Gadhwa stone inscription dated 88, Chhabra & Gai (ed.), *CII*, III, 244.
10. Sanchi railing inscription of Chandragupta II dated 93, Chhabra & Gai (ed.), *CII*, III, 247.
11. Mathura fragmentary stone inscription of Chandragupta II, Chhabra & Gai (ed.), *CII*, III, 252.
12. Mehrauli iron pillar inscription of king Chandra, Chhabra & Gai (ed.), *CII*, III, 257.

13. Basarh clay sealing of Dhruvasvāminī, Queen of Chandragupta II, Chhabra & Gai (ed.), *CII*, III, 260.
14. Poona copper plates of the Vākāṭaka queen Prabhāvatīguptā (regnal year 13), *CII*, V, 7.
15. Riddhapur copper plates of the queen Prabhāvatīguptā, *CII*, V, 33.
16. Bilsad stone pillar inscription dated 96, Chhabra & Gai (ed.), *CII*, III, 267.
17. Gadhwa stone inscription dated 98, Chhabra & Gai (ed), *CII*, III, 270.
18. Gadhwa undated stone inscription, Chhabra & Gai, (ed.), *CII*, III, 293.
19. Udayagiri cave inscription dated 106, Fleet, *CII*, III 258.
20. Mathura Jain image inscription dated 107, Chhabra & Gai, (ed.), *CII*, III, 272.
21. Dhanaidah copper plate inscription dated 113, Chhabra & Gai (ed.), *CII*, III, 273.
22. Tumain stone inscription dated 116, Chhabra & Gai (ed.), *CII*, III, 276.
23. Karmadanda *liṅgam* inscription dated 117, Chhabra & Gai (ed.), *CII*, III, 280.
24. Kulaikuri copper plate inscription dated 120, *IHQ*, XIX, 12.
25. Damodarpur copper plate inscription dated 124 Chhabra & Gai (ed.), *CII*, 282.
26. Mathura pedestal inscription of the reign of Kumāragupta I dated 125, Chhabra & Gai (ed), *CII*, III, 287.
27. Damodarpur copper plate inscription dated 128, Chhabra & Gai (ed.), *CII*, III, 288.
28. Baigram copper plate inscription dated 128, *EI*, XXI, 78.
29. Mankuwar image inscription dated 129, Chhabra & Gai (ed.), *CII*, III, 291.
30. Junagadh rock inscription of Skandagupta dated 136, 137 & 138, Chhabra & Gai (ed.), *CII*, III, 296.
31. Kahaum stone pillar inscription dated 141, Chhabra & Gai (ed.), *CII*, III, 305.
32. Supia stone pillar inscription dated 141, Chhabra & Gai (ed.), *CII*, III, 317.
33. Indore copper plate of Skandagupta dated 146, Chhabra & Gai (ed.), *CII*, III, 308.

34. Bhitari stone pillar inscription of Skandagupta, Chhabra & Gai (ed.), *CII*, III, 312.
35. Basarh sealing of Ghaṭotkachagupta, Chhabra & Gai (ed.), *CII*, III, 294.
36. Bihar pillar inscription of Budhagupta (?), Chhabra & Gai (ed.), *CII*, III, 345.
37. Mandasor stone slab inscription of M.S. 524, *EI*, XXVII, 12.
38. Mandasor stone slab inscription of the Guild of Silk-weavers dated M.S. 493 & 529, Chhabra & Gai (ed.), *CII*, III, 322.
39. Sarnath Buddha image inscription of Kumāragupta dated 154, Chhabra & Gai (ed.), *CII*, III, 321.
40. Sarnath Buddha image inscription dated 157, Chhabra & Gai, (ed.), *CII*, III, 332.
41. Sarnath (second) image inscription dated 157, *Ibid.*
42. Rajghat (Varanasi) stone pillar inscription dated 159, Chhabra & Gai (ed.), *CII*, III, 334.
43. Paharpur copper plate inscription dated 159, *EI*, XX, 61.
44. Mathura inscription of the reign of Budhagupta dated 161, *JESI*, XI, 6.
45. Damodarpur Copper plate of Buddhagupta dated 163, Chhabra & Gai (ed.), *CII*, III, 335.
46. Damodarpur copper plate (date lost) of Budhagupta, Chhabra & Gai (ed.), *CII* III, 342.
47. Eran stone pillar inscription of Budhagupta dated 165, Chhabra & Gai (ed.), *CII*, III, 339.
48. Shankarpur copper plate inscription of Budhagupta and Harivarman dated 168, *JSEI*, IV, 62.
49. Nandpur copper plate inscription dated 169, *EI*, XXIII, 52.
50. Nalanda clay seal (fragmentary) of Budhagupta, Chhabra & Gai (ed,), *CII*, III, 350.
51. Gunaighar copper plate inscription of Vainyagupta dated 188, *IHQ*, VI, 45.
52. Nalanda clay sealing of Vainyagupta, Chhabra & Gai (ed.), *CII*, III, 319.
53. Eran pillar inscription dated 191 of Goparāja (Bhānugupta's reign), Chhabra & Gai (ed.), *CII*, III, 352.
54. Damodarpur copper plate inscription of the year 224, Chhabra & Gai (ed.), *CII*, III, 360.

55. Nalanda clay seal of Narasiṁhagupta, Chhabra & Gai (ed.), *CII*, III, 354.
56. Bhitari copper-silver seal of Kumāragupta III, Chhabra & Gai (ed.), *CII*, III, 358.
57. Nalanda clay seal of Kumāragupta III, Chhabra & Gai (ed.), *CII*, III, 355.
58. Nalanda clay seal of Vishṇugupta, Chhabra & Gai (ed.), *CII*, III, 364.
59. Jagdishpur (Rajshahi) copper plate inscription, Gupta, P.L., *Gupta Sāmrājya*, Introduction, 22.

INSCRIPTIONS OF CONTEMPORARY RULERS & DYNASTIES:

60. Mandasor stone inscription of Naravarman dated *Kṛita* year 461, Chhabra & Gai (ed.), *CII*, III, 261.
61. Bihar-Kotra inscription of Naravarman of *Kṛita* year 474, Chhabra & Gai (ed.), *CII*, III, 266.
62. Gangadhar stone inscription of Viśvavarman dated *Kṛita* year 480, Fleet, *CII*, III 72.
63. Khoh copper plate of Mahārāja Hastin dated 156, Fleet, *CII*, III, 93.
64. Singrauli copper plate of Lakshmaṇa dated 158, *ASI.AR*, 1936-37, 88.
65. Pali copper plate of Lakshmaṇa dated 158, *EI*, II, 364.
66. Khoh copper plate of Hastin dated 163, Fleet, *CII*, III, 100.
67. Barwani copper plate of Subandhu dated 167, *EI*, XIX, 262.
68. Majhgwan copper plate of Hastin dated 191, Fleet, *CII*, III, 106.
69. Navagram copper plate of Hastin dated 198, *EI*, XXI, 124.
70. Betul copper plate of Saṁkshobha dated 199, *EI*, VIII, 284.
71. Khoh copper plate of Saṁkshobha dated 209, Fleet, *CII*, III, 112.
72. Bhumra Stone pillar inscription of Hastin and Śarvanātha, Fleet, *CII*, III, 110.
73. Karitalai copper plate of Jayanātha dated 174, Fleet, *CII*, III, 117.
74. Khoh copper plate of Jayanātha, dated 177 Fleet, *CII*, III, 121.
75. Sohaval copper plate of Śarvanātha dated 191, *EI*, XIX, 129
76. Khoh copper plate of Śarvanātha dated 193, Fleet, *CII*,III, 125.

77. Khoh copper plate of Śarvanātha dated 197, Fleet, *CII*, III, 132.
78. Khoh copper plate of Śarvanātha dated 214, Fleet, *CII*, III, 135.
79. Khoh copper plate of Śarvanātha (undated), Fleet, *CII*, III 129.
80. Bhamodara Mohatta copper plate inscription of Droṇasiṁha, dated 183, *EI*, XVI, 18.
81. Eran stone Boar inscription of Toramāṇa (regnal year 1), Fleet, *CII*, III, 158.
82. Khewda (Kura) inscription of Toramāṇa, *EI*, I, 239.
83. Gwalior stone inscription of Mihirakula, (regnal year 15), Fleet, *CII*, III, 162.
84. Three Sanjeli copper plate inscriptions, *M.S. University, Baroda, Archaeological Series*, No. 14.
85. Risthal stone slab inscription of Prakāśadharmā dated 572, *JESI*, X, 93.
86. Mandasor stone inscription of Yaśodharman dated 589, Fleet, *CII*, III, 150.
87. Mandasor stone pillar inscription of Yaśodharman, Fleet, *CII*, III, 142.

Coins

Allan, John: *Catalogue of the Coins of the Gupta Dynasties*, London, 1914. *Catalogue of Coins of Ancient India in the British Museum*, London, 1936.

Altekar, A.S. : *The Coinage of the Gupta Empire*, Varanasi, 1957. *Catalogue of the Gupta Gold Coins in the Bayana Hoard*, Bombay, 1954.

Brown, C.J.: *Catalogue of the Coins of the Guptas, Maukharis etc. in the Provincial Museum Lucknow*, Allahabad, 1920.

Chhabra, B. Ch.: *Catalogue of the Gupta Gold Coins of Bayana Hoard in the National Museum*, New Delhi, 1986.

Cunningham, A.: *Later Indo-Scythians*, London, 1893-95.

Rapson, E.J.: *Indian Coins*, Strasburg, 1897. *Catalogue of the Coins of Andhra Dynasty, the Western Kshatrapas, the Traikuṭaka Dynasty and the Bodhi Dynasty*, London, 1908.

Saran, P.: *Tribal Coins—A Study*, Delhi, 1972.

Shastri, A.M.: *Kauśāmbī Hoard of Magha Coins*, Nagpur, 1979.

Smith, V.A.: *Catalogue of the Coins in the Indian Museum, Calcutta*, Vol. I, Oxford, 1906.

White, R.B.: *Catalogue of the Coins in the Punjab Museum*,

MODERN WORKS ON GUPTA HISTORY

Aiyangar, S.K.: *Studies in Gupta History*, Madras, 1928.

Altekar, A.S. & Majumdar, R.C.: *The Vākāṭaka Gupta Age*, Lahore, 1946; Reprint, Delhi, 1967.

Banerji, R.D.: *The Age of the Imperial Guptas*, Benaras, 1933.

Chakraborty, H.P.: *India as Reflected in the Inscriptions of Gupta Period*, Delhi, 1978.

Dandekar, R.N.: *A History of the Guptas*, Poona, 1941.

Dikshitar, V.R.R.: *Gupta Polity*, Madras, 1952.

Gokhale, B.G.: *Samudragupta and his Times.*

Goyal, S.R.: *A History of the Imperial Guptas*, Allahabad, 1967.

Gupta, P.L.: *Gupta Sāmrājya*, (Hindi), Varanasi, 1972. *Imperial Guptas*, Varanasi, 1974.

Maity, S.K.: *The Imperial Guptas and Their Times*, Delhi, 1975. *Economic Life of Northern India in the Gupta Period*, Calcutta, 1958.

Majumdar, R.C. (ed.): *The Classical Age*, Bharatiya Vidya Bhavan, Bombay, 1970. *Comprehensive History of India*, Vol. III, Delhi, 1981.

Mehta, G.P.: *Chandragupta Vikramāditya* (Hindi), Allahabad, 1932.

Mookerji, R.K.: *The Gupta Empire*, Bombay, 1948.

Pandey, R.B.: *Vikramāditya of Ujjaini*, Benaras, 1951.

Saletore, R.N.: *Life in the Gupta Age*, Bombay, 1943.

Shastri, Raghunandan: *Gupta Vaṁśa kā Itihāsa*,(Hindi), Lahore, 1932.

Shembavnekar, K.M.: *The Glamour about the Guptas*, Bombay, 1953.

Sinha, B.P.: *The Decline of the Kingdom of Magadha*, Patna, 1954.

Smith, B.L. (ed.): *Essays on Gupta Culture*, Delhi, 1983.

Upadhyaya, B.S.: *Gupta Sāmrājya kā Itihāsa*, (Hindi), 2 Vols., Allahabad, 1939. *India in Kālidāsa*, Allahabad.

General Histories of Ancient India

Aiyangar, S.K.: *Ancient India*, Vol. I, Poona, 1941. *The Vākāṭakas and Their Place in Indian History*, Madras.

Altekar, A.S.: *State and Government in Ancient India*, Benaras, 1955.

Basak, R.G.: *History of North-Eastern India*, Calcutta, 1934.

Basham, A.L.: *The Wonder that was India*, London, 1954.

Bhandarkar, R.G.: *A Peep into the Early History of India*, Bombay, 1920.

Biswas, Atreyi: *The Political History of the Hūṇas in India*.

Buddha Prakash: *Studies in Indian History and Civilization*, Agra, 1962. *Aspects of Indian History and Civilization*, Agra, 1965.

Chattopadhyaya, K.C.: *Date of Kālidāsa*, Allahabad, 1926.

Chattopadhyaya, S.: *Early History of North India*, Calcutta, 1958. *Some Early Dynasties of South India*, Delhi, 1974.

Clevson: *Turkish and Mongolian Studies*, London, 1962.

Coomaraswamy, A.K.: *History of Indian and Indonesian Art*, London, 1927.

Cunningham, A.: *The Ancient Geography of India*, Calcutta, 1924.

Dasgupta, K.K.: *Tribal History of Ancient India*, Calcutta, 1974. *The Mālavas*, Calcutta, 1966.

De, S.C.: *Kālidāsa and Vikrāmaditya*, Calcutta, 1928.

Dey, N.L.: *The Geographical Dictionary of Ancient and Mediaeval India*, London, 1927.

Dubreuil, J. : *Ancient History of Deccan*, London.

Ghoshal, U.N.: *Contributions to the History of the Hindu Revenue System*, Calcutta, 1929. *A History of Indian Political Ideas*, Bombay, 1959.

Gopalachari, K. : *Early History of the Andhra Country*, Madras, 1941.

Jayaswal, K.P. : *History of India*, 150 *to* 350 *A.D.*, Lahore, 1933. *Imperial History of India*, Lahore, 1934. *Hindu Polity*, Calcutta, 1924.

Kane, P.V. : *History of Dharmaśāstra*, Poona, 1930-46.

Keith, A.B. : *History of Sanskrit Literature*, Oxford, 1928.

Krishnarao, B.V. : *Early Dynasties of Andhradeśa*, Madras, 1942.

Law, B.C. : *Tribes in Ancient India*, 2nd ed., Poona, 1973.

Majumdar, R.C. (Ed. Gupta, S.P.): *Readings in Political History of India*, New Delhi, 1976. Ed. *History of Bengal*, Vol. I, Dacca, 1943. Ed. *The Age of Imperial Unity*, Bombay, 1980.

Marshall, John : *Guide to Sanchi*, Delhi, 1936. *Guide to Taxila*, Delhi, 1936.

Masson-Oursel, P. : *Ancient India and Indian Civilization*, London 1943.

McGovern, W.M.: *The Early Empires of Central Asia*, New York, 1939.

Mirashi, V.V. : *Studies in Indology*, 3 Vols., Nagpur, 1968. *Vākāṭaka Rājavaṃśa kā Itihāsa tathā Abhilekha* (Hindi), Varanasi, 1964. *Indological Research Papers*, Vol. I, Nagpur, 1982. *Studies in Ancient Indian History*, Bombay, 1984.

Mookerji, Shobha : *The Republican Trends in Ancient India.*

Munshi, K.M. : *Indian Inheritence*, Bombay, 1955.

Pandey, V.C. : *Prāchīna Bhārata kā Itihāsa*, (Hindi), Meerut, 1978.

Pires, E. : *The Maukharis*, Madras, 1934.

Ray, H.C. : *Dynastic History of North India*, 2 Vols., Calcutta, 1931 & 1936.

Raychaudhuri, H.C. : *Political History of Ancient India*, Calcutta 1954.

Saletore, R.N. : *Early Indian Economic History.*

Sastri, K.A.N. (ed.) : *A History of South India*, 2nd. ed., 1958. *Comprehensive History of India*, Vol. II, 1957.

Sharma, R.S. : *Aspects of Political Ideas and Institutions in Ancient India*, Delhi, 1959. *Indian Feudalism*, Calcutta, 1965.

Sinha, B.P. : *Dynastic History of Magadha*, New Delhi, 1977. *Readings in History and Culture*, Delhi, 1978. (ed.) *Comprehensive History of Bihar*, Vol. I, Parts I & II, Patna.

Sircar, D.C.: *Ancient Malwa and the Vikramāditya Tradition*, Delhi, 1969.

Smith, V.A.: *Early History of India*, Oxford, 1924.

Subramaniam, K.R.: *Buddhist Remains in Andhra and Andhra History.*

Thakur, Upendra: *The Hūṇas in India*, Varanasi, 1967.

Tripathi, R.S.: *History of Kanauj*, Benaras, 1937. *History of Ancient India*, Delhi, 1967.

Vaidya, C.V.: *History of Mediaeval Hindu India*, 3 Vols., Poona, 1921-26.

Virji, K.K.J.: *Ancient History of Surāshṭra*, Bombay, 1952.

Winternitz, M.: *History of Indian Literature*, 3 Vols., Delhi, 19—1983.

Yazdani, G.: *The Early History of Deccan*, 2 Vols., London, 1960.

SELECT ARTICLES

Epigraphy

Agrawal, Ashvini: Dhāraṇa Gotra of the Vākāṭaka Queen Prabhāvatīguptā, *Annali*, Rome, 1986, lf. Is Mehrauli Pillar Inscription of Chandra Posthumous?, *HSAJIS*, II.

Agrawal, Jagannath: The Pushyamitras of the Bhitari Pillar Inscription, *IHQ*. XXII. 112ff. Eran Inscription of Samudragupta, *JIH*, XIX, 27ff. Some Observations on the Bihar Stone Pillar Inscription, *JOI*, XX, 44-47. Some Further Observations on the Eran Inscription of Samudragupta, *PIHC*, 1967, 61ff. Is Bhamodramohotta Copper Plate of Droṇa-Siṁha Spurious?, *PIHC*, 1954, 87ff. Notes on Eran Stone Inscription of Samudragupta, *PIHC*, 1951, 62ff. Epigraphical Notes, *BV*, IX, 277-83. A Passage in the Sarnath Inscription of Kumāragupta and Budhagupta, *VIJ* XV, 121f. Some Observations on the Bhitari Stone Pillar Inscription of Skandagupta, *VIJ*, XVII, 192ff. A Disputed Reading in the Bhitari Stone Pillar Inscription of Skandagupta, *VIJ*, XX, 184ff.

Bajpai, K.D.: A Note on the *Svabhoga-nagara* in the Eran Inscription of Samudragupta, *BAIHA*, I, 1967, 69f.

Banerji, A.: Studies in Basarh Sealings, *IHQ*, XXXI, 330-38.

Banerji, R.D.: A Note on King Chandra of the Mehrauli Inscription, *EI*, XIV, 367-71. Two Inscriptions of Kumāragupta I *JASB, NS*, V, 457-461.

Basak, R.G.: Dhanaidah Copper Plate Inscription of the Time of Kumāragupta I of the G.E. 113, *EI*, XVI, 345ff. Baigram Copper Plate Inscription of the G.E. 128, *EI*, XX, 78ff. The Five Damodarpur Copper Plate Inscriptions of the Gupta Period, *EI*, XV, 113-145.

Bhandarkar, D.R.: Identification of Princes and Territories in the Allahabad Pillar Inscription of Samudragupta, *IHQ*, I, 250ff. Notes on Ancient History of India, *IC*, III, 511f. Mehrauli Pillar Inscription of Chandra, *JAHRS* X, 86-88. Epigraphic Notes and Questions, *IA*, LXI, 101-03. Mathura Pillar Inscription of Chandragupta II, GE 61, *EI*, XXI, 1-9. Mahendragiri, Ruler of Pishṭapura, *S.K. Aiyangar Commemoration Volume*, 155ff. Chatsu Inscription of Bālāditya, *EI*, XII, 10-17. An *Ekaliṅgajī* Stone Inscription and the Origin and History of the Lakulīśa Sect, *JBBRAS*, XXII, 151-65.

Bhandarkar, R.G.: Note on the Mandasor Inscription of Naravarman, *IA*, XLII, 199f.

Bhattacharya, D.C.: A Newly Discovered Copper Plate from Tippera, *IHQ*, VI, 45-60.

Bhattacharya, S.C.: A Note on an Expression in the Allahabad *Praśasti* of Samudragupta, *PIHC*, 1961, 50f.

Bhattasali, N.K.: On Pushyamitras, *IHQ*, XXI, 24f.

Buddha Prakash: *Daivaputra-Shāhi-shāhānushāhi*' in the Allahabad Pillar Inscription of Samudragupta, *IHQ*, XXXIII, 119-128. A Reference to the '*Daivaputra-Shāhi-Shāhānushāhi*' in the Allahabad Pillar Inscription of Samudragupta, *PIHC*, 1956 144ff.

Buhler, Geogre: The Illichpur Grant of Pravarsena II of Vākāṭaka, *IA*, XII, 239-46. Banskhera Plate of Harsha, *EI*, IV, 208-11. The Madhuban Copper Plate of Harsha, *EI*, I, 67ff. Indian Inscriptions & the Art of Poetry, *IA*, 1912-13.

Chattopadhyaya, K.: *Tat-pādānudhyāta*, *IHQ*, XVIII, 43f.

Chaudhary, R.K.: Govindagupta of Vaiśālī Seal and Mandasor Inscription (A Gupta Emperor Between G.E. 93 and 96), *JOI*, XII, 370-76. A Rare Terracotta Seal of Samudragupta from Nalagarh, *PIHC*, 1964, 137. Govindagupta of Vaiśālī Seal and Mandasor Inscription, *PIHC*, 1960, 50.

Chhabra, B. Ch.: Allahabad Inscription of Samudragupta is not Posthumous, *IHQ*, XXIV, 104-13. A Note on Tumain Inscription, *JOR*, XVII, 205-08. Some Observations on Bhitari Inscription of Skandagupta, *JIH*, XLI, 543-49.

Beauties of the Bhitari Inscription of Skandagupta, *V. V. Mirashi Felicitation Volume*, 362ff.

Dikshit, K.A.: The Nalanda Seal of Kumāra Bhāskaravarman, *JBORS*, VI, 151-52.

Dikshit, K.N.: Paharpur Copper Plate Grant of the Gupta Era 159, *EI*, XX, 59-64.

Diskalkar, D.B.: A New Inscription of Chandragupta II of G.S. 61 found in Mathura, *ABORI*, XVIII, 166ff.

Epigraphic Notes and Questions, *JBBRAS*, *NS*., II, 176-83.

Dubreuil, J.: Vyāghra, the Uchchakalpa, *IA*, LV, 103f.

Fleet, J.F.: Conquests of Samudragupta, *JRAS*, 1898, 368ff.

The Bhitari Seal of Kumāragupta II, *IA*, XIX, 224ff.

Mandasor Inscription of Kumāragupta and Bandhuvarman, *IA*, XV, 194-221.

Mandasor Inscription of Yaśodharman and Vishṇuvardhan, *IA*, XV; 222ff.; and XVIII, 220f.

Mandasor Inscriptions of Yaśodharman, *IA*, XV, 253-56.

The Use of Twelve Year Cycle of Jupiter in Records of the Early Gupta Period, *IA*, XVII, 131-39.

Corpus Inscriptionum Indicarum, III, Corrections, *IA*, XVIII, 219-20.

Epigraphy, *Imperial Gazetteer of India*, 1909, *The Indian Empire*, Vol. II, 1-88.

Ganguly, D.C.: A Note on the Bhumra Inscription of the time of the Imperial Guptas, *IHQ*, XXI, 137ff.

Garde, M.B.: Tumain Inscription of Kumāragupta and Ghaṭotkachagupta, *EI*, XXVI, 115-118.

Mandaśor Stone inscription dated Mālava Samvat 524, *EI*, XXVI.

Gawronski. Andrzej: The Date of the Allahabad Stone Pillar Inscription, *Festschrift Fur Ernst Windisch*, Leipzig, 1914, 170-72.

Ghosh, A.: Nalanda Seals of Budhagupta and Vishṇugupta, *IHQ*, XIX, 119-125.

Ghosh, A. & Krishnaswamy, R.S.: Note on the Allahabad Pillar of Aśoka, *JRAS*, 1935, 697-706.

Ghosh, J.C.: *Vishṇupadagiri*, *IC*, I, 515-19. Antiquity of Gaya, *JBORS*, 1938, 93-95.

Ghose, M.: The Newly Discovered Gunaighar Grant, *IHQ*, VI, 561.

Goyal, S.R.: Nalanda and Gaya Records of Samudragupta,

JBRS, LII, 52-55. Bihar Stone Pillar Inscription of the Imperial Guptas, *JESI*, VII, 49ff.

Gupta, P.L.: The Dates of Copper Plates of Samudragupta, *PIHC*, 1953, 94.

Gupte, Y.R.: A Grant of the Vākāṭaka Queen Prabhāvatīguptā, the Year 19 of Pravarasena II, *JRAS*, 1924, 94-96. A Grant of the Vākāṭaka Queen Prabhāvatīguptā, *IA*, LIII, 248.

Hoernle, A.F.R.: Inscribed Seal of Kumāragupta, *JASB*, LVIII, 84-105.

Indraji, Bhagwanlal: Bhitari *Lāṭa* Inscription, *JBBRAS*, XVI, 349-56.

Indraji, B. & Burgess, James: The Kahaum Inscription of Skandagupta, *IA*, X, 125-26.

Jamshedji, K.B.A.: The Sudarśana or Lake Beautiful of the Girnar Inscription dated B.C. 300-A.D. 450, *JBBRAS*, XVIII, 47-55.

Jayaswal, K.P.: The Kākas—Their Location, *JBBRAS*, XVIII, 212f. Some Unpublished Seals, *JBBRAS*, XX, 1-6. Airikiṇa and Sanchi, *IA*, LXI, 159-60. A Passage in Samudragupta's Inscription at Allahabad and Gupta Coins, *JBBRAS*, XVIII, 207-11.

Kar, R.C.: King Chandra of Mehrauli Iron Pillar Inscription, *IHQ*, XXVI, 184-92.

Kielhorn, F.: Madhuban Plates of Harsha, the Year 25, *EI*, VII, 155-60.

Konow, Sten: Karamdanda Inscription of the Reign of Kumāragupta, *EI*, X, 70-72.

Krishnadeva: Nalanda Seal of Vishṇugupta, *EI*, XXVI, 235-39.

Majumdar, R.C.: The Gaya and Nalanda Plates of Samudragupta, *IC*, XI, 225-30. The Seal of Vainyagupta, *IHQ*, XXIV, 67-68. Bihar Stone Pillar Inscription of Skandagupta, *IC*, X, 170ff. Interpretation of *Digvijaya Praśastis*, *JIH*, XLII, 651ff.

Marshall, John: Excavations at Bhita, *ASIAR*, 1911-12, 44ff.

Mehta, N.C.: Jain Record on Tormāṇa, *JBORS*, XIV, 28-38.

Mirashi, V.V.: Eran Pillar Inscription of Śrīdharavarman, *PIHC* 1951, 23. Bhitari Stone Inscription of Skandagupta, *JESI*, VII, 86ff. Some Aspects of Rāmagupta Problem, *JOI*,

XIX, 139ff. An Unfinished Vākāṭaka Plate from Drug, *EI*, *XXII*, 207-212. Epigraphic Notes, *IA*, I, (1964), 174-76.

Misra, Padma: Vāhīka and Bāhlīka, *IC*, VIII, 85-89.

Mishra, P.L.: King Mahendra of Allahabad *Praśasti*, *IHQ*, XXXVII, 23-30.

Mookerji, D.N.: Mandasor Inscription of Kumāragupta I, *IC*, V, 331-32. The Haraha Inscription of *Mahārājādhirāja* Īśānavarman, *IC*, V, 104-05.

Mukherji, B.N.: A Note on a Passage in the Allahabad Pillar Inscription, *PIHC*, 1955, 76.

Narasimhachari, R. & Pran Nath: The Mathura Pillar Inscription of Chandragupta II, *IA*, LXI, 117-18.

Pandey, V.C.: Vaṅga and Vāhlīkas of the Mehrauli Pillar Inscription, *VIJ*, XII, 241-45. The Bhitari Pillar Inscription: Some Observations *VIJ*, XVI, 74-78. The Bhitari Pillar Inscription of Skandagupta: A Controversy, *VIJ*, XVIII, 435-38.

Pandeya, R.B.: The Kahaum Stone Pillar Inscription of Skandagupta, *IHQ*, XXVIII, 298-300.

Pisharoti, K.R.: Vatsabhaṭṭi's *Praśasti*, *IC*, IV, 110f. Vatsabhaṭṭi's *Prasasti*, *IC*, IV, 339-41.

Raghvan, V.: Allahabad Pillar Inscription Verses 3 and 8, *JOR*, XVI, 159-62.

Ramdas, G.: Kingdoms of the Deccan (Mentioned in the Allahabad Pillar Inscription of Samudragupta), *IHQ*, I, 679-89.

Ramesh, K. V. & Tewari, S. P.: Risthal Inscription of Aulikara Prakāśadharmā, (Vikrama) year 572, *JESI*, X, 96ff. Vyāghradeva of the Vākāṭaka Inscription of Ganj, *JAHRS* I, 228-33.

Rana, S.S.: King Chandra of Mehrauli Pillar Inscription, *JOI*, XVIII, 326-30.

Sadhu Ram: A New Pillar Inscription from Mandasor, *IHQ*, XXXIII, 62-64. Eran Stone Inscription of Samudragupta, *KURJ*, I, 13. Importance of a Verse in the Prayāga *Praśasti* of Samudragupta, *VIJ*, XVII, 203-05.

Samaddar, J.N.: The Gupta Pillar at Bihar, *JBORS*, V, 541-42.

Sen, Sukumar: On the *Aira* in the Udayagiri Cave Inscription, *PIHC*, 1953, 34.

Sharma, Dashrath: Vatsabhaṭṭi's *Praśasti*, *IC*, VI, 110. A Supplementary Note on the Mandasor Inscription of the Silk-weavers' Guild, *IC*, IV, 262f. The Mandasor Inscription of the Silk-weavers' Guild, *IC*, III, 379-81. The Mehrauli Iron Pillar Inscription, *JIH*, XVI, 13-18. *Mahādevī* Prabhudāmā of the Vaiśālī Seal, A Gupta Queen, *PIHC*, 1956, 146. The Interpretation of *ā kumāraṁ manushyaiḥ* of Skandagupta's Bhitari Inscription and connected Problems, *PIHC*, 1956, 148. Three Short Notes on Samudragupta's Allahabad Pillar Inscription, *PIHC*, 1954, 83. On the Eran Inscription of About 350 A.D., *JIH*, XIV, 27-29.

Sharma, G. R.: Chandra of the Mehrauli Pillar Inscription, *IHQ*, XXI, 202-12.

Sharma. I.K.: Bihar Stone Pillar Inscription—A Revised Study, *JOI*, XVII, 267-74.

Shastri, A.M.: Sanchi Inscription of Chandragupta II, *JAIH*, V, 199-203.

Sastri, Harprasad: King Chandra of the Mehrauli Iron Pillar Inscription, *IA*, XLII, 217-19. The Susunia Rock Inscription of Chandravarman, *EI*, XII, 133ff. Mandasor Inscription of the Time of Naravarman, *EI*, XII, 315-21.

Sastri, Hiranand: Clay Seals of Nalanda, *EI*, XXI, 72-77.

Sastri, Sakuntala Rao: The Nalanda and Gaya Plates of Samudragupta, *IC*, X, 77. *Paramabhāgavata* Samudragupta, *IC*, X, 78.

Shastri, R.M.: Mandasor Inscription of Vatsabhaṭṭi, *IC*, VI, 361ff.

Sinha, B.P.: Some Fresh Light on the Mehrauli Pillar Inscription of Chandra, *PIHC*, 1943, 124.

Sircar, D.C.: Note on the Mathura Inscription of Chandragupta II, *IHQ*, XVIII, 271-75. Kulaikuri Copper Plate Inscription of the Gupta Year 120, *IHQ*, XIX, 12-26. Evidence of the Nalanda Seal, *IHQ*, XIX, 272-81. Notes and Queries: Ghaṭotkachagupta; Govindagupta; *Paramabhaṭṭāraka-pādānudhyāta-mahārājas*, *IHQ*, XXIV, & 71-79. Maukhari Inscription from Jaunpur, *JIH*, XLII, 127. Indological Notes, *JAIH*, III, 133-51. A Passage of the Eran Inscription of Samudragupta, *PIHC*, 1954, 72. Supia Pillar Inscription of Skandagupta, 141, *EI*, XXXIII, 306.

A Note on the Damodarpur Grant of the Time of Budhagupta and Jayadatta, *IC*, V, 432-33. Spuriousness of the Nalanda Plate of Samudragupta, *EI*, XXVI, 135-36. Two Inscriptions of Gupta Age, *EI*, XXXIII, 303ff.

Smith, V.A.: The Iron Pillar of Delhi (Mehrauli) and the Emperor Chandra, *JRAS*, 1897, 1ff. The Conquests of Samudragupta, *JRAS*, 1897, 859ff. The Vaiśālī Seals of the Gupta Period, *JRAS*, 1905, 152-53.

Sohoni, S.V.: First Part of Samudragupta's *Praśasti*, *ABORI*, XXXIX, 34-46. Epigraphical Notes, *JBRS*. L, 125-29. Notes on Prayāga-*Praśasti* of Samudragupta, *JBRS*, LI, 22-49. So-called Bihar Stone Pillar Inscription of Skandagupta, *JBRS*, XLIX, 170-77. Nalanda and Gaya Copper Plate Grants of Samudragupta, *JBRS*, LII, 20-28. A Note on Eran Inscription of Samudragupta, *JBṘS*, LI, 50-52.

Srinivasan, P.R.: Mathura Pillar Inscription of the Gupta Year 61, *JAIH*, III, 113-22. Note on Eran Stone Pillar Inscription of Śrivikrama, *JOI*, XX, 51-55.

Thakur, Upendra: A Note on the Pushyamitras of Bhitari Pillar Inscription, *IHQ*, XXXVII, 279-86.

Thaplyal, K.K.: Imperial Gupta Seals: A Review, *JNSI*, XXXIII, 49ff. The Nalanda Seal of Vishṇugupta—Some Problems, *JNSI* XXXV, 166-70.

Thaplyal, K.K. & Srivastava, A.: Mathura Stone Pedestal Inscription of the Time of Budhagupta, Year 161, *JESI*, IX, 6ff.

Trivedi, H.V.: A New Mandasor Stone Inscription *PIHC*, 1954-94.

Vajpeyi, Raghavendra: A Note on the Term *Chatursamudrānta-pṛithivi* in the Mandasor Stone Inscription of Kumāragupta I, *ABORI*, LIII, 212-220.

Vidyalankara, J.C.: Mount Vishṇupada, *JBORS*, XX, 97-100.

NUMISMATICS

Acharya, G.V.: A Unique Half-Dinar of Chandragupta II, *JNSI*, I, 27.

Agrawal, Ashvini: The Place of Kācha in Gupta Chronology, *JNSI*, XLIII, 71-74. The Kotas and Their Coinage, *JNSI*, XLVIII.

Agrawal, Jagannath: An Interesting Type of Skandagupta's Coins, *JNSI*, VIII, 48.

Agrawal, J.K.: Some New Varieties of Gupta Coinage, *JNSI*, III 83. A Chhatra Type Coin of Chandragupta II, *JNSI*, IV, 59. A New Sub-variety of the Chhatra Type Coins of Chandragupta II, *JNSI* XI, 32ff.

Agrawala, P.K.: A Note on Kārtikeya Type, *JNSI*, XXX, 203-06.

Agrawala, V.S.: An explanation of the Chakravikrama Type Coins of Chandragupta II, *JNSI*, XVI, 97-101.

Ahmad, Nisar: A Silver Coin of Budhagupta With the New Date, *JNSI*, XXXIII, 122. Classification of the Repousse Gold Coins of Mahendrāditya, *JNSI*, XXXI, 160. On Identification of Mahendrāditya and Kramāditya of Repousse Gold Coins, *JNSI*, XXIV, 31. Chronology of the Rulers known from the Repousse Gold Coins of the Garuḍa Type, *JNSI*, XXXIII, 61f. Chandragupta III, *JNSI*, XLVI, 91ff. Harigupta a Successor of Kumāragupta I, *PIHC*, 1984, 892. On a Bayana Horad Coin of Chhatra Type Bearing the Legend Kramāditya, *JNSI*, XXX, 84ff. On the Copper Coins of Rāmagupta, *JNSI*, XXV, 105ff. On Some *Suvarṇa* Standard Coins of Chandragupta, *JNSI*, XXVII, 177ff.

Altekar, A.S.: King and Queen on Couch Type Coin of Chandragupta II, *JNSI*, XVIII, 51-55. A New Variety of the Archer Type of Kumāragupta, *JNSI*, XII, 124-25. Gold Coins of Budhagupta, *JNSI*, X, 78. Some Rare and Unique Coins in the Prince of Wales Museum, *JNSI*, XI, 44-63. The Date and Attribution of the Coins of Vishṇugupta, *JNSI*, III, 57 and 103. The Chandragupta-Kumāradevī Type, *JNSI*, V, 145. Identity of Kāchagupta, *JNSI*, IX 131. Bayana Hoard of the Gupta Gold Coins, *JNSI*, VIII, 179. Rare and Unique Coin from Bayana Gupta Hoard, *JNSI*, X, 95. Apratigha Coins, *JNSI*, XI, 64. A Note on Apratigha Type, *JNSI*, XXI, 71ff. Lyrist Type of Samudragupta in Silver, *JNSI*, XXI, 191-92 Under Weight Gupta Gold Coins, *JNSI*, XXI, 191.

Altekar, Padma: The Chhatra Type of Chandragupta II—A New variety, *JNSI*, XIV, 66. Some Rare Gupta Coins of Mr. Poddar's Collection, *JNSI*, XIV, 67-70.

Bajpai, K.D.: A Rare Gupta Coin from Sanchi, *JNSI*, XXXIII,

120. A New Copper Coin of Rāmagupta, *JNSI*, XVIII, 108. Samudragupta's Copper Coin, *JNSI*, XXVII, 190-92.

Bajpai, S.K.: A New Silver Coin of Skandagupta bearing the Date 141, *JNSI*, XXXVIII, 73-73. Pagara-Hoard of Gupta Gold Coins, *JNSI*. XLIV, 52ff.

Banerjea, J.N.: The King to R'Variety of the Standard Type Coins of Samudragupta, *JNSI* XII, 116-17.

Banerji, R.D.: Coinage of the Later Guptas, *ASI.AR*, 1913-14, 258ff. Notes on Indian Numismatics, *JBORS*, V, 82-89.

Burn, Richard: The Attribution of Ancient Indian Coins, *Bharata Kaumudi*, I, 147ff.

Chandra, R.G.: A New Chakravikrama of Chandragupta II, *JNSI*, XXII, 261-62. Two Gold Coins of Chandragupta II, *JNSI*, XIX, 190-91. Another Standard Type Coin of Chandragupta II, *JNSI*, XXX, 202-03.

Chatterjee, C.D.: Gold Coins of Standard Type (Class I) of Chandragupta II, *JNSI*, XXXVII, 85-99.

Chattopadhyaya, B.D.: Political Significance of the Altar Type Coins of Skandagupta, *JNSI*, XXVII, 37-40.

Chaudhary, K.: Unique Gold Coin of Samudragupta, *JNSI*, XLVI, 49f.

Chaudhary, R.K.: A Critical Study of the So-Called Apratigha Type of Kumāragupta I, *JNSI*, XXVI, 15-26.

Chhabra, B. Ch.: A Unique Gold Coin of Chandragupta I, *JNSI*, XI, 15-31. Coin Legends of the Gupta Emperors and *Vishṇusahasranāma*, *JNSI*, IX, 137.

Chinmulgund, P.J.: Another Rhinoceros-Slayer Type Coin of Kumāragupta I, *JNSI*, XVII, 104-06. A New Variety of Kārtikeya Type Coin of Kumāragupta I, *JNSI*, XXI, 72-73.

Curtis, J.W.; Bhānugupta Prakāśāditya: Aspects of His Reign in the Light of a New *Suvarṇa* Variety, *JNSI*, XX, 73-76.

Dani, A.H.: Chandragupta I—Kumāradevī Coin Type, *JNSI*, XX, 4-8 Rāmagupta Problem—A New Solution, *JNSI*, XXVI, 11ff. A Dated Silver Coin of Kumāragupta I, in Watson Museum Rajkot, *JNSI*, XXVI, 104-06.

Dasgupta, K.K.: Kushāṇa Influence on Apratigha Coins, *IHQ* XXXV, 265-70.

Dhavalikar, M.K.: On the Attribution of the Aśvamedha Type of Samudragupta, *JNSI*, XX, 175-77.

Dikshit, R.K.: Siṁhavāhinī Lakshmī, *JNSI*, XXVI, 102.

Diskalkar, D.B.: Bamnala Find of Twentyone Gold Coins of Gupta Dynasty, *JNSI*, V, 135.

Dudley, Hamilton: A New Type of Copper Coinage of Chandragupta II, *JNSI*, XIII, 103-04. A Rare Variety of the Aśvamedha Type of Samudragupta, *JNSI*, XIII, 105-06.

Ghosh Ajit: Discovery of a Second Gold Coin of Ghaṭotkachagupta, *JNSI*, XXII, 260. Five Rare Gupta Gold Coins from the Bayana Hoard, *JNSI*, XXII, 177-83. A New Variety of Lion Slayer Type of Chandragupta II, *JNSI*, I 28.

Goyal, S.R.: Attribution of the Coins of Prakāśāditya, *JNSI*, XXVIII, 17. Some Observations on the Śrivikrama Coin of Samudragupta, *JNSI*, XXVII, 142ff.

Gupta, P.L.: The Coins of Rāmagupta, *JNSI*, XII, 103-11. An Unexplained Archer Type Coin of Samudragupta, *JNSI*, XVI, 102-04. Chandragupta II's Standard Type Coin, its Attribution, *JNSI*, XI, 104-07. The Gold Coins of Kumāragupta II & III, *JNSI* XII, 31-33. The Attributlon of the Coins of Prakāśāśāditya, *JNSI*, XII, 34-35. A Note on the Gold Coins of Budhagupta, *JNSI*, XV, 193-94. Kumarkhan Hoard of Gupta Gold Coins, *JNSI*, XXII, 265. King and Queen on Couch Type Coin of Chandragupta II, *JNSI*, XVIII, 222. The Metrology of the Gold Coins of the Gupta Dynasty, *JNSI*, XIV, 118-21. Place of Ghaṭotkachagupta in the Gupta Chronology, *JNSI*, XIV, 99-102. Kācha a Step Brother of Samudragupta, *JNSI*, V, 33. A Standard Type coin of Samudragupta, *JNSI*, VIII, 44.

Jai Prakash: Observations on the So-called *Khaḍgatrātā* Coin Type of Kumāragupta I, *JNSI*, XXV, 29-35. On the Rāmagupta Coins, *JNSI*, XXV, 165-71. Observations on the Battle-axe Coin Type of Samudragupta, *JNSI*, XXVII, 12-16.

Jain, B.C. : A Rare Chhatra Type Coin of Chandragupta II, *JNSI*, XVII, 103-04. Hitherto Unknown Repousse Coins of Kramāditya, *JNSI*, XXII, 184-87.

Jayaswal, P.K.: On Attribution of the Coins of Prakāśāditya, *JNSI*, XXVIII, 65.

Joshi, M.C.: The king and Lakshmī or Queen Type Coin of Skandagupta *JNSI*, XXII, 263-64. The Probable Background of the Standard Type Coin of Samudragupta,

JNSI, XIX, 14-19. Apratigha Type—A Study, *JNSI*, XXI, 34-36. Notes on Some Gold Coin Types of the Guptas, *JNSI*, XXIV, 34-40. Samudragupta's Standard Type: A Further Consideration, *JNSI*, XXI, 70.

Kar, R.C.: The Fire Altar on Gupta Gold Coins, *JNSI*, XII, 48-49. The Vāmana Attendant on Gupta Coins, *IHQ*, XXIII, 113-22. A New Interpretation of the Gupta Chhatra and Battle-axe Types, *JNSI*, VI, 27.

Maity, S.K.: The Gold Contents of Gupta Coins, *JNSI*, XVIII, 187-97. The Gold Content of Gupta Coins from the Indian Museum, *JNSI*, XX, 183-88. The Gold Contents of the Later Imperial Gupta Coins, *JNSI*, XXII, 266f.

Majumdar, R.C.: Apratigha Coins of Kumāragupta I, *JNSI*, XII, 72-73.

Mani, B.R.: New Evidence Concerning Gold Proto-Type Silver Coins of the Gupta Emperors, *JNSI*, XLIII, 54ff.

Martin, M.F.C.: Coins of Kidāra and the Little Kushāṇas, *JRASB. L*, III, *N.S.*, XLVII, 23-50.

Mehta, R.N. & Mankad, B.L.: Some Interesting Coins from Karvan, *JNSI*, XIII, 219-22

Mirashi, V.V.: A Note on the Khairtal Hoard of the Coins of Mahendrāditya, *JNSI*, XI, 108-10. The Apratigha Coins of Kumāragupta I, *JNSI*, XII, 68-71.

Mishra, S.N.: Siṁhavāhini on the Gupta Coins, *JNSI*, XXX, 80ff.

Mookerji, R.K.: Some Aspects of Gupta Coinage, *JNSI*, V, 151.

Mukharji, B.N.: Rhino-Slayer Type of Coin of Kumāragupta, (Its Historical Significance), *IH*Q, XXXI, 175-81.

Nagar, M.M.: Rhinoceros Type Coin of Kumāragupta I, *JNSI*, XI, 7-8. New Gupta Coins in the State Museum, Lucknow, *JNSI*. XV, 80-84.

Narain, A.K.: A Very Rare Silver Plaited Coin of Kumāragupta I, *JNSI*, XIII, 76-77. Budhagupta and his Gold Coins, *JNSI*, XII, 112-15. The Coins of Rāmagupta, *JNSI*, XII, 103-11. Numismatic Evidence and Historical Writings, *JNSI*, XVIII, 157-162.

Nath, B.B.: Recent Numismatic Discoveries in Orissa, *JNSI*, XIII, 92-94.

Pandey, V.C.: Chandragupta-Kumāradevī Type of Coins and the Dual Character of Samudragupta's Royalty, *JNSI*,

XXXVIII, 58-64. A Note on *Apratirathaḥ*, *JIH*, LI, ii, 345-48.

Pathak, V.S.: Notes on the Gupta Coinage, *JNSI*, XIX, 135ff.

Rade, V.P.: Khairtal Hoard of the Coins of Mahendrāditya, *JNSI*, X, 137-42.

Rapson, E.J.: Coins of Vainyagupta, *Num. Chr.*, 1891, 57.

Ray, S.C.: On Coins Recovered from Nalanda Excavations, *JNSI*, XVIII, 101-07.

Roy, B.P.: The So-called Apratigha Coin Type of Kumāragupta I, *JNSI*, XXIV, 164-67.

Roychaudhury, C.: Observations on the Apratigha Coins of Kumāragupta I, *IH*Q, XXXIV, 270-75.

Saraswati, S.K.: A Gold Coin of Budhagupta, *IC*, I, 691-92.

Sethi, R.K.: The Problem of Mahārāja Śri-Gupta, *JNSI*, XLIII, 63ff.

Sharma, Dashrath: The Expression *Samara-śata-vitata-vijayo* in Relation to the Chronological Position of Samudragupta's Standard Type Coins, *JNSI*, XXVIII, 62-63.

Shastri, A.M.: Contemporary Forgeries of Silver Coins of Kumāragupta I, *Dineśa Candrika* (*D.C. Sircar Felicitation Volume*), 97-102. The Couch Type Coins of Chandragupta II, *JNSI*, XLVI, 86ff.

Shukla, S.M.: Some Interesting sub-varieties of the Gupta Coins, *JNSI*, XXII, 188-92.

Singh, A.N.: The Rhinoceros Slayer Type of Kumāragupta I and its Significance, *JNSI*, XLV, 150ff.

Singh, J.P.: The King and Queen Type of Skandagupta, *JNSI* XXXI, 155ff. Observations on the So-called *Khaḍgatrātā* Coin Type of Kumāragupta I, *JNSI*, XXV, 29-35.

Singh, O.P.: Obverse Device of Horseman-Lion Slayer Type of Prakāśāditya's Coins, *JNSI*, XXXIII, 122. A Note on Silver Coin of Chandragupta I and Kumāradevī, *JNSI*, XLIV, 48ff.

Singh, Y.B.: A Note on Rhinoceros Type Coins of Kumāragupta I, *JNSI*, XLIII, 67ff.

Singhal, C.R.: A Hoard of Gupta Gold Coins Found in Gujrat, *JNSI*, XV, 195-96.

Sinha, B.P.: Apratigha Coins, *JNSI*, XVI, 210-14. Remarks on Apratigha Coins, *PIHC*, 1954, 104.

Sircar, D.C.: Rhinoceros-Slayer Type Coins of Kumāragupta I, *JNSI*, XXVIII, 211ff. *Bhavishyottarapurāṇa* and Early Gupta History, *JNSI*, VI, 34.

Sitholey, B.S.: The Origin of Samudragupta's Standard Type Coins, *JNSI*, X, 64-71. Art of the Gupta Coins, *JNSI*, X, 119-31. Symbols on Gupta Coins, *JNSI*, XI, 111-13. Was Kācha a Gupta Monarch?, *JNSI*, XII, 38-40.

Sivaramamurti, C.: Chakravikrama Type, *JNSI*, XIII, 180-82.

Smith, V.A.: Catalogue of the Coins of Gupta Dynasty, *JASB*, 1884, 119ff. Catalogue of the Coins of Gupta Dynasty, *JRAS*, 1889, 1-159.

Sohoni, S.V.: Apratigha Coin Type of Kumāragupta I, *JNSI*, XVIII, 56-63. Chandragupta I—Kumāradevī Coin Type, A Reexamination, *JNSI*, XIX, 145-54. Chandragupta-Kumāradevī Type, *JNSI*, V, 37. Vīṇā Coin Type of Samudragupta and Kumāragupta, *JNSI*, XIX, 155-61. Battle Axe Type Coins of Samudragupta, *JBRS*, 1956, 157. *Khaḍgatrātā* Coins of Kumāragupta, I, *JNSI*, XVIII, 178-86. On the King and Queen on Couch Type Coin of Chandragupta II, *JNSI*, XX, 178-82. Eagle on the Gupta Coins, *JBRS*, 1956, 152. Alleged Cornucopiae and Fillet in Gupta Coinage, *JNSI*, XIX, 162-67. So-called Apratigha Coin Type of Kumāragupta I, *JNSI*, XXIII, 345-56. Standard Type of Samudragupta, *JNSI*, XIX, 186-90. Elephant-Rider Coin Type of Kumāragupta I, *JNSI*, XIX, 191-93. The Repousse pieces of Mahendrāditya etc., *JNSI*, XLV, 152ff.

Soundarajan, K.V.: Three Silver Plated Gupta Coins from Sherdi, Junagadh District (Gujarat State), *JNSI*, XXVI, 27ff.

Srivastava, A.L.: A Silver Coin of Chandragupta-Kumāradevī Type, *JNSI*, XXXVII, 83-84.

Thakur, V.K. : The Place of Kācha in Gupta Chronology, *JNSI*, XXXIX, 108-113.

Thakur, Upendra: A Unique Coin of Samudragupta, *E & W*, XXIV, 121ff. Some Observations on Chandragupta I-Kumāradevī Coin Type, *JNSI*, XXII, 172-76. A Study of Copper Coins of Rāmagupta, *JNSI*, XXVI, 162-70. The Hūṇa Coinage, *JNSI*, XXIX, 9-21.

Trivedi, H.V. : Some More Copper Coins of Rāmagupta, *JNSI*,

XIII, 128-30. The Chakravikrama Coin of Chandragupta II, *JNSI*, XVII, 108.

Upasak, C.S.: Some Salient Features of Brāhmī on Gupta Coins, *JNSI*, XXIII, 216-40.

Vatsa, M.S.: A Gold Coin of Samudragupta, *ASIAR*, 1923-24, 124.

Verma, T.P.: Chandragupta-Kumāradevī Coin Type, *JNSI*, XXXIII, 44-48.

Vidya Prakash: Some Aspects of Material Life on Gupta Coins, *JNSI*, XXIII, 267-96.

CHAPTERS II, III & IV:

Agrawal, Ashvini: Maruṇḍa Problem—Re-Examined, *VIJ*, XVIII, 461ff. The So-Called Maruṇḍa Rule in Orissa, *Ajaya Śrī, Prof. A.M. Shastri, Felicitation Volume.*

Agrawal, Jagannath: Political Situation in Magadha in the Third century A.D., *JUPHS*, XVIII, 101-06. The Location of T'China Temple and the Original Home of the Guptas, *IHQ*, 1946, 28-33. Predecessors of the Guptas in Magadha, *PIHC*, 1948, 93-95. An Ancient Republic of the Panjab—The Yaudheya Gaṇa, *M.S. Randhawa Felicitation Volume*, 1970, 49-55.

Altekar, A.S.: Who were Bhāraśivas? *NIA*, VI, 119ff. Did Bhāraśivas Overthrow the Kushāṇas?, *IC*, XII, 119-22.

Banerji, Adris: Eastern Expansion of the Kushāṇa Empire, *IHQ*, XXVII, 294ff.

Bhandarkar, D.R.: New Light on the Early Gupta History, *Mālavīya Commemoration Volume*, 189-211.

Bhattacharya, B.: New Light on the History of the Imperial Gupta Dynasty, *JBRS*, XXX, 1-46.

Buddha Prakash: The Political Geography of India on the Eve of Gupta Ascendency, *IC*, XIII, 85-90. Kushāṇa Invasion of India Under Kumāragupta, *IHQ*, XXX, 219-36.

Dwivedi, Gautam N.: Tribal Communities in the Gupta Age, *PIHC*, 1974, 86-88.

Ganguly, D.C.: Early Home of the Imperial Guptas, *IHQ*, XIV, 532-36. The Original Home of the Imperial Guptas, *IHQ*, XVIII, 386-91.

Ghosh, B.: *Pādānudhyāta*, *IC*, IX, 118f.

Gokhale, B.G.: The Origin of the Imperial Guptas, *JBBRAS*, XXVII, (Supplement), 275-78.

Gupta, K.K.: Mr. K.P. Jayaswal on the Bhāraśivas, *IC*, I, 635-42.

Gupta, P.L.: The Predecessors of the Guptas in Magadha, *IC*, XI, 137-41. Kushāṇa-Muruṇḍa Rule in Eastern India, *JNSI*, XXXVI, 25ff. Eastern Expansion of the Kushāṇa Empire, *IHQ*, XXIX, 205ff. Bearing of Numismatics on the History of the Tribal Republics in Ancient India, *IHQ* XXVII, 197-209.

Jackson, V.H.: Hiuen Tsang's Route in South Bihar, *JBORS*, III, 293-316.

Jayaswal, K.P.: Nepal Chronicles on the Caste of the Guptas, *JBORS*, 1936, 108-10. Historical Data in *Kaumudīmahotsava*, *ABORI*, XII, 50.

Law, B.C.: Some Ancient Indian Tribes, *IC*, I, 381-91.

Majumdar, R.C.: Original Home of the Imperial Guptas, *JBRS*, XXXVIII, 410ff. The Chinese Temple of Śri Gupta, *PIHC*, 1952, 45ff.

Pires, E.A.: Who Were the Rulers of Pāṭaliputra Before the Guptas? *The Maukharis*, Bombay.

Sastri, Rao, S.: Chaṇḍasena of *Kaumudīmahotsava*, *IC*, IX, 232ff. *Kaumudīmahotsava*, *IC*, X, 29ff. *Kaumudīmahotsava*, *IC*, XI, 86ff.

Sharma, Dashrath: Chaṇḍasena of the *Kaumudīmahotsava*, *JBORS*, 1935, 77ff. The Origin and Original Home of the Imperial Guptas, *JBRS*, XXXIX, 265-68. Dhāraṇa Gotra of the Guptas, *JBORS*, XX, 225ff. *Kaumudīmahotsava* & the Date of Kālidāsa, *IHQ*, X, 763ff.

Singh, B.P.: Original Home of the Guptas, *JBRS*, XXXVII, 138ff. Original Home of the Guptas, *JBRS*, XXXVIII.

Singh, S P.: Numismatic Evidence of Kushāṇa-Muruṇḍa Rule in Eastern India, *JNSI*, XXXV, 127ff.

Vidya-Bhushan, S. C.: The Licchavi Race of Ancient India, *JASB*, LXXX, 142-48.

CHAPTER V

Agrawal, Jagannath: *Kaumudīmahotsava* as a Historical Play, *Festschrift F.W. Thomas*, Bombay, 1938, 115-20. The Bearing of Haraha Inscription on the Epoch of the Gupta Era, *IC*, V, 335-37.

Barua, K.L.: The Gupta Era, *IC*, V, 114-15.

Bhandarkar, R.G.: A Note on the Gupta Era, *Collected Works*, III, 176-85. The Epoch of the Gupta Era, *JBBRAS*, XVII, 80ff.

Buhler, George: The Origin of the Gupta-Valabhī Era, *VOJ*, V, 215ff.

Chakravarti, B.: The Chronology of the Kāmarūpa Kings, *IC*, VI, 341-45.

Chattopadhyaya, K.C.: Date of the *Kaumudīmahotsava*, *IHQ*, XIV, 582ff.

Chhabra, B.Ch.: Chandragupta's Abdication, *IC*, XIV, 141-50.

Cunningham, A.: Coins of Nine Nāga Kings, *JASB*, XXXIV, 115-19. Bhilsa Topes, *JASB*, XXXII.

Fergusson, J.: On Indian Chronology, *JRAS*, 1870, (N.S.), 81ff. On the Śaka *Saṁvat* and the Gupta Eras, *JRAS*, XII, (N.S.). 259-85.

Fleet, J.F.: The Epoch of Gupta Era, *IA*, XV, 189. Note on the Origin of the Gupta Era, *IA*, XV, 278-79. The Scheme and Equation of the Years of the Gupta Era, *IA*, XVI, 141ff. A Note on a Matter Arising Out of the Gupta Era, *JBBRAS*, XVIII, 71-87. The Gupta-Valabhī Era, *IA*, XX, 376ff. Summary of the Results Regarding the Epoch & Origin of the Gupta Era, *IA*, XVII, 359-69.

Gupta, K.K.: Some Recent Views on the Gupta Era, *IC*, III, 47-61.

Gupta, P.C.: The Gupta Era, *JASB*, 1942, 41-56.

Gupta, P.L.: Gupta Era: A Re-Assessment, *JBRS*, XLIX, 71-87.

Jayaswal, K.P.: Historical Data in Kaumudīmahotsava, *ABORI*, XII, 50.

Joshi, N.P.: New Light on the Gupta Era and the Chronology of the Early Gupta Kings, *VIJ*, XIV, 245-60.

Mukherjee, D.N.: Chronology of the Kāmarūpa Kings, *IC*, V, 367-68. The Haraha Inscription of Maukhari *Mahārājādhirāja*, Īśānavarman, *IC*, V, 104-05. Āchārya Vasubandhu, the Teacher of Sthiramati, *IC*, IV, 520-22. The Gupta Era, *IHQ*, VIII, 85-92. The Gupta Era, *JIH*, XVII, 293-316. The Identity of Gupta and Vikram Eras, *JIH*, XVIII, 64-69. The Valabhī Rulers and the Gupta Era, *PIHC*,

1939, 419-32. The Gupta Era, *JIH*, XX, 71-84. Chronology and Genealogy of the Early Imperial Guptas, *JIH*, XXI, 34-56.

Ojha, K.C.: The *Āryamañjuśrīmūlakalpa* on Chandragupta I, *IHQ*, XXVII, 170ff.

Oldenberg, H.: On the Dates of Ancient Indian Inscriptions and Coins, *IA*, X, 213ff.

Pai, M.G.: The Gupta and the Valabhī Eras, *JIH*, XI, 175-89. The Gupta and the Valabhī Eras, *JIH*, XII, 215ff.

Pathak, K.B.: New Light on Gupta Era and Mihirakula, *IA*, XLVI, 287-96. New Light on Gupta Era and Mihirakula, *IA*, XLVII, 16-22.

Peterson: An Inscription from Kotah, *JBBRAS*, XVI, 378-89.

Sankar, K.G.: The Epoch of the Gupta Era, *NIA*, III.

Sastri, S.R.: Chaṇḍasena of *Kaumudīmahotsava*, *IC*, IX, 232-34.

Sengupta, P.C.: Gupta Era, *JRASB*, *L*, VIII, 41-56.

Sharma, Dashrath: Chaṇḍasena of the *Kaumudīmahotsava*, *JBORS*, 1935, 77ff.

Sundararaman, R.P.: A New Epoch for the Gupta Era, *JIH*, XVI, 132ff.

Winternitz, M.: Some Historical Plays in Indian Literature, *Dr. S.K. Aiyangar Commemoration Volume*.

CHAPTER VI:

Agrawal, Ashvini: Can Kācha of the Gupta Gold Coins be Identified with Bhasma of the *Āryamañjuśrimūlakalpa*?, *Vājapeya*, *K.D. Bajpai Felicitation Volume*, 329ff. *Ārya-mañjuśrīmūlakalpa's* Account of Bhasma's Invasion of the North-West—A Re-appraisal, *PPHC*, 1982.

Agrawal, Jagannath: Samudragupta's *Aśvamedha*, *Essays Presented to Sir Jadunath Sarkar*, Vol. II, 10ff.

Altekar, A.S.: Were the Vākāṭakas defeated by Samudragupta in c. A.D. 350?, *IC*, IX, 99ff.

Bhandarkar, D.R.: *Aśvamedha* by Samudragupta, *IC*, I, 115-18.

Bhattacharya, A.: A Note on the Expression *Lichchhavidauhitra*, *PIHC*, 1963, 90ff.

Bhattacharya, A.K.: A Note on Samudragupta's Southern Campaign, *PIHC*, 1963, 50ff.

Bhattacharya, S.: Kācha Problem, *JIH*, XLV, 727-36.

Chattopadhyaya, A.: A Note on the Kācha Problem of Gupta History, *JOI*, XXII, 64-67.

Chaudhuri, S.B.: Āryāvarta, *IHQ*, XXV, 110-22. The Mālavas, *IHQ*, XXIV, 171-79.

Dasgupta, N.N.: The Kācha Problem, *IHQ*, XX, 351-53.

Ghosh, A. & Krishnaswami, R.S.: A Note on Allahabad Pillar of Aśoka, *JRAS*, 1935, 697.

Gupta, P.L.: Can Kācha be Identified with Rāmagupta?, *JNSI*, XI, 33-37. The Place of Kāchagupta in the Gupta Chronology, *JNSI*, XII, 36-37. Kācha a Brother of Samudragupta, *JNSI*, V, 33ff. Kācha Problem Solved, *IHQ*, XXII, 60-61.

Heras, H.: Kāchagupta and Rāmagupta, *JBRS*, XXXIV, 19-28. Two Controversial Events in the Reign of Samudragupta, *ABORI*, IX, 83-90.

Lakshminarayana, V.: The Contemporaneity of Samudragupta and Augustus Caesar of Rome and the Problem of the Epoch of the Gupta Era, *PIHC*, 1944, 136ff.

Law, B.C.: Samudragupta and Śrimeghavarṇa, *JBBRAS*, 1951, 88-93. Ārjunāyanas, *NIA*, I, 460ff.

Maity, S.K.: Kācha Coins, *BSOAS*, XIX, 390ff.

Majumdar, R.C.: Literary References to Samudragupta, *IHQ*, IX, 930-33.

Mookerji, R.K.: Character of Samudragupta from his Inscriptions and Coins, *IC*, IX, 177-79.

Mukherjee, D.N.: Contemporaneity of Samudragupta and Augustus Caesar, *ABORI*, XXII.

Narayanan, M.G.S.: A Re-appraisal of Samudragupta's Digvijaya, *Dinesha Chandrika, D.C. Sircar Felicitation Volume* 283-93.

Ojha, K.C.: Was Kācha a Brother of Samudragupta?, *JNSI*, XII, 170-75.

Pandey, L.P.: Identification of Mahākāntāra, *PIHC*, 1947, 176-79.

Pandey, V.C.: Samudragupta's *Aśvamedha*—A Re-appraisal, *ABORI*, LIII, 228-32.

Ramachandramurty, V.S.: Mahendragiri Ruler of Pishṭapura, *IC*, III, 230f.

Raychaudhury, C.: New Light on the Identification of Kācha, *IHQ*, XXXV, 333-39.

Saletore, B.A.: Samudragupta's Conquest of Koṭṭūra, *ABORI*, XXVI, 120-41.

Sircar, D.C.: Rudradeva and Nāgadatta of Allahabad Pillar Inscription, *PIHC*, 1944, 78ff. Samudragupta's *Aśvamedha* Sacrifice, *JIH*, XIII, 35-40.

Smith, V.A.: Samudragupta, *JRAS*, 1897, 19-35. Conquests of Samudragupta, *JRAS*, 1897, 859-910.

Trautmann, Thomas R.: *Licchavidauhitra*, *JRAS*, 1972, 1-15.

CHAPTER VIII

Agrawala, R.C.: Newly Discovered Sculptures from Vidiśā, *JOI*, XVIII, 252-53.

Altekar, A.S.: A New Gupta King, *JBORS*, XIV, 223ff. Further Discussion About Ramagupta, *JBORS*, XV, 134-41

Bajpai, K.D.: Rāmagupta, A New Gupta King, *JNSI*, XXIII, 340ff. Identification of Rāmagupta, *JIH*, XLII, 389ff. Fresh Light on the Problem of Rāmagupta, *PIHC*, 1961, 53f. Fresh Light on the Problem of Rāmagupta, *IHQ*, XXXVIII, 80-85.

Bhandarkar, D.R.: New Light on Early Gupta History, *Mālavīya Commemoration Volume*, 189-211.

Chattopadhyaya, A.: *Mujmal-ut-Twarikh* and the Rāmagupta Problem of Gupta History, *JOI*, XVIII, 331-36.

Chattopadhyaya, K.C.: Rāmagupta, *IC*, IV, 216-22.

Dani, A.H.: Rāmagupta Problem—A New Solution, *JNSI*, XXVI, 11-14.

Dasgupta, C.C.: A Note on the Interpretation of *Devīchandraguptam PIHC*, 1956, 79f.

Gai, G.S.: Three Inscriptions of Rāmagupta, *JOI*. XVIII, 247-51.

Jai Prakash: Observations on the Rāmagupta Legend, *JNSI*, XXVIII; 157ff.

Jayaswal, K.P.: Rāmagupta, *JBORS*, XVIII, 35-36. Alipura of the Gupta History, *IA*, LXII, 119ff. Chandragupta II and his Predecessors, *JBORS*, 1932, 17-36.

Konow, Sten: *Devīchandraguptam*, *JBORS*, 1937, 449ff.

Mirashi, V.V.: Further Light on Rāmagupta, *IA*, LXII, 201-05. Some Aspects of Rāmagupta Problem, *JOI*, XIX, 139-51.

Ojha, K.C.: An Analysis of the Rāmagupta Tradition, *JBRS*, XXXVII, 39ff.

Shah, U.P.: Some Aspects of Rāmagupta Problem—A Reply to V. V. Mirashi, *JOI*, XIX, 152-56. A Further Note on Rāmagupta Inscription, *JOI*, XVIII, 254-55.

Sharma, Dashrath: The Śaka Rival of Rāmagupta, *IC*, V, 228-30.

Sircar, D.C.: Copper Coins of Rāmagupta, *JIH*, XL, 533-36.

Sohoni, S.V.: Viśākhadatta's *Devīchandraguptam*, *ABORI*, LXII, 169-92.

Thakur, Upendra: Historicity of Rāmagupta, *PIHC*, 1957, 79ff. A Study in the Copper Coins of Rāmagupta, *JNSI*, XXVI, 162-70.

CHAPTER VIII

Agrawal, Jagannath: Some Observations on the Reign of Chandragupta II Vikramāditya, *NIA*, II, 685ff. Some Observations on the Character and achievements of Chandragupta II, *JIH*, XIX, 158ff.

Agrawala, R.C.: Carved Pillar of Gupta Year 61, *JOI*, XIX, 355-56.

Aiyangar, S.K.: Vikramāditya, *Sir Ashutosh Memorial Volume*, I, 143-63.

Buddha Prakash: The Central Asian Expedition of Chandragupta Vikramāditya, *JRASB*, XIII, 31-39.

Chakladar, H.C.: Geography of Kālidāsa, *Indian Studies—Past and Present*, IV, 375-78.

Dikshit, S.K.: Chandragupta II, Sāhasāṅka Alias Vikramāditya and the Nine Jewels, *IC*, VI, 191-210 & 377-92.

Dwivedi, Gautam N.: Western Limits of the Gupta Empire, *PIHC*, 1973, 76-79.

Heras, H.: Relations Between Kadambas, Vākāṭakas and Guptas, *JBORS*, XII, 455ff.

Jayaswal, K.P.: The Historical Position of Kalki & His Identification with Yaśodharmā, *IA*, XLVI, 145ff. The Book on Political Science by Śikhara, Prime-Minister of Chandra-Gupta II, *JBORS*, 1932, 37-39.

Mirashi, V.V.: Chandragupta Vikramāditya and Govinda, *IHQ*, X, 48-53. Did Chandragupta II Sell his own Palace at

Vidiśā?, *ABORI*, LXIII, 221-23. Did Chandragupta II Become a *Vānaprastha*?, *VIJ*, XX, 76-83.

Shah, U.P.: Vikramāditya Saga, *JOI*, IV, 69-84 and 218-39.

Sharma, Dashrath: Chandragupta of Vāmana's *Kāvyalaṅkāra-sūtravṛitti*, *IHQ*, X, 761ff.

Shastri, A.M.: Chandragupta II Vikramāditya as a Poet, *PIHC*, 1965, 109ff. Chandragupta II Vikramāditya and King Pramati of the *Matsya Purāṇa*, *NUJ*, XVII, 150-57.

Sohoni, S.V.: Western Front of Chandragupta II and Kumāra-gupta, *JBRS*, 1956, 396ff.

Tripathi, K.B.: Geography of India in Kālidāsa with Special Reference to Raghu's Campaign of Conquest, *OHRJ*, XI, 234-37.

Vajpeyi, Raghvendra: The Vāhlīkas of the Mehrauli Iron Pillar Inscription, *PIHC*, 1977, 783-89.

CHAPTER IX

Agarawal, Jagannath: Are Govindagupta and Kumāragupta Identical?, *IC*, XII, 167-69. Govindagupta, A New Gupta Emperor, *IHQ*, XXII, 286ff. The Status of Govindagupta, *PAIOC*, 1968, Govindagupta—A New Gupta Emperor, *PIHC*, 1946, 78ff.

Bhandarkar, D. R.: Govindagupta and Purugupta, *IC*, XI, 231ff.

Chaudhary, R.K.: Govindagupta of Vaiśālī Seal and Mandasor Inscription, (A Gupta Emperor Between G.E. 93 & 96), *JOI*, XII, 370-76.

Sircar, D.C.: Notes and Queries: Govindagupta, *IHQ*, XXIV, 71ff.

CHAPTER X

Agrawal, Ashvini: Did Kumāragupta I Abdicate—A Study of the Numismatic and Epigraphic Data, *Indologica Taurnesia*, 1987.

Bhattacharya, A.: A Note on the Conquest of the Region of Mandasor by Kumāragupta I, *PIHC*, 1964, 70ff.

Buddha Prakash: The Kushāṇa Invasion of India Under Kumāragupta, *IHQ*, XXX, 219ff.

Pathak, K.B.: Kumāragupta I, The Patron of Vasubandhu, *JBBRAS*, XXIII, 185ff.

CHAPTER XI

Agrawal, Jagannath: Are Skandagupta and Purugupta Identical?, *BV*, VIII, 7-10. The Status of Skandagupta's Mother, *ABORI*, XLVIII-XLIX, 325-327.

Basham, A.L.: The Date of the End of the Reign of Kumāragupta I and the Succession After his Death, *BSOAS*, XVII, 367ff.

Bhattacharya, T.: Was Anantadevī the Mother of Skandagupta?, *JBRS*, XXXII, 182-83.

Charpentier, Jarl : A Remark on Two Indian Names, *JRAS*, 1928, 902ff.

Chowdhury, P.C. : Ajapura of Skandagupta and the Area Round Bihar, *JBORS*, III.

Gupta, P.L. : The Legitimacy of Skandagupta's Succession, *JIH* XL, 243-52.

Lakshminarayan, V. : A Note on the Identity of Purugupta and Skandagupta, *PIHC*, VI, 86-89.

Panna Lal : The Date of Skandagupta and his Successors, *Hindustan Review*, 1918.

Sastry, S.A. : A post Script on Sudarśana Lake, *JOI*, XXII, 153-55.

Sharma, Dashrath : The Legitimacy of Skandagupta's Succession *JIH*, XLIII, 219-26. The Legitimacy of Skandagupta's Succession and Connected Problems, *JIH*, XXXVII, 145-52. Significance of Two old Historical Titles, *IHQ*, XXVII, 337-39.

Sinha, B.P. : Purugupta and Skandagupta, *JBRS*, XXXVI, 53ff.

Vajpeyi, Raghvendra : Skandagupta's Bhitari Grant to Vishṇu-Śārṅgin and Bhitari Excavations, *PIHC*, 1983, 70ff.

CHAPTERS XII TO XV:

Agrawal, Ashvini : Place of Ghaṭotkachagupta in the Gupta History, *PURB* (*Arts*), XVII, 141-46. New Light on the Aulikaras and Hūṇas in India, *HSAJIS*, I, 13-18.

Agrawal, Jagannath : Identification of Budhagupta with Purugupta, *BV*, VI, 235-36. The Hūṇas in India, *NIA*, V, 249ff. The Route of Hūṇa Invasion, *PIHC*, 1958, 160-61. Nalanda Clay Sealing of Vainyagupta, *JNSI*, 1968, 206-07.

Aiyanagar, S.K. : The Hūṇa Problem in Indian History, *IA*, 1919, 65ff.

Banerji, R.D. : Chronology of the Late Imperial Guptas, *ABORI* I, 67-80.

Bhandarkar, D.R. : Foreign Elements in Indian Population, *IA*, 1911.

Buddha Prakash : Kālidāsa and the Hūṇas, *JIH*, XXXV, 91ff.

Chatterji, K.C. : Kālidāsa and the Hūṇas, *JIH*, 1936, 93-102.

Chattopadhyaya, S. : Later Imperial Guptas, *IHQ*, XXIX, 156-61. The Epthalite Invasion, *PIHC*, 1956, 178ff.

Dasgupta, N. N. : On Vainyagupta, *IC*, V, 297-303.

Dikshit, S.K. : Some Light on the Chronology of the Later Imperial Guptas, *IC*, V, 425-29.

Fleet, J.F. : The History and Date of Mihirakula, *IA*, XV, 245ff. The Coins & History of Toramāṇa, *IA*, 1889, 225ff.

Ganguly, D.C. : Vainyagupta Dvādaśāditya, *IHQ*, IX, 784-88. Vainyagupta Dvādaśāditya, *IHQ*, X, 154-56.

Ghosh, J.C. : Additional Notes on Foreign Elements in Hindu Population, *ABORI*, XII, 164-70.

Goyal, S.R.: The Problem of Bālādityas in the Gupta Period, *S.K. Bhuyan Commemoration Volume*, 1966, 200-14.

Gupta, P.L.: Ghaṭotkachagupta *IHQ*, XXII, 316-19. Later Imperial Guptas, *IHQ* XXIV, 253-62. Place of Ghaṭotkachagupta in the Gupta Chronology, *JNSI*, XIV, 99-102.

Heras, H.: Final Defeat of Mihirakula. *IHQ*, III, 1ff.

Hoernle, A.F.R.: Mihirakula is Identical with Mātṛigupta, *JASB*, 1889-94-100.

Hultzsch, E.: Extracts from Rājataraṅgiṇi, *IA*, XIX, 261ff.

Konow, Sten: Notes on Toramāṇa, *IHQ*, XII. 530ff.

Lakshminarayan, V.: A Note on Dr. Fleet's Parivrājaka Mahārājas, *NIA*, VI, 69-72.

Majumdar, R.C.: Successors of Kumāragupta I *JABS*, XVII, 249-55. The Revised Chronology of the Last Gupta Emperors *IA*, XLVII, 161-67. The Successors of Skandagupta, *JUPHS* XVIII, 70ff. Vainyagupta Dvādaśāditya, *IHQ*, IX, 989-91.

Mehta, N.C.: Toramāṇa *JBORS*, 1928, 28-38.

Modi, J.J.: The Early History of the Hūṇas, *JBBRAS*, XXIV, 539ff.

Mookerji. R.K.: Later Guptas of Magadha, *JBORS*, 1929, 251ff. Later Gupta History and Chronology, *JIH*, IV, 17ff.

Mukherji, B.N.: Did Purugupta Issue Coins?, *PIHC*, 1958, 77ff.

Mukherji, D.N.: The Genealogy and Chronology of the Early Imperial Guptas, *JIH*, XXI, 34-56.

Rao, G.V.: The Problem of Bālādityas in Gupta Period, *PIHC*, 1952, 51ff.

Ray, Atreyi: Origin and Ethnology of the Hūṇas in India, *JIH*, XLIII, 493-512.

Raychaudhuri, H.C.: The Successors of Kumāragupta I, *IHQ*, VIII, 352. The Order of Successions of the Later Imperial Guptas, *PAIOC*, 1922, 335-38.

Shankar, K.G.: Hūṇa Invasion of Hindustan, *NIA*, IV, 36ff.

Sinha, B.P.: Kumāragupta III, *JBRS*, XXXVI, Bearing of Numismatics on the History of the Later Imperial Guptas, *JBRS*, XXXIV, 18-26.

Sircar, D.C.: Ghaṭotkachagupta and Govindagupta, *IHQ*, XXIV 71ff.

Smith, V.A.: Coins of Toramāṇa and Mihirakula, *JASB*, LXIII, 195ff. White Hūṇa Coins from the Panjab, *JRAS*, 1907, 91ff. Revised Chronology of the Early Gupta Dynasty, *IA* XXXI, 257-66.

Stein, M.A.: White Huṇas and Kindred Tribes in the History of the Indian North-West Frontier, *IA*, 1905, 73-87.

Thakur, Upendra: The Second Phase of the Hūṇa Invasion of India, *JIH*, XLIV, 67-92

Upadhyaya, B.S.: The Final Defeat of Mihirakula, *IHQ* XV, 302ff.

EPILOGUE:

Agrawal, Jagannath: Early History of the Maitrakas of Valabhī, *IC*, V. 407ff. New Light on the Maukhari Genealogy, *Dr. A.C. Woolner Commemoration Volume*, 116-18.

Jayaswal, K.P.: An Observation on the Origin of Maitrakas of Valabhī, *JBRS*, XLIX. 111-18.

Ray, H.C.: The Line of Kṛishṇagupta, *IC*, VIII, 133-36.

GENERAL:

Agrawal, Jagannath: Kaliyugarājavṛittānta and the Imperial Guptas, *JBRS*, XXXI, 1-6. Kaliyugarājavṛittānta and the Imperial Guptas, *PIHC*, 1944, 119ff.

Basak, R.G.: Historical Basis of Raghu's Conquests, *PAIOC*, 1922, 325-34.

Bose, S.K.: Studies in Gupta Palaeography, *IC*, IV, 325-46.

Chhabra, B. Ch.: Garuḍa of Vishṇu, *JIH*, XLIII, 387-92.

Dandekar, R.N.: Society in Gupta Age, *JIH*, XL, 537-50.

Gupte, Y.R.: Gupta Chronology, *JIH*, IV, 118-19.

Majumdar, N,G,: Home of Kālidāsa, *IA*, 1918, 264ff.

Mirashi, V.V.: Rāmagiri of Kālidāsa, *JIH*, XLII, 131-43. Were the Mahārājas of Khandesh Feudatories of the Guptas?, *IHQ*, XXIII, 156ff. D.R. Bhandarkar's Researches About Kālidāsa, *ABORI*, LXIV, 197-203.

Munshi, K.M. The Golden Age of the Imperial Guptas, *BV*, III, 113ff.

Sircar, D.C.: Gupta Rule in Orissa, *IHQ*, XXVI, 75ff.

Sohoni, S.V.: Guptaṣ, Kadambas, Pallavas and Kālidāsa, *ABORI*, LX, 1-40. Raghu's Digvijaya in the Himalayas, *ABORI*, LXV, 163-94.

Venkatramayya, M.: Rāmagiri of Kālidāsa, *JIH*, XLI, 69ff.

INDEX